# it's ~~im~~possible!

a leadership plan for implementing quality

reading instruction and **ensuring literacy for all**

# pati montgomery
## and **angela hanlin**

*foreword by jan hasbrouck*

Solution Tree | Press
a division of
Solution Tree

555 North Morton Street
Bloomington, IN 47404
800.733.6786 (toll free) / 812.336.7700
FAX: 812.336.7790

email: info@SolutionTree.com
SolutionTree.com
Visit **go.SolutionTree.com/literacy** to download the free reproducibles in this book.

Printed in the United States of America

Library of Congress Cataloging-in-Publication Data

Names: Montgomery, Pati, author. | Hanlin, Angela, author.
Title: It's possible! : a leadership plan for implementing quality reading
   instruction and ensuring literacy for all / Pati Montgomery, Angela
   Hanlin.
Description: Bloomington, IN : Solution Tree Press, 2025. | Includes
   bibliographical references and index.
Identifiers: LCCN 2024032903 (print) | LCCN 2024032904 (ebook) | ISBN
   9781958590935 (paperback) | ISBN 9781958590942 (ebook)
Subjects: LCSH: Reading--United States. | Literacy--United States. |
   Reading--Phonetic method. | Reading comprehension.
Classification: LCC LB1050 .M568 2025  (print) | LCC LB1050  (ebook) | DDC
   379.2/4--dc23/eng/20240821
LC record available at https://lccn.loc.gov/2024032903
LC ebook record available at https://lccn.loc.gov/2024032904

**Solution Tree**
Jeffrey C. Jones, CEO
Edmund M. Ackerman, President

**Solution Tree Press**
*President and Publisher:* Douglas M. Rife
*Associate Publishers:* Todd Brakke and Kendra Slayton
*Art Director:* Rian Anderson
*Copy Chief:* Jessi Finn
*Production Editor:* Gabriella Jones-Monserrate
*Copy Editor:* Charlotte Jones
*Text and Cover Designer:* Kelsey Hoover
*Acquisitions Editors:* Carol Collins and Hilary Goff
*Content Development Specialist:* Amy Rubenstein
*Associate Editors:* Sarah Ludwig and Elijah Oates
*Editorial Assistant:* Madison Chartier

*This book is dedicated to the millions of students who struggled to learn to read thinking there was something wrong with them and to the millions of principals and school leaders who have found the courage to lead the way and do what is right for those students.*

# Acknowledgments

## From Pati:

This book would not be possible without the many wonderful school partners with whom I have had the opportunity to work. Each of you contributed to my own knowledge and repertoire regarding how it's possible to substantially increase reading outcomes for all students. I am particularly proud of the work with the school and district leaders in Chippewa Valley, Cudahy, Davis School Districts, and Quest Academy.

I would also like to acknowledge my fellow Schools Cubed consultants and Taylor. What a wealth of knowledge each of you hold, and it is working together that makes us great. I appreciate you tolerating my busyness and sometimes—OK, maybe often—crankiness.

Finally, to Hilary Goff at Solution Tree. It was your passion and priority to ensure that there were quality books on literacy instruction for all educators, including leadership.

## From Angie:

I am forever grateful to Vicki Gibson, Jan Hasbrouck, Laura Stewart, and Pati Montgomery for shaping and defining my career. Thank you for teaching me the Science of Reading, research-based instructional practices, and the systems and structures that successful schools need to ensure that all students learn to read. A special acknowledgment goes to the staff and students of Matthews Elementary. You hold a special place in my heart, and you always will. Our time together was the most magical and meaningful of my career! Thanks to Hilary Goff for believing in this book and making it happen. Finally, a heartfelt thank you to Jeremy, Gretchen, Garrett, Cana, and Samuel for always believing in me and offering endless support and encouragement! None of this would be possible without all of you.

Solution Tree Press would like to thank the following reviewers:

Doug Crowley
Assistant Principal
DeForest Area High School
DeForest, Wisconsin

John D. Ewald
Educator, Consultant, Presenter, Coach
Retired Superintendent, Principal, Teacher
Frederick, Maryland

Louis Lim
Vice Principal
Richmond Green Secondary School
Richmond Hill, Ontario, Canada

Laura J. Quillen
Retired Principal
Fairview Elementary School
Rogers, Arkansas

Matthew Rodney
Education Specialist
VanderMolen Elementary School
Jurupa Valley, California

Katie Saunders
Principal
Anglophone School District West
Fredericton, New Brunswick, Canada

Jennifer Shaver
Principal
Deer Creek 4th & 5th Center
Edmond, Oklahoma

Kim Timmerman
Principal
ADM Middle School
Adel, Iowa

Vicki Wilson
Principal
Monroe Elementary School
Wyandotte, Michigan

Visit **go.SolutionTree.com/literacy** to download the free reproducibles in this book.

# Table of Contents

*Reproducible pages are in italics.*

## chapter three
# Creating a Comprehensive Assessment Plan ⟶ 57

## chapter four
# Intervening Quickly ⟶ 83

## chapter five
# Conducting Effective Data Analysis ⟶ 111

chapter six
# Aligning Instructional Strategies With Data 145

## Appendix A: Science of Reading Overview     253

## Appendix B: Lesson Plan Template     259

## Appendix C: Performance Level Profiles With Small-Group Suggestions     265

## References and Resources     275

## Index     291

# About the Authors

**Pati Montgomery** is the founder of Schools Cubed, a school consulting firm that specializes in collaborating with school and district leadership to increase reading outcomes and, therefore, educational outcomes for all students. Schools Cubed's focus is coaching and mentoring school and district leadership to implement evidence-based practices in literacy.

Pati has held the roles of classroom teacher, elementary and middle school principal, district leadership, and executive director of literacy for the state of Colorado, where she led the implementation of one of the first evidence-based literacy legislations in the country.

Pati has been recognized by the International Dyslexia Association, ARC, and ExcelED for her outstanding leadership in the area of literacy. She speaks nationally about leadership and literacy and specifically on the systems and structures that should be implemented in schools to increase literacy outcomes for students. She serves as an expert and advisor on several literacy panels for states and school districts. Pati was the lead author for the book *A Principal's Primer for Raising Reading Achievement*, a Lexia LETRS for Administrators module.

Pati received a bachelor of arts in elementary education from Indiana University of Pennsylvania, a master of arts in special education from the University of Northern Colorado, and a specialized certificate in administration from the University of Denver.

To learn more about Pati's work, visit www.schoolscubed.com.

**Angela Hanlin** is the owner of the educational consulting company Angela Hanlin & Associates. She is a dedicated and passionate leader for change in schools and classrooms. She works tirelessly to positively transform teacher practice and student achievement. She bases her career on the belief that all students can learn and perform at high levels of achievement when they are given highly engaging, research-based instructional practices and targeted, specific interventions. She feels it is our moral obligation to ensure literacy for all students. She creates a growth mindset among her students, staff, and community and uses character education to shape and sustain a positive culture of collaboration and growth that is focused on learning.

Since 1996, Angie has served as a classroom teacher, curriculum coordinator, instructional coach, professional development coordinator who worked to train and coach teachers on research-based instructional practices and strategies, as a building principal at Matthews Elementary in the New Madrid County R-1 School District, and as a superintendent. She has received numerous awards for her performance in the classroom and as a school leader, and she has found a new passion for working with school districts and building leaders to promote systems and structures to improve literacy for all students. The Matthews Elementary staff were able to dramatically transform their school and reach proficiency levels of 100 percent!

Angie received the 2019–2020 Outstanding Rural Administrator Award from the Missouri Association of Rural Educators. She also led a journey of literacy improvement, systems, and structure work.

Angie received a bachelor's degree in elementary education from Southeast Missouri State University, a master's degree in administration, and an education specialist degree in educational leadership from William Woods University.

To learn more about Angie's work, visit www.angelahanlin.com.

To book Angela Hanlin for professional development, contact pd@solutiontree.com.

# Foreword

*By Jan Hasbrouck*

I have worked in the literacy education field for over four decades—first as a reading specialist and literacy coach and later as a professor, researcher, and author. I consult with schools and agencies across the United States and internationally. The focus of my life's work has always been to help struggling readers become successful readers.

During my career, I learned that providing effective support to students requires more than just highly qualified, excellent teachers using high-quality, evidence-based materials, especially in today's increasingly challenging classrooms. Students' successes also require leadership from well-informed, supportive (and supported), focused, and skillful administrators.

I have had the privilege to work under and alongside many amazing principals and district leaders in my long career. I know those jobs are incredibly challenging. The authors of this book also understand that very well. They write, "We all know that principals are overworked, overburdened, over-everything!" (page 200). I also understand that far too few of our school leaders have received adequate support, including the extensive training and professional development that is necessary to lead schools to achieve literacy success for all students. This is extremely complex work, and every school leader deserves this support.

I was so excited when my longtime friends (and highly esteemed colleagues) Pati Montgomery and Angie Hanlin told me they were writing this book to share the tremendously successful systems and strategies they had developed and—most importantly—had used to turn around challenged schools. I have watched these two in action in the field over many years as they did the work described in this wonderful book. I promise you, they have walked the walk!

I first met Pati when she reached out to me to consult with her district in Colorado. Pati was (and still is) deeply committed to helping every student achieve literacy success and doing so using the most accurate, up-to-date evidence possible. Her district at the time was not having the success with student literacy that Pati knew was possible. She also knew that the district's adherence to a faulty theory of reading instruction, based in whole-language principles, was not going to achieve the goals she expected.

As Pati's roles changed in subsequent years, we stayed in touch and looked for more opportunities to collaborate. We have worked together on other projects including developing a literacy assessment plan for the state of Colorado and conducting an evaluation of the Colorado state literacy plan (the READ Act) that Pati helped develop and implement.

As Pati continues to provide training and support to school leaders through her amazing team at Schools Cubed, we stay in touch. We often meet up at literacy conferences and frequently share research articles and suggest relevant books, curriculum materials, and assessment tools to continue our work supporting student literacy.

I recall first meeting Angie Hanlin many years ago at one of those literacy conferences. Angie had recently read some of the materials that my colleague Vicki Gibson had written about optimal classroom organizational strategies to support differentiated instruction. Angie was clearly hungry to learn everything she possibly could about the best ways to support student literacy success. Vicki had suggested that Angie could learn more about assessments and science of reading instructional strategies and instructional coaching from me. Year after year, Angie would reappear at that same conference, always sitting in the front row, often bringing along colleagues (including building and district leaders) who she knew would benefit from hearing about evidence-based practices. At first it surprised me to see her returning repeatedly, but it made sense after getting to know Angie better. I learned that Angie Hanlin will never be satisfied or convinced that she has learned enough to accomplish the high goal she sets for herself and all her colleagues—that *all* students deserve the best possible support, and *all* students can be successful. She knows it is not just going through the motions of teaching but rather it is the learning—the actual student outcomes—that must be the focus of our efforts.

When Angie became a building principal in her district, she invited me to come and provide the same kind of consultation support and training I had provided for Pati all those years earlier. I was thrilled when Angie and Pati connected and started working together to build the effective systems and structures necessary for student success.

The outcome of their collaboration is this book, *It's Possible!: A Leadership Plan for Implementing Quality Reading Instruction and Ensuring Literacy for All.* If you are a school leader, you are in luck! You will find clear, accurate, evidence-based, field-tested directions to help you achieve your highest goals for your students' literacy success.

This book has guidance for providing optimal and effective leadership along with a wealth of information regarding what we know about literacy instruction based on the most current evidence. Because scientific evidence is always growing and evolving—after all, that is the purpose of science, to uncover and share new knowledge and understandings—these authors make this important statement:

"As a group of practitioners highly reliant on and aware of the research, we will continue to monitor these findings" (page 42).

As professional educators, it is our responsibility to follow updates in the science of reading and learning and modify our classroom practices accordingly.

As these authors so clearly state in their title, they want to ensure literacy for all. Using the wealth of clear and helpful guidance provided here, you can help make that a possibility for your students in your schools.

Onward—for *all* students. It's possible!

# Introduction

*By Pati Montgomery*

The landscape of literacy instruction is changing at an abrupt pace in American classrooms. Many schools are shifting from a balanced literacy approach to one called a structured literacy approach. As of this writing, and as results from the 2022 National Assessment of Educational Progress (NAEP) indicate, only 33 percent of our fourth-grade students read at grade level (Nation's Report Card, 2022). No wonder our schools are desperately trying to find solutions to this atrocious problem. The truth is, reading results for American students have been abysmal since we began measuring their progress in 1969.

The reading research behind how students learn to read is not new. In 2000, the National Reading Panel delivered a much-anticipated report aimed at assessing the effectiveness of various approaches to teaching reading. Though this research has been updated since then, the primary findings of that research have remained solid. Literacy instruction should explicitly include five areas of reading: (1) phonemic awareness, (2) phonics, (3) fluency, (4) vocabulary, and (5) comprehension. Regrettably, the application of these findings on reading instruction seemed to elude our schools in the years that followed the panel's report. Finally, however, schools seem to be taking note.

There appear to be several reasons for this sudden interest in a "new" method of reading instruction. Beginning in 2020, the COVID-19 pandemic and home schooling made the lack of quality reading instruction glaringly obvious to parents as they watched their students learn how to read via remote learning. Emily Hanford (2022) published her eye-opening podcast series *Sold a Story*, which chronicles both the how and why of the unfortunate way students have been taught to read over the past forty years. Social media pages, such as the Facebook group "The Science of Reading–What I Should Have Learned in College," which has more than 200,000 members, have been created so that teachers can educate themselves on how to best teach literacy instruction. State legislators, recognizing the poor outcomes of their students' reading abilities on state summative assessments, have enacted legislative mandates that require students to receive instruction in a structured literacy format and have teachers trained in said format. As of this writing, thirty-two states and the District of Columbia have passed laws or implemented new policies related to evidence-based reading instruction (Schwartz, 2022a). It appears that America has finally and pressingly recognized our literacy issue.

This work is not new to me. The first year that I led a school as a principal using structured literacy practices was 2000, the very year that the National Reading Panel (2000) released its findings. To implement structured literacy practices at that time, I had to rely on the research that began in 1986. Since that time, at various capacities, and now as the founder of Schools Cubed—a firm solely devoted to improving literacy outcomes for students by working with building principals to implement the science of reading—I have literally, along with my team of consultants, observed in thousands and thousands of classrooms and worked with thousands of principals to implement a structured literacy approach to reading. All of these schools are on the path to ensure that all students can read at grade level and to drastically improve the current reading outcomes for their students.

To ensure that all students can read at grade level requires much more than providing professional development to teachers. In fact, the work of ensuring that all students read at grade level cannot be on the backs of teachers. Learning how students learn to read is simply the first step. Teachers must then learn how to *implement* quality literacy instruction. Regrettably, it is that implementation that is being left out of the professional development to teachers.

What we have learned in our work with so many schools is that getting students to read at grade level requires the work of all school personnel. It requires principals to guarantee that specific systems and structures are in place that support teachers and students in higher reading expectations. There is a gap between the urgency schools now feel to increase reading achievement and their ability to do so, and that gap is the knowledge of what quality implementation looks like.

This book provides schools with a manual that will teach school leadership how to implement a structured literacy approach in schools as well as what quality literacy instruction looks like in classrooms. What you will find in the following pages is a blueprint to assure you that *it's possible* for all students to read at grade level.

# The Path to This Book

I have been working in schools since 1980. I can envision in my sleep the polished gleam of linoleum at the beginning of each school year; I can hear the clanking chains of empty swing sets on the playground after students have gone home and smell the scent of turkey coming from the cafeteria every Thursday before Thanksgiving. I am the great grandniece of one of the first female superintendents in the state of Nebraska. My grandmother attended a traditional college and then went back to finish her education degree (that required a bachelor's degree) when she found herself a widow with seven children to feed. Shortly after, she became the president of the teachers' union, leading for the rights of educators in her district in the 1960s. Educational leadership is in my bones.

This profession is not perfect—it is a profession of humans working with humans. It is built on the premise of service to our fellow humans, of educating the next generation so they achieve great success, invent new things, concoct new ideas, and make the world a greater place. It is one group of humans bestowing to a younger group of humans new knowledge, new abilities, and a compass with which to navigate the world. Humans, whether age six or sixty-six, are not widgets, and because of that, they bring to this splendid field imperfections. As educators, we have made mistakes along the way. It is these imperfections and mistakes that have provided me with both the greatest joys and frustrations of my career.

I am also a mother. I am the mother of a son who struggled to learn to read. One of the greatest mistakes in my profession that I have witnessed has been with the most fundamental right every student should have: the ability to read at grade level. My son was born to two educated parents, he was read to since infancy, conversation and language were a large part of our home, his room was full of books, he went to museums, he traveled, and he had every opportunity that parents provide their children—yet he struggled with learning to read.

My son was born in 1984; in 1986, the National Institute of Student Health and Human Development began one of the biggest research studies ever created in education. That research study was on how students learn to read and what we can do when some students struggle to learn to read. Little did I know then that the research from that study, started when my son was just two years old, would become the centrality of both my profession and my motherhood.

My son began kindergarten in 1991. It was the height of the whole-language movement, and my son's school was well steeped in its beliefs and practices. I, on the other hand, had just finished my master's degree in special education. At the time, for a master's in special education with an emphasis on learning disabilities, I had to take two reading courses and a linguistics class. My reading courses could not have been more opposite to one another. One reading course was on the language experience approach to reading—an offshoot of the whole-language movement—and the other (taught by a visiting professor from Oklahoma State University) was strongly rooted in a phonics approach, with a scope and sequence and an explicit format. My head was spinning. I wasn't quite sure what the right approach should be with two such divergent methods. It was in my linguistics course, which taught me the fundamental principles of language, that I began to understand the premise of phonemes and the relationship of phonics to reading. It made sense to me that learning to read was based on a code. It was at that point I knew exactly which approach to the teaching of reading was correct, and I've never doubted it.

By the time my son was in second grade, I knew he was struggling, and I was desperately trying to help him. When I attended his parent-teacher conference, I asked the teacher what books he was reading and what reading instruction was like in her classroom. She told me, "Ben reads the drawing books." I retorted, "But there are no words in the drawing books for him to read." She replied, "Those are the books that he enjoys. If we let him read the books that he loves, then he will learn to love to read." At that moment, I remember feeling like every organ in my body had turned upside down, and I wanted to run home and move to another school that understood reading. I mentally vowed to ensure that if given the chance, all students under my charge would learn to read correctly so that they *could* love to read!

Like so many parents, though my own education was devoted to helping students who struggled with learning, I found that tutoring my own child was a catastrophe. There were tears (both his and mine), there was frustration, and there was not a lot of fun. When my son was approaching middle school, his grandparents provided him with private tutoring at a summer reading camp that focused on a structured literacy approach. Ben learned to read.

He finished high school and went on to a year of college, and though he did well in his courses, his self-esteem had taken a huge hit, as it does for many students who struggle to learn to read. He had no interest in finishing his degree. School had become "not his thing." Ben's experience was like that of so many other students who began and ended school with reading difficulties. Multiple studies show that students with reading difficulties are at an increased risk for mental health problems, such as anxiety and depression (McArthur, Castles, Kohnen, & Banales, 2016; Yasir et al., 2023). Thankfully, Ben's story does have a happy ending. He has a terrific job and is a leader in the field of traffic maintenance, and I am hugely proud of what he has accomplished.

As a teacher, my training was in Reading Recovery, a short-term, first-grade intervention that relied on guessing and picture clues to decipher words. My district had a bastardized version that they used for all students receiving Title I, and because I was a special education teacher, they encouraged me to use it as well. It just didn't seem to stick. I felt like students were memorizing. Instead, I would readily go back to the scope and sequence I had acquired in graduate school and pair it with Primary Phonics books—the earliest decodable books. Students became readers. I spent several years teaching; I became a special education administrator and then an elementary school principal. At each career stop, I searched for the best evidence-based literacy practices for whatever group of teachers and students were under my watch.

To ensure that I knew how to help my son and my students, I devoured research articles on reading instruction. In doing so, I stumbled on two names: Louisa Moats and Barbara Foorman. Both were working on research projects on early literacy associated with the National Institute on Student Health and Human Development. As luck would have it, many years later, Moats spent a great deal of time training my teachers at the elementary school where I was the principal while she was writing Module 4 of the original LETRS modules. She later was a coauthor of my first book, *A Principal's Primer for Raising Reading Achievement* (Montgomery, Ilk, & Moats, 2013).

In 2017, I was speaking at a convocation of principals and district leaders in Mississippi. My topic was related to my belief that making change in schools is really on the shoulders of our principals, yet a fellow panel member informed the audience that my expectation of principals was much too high! As I was leaving the conference, a tiny, confident-looking woman tapped me on my shoulder. I turned around, and there was Foorman herself! She said she was a fan of my work and agreed with what I had just said to the audience of principals, that raising reading achievement was indeed dependent on our school leaders. I immediately went to my car and started to cry. At that moment, I was so touched that, in my career, I had been able to work with and meet the two women who had most guided my professional life—whether they knew it or not.

For some, my journey may sound a bit lucky. I cannot underscore how fortunate I have been to work with so many brilliant minds in education, such as Jan Hasbrouck, who wrote the foreword for this book. It has not been without its share of hoopla. My own district, where I spent over twenty-two years of my career serving mostly as a school leader, thought my ideas on reading should be reserved for students from impoverished backgrounds or special education students, certainly not for those from middle class and affluent families.

"Those" students certainly need phonics—not middle class or affluent students. When I was at the Colorado Department of Education, leading the implementation of the READ Act—one of the first state legislation mandates based on the science of reading—I was told that all districts shouldn't have to teach reading "my way" (as if I had created the findings from the research on how students learn to read). In that time, my fellow educators judged my reading views and told me I was taking the love of reading away from students.

I was not, and have not ever been, deterred. I knew then, and now, that *it's possible* for all students to read at grade level. While I was a principal in that district—which I both loved for the camaraderie and the graciousness they showed when letting me do my "reading thing" yet loathed for its view on how to teach reading to my children and thousands of others—I wrote a grant called the Alameda Literacy Project. The project consisted of five elementary schools, a middle school, and a high school. One of the elementary schools, using many of the concepts and principles outlined in this book, saw 100 percent of their students read at grade level in the first year of implementation. Others, with poverty rates of nearly 100 percent of students, saw results of nearly 90 percent of their students reading at grade level. My coauthor on this book, Angie Hanlin, saw the students in her district in New Madrid, Missouri (where 100 percent of students receive free and reduced lunch), move from a low of just 15 percent reading at grade level to as high as 100 percent. It can't be said enough: It's possible that all students can read at grade level.

I met Angie at the Plain Talk About Literacy and Learning Conference in 2014. Angie had been the district instructional coach in the New Madrid County R-1 School District and was interviewing for her first principal position at Matthews Elementary. We had mutual friends in Jan Hasbrouck and Vicki Gibson, who introduced us to one another. Angie did go on to get that principal position. Shortly after becoming the principal, she discovered that her school was deemed a focus school, meaning the school's performance was in the bottom 15 percent of all schools statewide. She was mortified and didn't know what to do. She once again reached out to Jan Hasbrouck and Vicki Gibson, and they said to her, "call Pati." She did, about thirty seconds later.

I had retired from the Colorado Department of Education and was starting a consulting firm, turning around struggling schools by implementing the science of reading and putting into practice the systems and structures necessary for supporting teachers and students in reading. Angie was literally my first school partner. How could I have ever gotten so lucky that my first consulting experience would be with a principal so willing to take on the work! Angie was eager to ensure all students could read at grade level.

What I have come to know is that teachers are made, not born. I have witnessed this over and over. When I walked into Matthews Elementary and first observed each classroom, I remember thinking, "How will we ever move these students?" The innate teaching talent I was hoping for was not abundantly evident. But things quickly changed. Angie ran with every piece of advice I gave her and added her own spin. The teachers listened and went even further; every single soul stepped up to the plate. By the last year of our partnership, when I observed the teachers teaching, I couldn't tear myself away from the classrooms. I wanted to see the teachers' next moves. I was mesmerized. Lessons were magical. Not a fairy tale sort of magic, but a method of teaching that assured every student would be successful. The whole-group lesson, in which every student participated, typically started with directly teaching the code for the words they would encounter and then moved to learning new vocabulary words, often at levels I couldn't imagine six- and seven-year-olds possibly understanding. They would then discuss the story they were about to encounter, listen to the teacher model what reading the passage should sound like, and finally pass it over to the students to read and discuss themselves with guidance provided by the teacher along the way. Imagine the feelings of the students in those classrooms! They, too, were mesmerized, and their faces and engagement proved it! Teachers who hadn't undergone the appropriate training to succeed became some of the highest achieving teachers I'd ever seen! They, like so many others, simply didn't know what to do at first. They needed coaching and the guidance and feedback of a wonderful principal.

# The Framework for This Book

Unfortunately, to ensure all students read at grade level takes time, tenacity, and a never-ending pursuit of refining practices. It's a continual strive, not a destination. Far too often in education, we seem to lack the fortitude that the path requires. We seem to be in search of a silver bullet or magic elixir to solve the issue. Unfortunately, what results is one program after another being used in schools, a little of this and a little of that—sometimes, all evidence-based programs—with the hopes that one or all of those will fix the problem. In fact, I have found the opposite to be true. What schools need is to focus on the most fundamental reading principles through a comprehensive, quality reading curriculum, delivered in an explicit manner and with a doggedness to ensure students are reading to practice the skills they have been taught.

As Mike Schmoker (2018) writes in *Focus: Elevating the Essentials to Radically Improve Student Learning*, "the general underperformance of schools is a failure to implement three simple well-known elements: coherent curriculum, soundly structured lessons, and adequate amounts of fairly traditional literacy activities" (p. 7). I couldn't agree more. That is the premise of this book—implementing those principles, coupled with the necessary systems and structures that support teachers and students in their effort to ensure all students are reading at grade level. The answer could already be in your school. You may just need to reduce the number of programs and interventions being used and focus on exactly what matters for increasing literacy achievement.

This book is about a rubric comprised of the following six systems and structures that we have found necessary to increase reading achievement for all students.

1. Universal instruction
2. Comprehensive assessment
3. Intervention
4. Data-based decision making
5. Ongoing professional development
6. Collaborative teams

To ensure a smooth implementation, tackle them as rapidly as you can, but as slowly as you must. We have found there is a cadence to this work. Begin with implementing strong universal instruction and highly effective interventions. Doing this ensures that students stop falling behind and that those who are behind can catch up as quickly as possible. When you feel universal instruction and interventions are in place, focus on data-based decision making and school leadership teams. Teachers begin to hone their practices and are interested in seeing the outcomes of their labor through analyzing data. Teachers often begin to see enhancements they can make to the literacy initiative and want a voice through the school leadership team. Finally, in that ongoing pursuit of refining practices, ensure your staff has top-notch professional development through a collaborative culture.

Increasing reading achievement cannot be on the backs of teachers alone. I have never seen a school ensure that *it's possible* for all students to read at grade level without a strong leader at the helm. Leadership matters, and research bears that out. For a school as a whole, the effectiveness of the principal is more important than the effectiveness of a single teacher (Grissom, Egalite, & Lindsay, 2021). As a school or district begins to make a shift in their literacy practices to ensure students are reading at grade level, consider this: The reading gains from replacing a below average principal with an above average one would be larger than approximately 50 percent of the effects on reading achievement of various educational interventions in 747 studies (Kraft, Papay, & Chi, 2019). We don't suggest replacing anyone. In fact, I believe top-notch principals are also made and not born. But to become a top-notch principal, you must know what to do, and our principal development programs have failed even more woefully than those for our teachers. It is my hope that this book helps every principal become that top-notch principal—*it's possible*.

The contents of this book will lead you in implementing high-quality literacy instruction. It presents a framework that I have used and taught countless other school leaders to use to dramatically increase reading achievement and, for many, make *it possible* for all students to read at grade level. Whether you are charged with raising reading achievement for multiple schools or for one school, this book is for you.

# The Structure of This Book

Each chapter opens with a scenario from Angie Hanlin that details an experience leading this work in her school. Angie was a superintendent in Thorp, Wisconsin, but she began her school leadership career in the New Madrid County R-1 School District in Missouri, where she and I worked closely together for five years. She worked tirelessly to get Matthews Elementary out of focus school status as quickly as possible, which she did in just two years. Each of the chapters in this book opens with Angie's insights on how she took the information found within the chapter and implemented it in her school. We hope it will provide a real-life perspective of the daily work involved in accomplishing each portion of the rubric this book describes.

Chapter 1 begins by providing a background on the two main types of literacy instruction used in schools today as well as how they differ. You will also read a comparison between some common practices and what you might do in your school setting instead.

Chapter 2 explores the practices used during a literacy block at the various grade levels and why a universal instructional hierarchy in teaching is so important.

Chapter 3 discusses the assessment necessary for increasing reading proficiency as well as the frequency with which each type of assessment is used and at what grade levels.

Chapter 4 explains how to put into place a rigorous intervention system, what the various tiers of intervention look like, and who should be receiving what interventions.

Chapters 5 and 6 are both about data, with chapter 5 giving an overview and explanation of the data needed to analyze and chapter 6 digging in deeper regarding what teachers can do with the information gleaned from the assessments.

Chapter 7 discusses the many ways school leaders can enhance teachers' skills daily through job-embedded professional development beyond a "stand and deliver" sort, because none of this work can be accomplished without critical professional development.

Chapter 8 explains why teacher collaboration is such a crucial component for this endeavor.

Each of the chapters contains a spotlight story from educators who work with us in schools and districts across the United States. They tell a brief story about how they have implemented the work from that chapter into their schools and districts.

Appendix A includes a science of reading overview, which will provide you with a definition as well as a broad understanding of the science of reading. You may want to clip this section or print it separately for easy reference for yourself, parents, and staff as you begin this journey. Appendix B provides a generic lesson plan template for grades 3–5 for you to use following the completion of this book, and appendix C includes performance level profiles with small-group suggestions. We also offer access to additional tools at the Schools Cubed website (visit **https://itspossible.schoolscubed.com**).

We close with some final words and inspiration that we hope keep your eyes on the prize: Research bears out, and we have found to be true in our work, that 95 percent of all students can read at grade level (Al Otaiba et al., 2009; Allor et al., 2014; Foorman & Al Otaiba, 2009; Goldberg & Goldenberg, 2022; Hempenstall, 2013; Kilpatrick, 2015; Moats, 2020b; Vaughn & Fletcher, 2021). It's possible in your school as well.

Using the rubric found within this book (page 26) as a framework will help guide you and keep you on course for your literacy initiative. Go back to it frequently to see what pieces may be missing or what your next step might be. Share the rubric with your staff and leadership team so that they understand and become a part of the decision-making process. The systems and structures presented in this book are akin to cogs in a machine. Each domain outlined is a cog of the wheel. The more cogs or domains put into place, the better your machine operates. Get one in place, and the next is easier to implement. As you go along, you will begin to see students reading at much higher levels.

# A Call for Courage

Along with my children, my career was the love of my life. Being a school principal was the most fulfilling and rewarding job I ever had, but it was also the hardest. Every day of my career as a principal, I walked into my office with a framed poster of Eleanor Roosevelt hanging on my wall. The poster had a picture of Eleanor determinedly walking and contained one of her famous sayings, which is, "You must learn to do the things you think you cannot do." That poster was given to me by my own beloved principal, Irene Martinez Jordan, when I was a teacher. She saw something in me and knew I was an educational leader; she recognized my lineage.

As a leader, I did something I thought I couldn't do every day, whether it was corralling a nest of snakes, cleaning up vomit, finding coats and mittens for students who did not have them, chasing down suspicious intruders who had entered the building—the list goes on and on. Principals reading this, you know what I mean. Most importantly, in doing the things I thought I couldn't do, I confronted teachers who would not teach literacy in the manner we had agreed—the manner that ensures *it's possible* for all students to read at grade level. I didn't and couldn't tolerate the thought of any student not being able to read. It is incumbent on every leader to do what they think they cannot do in regard to students reading. Simply put, leadership takes courage.

Finally, in thinking back through the years of my career that the practices in this book were formulated, I can't help but remember the students running into my office with ear-to-ear grins telling me the percent their accuracy score had increased, or the second-grade student in the hall asking me if I knew what a diphthong was, and the pride on so many students' faces who finally found the love of reading because they had been taught how to read. Nothing warms one's soul quite like that. I hope this book brings you all of these joys, as well.

As you embark on this journey, and a journey it will be, you will be reminded each day of the courage you must find to lead this endeavor. You don't realize it today, but I can only imagine the lives that you will be changing. I gratefully thank you for having the courage and the fortitude to change the lives of the many, many Bens in your school. Ben thanks you, as well!

# Getting Started With Structured Literacy Instruction

## The Principal's Perspective

*By Angela Hanlin*

The journey began with a question. "What would you do if anything were possible?" The answer was easy. "Ensure that all students could read at or above grade level." The question came to me at one of the most challenging moments in my career. I had just left a meeting for focus school principals. During that meeting, I learned that schools identified as focus schools were in the lowest 15 percent of schools in the state. We would be given three years to demonstrate growth, but on average, most schools usually needed five to seven years. Our school was the newest school to be identified in our region, and I was the only first-year principal in the group. As if that information was not devastating enough, I then learned that most of the principals in the room had been stuck in this turnaround status for seven to nine years! As I left the meeting and sat in my car in tears, frustration hit. We did not have seven to nine years. With our school being an elementary building that served students from prekindergarten through grade 5, our students would be out of school in that amount of time. Spending seven to nine years turning our school around was simply not an option. I took a deep breath and asked myself, what would I do if I could do anything? What would I do if anything were possible? I would do whatever it took to make sure that every single student at school could read, and not just read, but read at or above grade level. So at that moment, sitting in the car as a brand new leader, discouraged by the grim data that was our current reality, I decided that I would completely throw out the idea of impossible. As a team, we would not even consider the idea that our students could not read. Every single student, regardless of background, previous failures, learning disabilities, or economic level, would read. I am proud to say that is exactly what we were able to accomplish. We were able to make what so many educators feel is impossible become possible. The beauty of our journey is that all schools can do exactly what we did.

In the spring of 2015, I was appointed the principal of Matthews Elementary, a small, rural school in the New Madrid County R-1 School District in southeast Missouri. I had been a classroom teacher at the school for ten years before leaving to be an instructional coach. I was so excited to be returning to my home school. What I found was very different from how things had been when I was a classroom teacher, different from what I thought I would be walking into. The current reality was chronic absenteeism, low staff morale, a one-size-fits-all approach to intervention, two years of extremely high rates of discipline referrals, dismal reading and mathematics data, a high rate of students in special education, inconsistent instructional practices, weak instructional materials, and a complete and total lack of systems and structures. How had things gotten to this point? The school had the lowest attendance rate in the district, a high number of students were tardy on a regular basis, and most absences were unexcused. Staff members were incredibly discouraged, and they didn't have a strong sense of community and belonging. Students were placed into pullout groups, but interventions were neither targeted nor specific. Teachers were spending the majority of their day dealing with behavior issues. Benchmark assessment data and scores from state achievement tests were incredibly low. Over 25 percent of the students had an individualized education program (IEP), and the gap widened after students were placed in special education. Instructional practices were not systematic throughout the building. Each teacher basically did their own thing. Reading materials were outdated, with no funds to purchase new resources.

The reality was completely overwhelming! Where does one even start? I immediately put a self-imposed improvement plan into place, which included research-based instructional practices from John Hattie (2012, 2023) and an emphasis on explicit instruction. I provided weekly professional development on foundational literacy skills and modeled the most effective literacy practices for both whole-group and small-group instruction. We had pockets of success, but we were nowhere near buildingwide success. I worked with a sense of urgency daily, but it was hard to create a sense of urgency with all staff members, because they did not seem to fully grasp just how low our data really was.

Data review was a practice that had taken place prior to my leadership, but it had not gone deep enough, and it was not impacting instruction. There was a complete disconnect between the data and what teachers did in the classrooms. Data revealed that less than 20 percent of the students could read at the 50th percentile, and less than 10 percent of students performed at the 50th percentile in mathematics. The previous year's state test scores revealed that only 13 percent of students in grades 3 through 5 scored proficient in reading, and less than 10 percent scored that in mathematics. There was only one student in the entire building that had scored advanced. Students in special education were stagnant and had scored below basic for the last three years. We could do better, and our students deserved better, but it was overwhelming with so many areas needing improvement. I was shocked that more people were not alarmed by the data and our current situation.

A few months into our school year, I received the news that Matthews Elementary had been identified as a focus school by the Department of Elementary and Secondary Education. With the previous three years of state achievement scores being so low, the school had fallen into the lowest 15 percent of schools in the state. A one-time blue-ribbon school was now a focus school. Instead of being discouraged by the turnaround status, I was actually encouraged. This could be used to create a sense of urgency!

This would be an opportunity to reach out and get help. The morning after that first focus-school meeting, I reached out to Pati Montgomery and asked for help. Together, we developed a plan of action, and our professional collaboration and journey began. Pati emailed a few questions to me before her first visit, and one of those asked about my vision for Matthews Elementary. I remember writing that I wanted to create something that would outlast my tenure as building principal, and that the expectation for how school was done no matter who was in the role of principal would become the norm. That was the dream, the vision, but I did not yet know how to make that a reality. I learned that the way to do that is to create strong systems and structures. That is where the work began. Since no systems were in place, we did not have to undo anything. Looking back, the school had been operating day to day without a structure for how the work needed to be done. We would need to start from the very beginning. We began by identifying our guiding beliefs and used those to create a vision statement. This was done by every single staff member, no exceptions. The vision was voted on by everyone, adopted, and displayed throughout the building. We frequently revisited the vision and used it to plan initiatives and make decisions. We routinely asked ourselves, "Is this who we are? Does this decision align with our vision? Does this decision align with our guiding beliefs?"

With those initial steps completed, it was time to create a detailed, comprehensive school-improvement plan and implement it. I knew what I wanted for the school, the teachers, and the students, so creating the plan was relatively easy and very satisfying. When it came time for the implementation of the plan, however, I was met with immediate resistance. Teachers had been doing things the same way for quite some time and were not open to change. Most had a fixed mindset and felt that our students were achieving to the best of their ability. The focus had always been on teaching, and teachers believed they were teaching in a manner that was effective because they were covering their content. Resistance can be incredibly defeating, but as the instructional leader, I had to keep my eye on the vision and the goals for the building. I had to take each day and press toward the goal. Little by little, we made progress. I have often shared with other building leaders that school turnaround work is daunting, relentless, and challenging. Challenges often come and threaten the work that is being done. That is why leadership is so important. With the comprehensive school-improvement plan in place, I continuously worked on the plan and never strayed from the work. I kept detailed records of the progress that was made each and every week. It helped tremendously to have a partner in Schools Cubed, and I reached out to Pati on a weekly basis in the beginning. Throughout this book, I will share more of our story and the steps we took to leave focus-school status and reach heights that we had only dreamed possible.

Angie Hanlin is not the first principal, and certainly not the last, to face similar circumstances. In fact, 2015 was Angie's first year as a building principal. Imagine the circumstances schools have faced in the years since. There seems to be one crisis in our schools after another.

The United States educational system wrestled with the insecurity of a global pandemic for over two school years beginning in 2020. The impact of this may be felt for decades, or at least until the students entering kindergarten in the fall of 2019 graduate from high school. As of this writing, we know that not only have our students suffered from the pandemic, but teachers, staff, and administrators have also faced devastating consequences.

Since the pandemic began, our educational system has seen the highest labor burn-out of any labor force in the United States (Marken & Agrawal, 2022). A study by the National Center for Educational Statistics (2022b) found that 44 percent of schools had teacher vacancies.

Student absenteeism has also increased dramatically. Although as of this writing, the national data for the 2021–2022 school year have not yet been released, early data indicate the chronic absentee rate in the United States may have doubled for students (Chang, Balfanz, & Byrnes, 2022). The national chronic absenteeism rate has skyrocketed since the pandemic, from 16 percent in 2019 to an estimated 33 percent in 2022. This is the highest rate since the U.S. Department of Education released its first national measurement of chronic absenteeism in 2016.

Students who met the criteria for depression more than doubled in just one year, from 2020 to 2021 (Elharake, Akbar, Malik, Gilliam, & Omer, 2023). The number of schools in the United States that have experienced shootings since the 2000–2001 school year to the 2022–2023 school year has risen from 31 to 349, an increase of 1,163 percent (Korhonen, 2024). In elementary schools, that increase is 1,475 percent (National Center for Education Statistics, 2023). In 2022, the National Center for Education Statistics (2022a) conducted a special reading assessment to capture the possible learning loss students may have suffered from the COVID-19 pandemic, which began in 2020. The results were staggering. The average scores for nine-year-old students dropped by five points in reading. This outcome was the largest decline since 1990 (The Nation's Report Card, n.d.).

The statistics seem overwhelming just writing this. What seems likely is that the issues within our educational system did not begin with the pandemic. Rather, longtime systemic failures have been exacerbated by the pandemic, leaving a principal or district leader with the question, "Where does one begin?" The preponderance of concerns in schools does seem insurmountable. However, the story of Matthews Elementary in New Madrid, Missouri, offers more than the tale of one school. Perhaps it offers a solution to many of the woes faced today by schools. We (as Schools Cubed consultants) have collaborated with countless schools, districts, and state departments of education throughout the United States, leaning on the research in very specific areas (that's to come in the following chapters) to create what we believe to be the secret sauce for school improvement.

School principals and district leadership cannot and should not expect to turn around schools in a year; there are no silver bullets. However, using a framework that is based on research in the areas of effective schools, school leadership, and scientifically based evidence in reading, a school can make significant strides one step at a time.

This chapter will introduce you to the full scope and data of the state of literacy in schools, the history of the development of the science of reading, and the benefits and necessity of installing science of reading-aligned instruction in your school.

# National Reading Outcomes and Debates

Angie's debut as a principal into a world where 15 percent of students are reading at grade level is not unusual. In the United States, only 33 percent of our fourth-grade students read at grade level. New Madrid School District is in southeast Missouri in a nearly high-poverty county, with over 17.3 percent of the population living in poverty and only 11.3 percent having bachelor's degrees (based on ICES). One might conclude that low literacy levels are a part of the problem.

Until the results in 2022, the results in our national scores in reading have remained fairly stable, and low, since 1992. In 2022, due to the COVID-19 pandemic, scores dropped to the lowest point since 1992 (see figure 1.1).

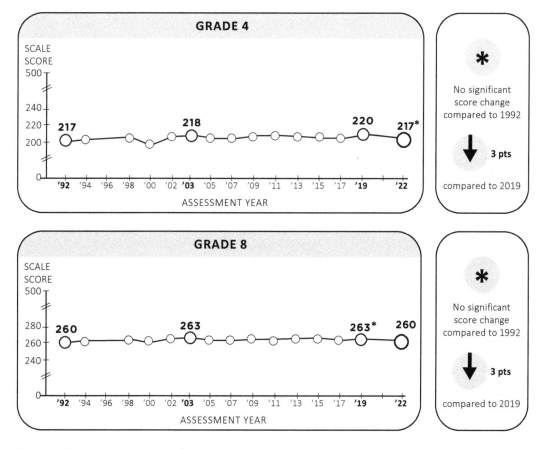

Source: *The Nation's Report Card, 2022.*

**FIGURE 1.1:** National average reading scores for fourth- and eighth-grade students since 1992.

Perhaps an even more concerning outcome regarding national reading ability is that, over the long term, higher-performing students have made gains while the lower-performing students have made no significant progress.

The long-term trend data that includes the impact of the COVID-19 pandemic shows an even more significant concern. Average scores for grade 4 students in 2022 declined 5 points in reading compared to 2020 (figure 1.2). This is the largest average score decline in reading since 1990 (The Nation's Report Card, n.d.).

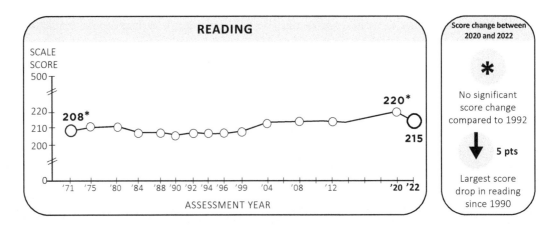

Source: *The Nation's Report Card, n.d.*

**FIGURE 1.2:** Reading score changes from 1971–2022.

Why such dismal outcomes in reading? There is no proof of a direct causal effect, but there is much debate in education and among parents and advocacy groups regarding how to best teach our students to read.

This debate has lingered for generations and centers on the question, Should reading be taught with a meaning-based, whole-word method, or a phonics-based approach? (Though in a phonics-based approach, it should be clear that no one is advocating the exclusion of meaning or comprehension.) In 1955, Rudolf Flesch published his book *Why Johnny Can't Read*. The book criticized the look-say and whole-word method taught in *Dick and Jane*–type books and instead insisted students were not reading adequately because they were not learning phonics. Though Flesch's (1955) book receives much regard for kicking off the reading wars, controversies have swirled on the best approach for literacy instruction since the McGuffey Readers, a phonics-based approach that was widely used in schools in the mid-19th to early 20th centuries.

In 1965, the National Institute of Student Health and Human Development (NICHD) began a research program seeking to understand how students learn to read, why some students and adults have difficulties learning to read, and effective ways to help students learn to read (Lyon, 2002b). This research continues today.

In 1997, the United States Congress asked the NICHD to convene a panel regarding the research-based knowledge of the teaching of reading that would include the effectiveness of various approaches to teaching students to read. That request led to the 2000 release of the National Reading Panel report. Its results identified the five components of how students learn to read, which includes phonics, phonemic awareness, fluency, vocabulary, and comprehension. These have remained the basic components of learning to read since the report's 2000 release.

The large body of evidence regarding how students learn to read is so extensive, one would assume it might have squashed the debate over how reading should be taught in our schools. Yet many educators have found the teaching of explicit phonics instruction (which was called for in the National Reading Panel findings) boring, tedious, and confusing, and they may have misunderstood how to teach it. To compromise, a "balance" of the scientific findings as well as a combination of a "whole-word" method became popular. This method has become known as the *balanced literacy* method and is the most prevailing method of teaching reading today; 72 percent of teachers report using a balanced literacy approach to reading (Schwartz, 2022b).

In 2013, the National Council on Teacher Quality (NCTQ) began analyzing how our universities are preparing teacher candidates in early reading. At that time, only 35 percent of our universities provided adequate instruction in at least four of the five components of science-based reading instruction. In 2021, that figure had risen to over 50 percent of traditional university programs providing adequate instruction, which may seem like a modest improvement. In 2023, the NCTQ found that only 28 percent of teacher preparation programs fully address all five components of reading. Of the components taught, however, the NCTQ found that comprehension was the component most covered by traditional teacher preparation programs, and phonemic awareness, which is essential to the development of word recognition, was covered the least (NCTQ, 2023a).

Initially, the purpose of a balanced literacy approach to reading instruction was to include scientific evidence. Many classrooms do include the teaching of phonics, many classrooms do indeed practice fluency or help students to become fluent readers, and certainly much attention is paid to reading comprehension. These are three of the five major components of structured literacy teaching. Unfortunately, in many balanced literacy classrooms, methods that are not scientifically sound are also put into practice. Some of these practices, to name just a few, include the three-cueing strategy, leveled instructional readers, and a mishmash of phonics instruction.

This debate over how to teach reading became more pervasive during the COVID-19 pandemic, when parents sat at home with their students participating in remote learning, as mentioned in the introduction (page 1). Suddenly, parents realized their students were not being adequately taught to read.

It seems that enough attention to the science of reading has finally taken grip. Forty-five states have passed literacy legislation with the hope of increasing our students' literacy outcomes. This focus on literacy legislation regarding increased reading outcomes for students has gained significant steam since the state of Mississippi passed its literacy laws in 2013. Mississippi has seen year-over-year progress in NAEP scores since passing this legislation. As of this writing, thirty-seven states and the District of Columbia have passed laws or implemented new policies related to evidence-based reading instruction (Schwartz, 2024). Dozens of states require professional development be provided to teachers in a structured literacy approach to reading.

# Instruction Aligned to the Science of Reading

It is important to note that though teachers are being trained in the content of how students learn to read, sadly, little of this coursework or professional development teaches teachers how to implement the research in their classroom. It simply provides the knowledge of how students learn to read with a void in the method or implementation in how to teach literacy. A structured literacy process is just that: a much more structured approach than what is outlined in other approaches to the teaching of reading. Teachers must understand these differences to teach reading correctly.

Various analyses of state legislative policies on literacy have indicated a need for principals and school leaders to also know how to implement structured literacy practices (Northern, 2023). Again, for the most part, professional development for teachers is devoid of implementation methods and practices aligned to the science of reading (Holston, 2024; Schwartz, 2022b). At the same time, school leaders, most often not trained in the science of reading, can become confused in understanding and knowing the difference between a structured literacy classroom and a balanced literacy classroom. After all, parts and pieces can sound the same. Colorado, North Dakota, Utah, and Wisconsin (as of this writing) are the only states that have a requirement for school leaders to be trained in the science of reading (The Reading League, 2021). Further, the method for evaluating teachers in thirty-one states and over half of the United States' twenty largest school districts is based on a *constructivist* approach to learning (The Danielson Group, n.d.). Constructivism relies on the teacher being a facilitator of learning to the students to build and create their own knowledge versus a direct approach to teaching or explicit instruction. This approach to instruction directly contradicts the explicit instruction model called for in a science of reading-aligned approach (more on this in chapter 2, page 27). No wonder our school leaders are confused, and no wonder our schools are underachieving.

To untangle the layers of confusion regarding what a science of reading approach is and what it is not, table 1.1 shows the differences among approaches in classrooms. In the following chapters, we will go deeper using this table in the various domains of a system devoted to the science of reading that will help to ensure *it's possible* for all students to read at grade level.

As you will come to see, how we teach students to read is indeed a critical component of improving our schools. In fact, we believe it is one of two key drivers—the second of which is systems and structures—in improving outcomes for our students.

Time, money, and legislation investments to ensure teachers have a science-based understanding of how students learn to read is a necessary first step, but to dramatically increase the outcomes of literacy for our students, ensuring teachers have the knowledge is not nearly sufficient. In fact, believing that schools will improve in literacy outcomes by simply increasing teachers' knowledge is an oversimplification of a complex problem.

**TABLE 1.1:** Differences in Literacy Instruction

| Component of Reading Instruction | Science of Reading-Aligned Practices | Classroom Practices Not Aligned to the Science of Reading Findings |
|---|---|---|
| **Phonemic Awareness Instruction** | Explicit and direct teaching in phoneme awareness linked with letter knowledge following a logical progression of development—easiest to more difficult | Incidental teaching of speech sounds—instruction is typically provided on an "as needed" basis. A lack of differentiation between, phonemic awareness, letter knowledge and phonics |
| **Phonics** | Explicit teaching of letter-sound correspondence—the ability to decode prefixes, suffixes, and word parts is highlighted; sounding out a word is a primary strategy when coming to an unknown word. | Phonics, if taught, is often through word sorts, three-cueing strategy, and typically no reliance on a phonetic scope and sequence. |
| **Fluency** | Measurable goals for accuracy and Words Correct Per Minute (WCPM) using an oral reading fluency (ORF) or Criteria Based Measure (CBM) | Reading practice in leveled readers with a focus on miscue analysis<br><br>Readers Theater and repeated readings of timed passages |
| **Vocabulary Instruction** | Direct preteaching of vocabulary words<br><br>Structured practice using new words<br><br>Words taught are embedded and connected to text read | Reading in leveled books and trade books<br><br>Lots of discussion around vocabulary words appearing in text |
| **Comprehension Instruction** | Direct teaching of structure of narrative and expository text<br><br>Emphasis on background knowledge<br><br>Language structure<br><br>Vocabulary<br><br>Comprehension strategies emphasized over comprehension skills | Student book choice emphasized—trade books, novels<br><br>Literature circles<br><br>Emphasis on comprehension skills—main idea, author's purpose, schema comparison |

*continued →*

| Component of Reading Instruction | Science of Reading-Aligned Practices | Classroom Practices Not Aligned to the Science of Reading Findings |
| --- | --- | --- |
| **Instructional Materials** | Decodable text used for beginning readers<br><br>Basal or Core Reading Program | Leveled texts used for beginning readers<br><br>Novel sets |
| **Instructional Strategies and Processes** | Explicit instruction—I do, we do, you do<br><br>Whole-group and small-group instruction<br><br>Linking of small-group instruction to data and the five components of literacy | Workshop Model of instruction<br><br>A constructivist approach to reading<br><br>Whole-group mini lesson of ten minutes typically based on a read aloud<br><br>Much discussion on schema, text to self<br><br>Peer conferencing<br><br>Teacher and student conferencing |
| **Interventions** | Sustained intervention for students reading well below or below grade level until they are at grade level | Students reading well below or below grade level typically have six-week sessions of fluency program or computer program. |
| **Assessments** | Measuring of foundational skills of literacy that include:<br><br>• Phonemic segmentation<br><br>• Nonsense word blending<br><br>• Oral reading fluency | Running records (a tool for coding, scoring, and analyzing a child's reading behaviors) with outcomes for placement within a leveled reading continuum, usually from A–Z, teacher-created formative assessments |

## The Principal's Role in Literacy Instruction

Let us turn our attention to the second largest influence on student achievement—the principal. In 2004, Kenneth Leithwood and colleagues said, "Leadership is second only to classroom instruction among all school-related factors that contribute to what students learn at school" (as cited in National Comprehensive Center for Teacher Quality, 2008, p. 5). It had been difficult to quantify the true effectiveness of school leadership before organizations like the National Comprehensive Center for Teacher Quality.

Both instinctively—as longtime school principals—and through the research on what effective schools do (Lezotte & Snyder, 2011), we understand that to make significant increases in school achievement, particularly in literacy outcomes, principals must be able to guide and lead this work. Many schools have turned to instructional coaching to propel or advance the outcomes for students. We are big proponents of instructional coaching, but the premise behind instructional coaching, and rightly so, is that it is nonevaluative in nature—and, in many settings, teachers receive coaching on a voluntary basis. We have observed that teachers who are already good teachers seek out further improvement from the instructional coach. Lower-performing teachers typically do not solicit the help of a coach. Consequently, to move the needle on increased literacy outcomes, principals must be able to provide instructional feedback in literacy instruction as part of the evaluation process. *It's possible* when all teachers are providing high-quality instruction.

In February of 2021, the Wallace Foundation released a systematic synthesis of two decades of research that enabled them to quantify how much principals truly do contribute to student achievement (Grissom et al., 2021). This synthesis found that a principal at the 75th percentile of the distribution of principal effectiveness has an effect on student achievement nearly as large as that of a teacher at the 75th percentile. In fact, the research goes on to say (Grissom et al., 2021):

> For a school as a whole, however, the effectiveness of the principal is more important than the effectiveness of a single teacher. Principals affect all 483 students in the typical elementary school, whereas teachers affect 21 in the average elementary school classroom. (p. 14)

Knowing that principals affect more than twenty times the number of students than a typical teacher, and knowing that low-performing teachers must become high-performing teachers, doesn't it seem logical to ensure that when addressing increased literacy outcomes, principals would be the first line of attack? Yet when states and policymakers began to require that educators understand the scientific evidence of how students learn to read, only four states mandated professional development for principals.

We must also follow the research on what effective schools and effective principals do and incorporate this research with the science of reading. Principals, for the most part, do not directly increase reading achievement through student instruction, but they can still have a dramatic effect in a more indirect manner. To do so, they must be able to set up the systems and structures that enable others to achieve more. They ensure that the school has an organized framework to get the job done. We believe that establishing efficient systems and structures in schools is the second key driver to increased literacy outcomes.

## The Distinction Between Structure and Systems

To understand what systems and structures are in schools, we must first understand what each is. A *system* is a collection of parts that interact with each other to function as a whole (Kauffman & Kauffman, 2021). There is no denying that schools today are busy. An exorbitant number of "things" are taking place. Staff members are often exhausted in an effort to "get things done." Simply doing "things"—whether it is assessments, behavioral management, standards, or data analysis—is not a system. That is simply busy, albeit meaningfully busy. Each time we implement or focus on something new in school, we add something additional for teachers to do, and we still have not created a system; we have created more busyness. No wonder principals are reluctant to introduce something new in schools. They worry about the burdens on teachers. However, elimination of busyness is dependent on the structures we put into place.

A *structure* is the network of relationships that creates a certain behavior. The structure is difficult to see. Internal structures are critically important to the systems we put into place. As an example, without a structure, a system of data analysis or a professional learning community is unlikely to succeed in dramatically increasing literacy outcomes for students.

Table 1.2 highlights examples of systems and structures that should be in place to support an increase in literacy outcomes.

**TABLE 1.2:** Examples of Systems and Structures That Support Literacy Instruction

| Structures That Support Literacy Instruction | Systems That Support Literacy Instruction |
| --- | --- |
| **Urgent Commitment to Literacy** | Master schedule that ensures a daily minimum of 120 minutes of reading instruction |
| | Interventions for all students who are reading below grade level |
| | Monitoring effectiveness of instruction through evaluation or pop-ins |
| | Analyzing personnel schedules to ensure the effective use of ancillary staff |
| | After-school tutoring that is aligned to instructional needs of students |
| **Culture of Collaboration** | Implementing and sustaining a school leadership team |
| | Establishing yearly goals and progress monitoring of said goals |
| | Grade-level PLCs to discuss and analyze data |
| **Highly Effective Professional Development for All** | Job-embedded professional coaching |
| | Responsible use of instructional coaches |
| | Ongoing professional development based on trend data |
| | Reliable and authentic instructional feedback |

In most states, schools deemed turnaround schools are the schools performing at the lowest 5 percent in each state in the United States. As a focus school, Matthews Elementary was in one rung higher than a turnaround school. Angie used her designation as a gift, a reason to spark a sense of urgency within her teachers. The training that Angie received from her state on how to turn around a school was typical. Some states require no specificity as to what avenue schools use to improve. In Angie's case, there were no systems or structures to rely on, just lots of busy.

One successful model often implemented to increase school outcomes is the four domains for rapid school improvement. The four domains for rapid school improvement is a framework developed in 2017 by the Center for School Turnaround and Improvement at WestEd. This framework is based on the research and best practices established through federal school improvement grants. It is a systems approach to school improvement.

It is important to remember that the four domains for rapid school improvement are implemented as a means for improving the school outcomes found within the lowest-performing schools. The four domains of rapid school improvement include: (1) turnaround, leadership focused on creating a sense of urgency, establishing a school leadership team, and creating and monitoring school goals; (2) talent development, ensuring there is recruitment of quality staff, targeting professional learning activities, leveraging highly effective teachers and coaches, and setting clear performance protocols; (3) instructional transformation, recognizing students' needs, prioritizing interventions, monitoring student data, and providing rigorous evidence-based instruction; and (4) culture shift, building a community based on student learning, ensuring all voices are heard, and engaging students and families in educational goals (Center for School Turnaround, 2017).

Yet, to become a turnaround school, the students in that school are performing on state assessments, as one predominant measure of school turnaround, at the lowest level in the state. I would argue that all state summative assessments are a reading test. They may be measuring reading in the topic of science, mathematics, or English language arts, but for students to perform well on the test, they must also be able to read well.

As indicated, we agree strongly with the four domains of rapid school improvement and have also found evidence that enacting such principles and practices will indeed move the needle on educational outcomes. However, these domains widely implemented to improve school performance have one glaring oversight: They lack a focus on increasing reading achievement. The instructional transformation domain of the four domains framework refers to state standards. We argue that if students cannot read, or read significantly below grade level, then they also cannot access the text within grade-level standards materials. Consequently, numerous schools across the United States are making these changes-based on misguided direction without enforcing the basic principle of ensuring students can read!

Principals desperately want to know how to increase achievement for all students. In a national survey conducted by the National Association of Secondary School Principals (2019) and the National Association of Elementary School Principals, with a total sampling of 836 school principals, 78 percent of respondents said they wanted more professional development in leading a schoolwide process to improve student achievement, 77 percent wanted more professional development in the use of student and school data for continuous school improvement, and 73 percent wanted professional development in leading instruction on raising achievement on standardized tests. All of these requests directly correlate to raising reading achievement for students.

## The Six Domains of Literacy Evaluation

The following literacy evaluation tool (LET) was developed over many years working with schools across the United States. It is a rubric for the systems and structures that we have found to prove highly effective in increasing literacy outcomes for students. We hope you find it as useful as we do to guide your journey as a framework for good literacy instruction in your school or district.

The reproducible at the end of this chapter (page 26) contains the six domains found within the LET along with an overall description of the construct for that domain. You can think of the domains as the systems necessary to increase reading achievement. As you will see in the complete rubric, each domain has numerous criteria. The criteria can be thought of as the necessary structures for the system.

The six domains are akin to cogs on a wheel (see figure 1.3). To create an efficient system of operation, they need to be working in sync. Removing or disabling one slows, drags, or even stalls the entire system. The reverse is also true; as you begin to implement these cogs, the system becomes more efficient and results in a smoothly operating machine.

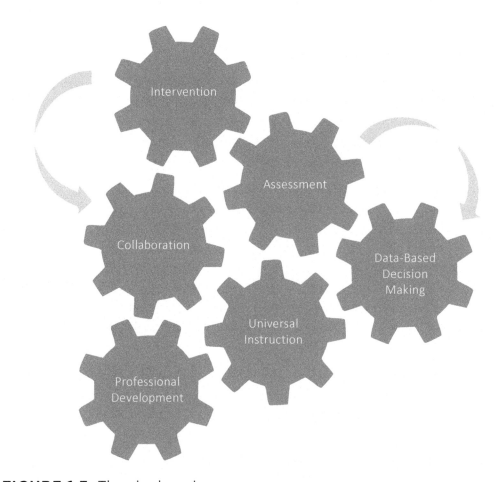

**FIGURE 1.3:** The six domains.

As we progress through the book, the LET and its components will be highlighted in each respective chapter. As you use this rubric, please keep in mind that it is best used in cooperation with someone outside of your own school or district setting. We find that the people "doing" the work either rank themselves too low (claiming "we aren't good enough yet"), or they rank themselves too high ("we've worked on this so much, it must be right"). These system evaluators should have a thorough understanding of the criteria found within each of the domains. We have found that when this instrument is only used internally, we become stilted in how we are truly creating these systems and structures and typically over or underrate our own progress.

If you are starting out in an endeavor to increase literacy outcomes or are hoping to move from a balanced literacy approach to a structured literacy approach, we suggest you perform a literacy audit on your school or district. Each chapter of this book ends with the domain of the literacy evaluation tool that corresponds to that chapter. As an example, at the end of chapter 2 (page 27) you will find the domain, or the portion, of the literacy evaluation tool that is about universal instruction. If you decide to complete an audit on the literacy instruction at your school, we suggest rating your school in each of the domains. Again, it is highly recommended that you engage with either district leadership or someone outside of your own school for an unbiased examination of how you are doing. You will see that the instrument self-calculates and provides a score from 0 percent to 100 percent. The criteria move from left to right. You will be introduced to this tool in chapter 2. To move from one criterion to the next, 80 to 90 percent of the staff should be implementing that criterion 80 to 90 percent of the time. This percentage is not intended to equal a grade; instead, it should be seen as a barometer for strengths and weaknesses within your literacy system and a direction for your next step.

## Summary

There is a preponderance of scientific evidence that outlines how best to teach reading. It is our belief that providing professional development to teachers is needed, but there is more to increasing outcomes. We must also provide professional development to principals.

Our experience indicates that not only do principals need a clear understanding of the science of reading, but they must also understand the systems and structures that should be put into place to support teachers and students. It is important to note that we recommend taking this one step at a time. We suggest conducting an audit of your system and determining the two or three items you can implement in the next month. Ensure that those you have put into place are operating smoothly, and then begin on the next step. *It's possible!*

In the reproducible titled "The Six Domains of Literacy Instruction" at the end of this chapter (page 26), we have outlined six domains that we feel strongly support the implementation of strong literacy instruction. We typically suggest that schools begin with the domain of universal instruction. This ensures that students are receiving the best literacy instruction possible so that no additional students slip back in their literacy acquisition. Chapter 2 will guide you through what we have found to be successful in implementing universal instruction. At the end of the chapter, you will find the rubric on what we feel is quality universal instruction.

# The Six Domains of Literacy Instruction

| Domain | Overall Description |
|---|---|
| **Universal Instruction** | All students receive highly effective literacy instruction that is comprehensive in its scope and delivered using highly effective research-based strategies. |
| **Assessment** | A valid and reliable foundational reading assessment is used for benchmark or screening three times per year in grades K–5. A progress monitoring tool that aligns with the screener is also used for all students reading below grade level. Additional assessments may be provided that help determine specific needs of students. |
| **Interventions** | Validated instructional programs and practices that are systematic, explicit, and delivered with a sense of urgency and a level of intensity to meet the needs of the students. Interventions are provided for a significantly extended duration of time that provides students extra practice and repetition with skills that address their specific deficiencies to move toward grade-level proficiency. |
| **Data-Based Decision Making** | Improving literacy achievement is urgent and is a shared school vision based on the current state of literacy achievement. Discussions regarding literacy data are a regular part of the school climate. |
| **Professional Development** | Professional development is an embedded part of the school and district culture that includes many avenues to increase educator effectiveness, such as workshops, courses, book studies, evaluation, peer mentoring, feedback, and coaching, which all increase literacy achievement. Professional development is aligned to evidence-based principles and instructional practices. |
| **Collaboration** | Various aspects of collaboration are evident. Teachers and grade-level teams have time to discuss and analyze student data, plan lessons, and engage in professional dialogue. Shared leadership is in place by an active school leadership team with the result of establishing a positive organizational climate and shared decision making. The school leadership team serves the purpose of leading the school's efforts to increase student achievement, determine professional development, and discuss building resources and practices of improvement. Representation consists of various grade levels and departments and an administrator. |

# Implementing Universal Instruction

## The Principal's Perspective

*By Angela Hanlin*

My favorite part of being a building principal is the opportunity to have conversations with teachers about their literacy instruction, including modeling in a classroom and providing feedback to help the teachers have a greater impact on their students' learning. As a former instructional coach, it had been a passion of mine for quite some time! But when I became a principal and began observing classrooms, I was surprised to discover that teachers had not implemented the information they were provided during professional development sessions. As I observed in the elementary classrooms throughout the building, I discovered many issues, but two were significant. First, no two teachers were teaching in the same way or consistently using the same materials. For example, vocabulary instruction looked different in every grade level. And second, teachers were not explicitly teaching. They provided instruction, but it was not explicit, and most was provided in whole group. Their "teaching" was actually facilitating worksheets. They were, however, explicitly explaining the directions of worksheets and activities. With the book *Explicit Instruction* by Anita L. Archer and Charles A. Hughes (2011) in hand, I modeled explicit instruction in classrooms so teachers could visibly see the difference. With discipline being a serious concern the previous two years, special education numbers being well above the state average, and the reading data being as low as they were, I knew we had to begin with strong, explicit instruction throughout the building.

### Consistent and Explicit Universal Instruction

We began by fixing our universal instruction, or Tier 1 instruction! I began by having all teachers, regardless of grade level or content area, start each lesson with a clear learner objective that was based on a state standard. We worked on one instructional practice at a time until at least 85 percent of teachers were consistently doing this 85 percent of the time.

As the instruction became more specific, discipline issues decreased, engagement of students increased, and students proficiently learned the content of lessons.

Our next step was to develop instructional practices that were consistent throughout the building. One of the first areas we tackled was the use of a focus wall that contained all of the key ideas students would learn that week. We also developed an explicit vocabulary procedure that was used by every single teacher in the building. Again, these practices had to be modeled multiple times in classrooms for teachers to become comfortable with the instruction. Teachers also needed feedback on their lesson delivery. It is important to note that there was resistance during this process, and some teachers were quite vocal about it. Change can be intimidating, and I was asking teachers to completely change the design and delivery of their lessons. Regardless of the level of resistance, these practices were an expectation for all, and feedback was given on a regular basis. In some rooms, the implementation of these practices was immediate.

One of the first teachers to embrace these expectations was the fifth-grade teacher, Christie Kenedy. One afternoon during her prep hour, we were discussing the changes in her instruction, and I asked why she thought teachers had not implemented the strategies and instructional practices they were shown during the time I had been the district instructional coach. She was honest and forthcoming in her response and said she believed the reason was that the information provided to teachers were looked at as "suggestions." She went on to explain that without an expectation of implementation by the building leader, most teachers looked at the practices as optional. Teachers would try things for a little while and then go back to their old habits. That conversation provided me with one of the greatest lessons I had learned up to that point as a principal. Expectations must be established, shared with all, monitored, and everyone had to be held accountable.

I think it is incredibly important to point out that teachers did not know what they did not know. They did not see an issue with the instruction they had been providing. Most were going straight through their curriculum resources and did not realize what was missing in their delivery. Another issue was that most lessons were not based on a grade-level standard. When this was explored at a deeper level, I learned that most classroom teachers were not even familiar with their grade-level standards. Professional development and coaching had to be provided in that area, as well.

## Aligning Instruction to the Science of Reading

After we addressed explicit instruction and established systematic practices throughout the building, we had to address the lack of knowledge that teachers had regarding the science of reading. Teachers genuinely believed that they were correctly teaching reading. They did not realize that their instruction did not include each of the five components of a structured literacy approach. It took a while for them to understand the difference, but the message that stuck with teachers was when I told them during a weekly professional development session that they were teaching the subject of reading, but they were not teaching students how to read. Teachers in grades K–2 were heavily teaching the skills of reading comprehension, such as sequence of events, cause-effect, and so on. It would take putting new reading curriculum resources in their hands that were founded on the science of reading for that knowledge to become concrete.

The transformation of instruction from start to finish was nothing short of miraculous! The teachers became masters in delivering explicit instruction, and no student was allowed to opt out. Students were engaged 100 percent of the time. Lessons were based on grade-level standards and delivered in a manner that was both systematic and explicit. Instruction was consistent throughout the building. It did not matter whose class you entered or what grade level you observed; the instructional routines were clear and consistent. Our vocabulary procedures were rock solid, with an overwhelming majority of students mastering the vocabulary assessment on a regular basis. By improving Tier 1 instruction, we were able to make significant gains with our special education students. The teachers developed a sense of self-efficacy. Their discussions changed, and they knew beyond a shadow of a doubt that their instruction was impacting their students. Honestly, my favorite place had always been in the classroom, but by doing this work, I realized the significant importance that a building leader brings to the work of literacy for all. We are called to be in classrooms observing, providing feedback, and having instructional conversations with our staff.

Literacy for all is not accidental. It happens as a result of good leadership, and it fails to happen without a strong instructional leader. All students and teachers deserve an instructional leader, and, when done correctly, it is the most rewarding work of all.

### *It's Possible* When Leaders Believe That:

- All lessons should be based on grade-level standards and delivered in a manner that is both systematic and explicit.

- Implementation of universal instruction and research-aligned instructional practices are an expectation for all.

- Teaching the subject of reading is not the same as teaching students how to read.

- The principal is the instructional leader responsible for driving literacy throughout the building.

Our belief is that you have to start in two places—universal instruction and Tier 3 interventions. (Tier 3 being instruction for students who scores in the lowest instructional level on a foundational reading assessment.) It is impossible and inappropriate to try to intervene your way out of the problem; however, in many schools, students are tremendously behind. If you begin with implementing good universal instruction or Tier 1 instruction in a structured literacy approach while at the same time putting into place highly effective Tier 3 interventions, the school quickly starts to make gains. (Our discussion on Tier 3 instruction and intervention occurs in chapter 3, page 57.)

It can't be emphasized enough: All students deserve and should receive high-quality universal instruction in alignment with their state standards. In order for all students to learn at high levels, educators must teach at high levels (Buffum, Mattos, & Malone, 2018). Many educators fret over the notion that students substantially lower in reading ability will only become frustrated. Many students below grade level in reading tend to misbehave when the literacy block starts; there is research that substantiates that students with low reading ability do display disruptive behaviors and create classroom difficulties (Boyes, Tebbutt, Preece, & Badcock, 2018). Teachers know this, as well, and may be relieved that a student is receiving instruction elsewhere. Struggling readers know what is coming, and for far too many students, literacy time is a trigger for failure. Instead of having to engage, struggling readers would rather hijack the instruction, hijack their friends, hijack the teacher, or often, all three! Clear behavioral expectations are a part of universal instruction, also referred to as Tier 1 instruction.

If you are a principal or district leader who is moving to a structured literacy approach or just seeking to increase literacy outcomes, you will see a striking difference between what you're currently doing and evidence-based literacy practices, although some common practices do overlap. Table 2.1 lists commonly found components in classrooms without a science of reading alignment compared to practices that align with evidence found within the research.

**TABLE 2.1:** Ineffective Versus Effective Literacy Practices

| Practices to Move Away From | Practices That Ensure *It's Possible* |
| --- | --- |
| Teacher observing reading behaviors | Teacher assessing on foundational reading skills |
| Minilessons | Whole-group instruction |
| Theme or comprehension-based instruction | Instructional hierarchy of the components of literacy |
| Workshop model—teacher conferencing | Explicit instruction |
| Leveled texts or trade books | Comprehensive Core reading program |
| Independent selected texts for silent reading | Decodable texts (K–3) |
| Small group may have blocks, Legos™, coloring books, mathematics activities—designed to be busywork | Small group based on the five components of literacy and on the students' areas of need |

As Angie pointed out regarding what was going on in her classrooms, there really was no clear understanding of what good literacy instruction was, whether it was a balanced literacy approach or a structured literacy approach. Like so many schools, it was a "little bit of everything" approach and a lot of noninstructional impact! Understand, this is not based on malintent from teachers; they simply don't know how to provide science-based instruction. There is a great deal of buzz among educators regarding what instructional strategies, materials, and philosophies they should be following and using. The cutest worksheet on Teachers Pay Teachers often makes the cut. Frankly, most of this is rarely based on research. As we discussed in the previous chapter, these unsound practices are often compounded not only by school leadership lacking the knowledge to provide quality instructional feedback but also by the emphasis on school leaders being school managers and not instructional leaders.

The awareness that the science of reading has sparked a movement for the professional development of teachers to become more knowledgeable in the area of reading has not necessarily ameliorated these practices. In fact, most of the common professional development for teachers in the science of reading lacks the development of the framework and understanding of the important instructional strategies used within a literacy block—put simply, they often lack how to implement the knowledge gained in professional development on structured literacy. One of the first places to begin implementation is with universal instruction.

# An Understanding of Universal Instruction

We have delineated eleven criteria that we believe should be found within the domain of universal instruction. The domain of universal instruction appears at the end of this chapter (page 53). When strongly implemented, these criteria make a significant difference in increasing literacy outcomes. This is not an end-all list but rather high-impact components that heavily influence positive results. As you will come to see throughout this book, each of the criteria found within the domains begins with the overall construct of that criterion. As you move from left to right on each criterion, it becomes more nuanced and student- or data-driven. Following this framework, your school will go from a culture of teaching to a culture of learning. In other words, as you begin to implement the ideas found within each of the domains, the understanding and implementation will be simple. As your school or district becomes more sophisticated in the application of this framework, so, too, will you refine your schoolwide practices.

The reproducible domain table at the end of this chapter outlines the critical components we find necessary to be included within strong universal instruction or Tier 1 during the literacy block. As we progress through this chapter, we will describe each of the criteria, discuss how they typically unfold in the classroom, and relate approaches that can be taken to improve outcomes. As a reminder, universal instruction is achieved when all students receive highly effective literacy instruction that is comprehensive in its scope and delivered through research-based strategies.

# The Schedule and the Structure of the Literacy Block

Students must receive, at minimum, 90 minutes of research-based reading instruction daily through fifth and sixth grades, and 120 minutes is ideal, as discussed in chapter 1 (page 11). Though the National Reading Panel in 2000 identified the five components of reading, it did not specify the number of minutes for each. Guidance documents from the U.S. Department of Education were the first to codify the expectation of an uninterrupted, 90-minute reading block (Denton, Foorman, & Mathses, 2003; Underwood, 2018; U.S. Department of Education, 2011). This amount of time changes for each component of reading as you increase through the grade levels. As an example, what a student receives in whole-group literacy instruction for phonics in the fifth grade would be of a much shorter duration than for phonics instruction in first grade.

## Creating a Master Schedule

Many teachers complain that they don't have time to provide 90 to 120 minutes of instructional time for literacy. We would assert that there should be two subjects, particularly in K–2 classrooms, that should take precedence—literacy and numeracy. This is critically important, especially due to consequences of the COVID-19 pandemic and the Nation's Report Card results. If students are unable to read, they are certainly unable to read textbooks in *every* subject.

To ensure students receive the adequate time for intervention, the master schedule becomes the linchpin for a successful literacy implementation. Because a school's master schedule impacts every grade level, department, and program in the school, creating such a schedule requires a schoolwide collaborative effort (Mattos et al., 2025). This is best accomplished through the school leadership team (see chapter 6, page 145).

Many schools still create a schoolwide literacy block. Though the principle of doing this is understood—a two-hour time block, at the same time, in every grade level, when all hands are on deck to increase literacy—we find it has more disadvantages than advantages. Staggering start and end times across the grade levels for literacy allows for a much more efficient system. As an example, interventions staggered at opposite times guarantee that students do not miss universal or Tier 1 instruction. Fifth grade has interventions while first grade is having whole-group instruction. Staggering start times permits a better use of human resources, particularly if you are implementing a push-in model for interventions. A push-in model is highly effective and ensures that paraprofessionals, special education personnel, and interventionists are providing additional services in a general classroom setting. These services are based on student need, delivered in a small-group setting and allow for students to receive another dose of instruction. Another advantage to this model is that two adults are providing services to students during small-group instructional time within the general classroom setting. Well-thought-out planning is an essential characteristic of successful push-in models. A push-in model cannot be achieved in a master schedule when the literacy block is for a common two-hour time schoolwide. Having a master schedule in which literacy is happening throughout the school day also ensures that the building principal can observe multiple literacy classrooms at multiple times during the day.

When scheduling literacy blocks, start with the non-negotiables in your building. This is often lunch and transportation. Often the organization of the time for specials will coincide with planning time for grade-level teachers. In other words, when students go to specials like art, music, and physical education is often when grade-level teachers can have common planning time. This is critical, and it is necessary to think this through. Whenever possible, all grade-level teachers should have a common planning time.

Once those have been determined, begin building your literacy blocks by grade level. Though we recommend scheduling literacy for the primary grades in the morning, we actually don't suggest literacy starting the day with kindergarten. Kindergarten needs time in the mornings for coats, mittens, tying shoes, and many other activities that may get in the way. We suggest beginning with first grade as early in the day as possible, then going to kindergarten thirty minutes later, and then second grade. From third grade and beyond, when each grade level begins their literacy block is not as important. In fact, we suggest rotating who goes next from year to year so that no grade level is always at the end of the day.

Figure 2.1 is an example of a master schedule. Listed with the recommended resources for universal instruction at the end of this chapter is a schedule maker that allows you to create a master schedule. Visit **https://schedule.schoolscubed.com** for a schedule maker.

## IT'S POSSIBLE

| Time Slot | Kinder-garten | First Grade | Second Grade | Third Grade | Fourth Grade | Fifth Grade | Sixth Grade |
|---|---|---|---|---|---|---|---|
| 08:05-08:10 | | | | | | | |
| 08:10-08:15 | | Literacy | | | | | |
| 08:15-08:20 | | | | | | | |
| 08:20-08:25 | | | | | | | |
| 08:25-08:30 | | | | | | | |
| 08:30-08:35 | | | | | | | |
| 08:35-08:40 | | | | | | | |
| 08:40-08:45 | | | Literacy | | | | |
| 08:45-08:50 | | | | | | | |
| 08:50-08:55 | | | | | | | |
| 08:55-09:00 | | | | | | | |
| 09:00-09:05 | | | | | | | |
| 09:05-09:10 | | | | | | | |
| 09:10-09:15 | Literacy | | | | | | |
| 09:15-09:20 | | | | | | | |
| 09:20-09:25 | | | | | | | |
| 09:25-09:30 | | | | | | | |
| 09:30-09:35 | | | | | | | |
| 09:35-09:40 | | | | | | | |
| 09:40-09:45 | | | | Literacy | | | |
| 09:45-09:50 | | | | | | | |

**FIGURE 2.1:** Sample master schedule. *continued →*

| Time Slot | Kinder-garten | First Grade | Second Grade | Third Grade | Fourth Grade | Fifth Grade | Sixth Grade |
|---|---|---|---|---|---|---|---|
| 09:50-09:55 | Literacy | | Literacy | Literacy | | | |
| 09:55-10:00 | | | | | | | |
| 10:00-10:05 | | | | | | | |
| 10:05-10:10 | | | | | | | |
| 10:10-10:15 | | | | | Literacy | | |
| 10:15-10:20 | | | | | | | |
| 10:20-10:25 | | | | | | | |
| 10:25-10:30 | | | | | | | |
| 10:30-10:35 | | | | | | | |
| 10:35-10:40 | | | | | | Literacy | |
| 10:40-10:45 | | | | | | | |
| 10:45-10:50 | | | | | | | |
| 10:50-10:55 | | | | | | | |
| 10:55-11:00 | | | | | | | |
| 11:00-11:05 | | | | | | | |
| 11:05-11:10 | | | | | | | |
| 11:10-11:15 | | | | | | | |
| 11:15-11:20 | | | | | | | |
| 11:20-11:25 | | | | | | | |
| 11:25-11:30 | | | | | | | |
| 11:30-11:35 | | | | | | | |
| 11:35-11:40 | | | | | | | |
| 11:40-11:45 | | | | | | Lunch | |
| 11:45-11:50 | | | | | | | |
| 11:50-11:55 | | | | | | | |
| 11:55-12:00 | | | | | | | |
| 12:00-12:05 | | | | | | | |
| 12:05-12:10 | | | | | | | |
| 12:10-12:15 | | | | | | Literacy | |

| Time Slot | Kinder-garten | First Grade | Second Grade | Third Grade | Fourth Grade | Fifth Grade | Sixth Grade |
|---|---|---|---|---|---|---|---|
| 12:15-12:20 | | | | | | Literacy | |
| 12:20-12:25 | | | | | | | |
| 12:25-12:30 | | | | | | | |
| 12:30-12:35 | | | | | | | |
| 12:35-12:40 | | | | | | | |
| 12:40-12:45 | | | | | | | |
| 12:45-12:50 | | | | | | | |
| 12:50-12:55 | | | | | | | |
| 12:55-01:00 | | | | | | | |
| 01:00-01:05 | | | | | | | |
| 01:05-01:10 | | | | | | | |
| 01:10-01:15 | | | | | | | |
| 01:15-01:20 | | | | | | | |
| 01:20-01:25 | | | | | | | |
| 01:25-01:30 | | | | | | | |
| 01:30-01:35 | | | | | | | |
| 01:35-01:40 | | | | | | | |
| 01:40-01:45 | | | | | | | |
| 01:45-01:50 | | | | | | | |
| 01:50-01:55 | | | | | | | |
| 01:55-02:00 | | | | | | | |
| 02:00-02:05 | | | | | | | |
| 02:05-02:10 | | | | | | | |
| 02:10-02:15 | | | | | | | |
| 02:15-02:20 | | | | | | | |
| 02:20-02:25 | | | | | | | |
| 02:25-02:30 | | | | | | | |
| 02:30-02:35 | | | | | | | |
| 02:35-02:40 | | | | | | | |

*Source: © 2015 by Schools Cubed (https://itspossible.schoolscubed.com). Used with permission.*

## Scheduling Whole-Group and Small-Group Instruction

A literacy block in a structured literacy classroom has two components: whole-group and small-group instruction. Again, we believe that all students should receive both whole-group and small-group instruction daily during the reading block. Whole-group instruction provides the instruction related to grade-level standards, and small-group instruction is additional time for students to receive differentiation during universal instruction or Tier 1 time. It should be noted that the English language arts standards of the Common Core, as well as all revised state standards, include a component called the foundational skills. These foundational skills of literacy include the five components of reading. As with the Common Core, we believe that students should receive comprehensive instruction in English language arts, which includes reading literature, reading nonfiction text, and the foundational skills. Though most or many states have stepped away from the Common Core state standards, I know of no state that does not include foundational reading skills in their standards.

Table 2.2 illustrates the time we suggest spending on the various components of literacy for each grade level during whole-group instruction.

**TABLE 2.2:** Time Spent on the Various Components of Literacy for Each Grade Level During Whole-Group Instruction

| **Kindergarten:** | **First Grade:** |
|---|---|
| Phonemic awareness and phonics: 25 minutes | Phonemic awareness and phonics: 25 minutes |
| Oral language development: 10 minutes | Vocabulary: 10 minutes |
| Listening comprehension: 20 minutes | Fluency: 10 minutes |
| | Reading comprehension: 20 minutes |
| **Second Grade:** | **Third Through Fifth or Sixth Grade:** |
| Phonemic awareness and phonics: 20 minutes | Phonics: 15 minutes |
| Vocabulary: 10 minutes | Vocabulary: 10 minutes |
| Fluency: 10 minutes | Fluency: 10 minutes |
| Reading comprehension: 20 minutes | Reading comprehension: 30 minutes |

The sequence in which the components are taught to students is also critical. This is called the instructional hierarchy (Cabell, Neuman, & Terry, 2023). The instructional hierarchy within a lesson should not be confused with an instructional hierarchy of academic skill development (such as acquisition, fluency, generalization, and adaptation). Instead, imagine a lesson that is linear in nature. In literacy instruction, pieces form the whole—sounds to letters, letters to words, words to sentences, sentences to passages and books. Instruction should address the multiple skills in a concerted manner, as the initial skill aids in the acquisition of the next skill.

The teacher begins with the phonemic awareness portion of the lesson, which feeds into the phonics portion, which in turn helps students to decode the words on the page, which then helps the students to read the vocabulary words, which finally helps them to comprehend the passage. Figure 2.2 illustrates an instructional hierarchy within a first-grade lesson.

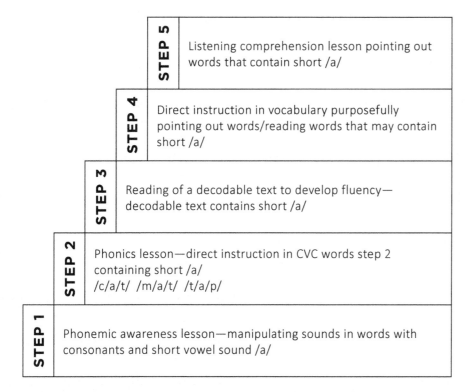

**FIGURE 2.2:** Instructional hierarchy of a first-grade lesson.

As you can see, phonemic awareness is taught first within the lesson. As you move up in grades, a similar progression occurs. Because most students would have acquired phonemic awareness by second grade, it would be dropped from the lesson. In third through fifth grade, we would begin with the phonics portion. Phonics occurs before vocabulary to assist with the decoding of words, and fluency and comprehension follow next to ensure the pieces form into the whole and help students through the learning progression.

## Starting With Whole-Group Instruction

A literacy block begins with whole-group instruction. Whole-group instruction typically lasts from forty-five to sixty minutes. In kindergarten, we recommend thirty minutes to forty-five minutes. When we tell teachers this, they often say, "my students can't sit that long." Though we agree it is a long stretch of time, we also assert that engaging teacher strategies, along with a perky pace, can hold students' attention. Examples of these strategies include turn and talk with your partner, let's reread together, and thumbs-up if you agree, to name just a few. We have seen many exciting classrooms where students were engaged for every minute of the literacy block and, quite frankly, didn't want it to end.

Engaging instruction should not be confused with lots of activities. A quality literacy block flows from one component to the next in a hierarchical fashion, directly and explicitly taught. In many schools that are moving from a balanced literacy approach to a structured literacy approach—even when professional development has been provided in structured literacy—teachers lack an understanding of explicit instruction, and we see many small groups going on instead. There may be a phonics group with activities or a vocabulary group with activities. This is not direct and explicit instruction.

Thoughtfully planned instructional routines should be a part of quality classroom instruction. Instructional routines are different from lesson planning—they are predictable methods for delivering the various components of instruction. Instructional routines ensure that all students are engaged and respond in a very short period of time. They generally are delivered with a perky pace with choral responses. Many quality core reading programs offer or contain suggestions for good instructional routines. It is imperative that teachers use them.

During whole-group instruction, teachers provide instruction in the five components of reading, depending on the grade level. In working with many schools, Schools Cubed consultants have found that basic phonemic awareness is secured by the majority of students by the end of first grade or the middle of second grade and does not need to be taught beyond that. This instruction should be based on grade-level material using a high-quality core reading curriculum and provided to *all* students. Though whole-group instruction is based on the five components of reading, it should also be thought of as having two big ideas: (1) the skills of reading, meaning phonemic awareness, phonics, and word recognition and (2) the knowledge portion of reading, meaning vocabulary, language, literacy knowledge, background knowledge, and so on. This understanding of whole-group instruction aligns with Scarborough's rope (see the overview of the science of reading in appendix A, page 253, for a further description of Scarborough's rope).

## Continuing With Small-Group Instruction

Typically, after whole-group instruction, small-group instruction begins. This is a time for differentiation to occur for universal or Tier 1 instruction. Again, *all* students should be receiving small-group, differentiated instruction. Small-group instruction, for the most part, should be aligned with whole-group instruction. When planning for teacher-led, small-group instruction, four considerations should be kept in mind. The purposes of the small group are as follows.

1. Provide more practice for the students.
2. Extend students' thinking about the topic being read or taught.
3. Reteach important, unacquired skills from whole-group instruction.
4. Front-load students' information for what is coming (vocabulary or background knowledge as an example).

To put the purposes of small-group instruction in context, it is important to remember the challenges found among struggling readers. About 70 percent of poor readers have weak word recognition and weak comprehension (Shankweiler et al., 1999). This is the most common profile of poor readers. About 10 percent of poor readers have good word recognition with specific language comprehension problems. This profile is very rare. About 20 percent of poor readers have inaccurate or slow word recognition with good comprehension (Shankweiler et al., 1999). Small-group instruction is based on data and the needs of the students; therefore, it consists of "like" students (those students having similar strengths or weaknesses in any of the five components of reading). The instructional needs of the students should be based on their instructional level as identified by their reading assessment. For most quality, foundational reading assessments, a student's outcome is based on four instructional levels that are usually (1) well below benchmark or grade level, (2) below benchmark or grade level, (3) at benchmark or grade level, and (4) above benchmark or grade level.

## Grouping Students Effectively

It can be tempting to group students based on these instructional levels—in other words, all students above grade level together, all students at grade level together, and so on. However, to ensure students' needs are truly being met, we must dig deeper into the assessments and form our small groups based on the subskill in need. Only students who are below in a subskill should receive small-group instruction based on the subskill. (How to analyze data will be discussed in chapter 5, page 111.) Though we will go into detail regarding small-group instruction based on subskills, in general, when thinking about small-group instruction, we can assume that our purpose for each instructional level of students will be the following.

- **Above grade level:** Extending learning on the standards being taught in whole-group instruction. This would be reading a text at a higher level, providing discourse in the text, and questioning students as it relates to the standard of instruction.

- **Grade level:** Ensuring students are meeting the grade-level standards associated with the unit of our core curriculum.

- **Below grade level:** Providing students the opportunity of rereading or reteaching the components of literacy that are connected to the core story in the curriculum. This would be another practice and more repetitions of receiving phonics instruction in the phonetic element being taught or enhancing vocabulary instruction and building background knowledge connected to the core story.

- **Well below grade level:** Students will typically need more instruction in a decodable text aligned with the phonetic element being taught or gaps identified in phonics elements. In the upper grades (grades 4 and 5), this may mean more practice in reading decoding patterns in the context of a larger narrative.

We recommend spending twenty minutes on each teacher-led small group. Since most classrooms have students who fall into each of the outlined instructional levels, four groups may be necessary in each classroom. This is an additional eighty minutes of instructional time. To reduce the time, we have found that two to three days a week of teacher-led small-group instruction (instead of five) is sufficient for the above grade-level group of students.

Understand that if the teacher is with one group of students for twenty minutes, there may be fifteen to twenty students working independently. In some cases, schools are able to provide paraprofessional assistance or another ancillary staff member to be a part of the classroom, known as a push-in model of instruction. Unfortunately, we see it used far too often as occupying (babysitting) students during independent work while small-group instruction is occurring. There are many excellent programs available for enhancing and providing opportunities for extension, enrichment, and extra practice in one of the components of reading with the use of technology. We believe strongly that ancillary technology use for increased literacy outcomes should be monitored closely. There are excellent reports available to teachers that can provide information on how students are doing. These reports should enhance teachers' instruction and give them more information on how to differentiate their instruction. See table 2.3, which illustrates the time allotted for the various components of literacy throughout the literacy block.

**TABLE 2.3:** Time Allotted for the Various Components of Literacy

| Whole-Group Instruction in the Five Components of Reading | | | | |
|---|---|---|---|---|
| | Phonemic Awareness | Phonics and Spelling | Oral Language and Vocabulary | Listening and Reading Comprehension *(To include background knowledge)* |
| **Kindergarten** | 5–7 minutes | 15–20 minutes | 5–15 minutes | 15–30 minutes |
| **Grade 1** | 5–7 minutes | 15–20 minutes | 5–15 minutes | 15–30 minutes |
| **Grade 2** | 5 minutes | 15–20 minutes | 5–15 minutes | 15–30 minutes |
| **Grade 3** | | 10 minutes | 5–15 minutes | 15–30 minutes |
| **Grade 4** | | 10 minutes | 5–15 minutes | 15–30 minutes |
| **Grade 5** | | 10 minutes | 5–15 minutes | 15–30 minutes |

| Small-Group Instruction | | |
|---|---|---|
| | **Duration** | **Frequency** |
| **Above Grade Level** | 20 minutes | 2–3 times per week |
| **Grade Level** | 20 minutes | 4–5 times per week |
| **Below Grade Level** | 20 minutes | 5 times per week |
| **Well Below Grade Level** | 20 minutes | 5 times per week |
| **Totals:** 35–45 minutes for kindergarten<br>45–60 minutes for grades 1–5 | | |

## Reteaching, Repetitions, and Alignment

Remember, all students need to receive small-group instruction as part of universal instruction. This is the opportunity to differentiate. For students who need Tier 2 intervention or strategic learners, those students just below benchmark, it should be a repetition or another dose or teaching opportunity to receive the main ideas or concept regarding what is being taught in whole-group instruction and should be based on their data.

Students need the opportunity to master what they have learned or a chance to master what they have not learned—the concept of *reteaching*. Mastery teaching requires that students need more time to practice. Regarding foundational skills of reading, overlearning of basic skills is required. To build on one skill to the next, students must first have mastery of the first skill. Regarding the learning of phoneme-grapheme (sound-letter) correspondence and many other components of reading, students must have automaticity.

In a rather old but often-cited study, good readers named words faster than poor readers, but when provided ample opportunities and adequate repetitions, variance of reading times decreased when poor readers had more repetitions to learn the new words (Lemoine, Levy, & Hutchinson, 1993). Table 2.4 (page 42) shows their findings.

Overlearning foundational skills is critical for skill reading. Overlearning requires many more opportunities for practice for poor readers than good readers. When students have an opportunity to practice, they are strengthening their neural pathways and ensuring they retain their new knowledge over the long term (Oakley, Rogowsky, & Sejnowski, 2021). If a teacher teaches CVC words with short /a/ in whole-group instruction and gives seven examples, then in small-group instruction, the strategic or Tier 2 reader or those students

### New Thinking on Phonemic Awareness

As this book goes to print, two controversial areas are shaking the literacy world on social media regarding the instruction of phonemic awareness. First, how much time should be devoted to the teaching of phonemic awareness, and second, should phonemic awareness be taught with letters or with sounds only? Though it is not our intent to finalize this discussion, the following provides a brief summary and references to the associated research.

### Devoting Time to Phonemic Awareness

Since time is a precious commodity in literacy instruction, knowing that we may be able to reduce the amount of time spent in certain areas of literacy components while still achieving satisfactory results for students is something that should strongly be considered. Texas A&M University created a meta-analysis on the optimal "amount of time/dosage" in phonemic awareness instruction needed to help preK through grade 1 students understand and use the alphabetic reading principle to read and spell (Erbeli, Rice, Xu, Bishop, & Goodrich, 2024).

The findings of this meta-analysis did indicate that optimal instruction of phonemic awareness in preschool through first grade was accomplished with 10.2 hours of instruction. They do go on to say that these "findings should not be used to dictate an oversimplified prescription regarding dosage. Students will differ in the time they need to acquire PA and bond orthographic and phonological representations" (Erbeli et al., 2024, p. 19).

## Teaching Phonemic Awareness With Letters or Sounds

Many providers of professional development for how students learn to read have advocated that teachers should teach and use materials that provide instruction in phonemic awareness by using sounds only. In this same meta-analysis conducted by Texas A&M University, researchers sought to answer the question, should phonemic awareness include letters?

Regarding phonemic awareness instruction incorporating letters, the Texas A&M study found that by, "coupling PA instruction with letter instruction, our results imply that after around sixteen hours of PA instruction with letters, the effectiveness of instruction will continually increase with increasing cumulative dosage" (Erbeli et al., 2024, p. 19).

As a group of practitioners highly reliant on and aware of the research, we will continue to monitor these findings. Currently, we do recommend that phonemic awareness instruction is provided to kindergarten students approximately fifteen minutes per day and to first-grade students approximately twenty-five minutes per day. We also recommend that this instruction should include and align with the letters of the sounds being taught in the phonics component of the lesson. As the next school year approaches, we will likely be conducting our own research to determine whether the amounts of time in this area can be condensed and continue to assure that students are more than adequately attaining reading proficiency.

**TABLE 2.4:** The Number of Repetitions Required for Students to Achieve Accuracy

| Good readers | 99 percent accurate after 4 repetitions |
| --- | --- |
| Strategic readers | 98 percent accurate after 5–25 repetitions |
| Truly struggling readers | Need many more repetitions |

who are in the instructional level of below benchmark on foundational reading assessments should have the opportunity to read it or spell it another seven times at minimum to as many as twenty-three more times. This is critical if we are ensuring all students are reading at grade level. It takes a great deal of practice and repetition.

It is important that the content of repetitions is aligned across whole group, small group, and interventions. In trying to switch from a balanced literacy approach, or even just trying to make sure their students are receiving the correct instruction, many schools are having to cobble together curriculum to align with the science of reading and provide quality structured literacy instruction. Very often, after examining what they are using for their core curriculum, schools often find inadequate literacy components, particularly for phonics or phonemic awareness. To correct this shortcoming in their curriculum, they may purchase a supplemental phonics program. Unfortunately, the best-laid plans can go awry. Imagine if you are a truly struggling reader, and in your whole-group instruction you receive instruction in CVC words with short /a/. When you go to small-group instruction, you again receive instruction with CVC words, but this time, it is short /o/. Because you are a strategic learner, you also receive twenty minutes of Tier 2 instruction, and this time the supplemental program is teaching CVCe, or silent *e*. And you are six years old! You have had multiple opportunities to learn, but each opportunity was a different skill. Not only are you confused, but you also were able to master nothing. We will talk more about intervention in the next chapter, but I am sure you can see how absolutely critical alignment is in our instruction.

# Explicit Instruction

In a structured literacy classroom, how we teach is just as important as, if not more important than, what we teach. Teachers absolutely must know how students learn to read. This is the content knowledge of what they are teaching. But, they also must know *how* to teach. The content knowledge or the subject matter of a teacher has an effect size of 0.13, but the craft of how we teach has an effect size of 0.60 (Hattie, 2023). An effect size is a statistical procedure to indicate the magnitude of change between one study and another study, such as a particular instructional procedure and how effective it is—in this case, at increasing academic achievement. An effect size of $d = 1.0$ indicates an increase of one standard deviation on the outcome, therefore the higher the effect size of an instructional method or strategy, the greater effect it has on academic achievement.

In the quest to maximize students' academic growth, one of the best tools available to educators is *explicit instruction*, a structured, systematic, and effective methodology for teaching academic skills (Archer & Hughes, 2011). The science of reading emphasizes an explicit model of instruction, and this type of instruction was called out in the report of the National Reading Panel (2000). It's important to note that the effect size of explicit instruction has been found to be from 0.60 (Hattie, 2023) to 0.75 (Adams & Engelmann, 1996).

When we compare the instructional model in a structured literacy classroom to that found within a balanced literacy classroom, vast differences surface. A balanced literacy classroom is focused on teacher conferencing, or a readers' workshop model. Typically, a smaller amount of time in this model is spent on direct teaching. The balanced literacy classroom portion of direct instruction focuses on teaching a procedure, reading strategy, or genre and is called a *minilesson* (Richardson, 2009). The majority of classroom instructional time in balanced literacy is provided by guiding reading instruction through a workshop model. In the book, *How to Reach and Teach All Students Through Balanced Literacy*, Sandra F. Rief and Julie A. Heimburge (2007) explain, "The workshop provides flexible instruction within a balanced curriculum of reading and writing experiences that include science, mathematics, social studies and visual and performing arts" (p. 29). The workshop model is based on a *constructivist* approach to education. In this model, students construct or discover knowledge themselves. The teachers' role is to guide students to the next level of learning. Again, looking at Hattie's (2012, 2023) ranking of effect sizes, a discovery instructional model to learning has an effect size of 0.21. Comparing discovery approach effect size found in most balanced literacy classrooms of 0.21, to an explicit model of instruction with an effect size of 0.75, one can't help but leave the reader scratching their head and wondering why this has perpetuated in our classrooms for so long.

At the teaching level, the notion of explicit instruction or direct instruction is often confused with lecture. In fact, explicit instruction requires student engagement and interaction with what is being taught, not simply listening to the teacher. We view explicit and direct instruction as synonymous, and in this book the terms are used interchangeably. Our focus here is to highlight the main ideas and provide resources for further learning.

The phrase, "I do, we do, you do," often used to describe explicit instruction, is a gross simplification and provides a disservice to what we should be seeing in literacy instruction if we intend to make significant increase in student outcomes. In fact, there are two major components to explicit instruction: (1) the design of the lesson and (2) the delivery of the lesson.

## Recommended Resources

- "A Meta-Analysis on the Optimal Cumulative Dosage of Early Phonemic Awareness Instruction" by Florina Erbeli, Marianne Rice, Ying Xu, Megan E. Bishop, and J. Marc Goodrich (2024)
- "How Much Time Should Teachers Spend on a Foundational Reading Skill? Research Offers Clues" by Sarah Schwartz (2024)

## Lesson Design Elements

The *design* of the lesson includes elements such as the big idea (lesson objective, target, or "I can" statement), background knowledge, mediated scaffolding ("I do, we do, and you do"), and judicious review. See the following list for detail on lesson design elements.

- **The big idea:** Simply put, what do we want students to learn in a particular skill, subskill, or strategy when they leave our classroom on that day? We want them to learn the objective, the learning target, or an "I can" statement. Lesson objectives or learning targets are the foundation of what is to be taught. In a literacy classroom, there may be multiple objectives or targets in a given day. We recommend that whole-group instruction should have two learning targets daily—a phonological awareness target (in lower grades, this may also include both phonemic awareness and a phonics target) and a comprehension target. In kindergarten and first grade, the comprehension learning target should be based on listening comprehension.

  Learning targets or objectives are not always easy for a teacher to understand. In our experience, we have found that the better the teacher is at implementing and understanding their learning objectives, the better they are at explicit instruction.

- **Conspicuous strategies:** This is the explicit teaching of helpful strategies available to students that will benefit their learning. They are made conspicuous by the manner in which they are taught, by providing visual maps or models and giving full, complete directions for use. A teacher should describe the strategy, include how it is helpful, demonstrate or model the strategy, provide adequate practice, and give feedback to students while they are using it.

- **Mediated scaffolding:** This provides help to students through steps and smaller tasks toward the whole. Reducing a task into smaller chunks helps the students master what they are learning. The teacher plans a gradual removal as the student becomes more independent in the task. The common expression of "I do, we do, you do" is an example of a mediated scaffold.

- **Strategic integration:** This is the student applying what has been learned and what they know and understand into new information. The teacher needs to make it clear how the previously mastered information will be used in the new information. Learning letters and sounds, forming them into words, and then progressing to decodable text is a perfect example of strategic integration in early reading instruction.

- **Judicious review:** Students are more likely to retain mastery of information if it is reviewed over time. Reviews in short spurts are more effective than amassed over a long period of time. An example of judicious review is, once students have mastered short /a/, and the teacher begins to teach short /o/, the wise teacher will continue to embed short /a/ words into the passage or lesson. Many quality interventions provide this type of instruction in their curriculum.

- **Background knowledge:** Acquiring new skills is based on what the student brings to the task, whether or not that information is accurate, and the ease at which they can access that information. As an example in literacy instruction, to decode a word a student must readily have access to the letters and sounds. For word recognition to be successful, the teacher must know what letters and sounds the student has. Priming background knowledge is also critically important to comprehension as well. If a student has no relevant background in a particular area that a story or passage is centered on, the likelihood of comprehending that passage is much more difficult. Priming students' background knowledge prior to reading a story increases comprehension.

It is not intended that a teacher uses each of these elements in every lesson. Certainly, every lesson needs to begin with the big idea. As mentioned above, the learning objective is the foundation of the lesson. Further, good reading instruction requires modeling by the teacher, whether it is a comprehension strategy or reading a CVC word, and students need a great deal of practice to master the skill being taught. Both of these are characteristics of mediated scaffolding. The more skilled the teacher, the more skilled they are at understanding the design of a quality lesson and weaving the various elements into the lesson as appropriate.

## Lesson Delivery Elements

The *delivery* of the lesson is *how* the teacher presents the information to be learned. It is what ensures students are engaged in the lesson. There are five elements found in the delivery of a lesson: (1) appropriate pacing, (2) adequate processing time, (3) frequent student responses, (4) monitoring students' responses, and (5) providing feedback.

- **Appropriate pacing:** The pacing of the lesson should be variable and is dependent on how difficult or easy a lesson is and if the lesson is new, review, or practice. The pacing, of course, is also dependent on the differences in students' abilities within the classroom. It's important to caution that many special education teachers believe that their students need a slower pace, when in fact special education students vary in their own capacity as well. We should not assume that special education students need a slow pace. A perky pace, when appropriate, provides students with more information and more opportunity for repetitions to hear, see, and digest information as well as minimizes behavioral problems.

- **Adequate processing time:** This is what we often think of as "think time." Processing time is also variable, as it depends on whether the information the students are receiving is new information or review information. It is also dependent on the complexity of the information. When students receive difficult information, they should have a longer time to process or answer a question.

- **Frequent student responses:** Students increase achievement when they actively participate in their learning. Students should not feel the need to put their heads down on their desks because of boredom or inattentiveness. Classrooms should be busy environments where students are engaged, because "highly interactive instructional procedures keep students actively engaged, provide students with adequate practice, and help them achieve greater success" (Hall & Vue, 2004, p. 6). Examples that would enhance student responses are teacher strategies such as personal response boards, choral responses, thumbs-up, talk to your neighbor, and so on.

- **Monitoring of students' responses:** Watching and listening to student responses provides the teacher with key instructional information. Adjustments may be made *during* instruction. When a teacher says, "Turn and talk to your partner," that is the optimal time to monitor and adjust student responses as needed.

- **Providing feedback:** Feedback to students has an effect size of 0.70 (Hattie, 2023). Feedback needs to be instructional and not accommodating. Feedback should be specific and should not interfere with the timing of the next question and response interaction between the teacher and student.

Explicit instruction is a critical component of a structured literacy block. Regrettably, teachers typically believe that they are teaching explicitly, but often, they are simply facilitating worksheets or continuing with a workshop model of instruction. The concept of explicit instruction is one of the hardest to implement in schools. If your school is going from a workshop model to one of explicit instruction, we recommend starting with the learning objective and building from there. Figure 2.3 is an explicit instruction observation checklist. You can use this to see where your teachers are in implementing the elements of explicit instruction.

| Design of Lesson | Evidence |
|---|---|
| **Big Idea**<br><br>What do you want students to learn by the end of the lesson?<br><br>Look fors:<br><br>• Today we will learn . . .<br><br>• By the end of literacy, we will know how to . . .<br><br>• [After a hook] What do you think we are learning today?<br><br>• Why are we learning this? | |
| **Conspicuous Strategies**<br><br>Teachers should explicitly teach helpful strategies to students that will benefit their learning.<br><br>Look fors:<br><br>• When I am reading a book or story, I visualize what I am reading about.<br><br>• To organize my thoughts, I like to create a web that helps me . . .<br><br>• Today I will teach you a strategy to use when . . . | |
| **Strategic Integration**<br><br>The student is applying what has been learned to new information.<br><br>Look fors:<br><br>• You know five consonant sounds and the short /a/ sound. Today we will make words from those.<br><br>• Yesterday you learned that we pause after a comma. Today we are going to read a passage that contains commas. I am going to listen to you read this passage . . .<br><br>• You have been working on CVC words. Today, we are going to put two CVC words together to make a word with two syllables. | |
| **Mediated Scaffolding**<br><br>Scaffolding is provided to students in the form of steps, tasks, materials, and personal support during initial learning that reduces task complexity.<br><br>Look fors:<br><br>• I will show you how to . . .<br><br>• First, we will . . .<br><br>• Watch as I do . . .<br><br>• Our first step will be . . .<br><br>• I will say, then you say . . .<br><br>• Follow me as I . . . | |

**FIGURE 2.3:** Explicit instruction observation checklist.

*continued* →

| Design of Lesson | Evidence |
|---|---|
| **Primed Background Knowledge**<br><br>Learning new skills and knowledge depends on (1) the knowledge the learner brings to the task, (2) the accuracy of that information, and (3) the degree to which the learner can access and use that information.<br><br>Look fors:<br><br>• K-W-L charts<br><br>• Showing two-minute videos<br><br>• Discussing previous experiences<br><br>• What does this remind you of?<br><br>• Have you ever seen . . . ?<br><br>• What do you know about this?<br><br>• Realia | |
| **Judicious Review**<br><br>Intentional review is essential to ensure students maintain a conceptual and procedural grasp of important skills and knowledge (big ideas). Information reviewed is useful and essential. Additionally, review should be distributed, cumulative, and varied. Review that is distributed over time, as opposed to massed in one learning event, contributes to long-term retention and problem solving.<br><br>Look fors:<br><br>• A question beginning the unit asking students about a previous unit<br><br>• Exit tickets of previously taught information<br><br>• A question asking for understanding of a previously learned big idea<br><br>• Not learning and moving on | |
| **Delivery of Lesson** | **Evidence** |
| **Frequent Student Response**<br><br>Teachers use engagement strategies that require student involvement.<br><br>Look fors:<br><br>• Personal response boards<br><br>• Teach/OK<br><br>• Thumbs-up | |
| **Appropriate Pacing**<br><br>Pacing is influenced by variables such as how difficult a task is, relative newness of the task, and the individual student differences within the class.<br><br>Look fors:<br><br>• Brisk pace<br><br>• Multiple repetitions<br><br>• Students are engaged in the instructional activity | |

| Delivery of Lesson | Evidence |
|---|---|
| **Adequate Processing Time**<br><br>Time to pause and think (think time) should vary based on the difficulty of the task relative to the students.<br><br>Look fors:<br><br>• Students' think time varies depending on task<br><br>  + Low-level questioning, such as facts, requires less time to process | |
| **Monitor Responses**<br><br>Watching and listening to student responses provide the teacher with key instructional information. Adjustments may be made during instruction. Teachers should be constantly scanning the classroom as students respond in any mode.<br><br>Look fors:<br><br>• Teacher listens to student responses as they interact with their shoulder partner<br><br>• Teacher moves around the classroom and listens to student responses during think-pair-share<br><br>• Teacher moves to students who look confused | |
| **Provide Feedback**<br><br>Feedback should be instructional and not accommodating.<br><br>Look fors:<br><br>• Feedback should be specific:<br><br>  + I like that you were careful to start that sentence with an uppercase letter.<br><br>  + I would make sure to . . .<br><br>  + Your first answer has more detail than your second; what did you do differently?<br><br>• Feedback doesn't become so involved that it interferes with the timing of the lesson. | |

*Visit* **go.SolutionTree.com/literacy** *for a free reproducible version of this figure.*

## Lesson Planning Templates

Explicit instruction requires planning. It is impossible for a teacher to explicitly teach the intricacies and components of literacy effectively without planning deeply. Unfortunately, most core reading programs offer more resources than a teacher can possibly teach in one literacy block. Consequently, teachers become overwhelmed and far too often pick the pieces in the core reading program that they like best or are most comfortable teaching. Because of this, we think it is critical for teachers to have a lesson plan template that helps them organize their lessons, ensuring that the most critical components are taught. We have included a sample lesson plan template for third through fifth grades (see appendix B, page 259). We have created sample lesson plans for the various grade levels with timestamps for each of the literacy components. These lesson plans are also available to download in the online resources.

## Helpful Resources for Digging Deeper into Explicit Instruction

- *Explicit Instruction: Effective and Efficient Teaching* by Anita L. Archer and Charles A. Hughes (2011)

- *Explicit Instruction: Effective Classroom Practices Report* by Tracey Hall and Ge Vue (2004)

- *Direct Instruction Reading, Sixth Edition* by Douglas W. Carnine, Jerry Silbert, Edward J. Kame'enui, Timothy A. Slocum, and Patricia A. Travers (2017)

- *The Handbook for the New Art and Science of Teaching* by Robert J. Marzano (2019; see chapter 3)

The templates are designed for teachers to reflect on the overview of what they will be teaching for the next week to two weeks of instruction. The big ideas for the weeks of instruction are laid out prior to the plans for the daily lessons. This layout is purposeful and inspires teachers to think deeply about what they will be teaching. When used appropriately, it ensures the correct instructional hierarchy. The included timestamps reinforce all of the components of literacy happening in the allotted amount of time.

## Materials for Instruction

Most of the legislation that states have created regarding literacy instruction in schools reference using or requiring evidence-based curriculum or science of reading curriculum. Unfortunately, this has become nothing more than a marketing label slapped onto curriculum that isn't evidence based at all. The consumer has to be savvy and know what to look for in the curriculum they choose. Further, high-quality materials matter. A Johns Hopkins study found that curriculum is deeply important (Steiner, 2017). Over time, a high-quality curriculum can yield an effect size of 0.60. That is approximately the equivalent of a student scoring in the 74th percentile versus the 50th percentile (Steiner, 2017).

To improve a school's ability to identify a truly evidence-based curriculum, the state of Utah has created an excellent core review checklist. It is referenced here: Teaching and Learning (https://schools.utah.gov/curr/index). We suggest using this resource to help identify quality evidence-based literacy materials.

## School Spotlight

### Kosciuszko Elementary School, Cudahy, Wisconsin

We were failing our students, particularly those from specific demographics. Despite an award from the state for exceeding average student growth, the glaring truth confronted us: Students were not learning to read. As a staff, we struggled with a sense of inefficacy, and students did not receive the instruction they deserved.

From the first time we rounded and did observations in all classrooms, it was evident that, as the building administrator and literacy specialist, we needed to become knowledgeable in systems, structures, and the science of reading to lead this change in our building. To drive the bus, we had to commit to learning and growing with our staff, and thus began an unimaginable journey.

Year one became an intense focus on Tier 1 instruction. This began with the crafting of a master schedule to guarantee every student received equitable, grade-level instruction. This was a significant change, as previously students would be pulled out for special education instruction or therapy, and now, that time was sacred. Systematic and explicit instructional routines took precedence. This process was complicated, as teachers were overwhelmed with information and the process of changing their teaching practice to include each of the five pillars. We focused on one pillar at a time to support classroom teachers, beginning with phonemic awareness. Observations were scheduled around phonemic awareness so we could give feedback on just that component until the routine was right and tight across classrooms and grade levels. We then moved on to the next pillar and completed the same process.

The weekly ritual of observations, initially perceived as a heavy burden by teachers accustomed to autonomy, transformed into a lifeline for growth. Reassurances were constant—these observations weren't evaluative but were rather a collective endeavor to enhance knowledge and skills. Trust became our foundation as teachers navigated the challenges of change, initially complying until the midyear data were presented. Students' unprecedented growth catapulted morale, and teachers moved from compliance to belief in the work. We moved students who had never moved in their reading and were considered long-term intervention students. Staff refer to this as the time when they drank the Kool-Aid.

In year one of implementation, we watched our students move from 22.4 percent being proficient on the state exam to 42 percent. The results were even better for our students with disabilities, who went from 4.3 percent being proficient on the state exam to 21.4 percent being proficient on the state exam.

One of the most essential components in implementing a change in universal instruction was using a lesson plan template aligned with structured literacy. We started with a basic template that included space for the five components of literacy. As we worked through implementation, the lesson plan was a living document that evolved with our growing understanding. We learned that we had to be in control of the resource, rather than the resource controlling us. Learning to be a good consumer of curriculum material meant that even with a resource change within our first two years of implementation, we were able to seamlessly continue the work, because good instruction is good instruction. Throughout the many iterations of our lesson plan template, the following components were included: timestamps for each pillar, explicit and systematic routines, learning objectives, scaffolded language, student engagement protocols, purposeful oral language opportunities, and culturally responsive teaching practices. Having a consistent lesson plan ensured a guaranteed and viable curriculum with equitable literacy instruction across all grade levels. Our teachers agree that being deeply planned is essential in doing this work.

Our mantra is the work is hard, but it's worth it. This journey has been life-changing for us as a staff, but more importantly, it has allowed us to give our students the gift of literacy.

---

*Melissa Kostka, Principal*
*Candice Johnson, Instructional Coach*

# Summary

Until quality universal or Tier 1 instruction is in place, students will continue to read below grade level. There are numerous instructional strategies that teachers can use. We believe, and research supports, that explicit instruction is the most effective manner in which to teach reading. Explicit instruction is much more than, "I do, we do, you do," and it is imperative that teachers know how to design and deliver their lessons based on explicit instruction.

The literacy block should include teaching both the knowledge and skills in reading. Quality literacy instruction contains an instructional hierarchy. To teach explicitly, ensure that teachers are teaching all the components of literacy in a manner that assures students will master reading acquisition, and make sure teachers have quality lesson plans. A lesson plan template can aid teachers in ensuring the layout of the lesson has an appropriate instructional hierarchy as well as the appropriate allotment of time for instruction. To ensure that students are learning what teachers are explicitly teaching in universal instruction, you will need to have a system to assess its effectiveness and ensure students are not falling behind. Chapter 3 will focus on how to establish a comprehensive assessment plan to do just that. You will also find in chapter 3 the evaluation domain for assessments that will help you establish a clear system for assessments.

# Universal Literacy Instruction

All students receive highly effective literacy instruction that is comprehensive in its scope and delivered through highly effective, research-based strategies.

| Big Idea | Basic (1) | Effective (2) | Proficient (3) | Exemplar (4) |
|---|---|---|---|---|
| **Students receive at least 90–120 minutes of research-based reading instruction daily.** | At least 90–120 minutes of grade-level comprehensive reading instruction is scheduled daily for all students. | The literacy block is protected time where only literacy instruction takes place. | Instruction during the literacy block is explicit, systematic, and research based. | Time and intensity of instruction are based on data and include both whole-group and differentiated small-group instruction. |
| **The literacy block is comprehensive and includes instruction in both knowledge and skills.** | Literacy instruction emphasizes either the knowledge strand of reading or the skills strand of reading. | Literacy instruction includes both knowledge and skills but may not address each appropriately based on the grade level. | The literacy instruction is both knowledge and skill based appropriately for the grade level. | Knowledge- and skill-based procedures are directly instructed based on the student data of the classroom. |
| **Daily reading instruction includes all components of literacy and is delivered in a systematic and explicit manner utilizing a research-based scope and sequence.** | Some components are taught during the literacy block. | All components are taught during the 90- to 120-minute literacy block. | Components are taught in an explicit and systematic manner using a research-based scope and sequence (intervention and small-group instruction are aligned to whole-group instruction). | Time and intensity of instruction for each component is consistently adjusted based on data and student needs. |
| **Literacy is taught daily in both differentiated whole-group and small-group formats based on students' needs.** | There is either whole-group or small-group instruction, but both do not exist. | Both whole-group and small-group instruction take place. | Whole-group instruction focuses on grade-level skills and small-group instruction is taught at the level of student need. | Whole-group instruction is taught with fidelity to the core program; small-group instruction is regularly adjusted (both concept and materials) based on student growth. |

**It's Possible!** © 2025 Solution Tree Press • SolutionTree.com
Visit **go.SolutionTree.com/literacy** to download this free reproducible.

| Big Idea | Basic (1) | Effective (2) | Proficient (3) | Exemplar (4) |
|---|---|---|---|---|
| **Small-group instruction is targeted and based on student need (including acceleration) and is of long enough duration for students to demonstrate mastery of the targeted skills or concepts.** | The school has adequate time for both whole-group and small-group instruction to occur daily. | Skills and concepts taught in small groups align to student data. | Teachers are routinely checking for mastery of skills taught in small groups. | Small-group instruction is consistently adjusted based on student data and is delivered at a pace that allows for multiple repetitions for students to master. |
| **Lesson objectives are clear, transferable, and communicated to students in a manner that is understandable.** | Instruction aligns to the lesson objectives. | Objectives are posted and referenced throughout the lesson. | Students can repeat the lesson objective. | Students understand and are able to reflect on lesson objectives and demonstrate understanding or mastery of the objectives. |
| **High-quality, research-based instructional materials for varied learning levels are readily available to teachers and students, and teachers are prepared to use the materials daily.** | There are enough materials available for all students, and teachers have been trained on how to use the materials. | All instructional materials are organized efficiently to maximize instructional time. | Instructional materials for students are differentiated during small-group instruction and based on student data and need. | Entrance and exit data are used to determine materials for all students during small-group instruction. |
| **Classroom instruction is student focused, engaging, predictable, and requires student interaction.** | The school's master schedule ensures that there is a predictable routine to the school day and teachers follow the schedule. | The classroom is organized, and there is evidence that routines for classroom procedures are in place. | Daily literacy lessons follow an appropriate instructional hierarchy. | Literacy instruction follows an instructional hierarchy, contains instructional routines, and is highly engaging for students. |

| Big Idea | Basic (1) | Effective (2) | Proficient (3) | Exemplar (4) |
|----------|-----------|---------------|----------------|--------------|
| **Technology is used appropriately to support and accelerate student learning and is aligned with the instructional focus.** | Reading technology programs are available for student use but may not be based on student needs. | Technology is aligned with instructional focus and learners are given the placement assessment if applicable. | Diagnostic data are used to adjust technology focus. | Student data from the technology program is used regularly to help track the effectiveness of the program, and there is evidence that supports technology is accelerating student learning. |
| **Literacy instruction is research based, is reflective of the population of students, and is implemented with fidelity.** | All instruction and materials are research based. | Instruction and materials reflect the student population and their needs. | Instruction is implemented with fidelity. | Instruction is responsive to the differing needs of students in the class or group. |

*Source: © 2024 by Schools Cubed (https://itspossible.schoolscubed.com). Used with permission.*

# Creating a Comprehensive Assessment Plan

## The Principal's Perspective

*By Angela Hanlin*

When I began my first year as elementary principal, the year began like any other, with staff members administering the beginning of year benchmark assessments using aimswebPlus. Our district had been doing this type of assessment for several years. Three times a year—beginning, middle, and end—all students were given a benchmark assessment in both reading and mathematics. Results were then used to identify which students needed an intervention. Data meetings were to follow each benchmark period, and results should be used to plan classroom instruction. I soon found a serious disconnect, however: The assessment data were not being used to plan instruction or interventions. Assessments were being done strictly for compliance. The data were not being used to improve student performance. Interventions were not targeted—instead there was a one-size-fits-all approach for any student scoring in Tier 3, which was anyone scoring below the 26th percentile. Meetings were held and assessment data were briefly discussed, but it stopped there. Staff members were not committed to the process, because they did not fully understand why the assessments were being given or how to use the results. The school had been conducting data meetings, but instructional decisions were not made based on data. Teachers would gather for a data meeting, review the benchmark results, and go back to their classrooms and pick up right where they had left off in their instruction. This explained the low scores and high number of students needing interventions. Assessment data were also not used to establish building goals or determine overall building success. Data were not kept in a common location and were not reviewed again until the next benchmarking cycle. For real change, we would need to really leverage the data and use it on a weekly basis to guide our instruction.

### Creating a Comprehensive Assessment Plan

We began by developing a comprehensive assessment plan. We mapped out three benchmarking periods: beginning of year, middle of year, and end of year. During each benchmark period, all students in grades K–5 were administered an assessment in both reading and mathematics. We held a data meeting after each benchmark assessment to identify students in need of intervention. Meetings were held with teachers at each grade level, and we looked at the assessment data for each individual student. Every single student not scoring at the 50th percentile in reading would receive an intervention. This was a significant change, since reading interventions had previously been given to students scoring below the 26th percentile. Prior to these changes, students were deemed OK, or not in need of an intervention, when really that was not the case.

Data were used to group students for small-group instruction as well. We reviewed the data to analyze the skill deficits for each student. Students with similar skill gaps were grouped together for small-group reading instruction in the regular classroom. Classroom teachers, special education teachers, and intervention teachers would use these data to plan instruction and set up progress monitoring to determine whether students were making progress or not.

We then planned six-week check-in meetings to review progress made by students whose progress was being monitored. This was the first time that teachers had ever reviewed the progress monitoring data, so they had to be taught how to analyze the data and use it to further plan instruction and interventions. This required coaching and modeling. It required instructional conversations between the building leader and teachers. They had been in the habit of simply going to the next lesson in their reading curriculum. Each small group had received the same instruction. At times, differentiation was done by different groups doing different activities but each receiving the same instruction. This was a significant change for teachers. They first had to understand that the instruction for each group was differentiated because the groups of students had different needs and skill deficits. Modeling was done in classrooms, and coaching was given on specifically planning differentiated lessons. It took some time before teachers felt confident in using the data to plan instruction. They needed feedback during their instruction in both whole group and small groups.

### Owning Our Assessment Data

As part of our comprehensive assessment plan, we used the benchmark data to set building goals for each grade level. This was met with significant resistance and hesitation! Teachers were incredibly nervous about working toward a goal that was based on data. They often asked what would happen if they did not reach their goals or provide reasons why they felt the goals might not be achieved. To put it simply, as a staff, we had never owned our data. We collected it, met to review it, but had never embraced and owned the data. Teachers saw data collection as something being done to them or that they had to do for compliance. Again, there was a serious disconnect.

To change the mindset of staff, I explained that we would take the focus off teaching and place it on *learning*. That was a complete shift in their thinking! Teachers had focused primarily on teaching the material instead of assessing whether students were learning the content. Staff did not realize the relationship or connection between the science of reading and the assessments being administered. Yes, they had received training in the science of reading, but they had missed the correlation between the assessments and the information that could be gained from the data. They definitely did not understand how to review progress monitoring data and use that to plan upcoming instruction. As we began this work, emotions ran high! Teachers were incredibly sensitive during data meetings and quickly became defensive. As their leader, the question became, "How do we make the data relevant and important on a weekly basis? How can I get teachers to embrace, and then own, the data?" My answer? Put the data on the walls! Up to this point, all assessment data were kept in three-ring binders. It was clunky and awkward at best! Each time Pati visited the building, I would drag out four thick binders of data. Getting the data out of the binders and putting them on the walls was a complete game changer and had a huge impact on student growth and teacher acceptance.

I took a small office-type space that had been used for storing assessment and intervention materials and created a data room. A sign was made and hung above the door that said, "Data Room," so that everyone who entered the building would see our data were important. Our student data would become a living, breathing space and would be used for daily decisions. Charts were hung around the room displaying the percentage of students in Tiers 1, 2, and 3 for each classroom. Goal posters were created that displayed the goals for each grade level. Information from each data meeting was also displayed to show which students were making progress, which were not making progress, and what our plan of action was in response to the data.

For starters, teachers began gathering in the data room to discuss the numbers, growth of students, and lack of growth. Over time, the dialogue changed. It is hard to ignore the data when they are visible in the school for all to see and are right in front of you at meetings. It is extremely important to point out that this is a process, and it requires diligence and persistence. Teachers need a strong leader for this process. It requires a system. We must put that system in place, and as building leaders, we cannot take a passive role in this work. We must lead the work! As a team, we developed protocols for data meetings and adhered to them consistently. We answered the exact same questions during all of our meetings: Who was making progress? Who was not making progress? Why did we get these results? What would we do in response to the data? Getting the teachers to understand how to use the data to plan upcoming instruction required extensive modeling. The step that solidified this in our staff was conducting a weekly meeting to review progress monitoring data. In the past, progress monitoring was done on a weekly basis, but nothing was done with the data. We began to meet on a weekly basis and had real, legitimate conversations about our students' progress or lack of progress. We worked as a team to brainstorm what would be done in response to the data. With a team approach, slowly but surely, teachers began to own the data and not be as defensive. If students were not making progress, we would not throw out excuses. We would respond by making instructional changes. Each week, teachers learned how to analyze the data and plan instruction to close the gaps in our students' learning.

I feel that it is important to point out that these meetings informed where I was needed the upcoming week. If one specific intervention group was not making progress, I observed that intervention group. If an entire class was not making progress, I observed the instruction in their classroom. Some teachers needed help developing small-group lesson plans that were directly tied to data. Others needed help differentiating their instruction. Often, student groups needed to be changed or interventions needed tweaking. It was a consistent, relentless response to the data. By modeling this to teachers, trust was built, and we developed team efficacy! We found that the more time we spent analyzing the data, the more growth our students made. Data meetings stopped being excuse sessions and became problem-solving opportunities. We kept a laser-like focus on the data and used it to make all instructional decisions. By doing this, our students made progress, and we began to close the gap. Teachers no longer complained about progress monitoring; instead, they embraced it and saw its importance. Teachers stopped complaining about weekly meetings and held them even when I was not in the building. Goals were met with excitement and determination. Students carried their goal cards with fierce determination and stopped me in the hallways to tell me their weekly progress monitoring results! The building had a different feel, an electric energy where everyone was working toward a common goal and speaking a common language. Teachers embraced feedback and saw it as a way to help their students make growth. We had daily conversations about assessments and instruction. Teachers sought other teachers and interventionists to ask for ideas about what to do with their students. We truly developed a system. When this is done correctly, it is powerful for all! We had bus drivers, maintenance staff, and cafeteria workers celebrate student success. Parents called to ask if their student had made progress on that week's progress monitoring assessment. As a team, we celebrated any and all success! Assessments were not something we had to do, but something we wanted to do to know how much progress was being made and what impact we were having on learning!

### *It's Possible* When Leaders Believe That:

- Assessment data must be reviewed on a regular basis for every single student.

- Data should be used to establish building goals, and goals should be revisited often.

- Data should be used to intentionally plan instruction and interventions that are specifically targeted to students' needs.

- Teachers should leave data team meetings with an instructional plan.

- Meaningful data review requires a system and leaders to take an active role in driving that system's implementation.

- Data should be visible for all to see.

- Data meetings are problem-solving opportunities.

Having engaged with thousands of schools and districts throughout the years, nothing seems as overdone and misunderstood as educational assessments. Angie, like so many principals across this country, knew that data were important and that assessments needed to be given to students. But where school systems can get lost is knowing what assessments to use when, and—most importantly—how to use data to effectuate change in instruction.

Truly understanding assessments, or *assessment literacy*, can be seen as dry, abstruse, and undesirable. Yet every school leader's goal should be to increase overall achievement outcomes for all students. Thus, it is imperative that we know what to assess, when to assess it, what the information is that we glean from the assessment, and how to generate instructional changes based on the information. Assessments assure that we maintain a laser-like focus on instruction.

As Paul Bambrick-Santoya (2012) claims, "data is the roadmap to rigor" (p. 25), and he is right! Whether students read below grade level, at grade level, or above grade level, we can't propel them to the next level and keep them there without good quality assessments.

In many instances, teachers are providing reading assessments as a school, district, or state compliance task. Too often, teachers do not understand the information the assessment is providing them to inform their instruction. We have found that because of the difficulty in the understanding of the assessments, teachers and schools continue to add assessments until they find one that seems to make sense to them or that aligns with their own beliefs about how students should be measured in reading. We have been in many schools that give students as many as four assessments to assess the same thing! In reality, the number of assessments needed to inform instruction is really quite minimal. Using too many assessments, assessing students too frequently, and not using the assessment to drive instruction are some of the key misunderstandings we find schools have. It's interesting to note that, as of this writing, twenty-nine states have enacted legislation that provides guidance on the usage of literacy assessments in grades K–3 (Olson, 2023); however, only thirteen states have identified specific literacy assessments that would be useful in addressing specific literacy deficits in students (The Reading League, n.d.).

When considering the assessments you are using in your school or district, it may be helpful to keep in mind some big ideas.

- **Redundancy in assessments:** Are we using different assessments that actually measure the same thing? Many schools use different assessments to measure the same skills. If you have multiple assessments for literacy, are they providing the same information?

- **Cost of assessments:** If you are using several assessments to measure the same item, then you are also doubling how much you are paying for assessments. The cost of the assessment could be better used going to cost for instruction. Cost doesn't stop at just the assessment. Time is also a cost, and if you are assessing students using multiple assessments, that time, too, could be going to instruction.

- **Use of assessments:** If teachers are not using the assessments they are giving to students, then the assessments are a waste of time. And a quality literacy assessment should never be a waste of time. Ensure the teachers understand what the assessments are saying about students' performance and about teacher performance. Is the assessment you are giving providing teachers with valuable information that will help them guide their instruction?

If you are a district or school moving from a balanced literacy approach to a structured literacy approach, assessment recommendations are quite different. Assessments in a structured literacy approach are typically valid and reliable instruments that leave little chance or judgment on what a student knows and doesn't know. Assessments are always timed to ensure that students have acquired the information with automaticity. Table 3.1 lists assessment practices commonly found in classrooms without a science of reading alignment, compared to assessment practices that align with evidence found within the research.

**TABLE 3.1:** Ineffective Versus Effective Assessment Practices

| Practices to Move Away From | Practices That Ensure *It's Possible* |
| --- | --- |
| Running records | Benchmark and screening assessments |
| Observational assessments | Progress monitoring probes |
| Reading level–based assessments | Diagnostic screeners and surveys |
| Standards-based assessments | Diagnostic assessments |
| Informal reading inventory | Outcome or summative assessments |
| Untimed assessments | Timed assessments |

# An Understanding of Reading Assessments

Overall, we believe the use of literacy assessments entails the following: clearly specifying and using valid and reliable instruments for screening and progress monitoring reading acquisition to guide instruction. Procedures for using assessments are specific, and the educational staff understand them. Students in grades K–5 take benchmark assessments at a minimum of three times a year, and students reading below grade level take them more often than that.

The terms *valid* and *reliable* are critical in making good decisions regarding test selection. A valid instrument is one that measures what it says it is measuring. In this case, the question to ask is, Is the test we are using truly measuring how a student is acquiring the skills necessary to read or progressing in their ability to read?

*Reliability* refers to whether or not the test will produce comparable outcomes under similar situations. What makes us excited as we see a student's growth in acquiring reading skills is the reliability of a test. We know that the student is "getting it." We know that the student's results are not arbitrary. Quality foundational reading assessments should provide a technical manual to show how the validity and reliability of a test has been determined. Be sure to examine any assessment you are considering to ensure the test you are using to determine students' reading progress is valid and reliable.

There are school factors that can impede a test's validity and reliability and should be given adequate consideration. Teachers who are not trained in administering the test and therefore do not adhere to testing procedures may invalidate the results. The subjectivity of an assessment can also make test results less valid. Last, how much influence assessment outcomes have on teachers' evaluations can unfortunately play a factor in how valid a test may be.

In a structured literacy approach, assessment is directly linked to identifying any student who may be below grade level so that interventions or help can be provided as quickly as possible. This initial assessment is called screening. All students should be screened to flag any student who may be below grade level in reading. When all students are screened, it is known as a *universal screener*. It is important to note that these sorts of assessments are identified with various names, but all have the same purpose. Commonly they are called universal, screening, or interim assessments. Screening is to identify who may be below grade level in reading, *universal* is to ensure all students are receiving the assessment, and *interim* means they are given at interim periods throughout the school year. All three terms will appear interchangeably throughout this book. All three terms come under the umbrella term of benchmark assessments.

In a structured literacy approach, not only are the types of assessment different, but what is being measured is also different. A structured literacy approach assesses *how* students are learning to read or, in other words, the *acquisition* of reading ability. Balanced literacy proponents, on the other hand, typically measure reading comprehension. This is a significant difference. One is measuring the *process* of how students read, while the other is measuring the outcome or the *product* of what students read.

In a structured literacy approach, curriculum-based measures are typically used for assessment. A curriculum-based measure is a set of methods for indexing academic competence and progress (Deno, Fuchs, Marston, & Shin, 2001). They are intended to be short probes of one or two minutes on a particular subskill of reading that a teacher could use to efficiently gather information as to whether or not a student is acquiring the academic knowledge or skill that is being taught. DIBELS 8 (Dynamic Indicators of Basic Early Literacy Skills), Acadience, and aimswebPlus were designed to be curriculum-based measures. These quick probes measure items like phonemic segmentation and oral reading fluency, concepts that are necessary at a particular grade level for reading, and they have expanded their scope and are much more than curriculum-based measures. We refer to these assessments as *foundational reading assessments*.

When measuring the *outcome* or *product* of what students read, balanced literacy advocates typically rely on a comprehension test that asks students questions indicating how well they understood what they have read. Often these assessments attempt to measure reading comprehension skills. These reading skills include such items as identifying the main idea and details, summarizing, describing the author's purpose, and sequencing, to name a few. In fairness, the English language arts portions in state standard assessments for the most part are based on these same reading skills. As explained in chapter 2 (page 27), we believe strongly in state accountability and standards, but reading comprehension tests do not provide us with information about why students fail to comprehend or fail such assessments. When we continue to measure students on product or outcome assessments, we fail to get to the root of why a student may not be able to comprehend what they are reading. Ensuring that students who do read at grade level are able to be proficient on the state summative assessment test is critical. In chapter 5 (page 111), we provide guidance on navigating this information.

# Types of Reading Assessments in a Comprehensive Plan

There are four types of assessment (screening, progress monitoring, diagnostic, and summative) that comprise a quality comprehensive reading plan. We will take a look at each and provide examples.

## Benchmark Assessments and Screening

Universal, screening, and interim assessments are all terms often used to describe the same assessment, though the meanings are slightly different. Universal assessment means all students receive the test, which we strongly support; screening assessment is the ongoing regular assessing of all students to make sure they are continuing to make gains; and interim assessments are used at intervals throughout the year. Generally, these terms may be used for the same assessment and should measure the foundational skills of literacy. They are typically given three times per year, at the beginning, middle, and end of the school year. These assessments are typically curriculum-based measures. Table 3.2 outlines the subskills that are measured each year. Tests vary regarding how long a subskill is measured and at what grade levels each are given, but overall, the following is a good descriptor. Some tests measure the subskill of letter naming fluency only in kindergarten. Some assessments measure it through first grade.

**TABLE 3.2:** The Subskills of Reading and In What Grade Level Each Is Assessed

| Structured Literacy Subskill | Purpose | Grade Assessed |
|---|---|---|
| **Letter naming fluency** | To identify the letter names students recognize | Kindergarten and the beginning of the year in first grade |
| **First sound fluency** | Phonemic awareness assessment that signals whether the student can recognize and produce the initial sound in a word | First semester of kindergarten |

| Structured Literacy Subskill | Purpose | Grade Assessed |
|---|---|---|
| **Onset-rime** | Phonological awareness assessment that separates a syllable into two parts— the onset or beginning and the rime or the end of the syllable | Preschool or beginning of the year in kindergarten |
| **Rhyming** | Phonological awareness assessment on the ability to recognize a rhyme | Preschool or beginning of the year in kindergarten |
| **Sentence segmentation** | Phonological awareness assessment to demonstrate the ability to recognize individual words within a sentence | Preschool or beginning of the year in kindergarten |
| **Phonemic segmentation** | Phonemic awareness assessment to ensure a student is able to recognize the individual sounds in a word | Middle of the year in kindergarten through first grade |
| **Nonsense word fluency** | Phonological awareness assessment to identify if a student has letter/sound correspondence necessary for phonics | Middle or end of the year in first grade through middle of the year in second grade |
| **Whole words read** | An assessment that measures how fluently students can accurately decode and blend letters and sounds to read whole words | Middle of the year in first grade through middle of the year in second grade |
| **Oral reading fluency (some assessments refer to this as a CBM)** | A standardized measure for passage fluency that indicates reading rate and reading accuracy | Beginning or middle of the year in first grade through eighth grade |
| **Retell** | Measures the students' ability to recall what happened in a passage | End of the year in first grade through sixth or eighth grade |
| **MAZE** | An indicator of a student's reading comprehension; students select a word from a list of three to five options to fill in a missing word in a sentence. | Beginning of the year in third grade through eighth grade |

Benchmark assessments need to be provided to students within the first thirty days of the school year, sooner if possible. Completing assessments as early in the year as possible encourages the following behaviors.

- Students in need of an intervention can begin an intervention as quickly as possible.

- Allocation of human resources to different classrooms or intervention settings can take place.

- Teachers will know which students need what and can immediately plan for their instruction in the general education setting.

In many school settings, teachers want to wait to provide assessments to kindergarten students until they have adapted to the school setting. We advise against this practice. Instead, we believe that the earlier a student can be identified as being below grade level, the quicker we can act, and the better the chances are of a student reaching grade level. For many kindergarten students, their entrance to public education is the first time that they have been exposed to letters, sounds, and the written word. We can and should provide this experience in the general education setting. We must know quickly who needs what instruction, repetitions for exposure, and adequate practice so that we can get students in kindergarten to grade level as soon as possible.

Table 3.2 (page 64) is a list of possible assessments of subskills found in early reading and beyond. Though the list may appear overwhelming, it is important to keep in mind that each of these are probes—those one-to-two-minute assessments discussed earlier in this chapter. Further, as you see in the right column labeled "Grade assessed," many subskills drop off based on appropriate reading development. As an example, we assume that by the middle of first grade, students know their letter names; therefore, we no longer measure that subskill. Typically, in kindergarten, most foundational reading assessments also assess rapid automatic naming (RAN), which is the ability to rapidly name any string of known items, such as letters, objects, or colors, under a timed circumstance and may indicate the ability to ultimately automatize words. Often, the subskill of letter naming is used to determine RAN.

Once given, the outcomes of how students performed on a reading screener are based on the instructional level as outlined on a specific assessment. Many educators recognize instructional levels by color and were originally designated as: green, on grade level or above; yellow, strategic or just below grade level; and red, well below grade-level expectations. Most screening assessments have moved to four levels of instruction and overall are, above grade level, on grade level, below grade level, and well below grade level.

Screening or benchmark assessments, as with all assessments in a science of reading world, should be considered formative assessments. Much can be gleaned from the information provided in these assessments. Any assessment given to a student without using it to inform instruction is a waste of teacher time and student time! How to disaggregate the data and make decisions from these data will be explored in chapter 5 (page 111).

# School Spotlight

## Remington Elementary, Colorado Springs, Colorado

During the fall of 2016, our school was awarded the Early Literacy Grant (ELG) from the Colorado Department of Education. Although our school was considered proficient according to the state's School Performance Framework, we were in a period of academic stagnation. We simply weren't moving students based on where students were currently performing. We hoped that with the support of the ELG, we would be able to leverage our data in meaningful ways to help all student populations at our school grow.

Through this grant, we had the opportunity to begin our work with Pati Montgomery. Although there were many adjustments we made during this time, one of the most impactful shifts we made was around the ways we were using our data. One of the questions Pati often asked our team to consider was, How are you using your data to identify specific literacy needs within your school? This was often followed up with, "Based on what you have learned from the data, what actionable steps can you take to improve those outcomes?" As our leadership team began to reflect on these questions, we realized that our emphasis within DIBELS was on the least-actionable part of the data. Up until this point, we had primarily been focused on the composite score. Although the composite score is great for identifying risk, the issue is that it doesn't identify a student's specific reading deficits.

As a result of these insights, we shifted our attention to the subscores within DIBELS. This adjustment had a profound impact, because it allowed us to pinpoint the exact needs of our students. So, if a group of students was struggling with reading fluency, we would look at their current and historical DIBELS data. The purpose was to identify any previous skills (accuracy, blending, phonemic awareness) that might be impeding their ability to read grade-level text fluently. Based on our findings, we would then administer a phonics or phonological awareness screener where necessary. By purposefully analyzing our subscore data, teachers were able to set meaningful goals, create action plans based on instructional needs, and monitor the impact of their instruction. Goals and action steps were regularly reviewed and adjusted throughout the year.

Three years before entering the ELG, 30 percent of our students were performing below or well below benchmark according to DIBELS. During the subsequent three years, that number was reduced to 18 percent and has been maintained since. In addition to this reduction, we have also seen an increase in rating within the state's School Performance Frameworks (SPF). Within the same time frame, our SPF rating has improved by an average of 11 percent, placing the school's rating in the low to mid-seventies. In fact, even through the pandemic and a change in leadership, scores have held consistently with no significant dips. We attribute this long-term success to the fact that when teachers know how to use the right data to improve outcomes, they take ownership of data because they see its value.

---

*Yuki Rockwell, District Instructional Coach (former instructional coach, Remington Elementary)*
*Lisa Fillo, Chief Academic Officer (former principal, Remington Elementary)*

## Diagnostic Assessments and Surveys

Benchmark assessments or universal screeners may not offer enough information when a student struggles to learn to read. It is at this point that we reach for a diagnostic assessment. Diagnostic assessments provide educators with more detailed or granular information that may help teachers make informed instructional decisions regarding next steps.

Diagnostic surveys are quick one-on-one assessments of various reading skills for students who are below grade level in one of the components of reading. Surveys are efficient and easy to administer, but they do not necessarily meet the criteria for being a reliable measure. As an example, many of these surveys have only one question for a student's ability to read CVC words, albeit with each of the vowels. Thinking of the definition for reliability—whether or not the test will produce comparable outcomes under similar situations—it may not be reliable. Having only one question regarding the ability to read a CVC word correctly with only one opportunity is not a reliable measure. That said, they do provide quality information which may help a teacher pinpoint what gaps may exist in a student's learning.

A diagnostic survey in the area of decoding is the most widely available. A decoding survey should not be given prior to the second semester of first grade, because not enough phonetic elements have been taught to determine whether a student has a gap in learning. Many surveys are free and downloadable. See the sidebar for a list of recommended diagnostic surveys.

Surveys are available in the area of phonemic awareness, phonological awareness, phonics, and vocabulary. For the most part, surveys are easy to use, and all staff should be able to be trained in how they are administered. They should not be given to everyone—we need all available instructional time that we can get. Instead, use surveys and screeners sparingly when students are struggling or as a guide to fill in instructional gaps for learners in Tier 2 intervention.

True diagnostic assessments are available for the most struggling readers. They are lengthy but provide very detailed and useful information regarding a student's weakness in the area of reading. We have found that when schools follow the advice provided in this book, very few students need a diagnostic assessment. These assessments should only be administered by highly skilled and trained individuals, such as special education teachers, educational specialists, and reading specialists. See the sidebar for a list of quality reading assessments.

## Progress Monitoring

Once a student has been identified as being below grade level on a reading screener, they then need to begin receiving interventions. Of course, the intensity of intervention will vary based on the need or the instructional level of the student as found on the screener.

Progress monitoring probes are used to identify whether or not the interventions are progressing the student toward the grade-level goal that the student is working toward. The progress monitoring tool should be aligned to the benchmark or screening assessment that the school is using. Frequently, intervention programs use a mastery test that may be confused with a progress monitoring tool. The progress monitoring tools that we recommend are brief "probes" that measure how well students are responding to the instruction that they are receiving, whether this intervention is in Tier 1 or universal instruction or through intensive intervention. In essence, progress monitoring answers the question, Is the help helping?

The probe that is used in progress monitoring should be the same skills that the teacher is directly teaching to increase the likelihood of meeting proficiency. Multiple equivalent forms—at least twenty and as many as thirty—should be available for progress monitoring as it may take many weeks for an intervention to be taught for a student to be at the desired goal.

Progress monitoring probes, as with screening assessments, are timed measures. It is critical that in basic word recognition skills, students demonstrate automaticity. Automaticity in word recognition skills demonstrates the ease of performance in these areas. Clearly, automatic word recognition is a critical factor in reading; therefore, so are the subskills required of reading acquisition.

The probes necessary for progress monitoring are the same subskills of reading that are outlined in table 3.2 (page 64).

## Frequency of Progress Monitoring

All students who are below grade level, as based on their screening assessment results, must be progress monitored to ensure they are making gains and that the intervention they are receiving is working. The frequency of progress monitoring varies based on the need of the student, as outlined in table 3.3 (page 70).

Students who are in the most intensive instructional level, typically called well below benchmark, should be progress monitored weekly to up to every ten days. Often, this level of instructional intervention is called Tier 3. Because of the intensive needs of these students, we must ensure that the interventions we are providing are working. There is no time to waste!

Students who receive Tier 2 intervention, often also called targeted or strategic students or those students in the instructional level identified as below grade level, should be progress monitored every two weeks or monthly. We also recommend students who may be just barely at the on-grade-level instructional level should be progress monitored monthly. We have found that these students, if not closely monitored, can quickly slip back.

## Regarding Diagnostic Surveys and Screeners

Many schools do indeed use a diagnostic survey or screener directly after discovering through a universal screening tool that a student is below grade level. This method will certainly identify specific gaps in a student's learning.

Instead of going directly from a universal screener to a diagnostic survey, however, we instead use the SIPPS placement test to determine the level of need within the SIPPS program and then place students into the appropriate intervention, thus using the placement test as a phonological diagnostic assessment.

Our organization has worked with hundreds of schools to administer the SIPPS placement test to literally thousands of students. Of those tested, 96 percent have qualified for a phonological intervention. (A phonics assessment used to place students in the Systematic Instruction in Phonological Awareness, Phonics, and Sight Words.) This test is administered to students scoring typically below 95 percent accuracy in a foundational reading assessment. We have found this method to be a much more effective means for identifying and providing interventions to students with phonological issues.

Since so many struggling students have a phonological processing issue, using a phonological intervention that identifies what level of issue a student has and then providing that intervention at the level of need saves a great deal of time.

## Recommendations for Screeners and Progress Monitoring Tools

- Acadience
  ⇨ https://acadiencelearning.org
- aimswebPlus
  ⇨ https://app.aimswebplus.com
- DIBELS 8
  ⇨ https://dibels.amplify.com
- FastBridge
  ⇨ www.illuminateed.com
  /products/fastbridge

## Recommendations for Quality Diagnostic Assessments

- *Assessing Reading Multiple Measures, Second Edition* by Linda Diamond and B. J. Thorsnes (2018)
- DAR-2: Diagnostic Assessments of Reading, Second Edition
  ⇨ www.proedinc.com/Products /13170/dar2-diagnostic -assessments-of -readingsecond-ed.aspx
- CTOPP-2: Comprehensive Test of Phonological Processing, Second Edition
  ⇨ www.pearsonassessments.com /store/usassessments/en/Store /Professional-Assessments /Speech-%26-Language /Comprehensive-Test-of- Phonological-Processing -%7C-Second-Edition /p/100000737.html
- WRMT-III: Woodcock Reading Mastery Tests, Third Edition
  ⇨ www.pearsonassessments.com /store/usassessments/en/Store /Professional-Assessments /Academic-Learning/Woodcock -Reading-Mastery-Tests -%7C-Third-Edition/p /100000264.html

**TABLE 3.3:** Frequency of Progress Monitoring by Instructional Level

| Assessment Instructional Level | Progress Monitoring Frequency |
| --- | --- |
| Students who score well above benchmark | Benchmark three times per year |
| Students who score well above but have a below-benchmark subskill | Progress monitor the below-benchmark subskill monthly |
| Students who score solidly at benchmark | Progress monitor three times per year |
| Students who score at benchmark but have a below-benchmark subskill | Progress monitor the below-benchmark subskill monthly |
| Students who score barely at benchmark | Progress monitor monthly |
| Students who score below benchmark | Progress monitor every two weeks |
| Students who score well below benchmark | Progress monitor weekly |

We often see schools that progress monitor students at their grade level only. This practice has consequences for both the teacher and the students. Advice from most assessment publishers is to progress monitor students at their current level of skills. To be able to show a student's progress, the assessment material must be at a level in which changes in student skills will be demonstrated. If the measure is too difficult, progress will not be apparent, and the student and teacher or interventionist may become discouraged. Further, if assessment materials are too difficult, educators may believe that the student is not making adequate progress and decisions whether or not an intervention is working may not be made accurately.

### Outcome or Summative Assessments

Beginning in third grade and continuing, we believe end-of-unit summative assessments from the core reading program should be given to students. There are numerous reasons for our thinking. First, typically end-of-unit assessments found in quality core reading programs measure how students are doing on the state standards. We think that is really important! Second, most reading program unit assessments mirror state assessments in length, question type, and standards measured. If regularly taking unit assessments is part of the literacy instruction routine, students will be more prepared to take the state summative assessment.

For many students, particularly those in schools where students are under performing, text and test stamina are legitimate issues. We believe that to enhance students' test stamina, a scaffolding approach for these unit assessments can be very helpful. Generally, core reading programs are divided into six units, each with an assessment.

Typically, each assessment has various sections that include a reading passage with multiple-choice questions, a vocabulary section, a phonics or structural analysis section, and a compare and contrast passage with an extended response section. For the first unit assessment, we recommend taking the test together as a whole class, focusing on test-taking strategies. The second unit assessment should be done 75 percent together as a class, again focusing on test-taking strategies and 25 percent taken independently. The third unit assessment should be 50 percent taken together and 50 percent taken independently. The fourth unit assessment should be taken 75 percent independently and 25 percent scaffolded. If following this procedure, the fifth unit assessment should occur shortly before the state assessment is given. Students should take this assessment independently. Teachers should analyze the outcomes with the opportunity to reteach students any standards that they seemed not to have mastered prior to the state assessment date. See table 3.4.

While the unit assessments are given, teachers should be paying close attention to any standards students may not have mastered. They should provide small-group reteaching opportunities in the next unit if a small number of students are not mastering a certain standard or whole-group reteaching if more than 50 percent of students have not mastered the standard.

**TABLE 3.4:** Scaffolding Schedule for Unit Assessments

| Unit Assessment | Suggested Schedule for Scaffolding |
| --- | --- |
| Unit 1 | Assessment is taken together as a whole class |
| Unit 2 | 75 percent of test is taken as a whole class, 25 percent is taken independently |
| Unit 3 | 50 percent of test is taken as a whole class, 50 percent is taken independently |
| Unit 4 | 25 percent of test is taken as a whole class, 75 percent is taken independently |
| Unit 5 | 100 percent of test is taken independently |
| Unit 6 | If the unit is completed prior to the end of the year, the test should be taken independently |

Struggling readers clearly do score lower on state summative assessments, but it sometimes isn't the standard that they don't understand, it is the reading of the test that tangles them up! It is our belief that all state assessments are reading tests with different topics. The more that students in a school or district improve their reading skills, the better scores in all state summative assessments will be, no matter the content area.

In the initial year of a literacy initiative, overall achievement on state assessments may not increase dramatically, but growth scores will. That is typically the first evidence that your initiative is working. In other words, don't be discouraged if, after working for one year on your literacy initiative, test scores remain the same. Instead, look for growth within the outcome bands of your state assessments. This should be reflected in your state's report of growth. Students will be increasing in raw score but may still be scoring within the same instructional band. It takes a bit of time to see tests scores on state summative assessments start to rise. We have found that special education students' scores rise the most.

## Organizational Practices and Procedures

As we began this chapter, we stated that the use and understanding of quality literacy assessments is one of the most misunderstood topics we encounter in schools. The educational purpose of assessments does not appear to be intuitive. This section outlines some organizational procedures and explanations for practice misperceptions that we think will help with the implementation of a comprehensive assessment plan that aligns with the science of reading.

The regular use of both benchmarking and progress monitoring can be enhanced by creating an instructional calendar. An instructional calendar provides staff with all of the imperative day-by-day routines, such as duty schedules, fire drills, concerts, field trips, and so on. It should also include dates for when benchmarking and progress monitoring assessments should be provided. If you are in a district that creates the assessment window for benchmarking students, this should also be included in your instructional calendar. If your district does not set an assessment window then you, the principal, should create the assessment windows. When assessment windows are provided to teachers, the individual management of assessing students becomes part of the instructional day. Figure 3.1 is an example of an instructional calendar. This example of an instructional calendar lets everyone in the school know what is going on. All staff can readily see when students are being taken out of class for picture day, or when field day is occurring, as examples. This knowledge of what is going on in the school alerts teachers to any alterations in the schedule so that they can plan accordingly.

| April 10–16 | April 10–16 | April 10–16 |
|---|---|---|
| • Monday, April 10<br>  + Report cards go home<br>• Tuesday, April 11<br>  + Elem SLT Meeting (3:30 p.m.)<br>  + Grades 6–8 Spring Concert (7 p.m.)<br>• Wednesday, April 12<br>  + Music field trip to Osseo-Fairchild for selected fifth-grade students (8:00 a.m.–2:30 p.m.)<br>• Thursday, April 13<br>  + Potluck Lunch—Salads!<br>• Friday, April 14<br>• Saturday, April 15<br>• Sunday, April 16 | • Monday, April 10<br>• Tuesday, April 11<br>  + Grades 6–8 Spring Concert (7 p.m.)<br>  + NHS Food Pantry (1:40 p.m.)<br>• Wednesday, April 12<br>  + Sped Meeting (3:05 p.m.)<br>• Thursday, April 13<br>  + Middle School Forward Test in a.m.<br>  + Potluck Lunch—Salads!<br>  + S/HS SLT Meeting (3:30 p.m.)<br>• Friday, April 14<br>  + HS Spanish trip to restaurant @?<br>• Saturday, April 15<br>• Sunday, April 16<br>  + FBLA State Comp in Green Bay | • Monday, April 10<br>• Tuesday, April 11<br>• Wednesday, April 12<br>  + Sped Meeting (3:05 p.m.)<br>• Thursday, April 13<br>  + Potluck Lunch—Salads!<br>• Friday, April 14<br>• Saturday, April 15<br>• Sunday, April 16 |
| April 17–23 | April 17–23 | April 17–23 |
| • Monday, April 17<br>• Tuesday, April 18<br>• Wednesday, April 19<br>• Thursday, April 20<br>• Friday, April 21<br>• Saturday, April 22<br>• Sunday, April 23 | • Monday, April 17<br>  + FBLA State Comp in Green Bay<br>• Tuesday, April 18<br>  + FBLA State Comp in Green Bay<br>  + MS Band & Choir Trip to MN Orchestra (7:30 a.m.–2:30 p.m.)<br>• Wednesday, April 19<br>  + Tech Ed trip to Coloma (7 a.m.–4 p.m.)<br>  + Reality Store<br>  + MS Forward Testing a.m.<br>• Thursday, April 20<br>  + Grade 7 to CVTC (8 a.m.–12 p.m.)<br>• Friday, April 21 | • Monday, April 17<br>  + FCCLA "Spring into Self-Care" drive begins<br>• Tuesday, April 18<br>• Wednesday, April 19<br>  + Staff Intruder Training<br>  + School Board Meeting (6:30 p.m.)<br>• Thursday, April 20<br>  + Grade 7 to CVTC: (8–12 a.m.)<br>• Friday, April 21 |

**FIGURE 3.1:** Sample instructional calendar.

As we have discussed, if staff have not been fully trained on how to administer assessments regularly, this can alter the validity of the outcomes of the assessments. We recommend having routine training practices in place not only for new staff to learn the basics of assessment administration but also for all staff to maintain ongoing inter-rater reliability on providing the assessment. Inter-rater reliability is simply the agreement between assessors on the administration and therefore outcome of the assessments. In other words, no matter who administers the assessment to the students, the outcome will be the same. This is particularly critical if others beyond the classroom teacher will be administering either the progress monitoring probes or screening assessments.

Regrettably, in many schools, when a majority of students are reading below grade level, there can be an overwhelming number of students who require progress monitoring. Remember, every student who is below benchmark must be progress monitored. Schools often develop a procedure to ensure all means all, and everyone helps get students progress monitored as needed. Often paraprofessionals, speech language pathologists, educational psychologists, interventionists, and other ancillary staff are trained on how to administer assessments. Again, ensuring testing validity is key!

# Development of a Comprehensive Assessment Plan

We have outlined eight criteria in the domain of assessments that we believe are key to developing an effective comprehensive assessment plan. The domain of assessments can be found at the end of this chapter and outlines these criteria. As with the domain in the previous chapter, the column on the left is the overall big idea. As you progress from left to right, the implementation of that criterion becomes more nuanced and sophisticated. Remember, a valid and reliable foundational reading assessment is used for benchmark or screening three times per year in kindergarten through fifth grade. Additional assessments may be provided that help determine specific needs of students.

As we have reiterated several times, many educators do not easily understand assessments that align with the science of reading. It takes time and knowledge to understand the subskills of reading and the instructional implications for each. Teachers want very much to see growth with their students, and a lack of understanding of the subskills may incentivize teachers to use assessments that they are familiar with or to simply get information that they understand. We have often walked into a classroom to see a teacher using a running record instead of a nonsense word probe to measure students decoding!

Classroom teachers, hoping to acquire instructional information about students, can become misguided in their approach. Table 3.5 displays a list of often-seen assessment practices, along with the information that the teacher is hoping to get. This chart also provides an alternative evidence-based practice and explains the rationale for why using the assessment might be flawed. We hope this provides school administrators with the communication tools and rationale to ensure teachers are using their time to assess students wisely.

**TABLE 3.5:** Typically Administered Assessments

| Intended Instructional Information | Purpose | Try This Instead | Rationale |
|---|---|---|---|
| **Letter naming** | To identify the letter names students recognize | Timed letter naming probes from the foundational skills assessment | These ensure students have automaticity with letter naming, timing is necessary. |
| **Sight word reading of high-frequency words** | Automaticity with high-frequency words | The subtest of nonsense word fluency demonstrates a student's ability to decode words. Oral reading passage errors should be analyzed to determine whether students are missing high-frequency words. | High-frequency words, though sometimes spelled irregularly, can be at least partially decoded. Students need to have letter/sound correspondence to decode even irregularly spelled words. Teacher should directly teach any combination of letters that are not spelled regularly. |
| **Dictated sentences** | Letter/sound correspondence information (phonics); sight word memorization knowledge | The mastering of letter-sound correspondence is best measured through nonsense word fluency and the accuracy measure of oral reading fluency. | Both oral reading fluency and nonsense word fluency are valid and reliable assessments. Dictated sentence—both the creation and scoring are subjective. |
| **Running record** | A way to record a student's performance during oral reading to guide teaching, assess text difficulty and measure progress (Clay, 2017) | Administer oral reading fluency probes | Oral reading fluency probes are valid and reliable assessments. A running record is subjective from the assessor's perspective. |

*continued* →

| Intended Instructional Information | Purpose | Try This Instead | Rationale |
|---|---|---|---|
| **Answering questions after passage reading** | To determine whether a student has secured reading comprehension | Use oral reading fluency, retell, and MAZE scores | See the subsection below for a more detailed description regarding the usage of reading comprehension assessments. |
| **Untimed assessments** | Teachers may feel that timed tests create anxiety behaviors for students. | Minimize assessing and increase practice so that skills can be gleaned more efficiently. Ensure that the student is being assessed by a person they feel comfortable with. | Students must be able to retrieve many of the subskills found within reading automatically (for example, letters/ sounds). Timed tests distinguish a student who needs more practice from one who has mastered it. Automaticity is required so that the retrieval process does not impede the cognitive ability for fluent word reading. |
| **Leveled readers** | A system for placing students with "like" reading ability. Levels go from A to Z. | Use the subskills for reading to group students together with similar reading needs. If teachers are looking for a reading grade equivalent score, most foundational reading tests have a Lexile level converter. | The foundational reading assessments found in this chapter and Lexile levels identified through MetaMetrics are valid and reliable. |

# Often Overlooked Ways to Use Assessment

I can't emphasize this enough: No assessment should be given without using it to guide instruction. That is simply a waste of instructional time. That said, there are many ways to use assessment that are often overlooked.

The outcomes on state summative assessments are far too often made available to schools after a prolonged period of time. Educators often think, "Those students have moved on to the next grade. How does it help us?" But state assessments can provide information that points to potential flaws or gaps in instruction. These flaws or gaps may be the result of the instructional materials, professional development necessary to understand the standards, or other factors. It is the trends of the outcomes from these assessments that should be analyzed.

State summative assessments in English language arts are typically broadly categorized into subtests of reading nonfictional text, reading literary text, vocabulary, and grammar as they relate to the state standards. There is also usually a writing portion valued at less than 25 percent of the assessment. By examining trends of the assessment, not only can you see what standards students are missing, but you can also see what areas may not be taught at the level of rigor necessary to score proficient on the state assessment.

As mentioned earlier, students reading below grade level should not be expected to be proficient on state summative assessments, but students who are reading proficiently certainly should. An examination of the outcomes on state summative assessments should analyze the following.

1. Who are the students passing the assessment?

2. What standards are those students proficient in?

3. In what class are non-struggling readers having the most success on the assessment?

Answers to each of those questions will provide school leaders with an abundance of information in increasing the outcomes for students.

Using assessments—regardless of whether it is a foundational reading assessment or a state summative assessment—to guide the professional development of teachers is often overlooked. Assessments are all about how students are learning, which is based on how and what teachers are teaching.

As a cursory example, examining how many students are mastering letter naming fluency in a kindergarten class is as much about how a teacher taught that skill as it is about how much the student learned that skill. Let's take that example further. While teaching letter names to the whole class during universal instruction, one kindergarten teacher may realize that a small group of students isn't mastering letter names, so the teacher will review them again when students are in small-group instruction. By the time the middle of the year assessment comes, 100 percent of their students have mastered letter naming fluency. Another teacher at the same school, also teaching kindergarten, directly teaches letter naming during universal instruction. They don't understand how to teach letter naming in small-group settings or don't even realize the importance of that skill. By the middle of the year assessment, only 65 percent of their students have mastered letter naming fluency.

## Oral Reading Fluency and Its Connection to Comprehension

Reading comprehension is not easily quantified, and it can be difficult to separate out the factors that contribute to reading comprehension (Farrall, 2012). Areas where students may struggle in comprehending a text include inferencing, language skills, monitoring their own comprehension, and background knowledge, to name just a few.

Fortunately, we do know that when students are fluent in their reading, without having to make a conscious effort to decode words on a page, there is immediate access to the meaning of the words. This allows a student to integrate all the processes of reading and allocate mental resources for understanding or comprehending the text.

In a study that Lynn S. Fuchs, Douglas Fuchs, Michelle K. Hosp, and Joseph R. Jenkins (2001) refer to, the correlation of oral reading fluency to comprehension was 0.91 as compared to tests of question answering (0.82), recall measures (0.70), and cloze measures of reading (0.72). In other words, using an oral reading fluency probe is the best proxy to determine whether a student can comprehend text.

Had our second teacher understood both how to teach letter naming in small-group instruction and the importance of the skill, 100 percent of students would have begun their first-grade year with the ability to name all letters, which in turn would have made a significant difference with their mastery of instruction in first grade. The effects of what would most likely have been a 30-minute professional development session can be huge!

The final example we would like to share regarding the often overlooked ways to use information from assessments is in regard to how we distribute human resources. In many schools, we distribute help to teachers evenly. For example, all teachers receive an equal amount of paraprofessional or teacher assistant time. The thinking is that all teachers deserve as much help as they can get, equally. Sometimes the help is distributed just among K–2 teachers, with the sole premise of getting K–2 students to grade level. We applaud all of the help educators can get, but if we really want to help, shouldn't we distribute our help based on what is available and who has the highest priority?

Figure 3.2 illustrates the vast difference in need between nine teachers in a particular building in any elementary school. As is usually the case, in kindergarten, which student goes to which teacher is usually the luck of the draw.

| Levels of Instruction | At or Above Benchmark | On Watch | Intervention | Urgent Intervention |
|---|---|---|---|---|
| **Kindergarten** | **17%** | **29%** | **37%** | **18%** |
| Mrs. Can | 19% | 30% | 37% | 14% |
| Mrs. Able | 16% | 24% | 34% | 27% |
| Ms. Free | 17% | 32% | 39% | 12% |
| **First Grade** | **58%** | **17%** | **19%** | **8%** |
| Mrs. Silk | 60% | 10% | 23% | 7% |
| Ms. Shippert | 57% | 21% | 17% | 6% |
| Mrs. Watson | 56% | 18% | 18% | 9% |
| **Second Grade** | **57%** | **15%** | **16%** | **12%** |
| Ms. Wildue | 57% | 18% | 9% | 16% |
| Mrs. Cotton | 55% | 15% | 15% | 15% |
| Ms. Furshur | 59% | 12% | 25% | 4% |

**FIGURE 3.2:** Beginning of the year screening information.

As illustrated in figure 3.2, Mrs. Able has a more significantly impacted class with 61 percent of her students in the urgent intervention and intervention instructional levels compared to Mrs. Can with 51 percent and Ms. Free with 51 percent. If we prioritize getting *all* students to benchmark, shouldn't Mrs. Able receive more help? She has a great deal more students in the two lowest instructional levels.

In second grade, though the classes are evening out, undoubtedly due to careful placement considerations, look at Mrs. Cotton. Many more of her students are further below grade level. Again, if all students are to reach benchmark, shouldn't Mrs. Cotton receive more help?

Paraprofessionals and teachers develop tremendous relationships and get used to their daily schedules quickly. Typically, once a schedule is established, principals are reluctant to change it. We suggest school leaders communicate to their staff that the paraprofessional or teacher aide schedule is temporary until benchmark assessments have been completed. At that point, using the benchmark data to determine what class needs the most help, a new paraprofessional schedule will be created. If this becomes part of the school norm, there are no hurt feelings to deal with. Some principals and school leaders go so far as to not create a paraprofessional schedule until after each benchmarking window and instead enlist the help of the trained paraprofessionals to help with benchmark testing. This method is a win for all!

# Summary

More than anything else, the assessments that we provide to students to determine whether they are adequately acquiring the ability to read must be valid, reliable and free from subjectivity. To this end, the number of assessments used in schools should be focused on the scientific evidence we know comprise the skills of how students learn to read. Minimizing the number of assessments given to students ensures that we have adequate time to focus on the main thing: instruction!

Assessments can be difficult to understand, and schools or districts should be sure to provide teachers with sufficient professional development so that the assessments provided can create meaningful change in instruction.

There are four types of assessments that schools should be using in a comprehensive assessment plan. Those four types of assessments are (1) benchmarking, (2) diagnostic survey, (3) progress monitoring, and (4) outcome assessments. An instructional calendar should be created in schools to ensure teachers are assessing as required.

Assessments can be useful for other decision-making purposes as well. Consideration should be given to the types of professional development individual teachers may need, and the distribution of human resources based on assessments. Assessments are able to tell us which students are making gains and which students are in need of intervention. In chapter 4, we will use the information from our assessments to understand who needs an intervention and what sort of intervention they might need. Further, after reading and using the domain of intervention found in chapter 4, you should have an understanding of the structure that you should put into place that will support quality intervention practices.

# Assessments

A valid and reliable foundational reading assessment is used for benchmark or screening three times per year in kindergarten through fifth grade. Additional assessments may be provided that help determine specific needs of students.

| Big Idea | Basic (1) | Effective (2) | Proficient (3) | Exemplar (4) |
|---|---|---|---|---|
| Within the first thirty days of enrollment, a universal screener is given to all students to identify those who may be reading above and below grade-level expectations. If the universal screener indicates that a student is below benchmark, plans are immediately developed in collaboration with parents to remediate any reading difficulties. | Universal screener or benchmark assessment is administered to all K–5 students within thirty calendar days of the start of the year. | Students who are in the lowest tier of instruction are identified within thirty days of the start of the school year. | On identification, a plan for intervention is developed/ updated for all students who are reading below grade level. | The plan for students identified as having intensive literacy needs includes goals that align to benchmark and diagnostic assessment/ survey results. |
| Students identified as needing targeted or strategic interventions are progress monitored at least monthly on a consistent basis. | All staff know the progress monitoring schedule and assess the appropriate students reading below grade level on a scheduled, routine basis. | Staff are aware of progress monitoring data. The data are not consistently used or understood. | Progress monitoring information is regularly examined and used to inform and align instruction. | Instructors know what students need based on data, have the materials to provide it, and intervention happens in both whole- and small-group instruction. |
| Students who are not progressing after appropriate interventions have been provided with fidelity are given additional assessments or surveys for diagnostic purposes. | There is one individual who can provide a diagnostic assessment or survey when appropriate. | Appropriate staff have been trained in the administration of the diagnostic assessments or survey. | The diagnostic assessments or surveys are used thoughtfully and with the correct students. | Use of diagnostic assessments or surveys are routine and appropriate; staff understand how to interpret the data and apply it to instruction. |

| Big Idea | Basic (1) | Effective (2) | Proficient (3) | Exemplar (4) |
|---|---|---|---|---|
| **Students identified as needing intensive interventions are progress monitored at minimum every seven to ten school days.** | Students below grade level have been identified. | Students reading well below benchmark are progress monitored as teacher determines. | Students reading well below benchmark are routinely progress monitored every seven to ten days. | Whole-group, small-group, and intervention instruction reflect the data and lead to continuous student growth. |
| **Students identified as reading above expected goals are progress monitored to ensure expected growth is taking place to maintain or exceed grade-level proficiency.** | A progress monitoring schedule is set for students above grade level. | Data are examined regularly to ensure students are maintaining growth. | Appropriate instruction is aligned to data to ensure continued growth. | Staff can easily adapt instruction to provide additional learning opportunities for students above grade level within regular classroom instruction. |
| **Assessment administration is frequently reviewed to ensure assessment data are valid and reliable, and fidelity of assessment administration is routinely verified.** | Assessors have been trained on administering the foundational reading assessment. | Routine check of assessment administration occurs, and a method of training new staff has been established. | Assessment observations and data outcomes rarely find lapses in fidelity. | Inter-rater reliability occurs on a consistent basis. |
| **Students who are below grade level are considered through a response to intervention (RTI) or a multitiered system of support (MTSS).** | Students below grade level have been identified. | A plan has been developed to assist these students in reaching grade-level expectations. | Consistent progress monitoring occurs to track progress toward goals. | A fluid process is in place for identifying, monitoring, and moving students off RTI or MTSS plans according to data. |

*Source: © 2024 by Schools Cubed (https://itspossible.schoolscubed.com). Used with permission.*

# Intervening Quickly

## The Principal's Perspective

*By Angela Hanlin*

In chapter 3, I explained how, as a staff, we embraced our data and owned it. Much easier said than done and it definitely took time and involved a process. Once we embraced the data, it was time to do something in response to our data: to intervene. When reviewing the benchmark results in reading using aimswebPlus reports, it was overwhelming to see that anywhere from 50–75 percent of students in some grade levels needed intervention because that many students were not reading at grade level! How on earth would we address that? It is tempting when looking at percentages that are that high to feel that intervening with that many students is not even possible. Teams might be tempted to say that they don't even have enough people to intervene with that many students. We were a very small staff, so I completely understand those feelings. Excuses can come even faster than ideas or solutions for how to address the need. We had decided as a team to throw out the idea of impossible and to look at every problem as an opportunity for student success. We looked at the data and knew the next question was, What is our plan in response to the data? So, we started the work. We did not wait until we had new reading curriculum or hired new intervention teachers. We started the work with the people we had. As a team, we discussed how unhappy we were about the data but quickly accepted it and knew that it was OK because we were not going to stay there! We believed that, as a team, we could change those percentages! Something had to be done as quickly as possible. We learned that schools cannot intervene their way out of a Tier 1 problem, so we started there.

### Starting with Tier 1 Instruction

Our first intervention was to completely redo our Tier 1 instruction in the regular education classrooms and improve the instruction all students received so every single student received instruction to help them grow and increase their learning. We began by doing a thorough review of state standards and created lesson plans that ensured each standard was not just taught, but was mastered. Our focus was on whether students learned the standard, not if it was taught. By reviewing the state standards as a team, we were able to see what students needed to learn by the end of each grade level. Teachers learned what they were responsible for and what their students needed to know to be successful in the next grade. We cannot simply assume that teachers know their state standards and use them weekly when planning lessons. As building leaders, we must have a process in place to ensure that it occurs. We must offer professional development to staff members so that they fully understand the standards and how to teach them. This became an expectation and lesson plans were submitted to the principal for review—not as a "got-cha" tool, but as a means for proof, or evidence, that lessons were planned using state standards and designed in an explicit manner. Feedback was then provided to teachers.

As a team, this also required us to look at the reading block and redesign what would be included during that block of time, whether it be 90 or 120 minutes. Every minute mattered when planning, so the design of the reading block became incredibly targeted. We first designed each minute of the reading block. We answered questions such as how many groups, how many students in each group, and how long each small group would last. Teachers had received training on the science of reading so they knew the important components that needed to be included in the reading block. Then it was time to take that further and truly differentiate the instruction for small groups and target the students who needed Tier 2 and Tier 3 intervention during whole-group instruction. All of these steps helped with what would be taught; now it was time to look at how to best deliver the instruction that was needed.

Teachers used explicit instruction and the instructional practices of John Hattie (2012, 2023) to deliver the instruction. Some of the most beneficial strategies that we implemented were explicit instruction, feedback, metacognitive strategies, reciprocal teaching, and developing assessment capable learners. Throughout this process, teachers saw the importance of feedback and the impact it could have on their instruction. We used their weekly progress monitoring data to determine whether their instruction had had an impact on student learning. In time, we also purchased new reading curriculum as well, but it is important to note that we doubled our state test scores in reading after our first year, and the only change we made was to our instruction. Teachers teaching effectively, using research-based instructional practices, impacted student achievement.

## Intervening at Tier 2 and Tier 3

Changing Tier 1 instruction ensured that all students were receiving the instruction, or interventions, that they needed from their classroom teacher. It is important to note that all teachers needed professional development on how to intervene. They needed to know what to do if a student was low in phonemic awareness, what that intervention would sound like, the difference between a fluency intervention and a decoding intervention, and more. By providing all teachers with that type of professional development, it made sure that all teachers were intervention teachers. Students would receive interventions from any adult they encountered through their school day. That meant that classroom teachers could reach a lot of the Tier 2 learners. That completely changed the dynamic of simply having two intervention teachers in the building. Students who were significantly below grade level, our students who needed Tier 3 intervention, required intensive intervention from another person in addition to what they received in the classroom from their regular teacher.

As for Tier 3 intervention, we had an all-hands-on-deck philosophy. Every person in the building became an option for intervention, but we zeroed in on staff members who had the knowledge to close the gap. For example, we tapped into the extensive knowledge of our speech and language pathologist (SLP). She was an incredible resource for both students and teachers, because SLPs have the knowledge base of phonemes, phonics, and foundational literacy skills. She could not be responsible for every student in the building, so we had to find other people to provide interventions. We used our school librarian because she was focused on promoting reading throughout the building, and she became an invested team player. We used classroom assistants and paraprofessionals. In the early years, I even taught intervention groups and had students that I personally progress monitored each week. When I say it was an all-hands-on-deck philosophy, that is exactly what it was! Creating a team of people to provide interventions meant providing professional development for staff members who had not received it in the past. Members of the building leadership team and I developed a schedule that would ensure that every Tier 3 student would receive an intervention on a daily basis. Every minute mattered, and we took a fresh look at our master schedule to determine where we could steal extra minutes. We actually planned out every minute of instruction for each calendar day. By working with Schools Cubed, we used a formula to see how many intervention minutes were needed in a day. Again, we planned for each and every minute. Some intervention groups began with as many as seven or more students in a group, so we had to rethink what an intervention room looked like. For some classrooms, we used a push-in model where an intervention teacher would push into a classroom and set up another teaching table to meet with numerous students in the class during a set block of time. For intervention rooms, we had more than one intervention teacher providing interventions in a room at the same time. The look of interventions from previous years was definitely altered, and it was challenging, but students immediately made progress, so we knew it was working.

Another important element of our work was to look at intervention materials and make changes. In the past, Tier 3 intervention had been a one-size-fits-all approach, and it was a label that stayed on for years. Students had not exited out of Tier 3 status. They were stuck. Some students had been Tier 3 students every year they had been in school. We knew our students deserved better, and we believed we could do better. We had to purchase new materials and decodable text. We used a checklist to ensure we were using and purchasing quality resources. One thing we learned was the importance of repetition! Were our students receiving enough repetitions to master the content? We found that they were not. We simply increased the number of repetitions that were given to students. Such a simple strategy yielded huge results! This happened due to explicit lesson planning and design. Building the repetitions into whole-group, small-group, and intervention instruction was critically important.

After analyzing data to develop intervention groups, reviewing intervention materials, and purchasing materials that were research-based, we had to determine whether what we were doing was working. For that, we established weekly data meetings to review progress monitoring data. This was a commitment by all staff members that led to growth by all students. All classroom teachers, special education teachers and paraprofessionals, and interventionists attended the weekly data meetings. We met each and every week to review progress monitoring data to see if our instruction and interventions were making an impact. If the interventions worked, if students made progress, then we continued what we were doing. If interventions were not working, or if students had not made progress three weeks in a row, then we tweaked the intervention. This often meant increasing the number of repetitions in instruction or possibly increasing the number of minutes students received intervention. The important thing to note is that everyone left those meetings with a plan! A plan for the classroom teacher, a plan for the intervention teacher, a plan for the special education teacher, and a plan for where I needed to be the upcoming week as well. We then carried out the plan and met the next week to review the data. This is an unending cycle of a data system that is relentlessly, continuously followed. It is an unending look at the questions, Did we have an impact? and Do we need to change our instruction? It is a process that is completely void of excuses and strictly involves problem solving. By talking about each student's progress, or lack of progress, each week, a school leader has a continuous pulse on the growth that is happening in the school. This knowledge drives the instruction and intervention provided to students. The students receive exactly what they need when they need it.

After discussing the approach of a weekly data meeting with many educators, I have heard some educators and building leaders say that they do not have time for weekly meetings to review data. I would counter with the statement that we do not have time not to conduct the weekly meetings. Without this type of meeting, how do we know if our instruction is having an impact on student learning? As a classroom teacher, I remember receiving beginning of the year benchmark data the first few weeks of school and not meeting on student data again until the middle of the year benchmark assessment in January. Half the year was gone! If I had known earlier, I could have intervened. As a teacher, a weekly data meeting provides the opportunity to review the data of the struggling students, discuss intervention ideas, and collaborate with other teachers. It is a chance to reflect on what worked and what didn't. These meetings provide the building leader, the instructional leader of the building, a real-time look at student data. Without reviewing the weekly data, we go blindly into the next week of instruction and intervention. We are guessing. Reviewing student data on a weekly basis takes the guessing out of it. It guarantees that all students in need of an intervention receive one. It ensures we are intervening as quickly as possible. And, it is how we reach 100 percent of our students.

### *It's Possible* When Leaders Believe That:

- We cannot intervene our way out of a Tier 1 problem. We must start with our Tier 1 instruction.

- When all teachers become intervention teachers, students can receive intervention from any adult they encounter through their school day.

- It is all hands on deck. Tap every person in the building to become an option for intervention, and zero in on staff members who have the knowledge to close the gap.

- We can rethink what Tier 3 intervention looks like and utilize every available minute.
- Weekly data meetings are essential. Relentlessly review progress monitoring data for every student every week and establish an action plan for the next week.

If a school is earnest in its attempts to ensure all students read at grade level as quickly as possible, then it is incumbent that schools start their initiative in two places—with universal instruction, as we discussed in chapter 2 (page 27), and with interventions. When I first visited Matthews Elementary School, Angie had two staff members who provided interventions. One was a speech language teacher who understood structured literacy and was trained in quality intervention but didn't have the time she needed to serve all the students who desperately needed her. Angie's other choice to provide interventions was a special education teacher who had previously taught at the secondary level. She didn't realize that, had they been given more explicit instruction in reading, all these students would have likely been able to read at grade level.

In reality, quality interventions can be provided in a much easier manner than schools seem to consider possible. It requires knowing what students need, delivering it in an explicit manner of teaching, and combining that with lots of practice and repetition and the belief and expectation that all students can achieve grade-level status.

It has been our experience that the implementation of highly effective quality interventions is one of the most rewarding situations that can happen in schools. Many schools and educators realize students are vastly behind where they should be. They desperately want all students to read at grade level, but they simply don't know how to achieve this goal. I can't count the number of times I have witnessed a school staff member, as we analyzed student data, shrug their shoulders and say a group of students "has been in intervention forever." Fortunately, it doesn't have to be that way. We know that 95 percent of students can achieve grade-level proficiency in reading. In fact, interventions that are appropriately responsive to individual needs have been shown to reduce the number of students with continuing difficulties in reading to below 2 percent of the population (Vellutino, Scanlon, & Zhang, 2007). Once students who have been deemed as eternal victims of intervention begin to see significant success, the school celebrates. In Angie's school, once the word got out regarding the gains her students were seeing in reading, families drove for miles to enroll their students! In fairness, however, interventions seem to be a quagmire for schools. The following questions swirl.

- Who gets an intervention?
- How long does an intervention last?
- Are interventions the same as universal instruction, just provided again in a double dose?
- Do we change interventions after so many weeks if a student isn't at grade level?
- Who provides the intervention?

This goes on and on. In this chapter, we hope to sort out those questions.

The importance of highly effective interventions can't be stressed enough. Whether public or private, if an education system cannot ensure all students know how to read at grade level, then I am not sure what we educators are responsible for. Isn't that our moral and professional obligation? To drive this point further, what happens to the students who cannot read at grade level? Data show 75 percent of students who drop out of high school have reading problems, and 85 percent of juveniles in the court system are functionally illiterate. Three out of four people on welfare can't read. Sixteen- to nineteen-year-old girls at the poverty level and below with below-average reading skills are six times more likely to have out-of-wedlock children than their reading counterparts (DoSomething.org, n.d.; Governor's Early Literacy Foundation, 2023; Parker, 2024).

For far too many years, many school districts, in an attempt to game the accountability system, focused intervention efforts on those students performing just below grade level on state summative assessments. They assumed that getting the lowest performing students to meet grade-level expectations was not realistic and regrettably used tactics that still did not get to the root cause of the issue. As we have stated previously, standards are critically important. In universal instruction, students reading at grade level must be taught the grade-level standards, and all students should receive grade-level content aligned with those standards. However, during interventions, the issue is not about failing to meet standards.

Rather, the inability to access *reading* the content in grade-level standards is the issue. I would also suppose that the students who were "just below grade level" on state summative assessments were also struggling readers!

Fortunately, *it's possible* to ensure all students can read at grade level. We know and have witnessed this firsthand, and in more than one setting. The research abounds that 90 to 95 percent of all students can learn to read when given appropriate instruction and intervention. Further, the research on implementing a clear multitiered system of supports substantiates these findings (Fletcher et al., 2019). We often see dubious educators question this research, believe that it can't happen in a school like theirs, think that the effort going into such outcomes must truly outweigh the gains, or, for general education students, *it's possible* but not those labeled as special education. Yet such assumptions are only that. In fact, one of the main factors contributing to the lack of such outcomes—even in schools that have gone to a structured literacy approach and have not seen the gains that they were hoping for—is a preponderance of doing too many things. There are too many different interventions being implemented, there are too many ways to analyze the data, and teachers receive too much professional development with little to no feedback from the instructional leaders. Alas, we find less to be more! Success, in our findings, particularly with the lowest readers, is reliant on focusing on what precisely it is they need!

As in our previous chapters, before going further, let us ground you in some practices seen in the world of intervention when using a structured literacy approach and compare them to what we often see in classrooms that are taking a different approach. Table 4.1 illustrates these differences.

**TABLE 4.1:** Ineffective Versus Effective Intervention Practices

| Practices to Move Away From | Practices That Ensure *It's Possible* |
|---|---|
| Data are obtained from running records and observational data | Data are obtained from foundational reading assessments, such as the components found within CBMs |
| Interventions are typically focused on fluency or comprehension | Interventions focus on the subskills of reading in which a student may be struggling |
| Reteaching of comprehension skills or standards | Rigorous instructional routines that follow a scope and sequence |
| Fix-up strategies during small-group instruction | Scripted program used to fidelity |

# An Understanding of Intervention

As observed in our countless visits to schools, the idea of what an intervention is can be as different and varied as the number of schools we have visited. To center our thinking, our definition of *interventions* is validated instructional programs and practices that are systematic, explicit, and delivered with a sense of urgency and a level of intensity to meet the needs of the students. Interventions are provided for an extended duration of time that provides students extra practice and repetition with skills that address their specific deficiencies to move toward grade-level proficiency.

In chapter 3 (page 57) we discussed the definition of *valid* in terms of assessments. When we apply the term *validated programs* to interventions, we are referring to those programs and practices that have at least one high-quality randomized controlled trial that indicates statistically significant and practically important effects on important outcomes, and other high-quality randomized controlled trials must not provide evidence to the contrary (Fletcher et al., 2019). In the simplest of terms, high-quality intervention programs are not likely found on a popular teacher-accessed website. Lightheartedness aside, we have seen materials used by teachers to provide interventions to the most struggling of readers downloaded from disreputable websites in more classrooms than not.

Systematic interventions are those where the instruction follows step-by-step procedures or routines in an explicit manner. (See the section Explicit Instruction in chapter 2, page 47, regarding its use in universal instruction. We believe those practices hold true with explicit instruction as it is implemented in the teaching of interventions.) Typically, a scripted intervention program will provide a teacher with a layout of the lesson using this step-by-step procedure. We will talk more about scripted programs and intervention materials later in this chapter.

## A Sense of Urgency

Not only should interventions be provided in a systematic and explicit fashion, but there also needs to be a sense of urgency, a schoolwide understanding and demonstration that all students in this school will read at grade level. A sense of urgency is clearly seen in the halls of schools where all students reading at grade level truly means *all* students will read at grade level. Angie describes such a school in her opening vignette. In schools where there is a sense of urgency, students receiving interventions don't slowly saunter down the halls toward their interventions. In schools with a sense of urgency, transitions from general classrooms to interventions, wherever they are located, are minimized. Students are excited to be there, and teachers are excited to deliver. Students and teachers are intervention ready with materials, lessons, and an upbeat attitude toward teaching and learning. That upbeat attitude is often called a perky pace. I prefer the description provided by Marina Licari, the Director of Elementary Education in Chippewa Valley Schools in Michigan. Marina says, "Intervention teachers need to have a caffeinated cadence!" (personal communication, November 2, 2023). We agree! The intervention room is where success and excitement occur. In many instances, students are learning to read for the very first time—often after years of failure. Who wouldn't be excited by that?

When teachers have a sense of urgency and deliver instruction in such a manner, the school displays an increased intensity to teaching and learning. The term *intensity* can be defined as instruction that is provided in a smaller group setting, focused on a smaller amount of skills, for a longer duration of time until the goal is achieved. We have found that in grades K–2, intervention groups can be successful in group sizes of three to five students. In grades 3 through 5 or 6, groups of six to eight are very manageable and successful.

## A Clear and Accurate Goal

Too often, schools understand that students need intervention, but because of a lack of understanding regarding how students learn to read, they are unclear on what goals in intervention should be. As an example, it is reasonable to think that if a student is performing poorly on a test of comprehension, they must then need an intervention on comprehension. Yet the intervention needs to address the underlying subskills needed to comprehend. Students with true comprehension deficits are between just 6 to 15 percent of struggling readers (Catts & Hogan, 2003; Leach, Scarborough, & Rescorla, 2003; Shaywitz et al., 1999). The same is true for fluency. It is reasonable to assume that if a student scores low in words read per minute, they must need more practice in reading passages. Again, consideration must be given to the underlying subskills needed to be a fluent reader that are currently lacking and are preventing the student from reading at the determined grade-level rate. Seldom do students show a deficit in just the area of fluency. Rather, struggling readers typically show a great deal of overlap in many areas of reading (Cerino, 2014). Simply put, more reading won't correct the issue.

## A Variable Time Frame

Interventions, particularly for students years behind in reading, may take time to help students attain grade-level status. Conversely, kindergarten and first grade students may catch up in a very short amount of time (Vellutino, Scanlon, Small, & Fanuele, 2006). Many students have been in interventions for years without success. This is not because students can't learn. In fact, it is usually an adult issue: low expectations, a misunderstanding of how students learn to read, the inability to analyze data correctly, or the lack of a structure to provide interventions to *all* students who need help!

Another tremendous defect we see occurring in schools is the notion that intervention happens in a set amount of time. Typically, we see this set amount of time at six weeks. We believe this stems from a belief or philosophy that sees response to intervention (RTI) as an avenue to enter special education rather than as an avenue to prevent special education. Also known as a multitiered system of supports (MTSS), RTI is a systematic process to ensure every student receives:

> The additional time and support needed to learn at high levels. RTI's underlying premise is that schools should not delay providing help of struggling students until they fall far enough behind to qualify for special education, but instead should provide timely, targeted, systematic interventions to all students who demonstrate the need. (Buffum, Mattos, & Malone, 2018, pp. 1–2)

If a student is making adequate progress and working toward grade level while in an intervention, as measured by a valid and reliable assessment such as a CBM probe, then intervention should continue, and no special education referral would be required.

# Tier 2 and Tier 3 Intervention

We are strong believers that you cannot intervene your way out of a schoolwide reading issue. Again, we can't stress enough: When over 50 percent of your students are not reading at grade level, then you must tackle two issues with an abundance of zeal—universal instruction and interventions.

As a school or district administrator, our end goal should always be that the minute a student enters our setting, be it in kindergarten or in the upper grades, we will ensure that they meet grade-level status in reading. Safeguarding the belief that every student who may be a struggling reader is provided with the best multitiered systems of support within the regular classroom can greatly reduce the number of students ever referred to remediation in reading of any sort, and this has been proven true, particularly as it relates to kindergarten instruction. One study (Scanlon, Gelzheiser, Vellutino, Schatschneider, & Sweeney, 2008) showed that the number of students who experienced early reading difficulties could be substantially reduced through the provision of a rather limited kindergarten intervention program (thirty minutes twice per week for twenty-five weeks) that supplemented the classroom program. That study also demonstrated that students who experienced reading difficulties, despite having the supplemental intervention in kindergarten, were much less likely to demonstrate severe reading difficulties at the end of first grade than were students who did not participate in kindergarten intervention (Scanlon et al., 2008).

When classroom instruction is comprehensive—including all components of literacy instruction—coupled with supplementary Tier 2 instruction that focuses on the individual needs of students, the number of students at risk appears to fall below 2 percent. Further, the outcome from that instruction remains through at least grade 5 (Blachman et al., 2004).

Yet when far too many schools create an RTI system, special education students are routinely excluded from these tiers of instruction. They are seemingly viewed as a different entity. RTI should be seen as an avenue to prevent special education and improve overall academic outcomes for all students. In schools that believe *it's possible* and recognize that all means *all*, students in special education are not seen as an excluded entity but rather as a part of the school where all tiers of instruction include all students, whatever their individual needs.

Intervention takes time, requires additional personnel and training, and can be a puzzle to put into place. Quality classroom instruction is the largest deterrent to initial reading failure. Many students identified as learning disabled would not have been identified if instruction had been appropriately provided in universal instruction (Clay, 1987; Denton et al., 2003; Lyon, Fletcher, Fuchs, & Chhabra, 2006; Scanlon, Vellutino, Small, Fanuele, & Sweeney, 2005; Snow, Griffin, & Burns, 2005; Vellutino et al., 1996).

## Tier 3 Intervention

We often hear that we must first focus on universal instruction to increase literacy outcomes for students. This thinking is absolutely correct. However, if a school or district is intent on making significant gains in reading quickly, then they must focus their efforts in two areas simultaneously: ensuring that there is quality universal instruction *and* robust, intensive Tier 3 intervention. When we speak of students who receive Tier 3 intervention, we refer to any student who is identified in the lowest instructional level on a quality, valid, and reliable reading assessment. On most assessments, these are the students who have tested in the lowest 9th percentile in reading. These students are significantly below grade-level reading and will require additional time, intensity, a smaller group size, and a concentrated focus on particular skills of instruction. Certainly not all students falling into this instructional range are special education students. Many students who have had years of reading instruction not based in scientific evidence will fall into this instructional range.

Since Tier 3 instruction is best accomplished through a concentrated focus on particular skills of instruction, it is achieved through materials outside the scope of a grade-level, comprehensive core reading program. Remember! Students in need of Tier 3 instruction must also receive grade-level core reading instruction. Tier 3 intervention is *in addition to* grade-level reading instruction. We will discuss appropriate intervention materials later in this chapter.

Students scoring in the Tier 3 range are students who are significantly behind in reading. This concentrated focus must be identified through valid and reliable assessments. As discussed earlier, a preponderance of intervention time is spent on comprehension and fluency, but by far the largest area of need for the greatest number of struggling readers is in the area of phonological processing. For example, P. G. Aaron, Malatesha Joshi, and Kathryn A. Williams (1999) identify three subgroups of struggling readers along with the percentage of students with that deficit of reading (see table 4.2).

**TABLE 4.2:** The Percentage of Struggling Readers Found in Various Deficit Areas

| Area of Deficit | Percentage of Struggling Readers |
|---|---|
| Phonological processing and weak comprehension | 70% |
| Good word recognition with weak comprehension | 10% |
| Slow reading deficits | 20% |

*Source: Aaron et al., 1999.*

In many situations, we often see schools providing Tier 3 instruction three times a week due to an overabundance of students needing intensive interventions, thinking that the rate is adequate or, more likely, better than nothing. To be effective, however, the frequency of Tier 3 intervention must be greater than the opportunity to receive regular instruction. In other words, if your school is providing reading instruction to all students for a minimum of ninety minutes per day, five days a week, then intensive interventions for students who need Tier 3 intervention three days a week have not accomplished the increased dosage to satisfy the definition of intensive intervention. Table 4.3 illustrates the number of minutes per day, five times per week, by grade level that we have found to be effective for Tier 3 interventions to students.

**TABLE 4.3:** The Number of Minutes Recommended for Intervention at Each of the Grade Levels

| Grade Level | Tier 3 Recommended Minutes per Day |
|---|---|
| Kindergarten | 15–25 minutes |
| First Grade | 15–25 minutes |
| Second Grade | 25–35 minutes |
| Third Grade | 35–45 minutes |

## Tier 2 Intervention

Most valid and reliable reading assessments generally consider students who need Tier 2 intervention as being those students who are scoring in the 10th to 29th percentile range. It is important to note that even though students' outcomes are reported by instructional levels, the results of various subtests within the assessment are what create the outcome of instructional levels. Consequently, instructional levels, though informative regarding the impact of the reading difficulty, should not be used for instructional decisions. Accordingly,

## Tiers of Instruction

When using a valid and reliable assessment, it is prudent to know how many students are at what level of instruction. This information will inform critical questions such as, How will it impact human resources? How will it impact school schedules? and How will it impact the results on state summative assessments? The tiers of instructional levels can also inform you of the severity of reading impact overall that students have.

For instructional purposes, to analyze and plan for interventions for students reading below grade level, you must "unpack" the subskills found within each students' benchmark.

Subskills are areas such as phonics or decoding deficits, phonemic awareness, vocabulary, orthographic mapping, fluency, and comprehension.

it is therefore not instructionally wise to make blanket statements regarding what materials and instruction work best for all students at the various tiers of instruction (see the sidebar on this page). We do note that for many students, Tier 2 instruction may sometimes be composed of materials associated with or that accommodate core reading programs. In chapter 5 (page 111), we will talk extensively about how to analyze student data to determine what focus of instruction is appropriate for various subskills of literacy and offer suggestions for materials and strategies to use based on identified subskills and instruction.

Once the subskill of reading in which a student is struggling has been identified, and direct instruction with many opportunities to practice the skill have been provided, we have observed most students who need Tier 2 intervention attain grade-level status quite quickly. Adequate Tier 2 instruction should occur for approximately twenty additional minutes per day beyond regular classroom reading instruction. Beyond our own findings, Jeanne Wanzek and colleagues (2016) found effect sizes ranging from 0.34 to 0.56 when effective Tier 2 interventions are in place.

# Creation of an Intervention Structure

As in the previous chapters, we have designed eight criteria under the domain of interventions that, once solidly implemented, will create success for all students in your school. This full domain, along with each criterion, appear as a reproducible at the end of this chapter (page 108). Examine where you are on each of the criteria. On which area would you like to begin working? Once started, you will see the excitement begin for your struggling readers. As you read this chapter, you will understand what quality intervention should look like that ensures *it's possible* all students can meet grade-level expectations. We define interventions as validated instructional programs and practices that are systematic, explicit, and delivered with a sense of urgency and a level of intensity to meet the needs of the students. Interventions are provided for a significantly extended duration of time that provides students extra practice and repetition with skills that address their specific deficiencies to move toward grade-level proficiency.

# Small-Group Instruction

Focusing instruction, rather than implementing more programs, is one of the most effective ways to increase outcomes for all students. Prevention is the best intervention, and the general education setting is where interventions should be provided as the first or second dose of instruction. The best way to accomplish differentiated instruction in the general education setting is through small-group instruction. When individual needs of students are analyzed, most classrooms will have at least three or four groups of students with common needs. During small-group instruction, the teacher works with one group of students—called the *teacher-led group*—and three or four groups work independently. Teacher-led instruction should ooccur, at minimum, five days per week for those students scoring below grade level on assessments, and in the best of scenarios, all students would receive small-group instruction every day. Depending on the numbers of students in need of intervention, all students receiving teacher-led small-group instruction isn't always possible. Consideration should first be given to those students below grade level.

If you are moving from a balanced literacy situation to a structured literacy situation, small-group instruction looks quite different. In many balanced literacy classrooms, teachers implement a menu approach to small-group instruction, in which students can choose activities to do while the teacher is working with a group of students. Often, this may include activities outside the realm of literacy, such as science and mathematics. We believe that all time during the literacy block should be devoted to literacy. There is plenty for students to be doing to increase their literacy skills.

To differentiate students' instruction, we first need to ensure that instruction aligns with the components within learning how to read. As mentioned previously, these components or subskills of reading include the following.

- Phonemic awareness—in grades K–2
- Phonics
- Vocabulary
- Fluency
- Comprehension

Students will be proficient at different levels of each of these components. Small groups, whether independent or teacher-led, will give the student another opportunity to master any skills that they may not have mastered in previously taught whole-group instruction.

There are also computer programs that offer students chances to practice these independent skills. It is important to note that we strongly believe a student's time on a computer to practice skills should be kept to no more than twenty minutes per day. If we determined anything during the pandemic, it was that students need teachers to learn. Practicing a skill on a computer is one thing, but it cannot and should not compare to being *taught* a skill by a highly trained teacher. That said, one rotation during independent time on a computer to practice a literacy skill is appropriate and helpful during small-group time. See the sidebar for a list of some digital programs we recommend during independent, small-group literacy time.

### Recommended Programs for Independent Groups

The following computer programs work well during independent small-group instruction.

- Lexia Core5 Reading
  - ⇨ www.lexialearning.com/core5
- Amira
  - ⇨ www.hmhco.com/programs/amira
- i-Ready Reading
  - ⇨ www.curriculumassociates.com/programs/i-ready-learning/personalized-instruction/reading

Small-group instruction is provided to all students and is based on their need as derived from the valid and reliable assessment. Generally, small-group instruction takes place directly after whole-group instruction. If your literacy block is 120 minutes, as we suggest, classrooms should be able to devote at least an hour to small-group instruction. As we recommended earlier, small-group instruction is not just based on the instructional levels of students, it is based on need of instruction or the subskill deficit. Students with good accuracy but low fluency would need one type of instruction and practice, while a student with poor accuracy would need a different sort of instruction. Understanding these differences will be clear after reading chapter 5 (page 111) on data analysis.

Small-group instruction provides students with the opportunity to have more time in a safer setting to respond to the teacher and for the teacher to provide feedback. In small-group settings, the teacher can hear how students are reading, students have opportunities to practice a new skill, and students may be able to respond differently. We suggest the following four purposes for small-group instruction.

1. Reteaching a skill that a student may not have mastered

2. Preteaching or front-loading skills such as vocabulary

3. Providing additional time for practice of a previously taught skill

4. Providing enrichment and advancement

In kindergarten through second grade, teacher-led small groups should be in numbers of three to five. In third through fifth or sixth grade, small groups can be provided in numbers of six to eight. It is important to note that many schools are concerned that tutoring, or interventions need to be delivered in one-on-one situations. Studies find that smaller groups are actually associated with better outcomes (Fletcher et al., 2019). Further, the cost of one-on-one interventions is simply not practical and is a barrier for all students receiving the intervention they need.

## Tier 2 Intervention Within Small Groups

To be the most effective, Tier 2 should be another opportunity for students to practice or master the skills they need, again based on a valid and reliable assessment. In some schools, districts, or state jurisdictions, this dose of instruction needs to be in *addition* to small-group instruction. In other situations, another round of small-group instruction, led by another professional such as a special education teacher, interventionist, or trained paraprofessional is also seen as an adequate dosage to qualify as Tier 2. In such cases, small-group instruction time may require two adults in the classroom to lead this instruction. The student receives one round of what they need from the classroom teacher, and the second round is provided by the ancillary personnel or tutor assigned to that class. Regardless, Tier 2 instruction should provide a minimum of an additional twenty minutes of intervention for those students in need.

Remembering that Tier 2 serves those students who are just below grade level, and often, reteaching or practicing the skill that was explicitly taught in whole-group instruction may be adequate. In lower grades, we have found that students just below grade level often need another opportunity to read decodable text or practice letter names and sounds; in the upper grades, they need to work on fluency of the core reading story. These are just examples of what occurs in teacher-led, small-group instruction. We will offer more guidance in the next chapter.

In chapter 3 (page 57), we discussed the importance of progress monitoring students who are receiving intervention to ensure that what we are providing is working. For students who need Tier 2 intervention, they should be monitored on a probe in their area of need and the area in which they are receiving intervention. This progress monitoring should occur every two weeks to one month. See table 3.3 (page 70) in chapter 3.

When teachers are planning for the instructional focus of Tier 2, alignment of what is being taught during whole-class instruction, rather than something different, is critical to ensure mastery of the content. As an example, let's imagine that a student has been taught the letter names and sounds of consonants, /s/, /t/, /l/, /m/, /r/, and /f/. Progress monitoring on these letters and sounds indicates that they have had a hard time mastering all the letters each time they are taught, but they appear to understand sometimes. In a teacher-led, small-group setting, the student should get another opportunity to master these same letters and sounds. New letters should not be taught in small groups since the student has not yet mastered these set of letters and sounds that are being taught in the whole group. Instead of learning new sounds, the student should have the opportunity in Tier 2 to practice learning these same sounds. More repetitions and practice increase their chances to master them.

This alignment to the instruction in the general classroom has advantages. A separate program for the instruction of Tier 2 intervention is rarely needed—assuming, of course, that the core reading program you are using contains all the components of literacy. Aside from decodable text in grades K–2, no additional program should be needed for Tier 2 instruction.

## Tier 3 Intervention Within Small Groups

Students who need Tier 3 intervention also need a dose of Tier 2 instruction. This means that a student in need of Tier 3 instruction should receive the following on a daily basis.

- Explicit instruction on grade-level reading in whole-group instruction
- Small-group instruction aimed at exactly their level of need
- An additional twenty minutes, or more, of another dose of what they need in Tier 2 small-group instruction
- An additional twenty-five to forty-five minutes, depending on grade level, of Tier 3 instruction of exactly what they need

Instead of students who need Tier 3 intervention receiving instruction that aligns to whole-group, grade-level content, we have found it helpful that students who need Tier 3 intervention receive instruction that aligns with their intensive interventions. To illustrate, let's assume our intensive intervention student is receiving a phonological processing intervention and is learning vowel pairs in that intervention. We recommend that during Tier 2 instruction, that student receives extra practice in a teacher-led or interventionist-led small group with other students, reading a decodable text containing vowel pairs.

In the preceding scenario, every student who is reading two to three years below grade level would likely receive 105 to 125 minutes of reading instruction per day! Such scenarios are certainly able to ensure all students are reading at grade level.

## School Spotlight

### Quest Academy, West Haven, Utah

What does reading intervention at Quest Academy look like? Well, this has changed drastically over the past few years. As our team came to recognize the various abilities and needs of our students, we quickly realized that teachers, alone, would not be able to provide the necessary reading interventions for all learners. Thus, an all hands on deck approach was implemented where administrators, instructional coaches, classroom teachers, teacher assistants, lunch room personnel, secretaries, recess aides, and the librarian were enlisted to provide small-group reading instruction. In short, it takes a village to raise a reader.

Early on, we realized that *all* students need intervention that's designed to help them grow, regardless of their current reading level. To promote this belief, we named our daily intervention "W. I. N. Time," which stands for "What I Need." Because every student participated in W. I. N. Time, we needed to be creative in utilizing all available building space. This meant that groups were being taught at lunchroom tables, in the principal's office, in the staff break room, in the library, in hallways, in classrooms, and every other nook and cranny throughout the school. This thirty-minute intervention time ensured high readers received enriched reading support, while other readers received either Tier 2 or Tier 3 foundational instruction.

W. I. N. Time was first introduced during the 2021–2022 school year. In August of that year, 304 students scored below grade level and began receiving interventions during W. I. N. time. By end of year testing, the number of students receiving intervention decreased by ninety-three students. The following school year, 101 students were exited from intervention, and, for the current school year—with only a middle of the year measurement so far—sixty-six students have exited intervention and are receiving instruction to maintain growth and extend their learning. Trends have also indicated that the number of students needing intervention at the beginning of each school year decreases. Another exciting development is the shift from spending money toward decodable books from trade books, which is needed to foster fluency in these developing readers.

For Quest, "all hands on deck" was not just a phrase but a commitment to ensuring every student had access to meaningful reading interventions. Through the collective effort of all school employees and the utilization of various spaces, our school was able to provide a supportive and engaging environment for students to improve their reading skills.

---

*David Bullock, Principal*
*Angelee Spader, Assistant Principal*
*Susan Goldsberry, Intervention Coordinator*
*Brittaney Zimmerman, Instructional Coach*

# The Intervention Calculator

Often, the thought of providing intervention to every student who needs it seems overwhelming and not feasible. We are here to tell you *it's possible*. The first step is to determine how many students actually need intervention. We have created a calculator that is available for your use (visit **https://itspossible.schoolscubed.com**).

We call this tool the intervention calculator, and its purpose is to determine how many sections of Tier 3 intervention you will need to ensure all students reading below grade level receive the necessary interventions.

The calculator can be adapted to meet the needs of your school, but we strongly recommend using the suggestions for group size and intervention times that we have discussed earlier in this chapter. The directions for using the calculator are as follows.

1.  Start with section 1. In column B, enter the number of students scoring on the lowest tier of instruction from a valid and reliable foundational reading assessment for each grade level.

2.  In column C, determine the number of students you will have in each intervention group. In grades K–2, we recommend putting three to five students in a group, and in grades 3–6 we recommend six to eight students per group.

3.  In column D, determine the number of minutes per grade level intervention. Remember, the earlier grades need less time than the upper grades. Adjusting the times appropriately also provides the availability of more sections of interventions.

4.  Once columns B through D have been completed, the number of sections will be automatically calculated. As you can see in the example below, the number of sections is typically not a whole number, meaning one section will have to be increased by one student.

5.  The total number of minutes of interventions you need in each grade level has also been calculated for you. The next step is to compare what is needed with what you have. In section 2 of the calculator, list the number and names of teachers or paraprofessionals who will be available to provide interventions.

6.  In column B of section 2, list the total number of minutes they work per day.

7.  In column C of section 2, list the number of minutes they will use for breaks, lunches, or other duties. Column D will calculate the total number of minutes available for each interventionist.

8.  Compare total number of minutes for intervention to total number of available minutes for interventionists.

Review the sample completed intervention calculator in figure 4.2 (page 100) to see it in action.

| Section 1 | | | | | | | |
|---|---|---|---|---|---|---|---|
| | Number of Students Needing a Tier 3 Intervention by Grade Level | Number of Students per Intervention Group | Minutes for Intervention | Number of Sections | Total Number of Minutes for Intervention | Total Number of Intervention Minutes Available from Section 2 | Difference in Time Available for Interventions |
| Kindergarten | 26 | 5 | 25 | 5.2 | 130 | | |
| First Grade | 32 | 5 | 30 | 6.4 | 192 | | |
| Second Grade | 43 | 5 | 30 | 8.6 | 258 | | |
| Third Grade | 19 | 6 | 40 | 3.2 | 127 | | |
| Fourth Grade | 17 | 6 | 45 | 2.8 | 128 | | |
| Fifth Grade | 22 | 7 | 45 | 3.1 | 141 | | |
| | | | | | | | |
| | | | | | | | |
| Total: | | | | | 976 | 1080 | 104 |

| Name of Interventionist | Minutes Worked per Day | Minutes for Lunch, Breaks, and Other Duties | Total Number of Intervention Time Available | | | | | | |
|---|---|---|---|---|---|---|---|---|---|
| | | | | | | | | | |
| Sarah Samual | 420 | 45 | 375 | | | | | | |
| Ben Meagan | 180 | 15 | 165 | | | | | | |
| Blake Master | 420 | 45 | 375 | | | | | | |
| Kent Bryan | 180 | 15 | 165 | | | | | | |
| | | | | | | | | | |
| | | | | | | | | | |
| | | | 1080 | | | | | | |

*Section 2*

*Source: © 2024 by Schools Cubed (http://itspossible.schoolscubed.com). Used with permission.*

**FIGURE 4.2:** Using the intervention calculator to determine number of intervention sections.

If you are short on minutes available to provide interventions, ask yourself the following before considering hiring an additional interventionist.

- Is there a person such as a librarian media specialist or school safety officer who may be able to provide interventions?

- Can you minimize the number of minutes that interventions are offered? Perhaps in kindergarten by going from twenty-five minutes to twenty minutes?

- Can you maximize the number of students in each group of interventions? Perhaps in fifth or sixth grade?

- Is there a grade level that has a particularly large number of students needing interventions that a general classroom teacher can be used for a small amount of time during the day?

In schools where administrators and staff see that *it's possible* in the first year of a reading initiative when a seemingly huge number of students need an intervention, they have been creative in ensuring who is trained to provide interventions so that all students can receive the help they need.

Once you have determined how many students need an intervention, how you schedule the intervention is the next priority. There is no single best way to ensure you have the best schedule. However, we have seen interventions provided throughout the day in a variety of ways. The following are several suggestions.

- Stagger interventions and reading blocks throughout the day (see chapter 4, page 83, for examples of both). This ensures that human resources available for interventions are available at various times during the school day.

- Designate a particular time for interventions for each grade level. Students receive interventions from the interventionist assigned to a particular intervention as designated by need, not teacher. Students then go to the teacher during the intervention time based on need. There is a walk to intervention time by grade level as opposed to at the same time for the entire school.

- Ensure all general education teachers are trained in the interventions provided and each grade level determines their own intervention time within the grade levels.

- Extend the daily schedule for interventionists so that they start the day earlier or later than the rest of the staff, and students needing an intervention begin school earlier or stay later.

Changing schedules is a significant shift to schools. This decision is one of the largest that needs to be made and likely will need to be adapted and changed from year to year. As you progress on your reading initiative, you will find that fewer students need intensive intervention. It is not a decision best served by the leadership alone. A collaborative process is highly recommended, and we suggest soliciting the help of your school leadership team. You and your staff know which situation works best for your school.

# How Interventions Will Be Selected

There is an abundance of intervention programs available to schools. Regrettably, there is a limited number of highly effective interventions available that produce significant results for students. To begin, any structured literacy intervention should contain a high-quality scope and sequence. Figure 4.3 is an example of a good beginning reading scope and sequence.

| Phonics concept | Example graphemes or patterns | Example words |
|---|---|---|
| Single, highly reliable consonants and a short vowel | b, s, t, d, m | sad, mat, mad, bat |
| More single consonants | r, l, f, z, v, g, p, n | red, fit, got, zip, pup |
| Short vowels /ă/, /ŏ/, /ĭ/, /ŭ/, /ĕ/, introduced gradually | a, o, i, u, e | wag, top, zip, rub, jet |
| Consonant digraphs | th, ch, sh, ng, wh, -ck | thing, chunk, shop, when |
| Consonant blends | st, lk, mp, br, cl | stop, milk, camp, bran, must |
| Inflections | -s, -ed, -ing | wishes, wished, wishing |
| VCe for long vowels | a_e, i_e, o_e, u_e | lake, ride, rope, cute |
| Odd consonants | x, qu | box, quit |
| "Floss" pattern | -ff, -ll, -ss, -zz | stuff, well, grass, jazz |
| Vowel teams | ee, ea, oa, ai, ay | meet, heap, boat, mail, play |
| Vowel-r patterns | er, or, ur, ar | her, for, fur, star |
| Complex consonants | ge/dge, ch/tch, hard and soft c and g | wage, dodge; church, catch; cell, city, gem, gym |
| Multisyllable words, gradual introduction | (six syllable types) | napkin, playground, compete |

*Source: Fletcher et al., 2019.*

**FIGURE 4.3:** Scope and sequence for electing a Tier 3 intervention.

We have developed criteria that we believe needs to be used when a school or district chooses a Tier 3 Intervention. This criterion appears in figure 4.4 (page 104). As it appears, the criteria are written in a format that can be used as a checklist if a committee of folks are choosing to purchase an intervention.

**Part I. Instructional Components and Design of the Intervention**

The program teaches one or all five of the components of reading thoroughly, explicitly, and with connections between each dependent on student need; includes assessments to assist with placement within the intervention and monitor progress; daily lesson plans include a structured language design with routines for each component that repeat on a daily and weekly basis; is systematic, sequential, and cumulative; provides multiple opportunities for review and practice of lessons taught; intervention has at least one high-quality randomized control trial that indicates statistically significant and practically important effects on important outcomes, and other high-quality randomized control trials must not provide evidence to the contrary.

*For each attribute found, give one point.*

| Points earned: | |
|---|---|
| | Explicit and clear routines are evident for each component being addressed in the intervention, and, as new skills are introduced, these patterns repeat. |
| | Systematic instruction is carefully sequenced and connected across each component, so that easier skills are taught before more difficult skills. |
| | Intervention provides explicit and systematic skill development in one or all of the following: phonemic awareness, phonics, vocabulary development, reading fluency including oral language skills, and reading comprehension. |
| | Phonological and phonemic awareness, letter-sound correspondences, and phonics skills (such as sounding out words and applying the "silent e rule") moves to advanced decoding and morphology and are taught in a predetermined order according to a clear scope and sequence so that there are no gaps in students' learning. |
| | Multiple hands-on manipulatives such as elkonin boxes, finger tapping or stretching, letter and word cards, phoneme and grapheme mapping charts, and grapheme tiles and magnetic boards support multisensory instruction. |
| | The pace of introduction of new material is reasonable to allow struggling learners to master key skills, and much of each lesson consists of practice of previously introduced skills, strategies, and concepts and the integration of these with the newly taught material. |
| | Intervention offers opportunities for extended guided practice, independent practice, and cumulative practice with teacher feedback. |
| | Specific positive feedback calls attention to behaviors and processes the student is implementing well. When errors are made by students, mistakes are corrected through corrective feedback. |
| | Cumulative practice is part of each lesson by offering repetition and practice of newly learned items mixed in with items learned earlier so that skills are not taught and dropped. |
| | Multiple opportunities for high student engagement and student responses are evident. |
| | Texts supporting the intervention are decodable and controlled for phonics or spelling skills introduced each week, follow the scope and sequence, and are cumulative as texts become more complex. |
| | Intervention has been proven to accelerate student progress in attaining reading competency. |
| | Intervention is the result of rigorous research studies or directly aligns to scientifically based reading research. |
| | **Total points for instructional components and design of the intervention** |

| | Part II. Assessments | | |
|---|---|---|---|
| | The intervention includes scientifically based and reliable assessments. The program provides initial and ongoing analysis of students' progress in attaining reading competency.<br>*For each attribute found, give one point.* | | |
| | The intervention includes assessments that are based on scientific reading research and are reliable. | | |
| | Students' learning is monitored on a daily and weekly basis so that teachers can reteach key skills when needed. | | |
| | There is initial and ongoing analyses of students' progress in attaining reading competency. | | |
| | The teacher can make clear instructional decisions based on the outcomes of the assessments. | | |
| | **Total points for intervention assessments** | | |
| **Total points for program:** | | | |

*Source: © 2024 by Schools Cubed (https://itspossible.schoolscubed.com). Used with permission.*

**FIGURE 4.4:** Intervention instructional review checklist.

*Visit **go.SolutionTree.com/literacy** for a free reproducible version of this figure.*

When selecting a program that has been shown to be effective with students who need Tier 3 intervention, it is important to ensure that it is implemented the way it was found to be effective. This is called *teaching to fidelity*. Typically, this is found in a scripted program. Why are so many interventions scripted programs? You can think of that script as an algorithm, so to speak. The design of a quality intervention is a set of steps carefully designed to solve a problem. In this case, the problem is getting the students to grade-level reading. That's why they are systematic in their approach—they are typical routines to which students can readily adjust and which provide a quality scope and sequence that builds on one skill to the next skill. The progression of skills is easier to more complex.

Often, teachers in interventions think scripted programs are boring, so they alter them or replace sections with another intervention or do not teach the lesson in its entirety. When the scripted program is changed, it discounts the very algorithm the intervention was based on, and, therefore, it becomes ineffective. We believe that it is the adults who are bored with the delivery of the scripted program. We rarely see students bored when they are learning to read. Remember, caffeinated cadence!

In describing intervention integrity, the National Center for Learning Disabilities outlines several recommendations (Cortiella, Gamm, Rinaldi, & Goodman, n.d.):

1. Evidence-based interventions and general education classroom curriculum are used to instruct students.

2. The intervention was appropriate for the student's instructional level.

3. The intervention has been proven efficacious with other students similar in age and level of performance (we would add area of need).

## Recommendations for Quality Tier 3 Interventions

- SIPPS, Collaborative Classroom
  - ⇨ www.collaborativeclassroom
    .org/programs/sipps
- Really Great Reading Company
  - ⇨ www.reallygreatreading.com
    /diagnostics
- 95 RAP, 95 Percent Group
  - ⇨ www.95percentgroup.com
    /products/95-rap

4. Educational professionals have appropriate training and demonstrable proficiency of delivering the intervention.

5. Implementation of fidelity to the program as designed by the developers was present and demonstrated.

6. The intervention was delivered with sufficient time to show an effect and with sufficient intensity.

To ensure that interventions are taught to fidelity, intervention providers need coaching—even for a scripted program—much like the advantages coaching affords to general education teachers. Yet so often, the staff providing the most intensive interventions to our neediest learners are forgotten when it comes to coaching and feedback. They are left to their own devices. This lack of oversight and independence is what often leads to special education and interventions being eternal placements. The very notion of an RTI system was to ensure that no placement in any tier was seen as a permanent condition. This is best addressed by ensuring that perpetual learning difficulties are not caused by a lack of quality instruction.

We have identified several interventions that we find effective for Tier 3 interventions in reading (please see the sidebar on this page). There are websites available to schools that show an analysis of an intervention or its effectiveness based on research. We caution the use of such sites as we find the research on which decisions are made are often supplied by the very intervention publishers they are reviewing, so the information may not be valid. Many schools visit the *What Works Clearinghouse*, but we find the research related to most of these programs limited in its scope. We find well-informed and trained educators using the information and checklists found within this chapter may make a more knowledgeable choice for interventions.

# Summary

Focusing instruction is a key ingredient to ensure all students read at grade level. Instead of having multiple programs and multiple interventions, we believe it is best to have a minimum number of highly effective, validated intervention programs. The use of such programs with students should be determined by student outcomes on valid and reliable reading assessments.

All students, including special education students, should be seen as part of the intervention process that is created in every school. Interventions should be provided to students based on need, no matter what label or designation they may have.

Interventions begin with small-group instruction. Small-group and Tier 2 interventions should be aligned to whole-group instruction whenever appropriate. To make adequate progress, students who need Tier 3 intervention should also receive additional Tier 2 instruction as well as general education Tier 1 instruction.

Most quality Tier 3 interventions are scripted programs. When teachers alter the script found within these programs, they are reducing the efficacy of such a program. To ensure interventionists are providing adequate instruction to students, the intervention staff should also receive instructional feedback and coaching.

Most importantly, moving students to grade-level reading expectations may take time for some students. It is prudent that schools and interventionists know that *it's possible* and keep a relentless eye on the goal for every student reading at grade level!

In chapter 5, we will describe how to set up the necessary systems to analyze the data to ensure that your interventions are helping students increase their literacy outcomes. In chapter 5, you will also find the domain of data-based decision making so that you can analyze your own structure regarding data-based decision making.

# Interventions

Validated instructional programs and practices are systematic, explicit, and delivered with a sense of urgency and a level of intensity to meet the needs of the students. Interventions are provided for a significantly extended duration of time that provides students extra practice and repetition with skills that address their specific deficiencies to move toward grade-level proficiency.

| Big Idea | Basic (1) | Effective (2) | Proficient (3) | Exemplar (4) |
|---|---|---|---|---|
| There is a sense of urgency for any student below grade level in reading. | A valid and reliable assessment is used to identify any student reading below grade level. | A schoolwide plan is in place to ensure all students reading below grade level receive an evidence-based intervention. | There is a regular routine to monitor the progress of all students below in reading. | There is a process that allows students to quickly move into interventions and move out of interventions when they are above and below grade level. |
| Interventions are provided daily to all students who are below grade level. | There is an intervention schedule that is based on students' grade levels and does not vary across the grades. | The staff understand the importance of students receiving the intervention, and intervention is rarely interrupted or rescheduled. | The intervention is specific to students' needs. | Intervention is a high priority; there is little time lost for transitions to and from interventions. |
| The intervention schedule is varied and based on the needs of students. | The intervention schedule is adult based and created by the staff providing the intervention. | The intervention time changes throughout the grade levels but is based on teacher availability. | The intervention schedule has been determined by the number of students who are reading below grade level. There are enough available staff for interventions. | The intervention schedule is precise, based on the number of students needing intervention and the grade level of students needing the intervention. There are an adequate number of interventionists trained to provide the interventions. |
| There are validated, evidence-based intervention materials for students reading just below and well below grade level, and they are aligned to the core reading program. | Students have been identified who are below grade level in reading, but there is no clear differentiation for instruction for Tier 2 and Tier 3 instruction. | Students who are below grade level in reading receive interventions that are evidence-based and at the level of need, based on data. | Students have been identified who are below grade level in reading. Teachers can determine the correct interventions/ materials that should be provided. | There are strong evidence-based materials for all levels of instruction. Staff have been trained on the materials. Students are appropriately moved in or out of interventions based on data. |

| Big Idea | Basic (1) | Effective (2) | Proficient (3) | Exemplar (4) |
|---|---|---|---|---|
| **Instruction of interventions is systematic, explicit, and delivered with a sense of urgency and intensity.** | Teachers and paraprofessionals provide interventions as time is available. | Interventionists provide an evidence-based program but often adapt it based on what they believe is best for students. | The evidence-based intervention is followed to fidelity and provided on a daily basis. | Evidence-based programming is used with fidelity. Interventionists have a perky pace, and the delivery of instruction is clear, concise, and consistent. |
| **The school has an intervention structure for all students below grade level. It is understood that interventions will be provided until students are at grade level.** | Students below grade level in reading needing intervention receive intervention as often as the school can provide. | Students below grade level in reading are identified and receive small-group instruction based on their need. | Students below grade level in reading are identified and receive small-group instruction and a daily, additional block of time, based on their needs. | Students below grade level in reading receive an adequate amount of intervention based on their needs. Adjustments are made to their instruction based on progress monitoring. |
| **Students who are above grade level receive interventions that are intended to extend their learning.** | Students who read above grade level have been identified. | Students who read above grade level have adequate materials to ensure growth. | Teachers have been trained on how to accelerate student learning in reading. | Students reading above grade level have the opportunity to extend their learning throughout the grades, and there is evidence that demonstrates their advanced level of reading is ongoing. |
| **There is ongoing progress monitoring of students receiving intervention with the intention of attaining grade-level proficiency.** | Some teachers progress monitor students who are receiving interventions. | All students who are receiving an intervention are progress monitored on a regular basis. | Teachers know the effectiveness of the intervention for students based on progress monitoring data. | The intervention provides a mastery test that is routinely given, and instruction is adjusted based on program recommendations. There is a placement test for appropriate entry into the intervention and mastery tests to determine progression. Interventionists have a system for tracking the progress of students within the intervention. Students have the opportunity to repeat lessons when necessary to ensure mastery. |

*Source: © 2024 by Schools Cubed (https://itspossible.schoolscubed.com). Used with permission.*

# Conducting Effective Data Analysis

## The Principal's Perspective

*By Angela Hanlin*

Data, data, data. Overwhelming, powerful, and a complete game changer! Data are the one area where I receive the most questions from teachers and leaders. Often the question is, Now that we've collected the data, what do we do with it? I remember having that same question. When we know what to do with our data, we can completely change the outcome for our students.

When Pati first visited Matthews Elementary, she asked to see our school data, and I pulled out four binders. I'll never forget the look on her face. We had data, we were collecting it and reviewing it, but it was not a structured system. We were using the data to set up interventions, but we were not using it to ensure that every single student was acquiring the state standards proficiently, mastering foundational literacy skills, or using it to plan specific, targeted instruction and interventions. We knew the answers were in our data, but we were lacking a system to effectively collect the data and share it with all stakeholders. We found that system through our work with Schools Cubed, and it put us on a path to 95 percent reading proficiency! Let's take a deep look at what we did.

### A New Plan for Data

We set up three benchmark periods: beginning of year, middle of year, and end of year. After each benchmark assessment, we held a data meeting to review the data for each class and grade level. We established six-week check-in meetings to review our progress monitoring data. Eventually, we created weekly data meetings to look at weekly progress monitoring data to determine whether our small-group instructional plans and intervention lessons were impacting our students. Did our instruction impact our students? If yes, then what would we do next? If not, then what would we do in response to the data?

## Establish Data Protocols

Once we had the assessments in place, we established data protocols for each meeting. This gave consistency to our data meetings and ensured that we went deep enough into the data and discussed every single student. The biggest change was the dialogue at these meetings. Previously, we talked about the data results. We used the data to establish groups, but we failed to look at every single student. We identified percentages of students who were or were not performing. We determined the percentage of students in Tier 1, Tier 2, and Tier 3. We had to go much deeper than that to make a difference in the lives of every single learner, though. Knowing that 35 percent of students are in Tier 3 let us know we had a problem, but it did not tell us what those students needed or what the teacher needed to do to move that student forward. Using the data protocol, we began each meeting with celebrations. This gave teachers a chance to review the data prior to meetings and find celebrations in the results. We then identified students who were and were not making progress and developed an instructional plan in response to the data for each student. When we went to the individual student level, things changed! Instruction changed. Lesson planning changed. Results changed. Our growth changed. We truly learned the power of data and assessment. We completely understood differentiated instruction and the power it has on individual students.

Another change was adding the question, Why? Which students made progress and why? Which students did not make progress and why? Finding the answer to why required us to dig deeper into our data and provided teachers with an answer as to how to close the gap. This also enabled teachers to determine which strategies were working and which were not. Teachers were able to determine exactly what they had done to get their results. This was empowering for all of us!

## Set Goals

We used the data to set goals. After the beginning of year benchmark period, we set goals for the middle of year and end of year. This answered the question, Where are we going? We revisited the goals at each data meeting and decided whether we were on track to meet our goals (Hattie, 2023). Again, this deepened our level of discussion and dialogue. This also helped us determine which specific instructional practices to implement in the classroom. If our students were two grade levels behind, then we needed an instructional practice with an effect size of more than one year's growth. These discussions were powerful and empowering for staff members. Teachers took control and ownership of their instruction and planning. The data truly guided instruction. Once we learned how to do that, instruction and intervention were forever changed. This also changed the intensity of our meetings. Instead of attending a data meeting as an act of compliance, there was a true commitment to the data because it was guiding every decision we made. Teachers were invested in the process because they were using the data to get results in the classroom.

## Make Data-Informed Decisions

A lot of schools say they use data-based decision making. It is a phrase that I have heard for decades. This new work made us confident that we were truly using data to make all our decisions. Our data determined which groups students were placed in, what instruction they would receive in small group, what intervention they received, the number of repetitions they would receive in small group, and so on. Our data also led us to purchase a new reading curriculum, and by using our data, we were able to determine what we needed in a reading program.

As building leaders, the data tell us where we need to spend our time. If a specific class is struggling, then we need to be in that classroom observing the instruction and providing feedback to the teacher. If a specific intervention group is not making progress, then we need to be in the room observing the intervention that is provided. Is the intervention being provided with fidelity to the program? Even with a scripted program, often the instruction is not being provided with 100 percent fidelity. Are the correct number of repetitions being given? Is the instruction at a brisk pace? We need to observe instructions and provide feedback. By looking at the data, we can determine exactly where we need to be and what we need to observe. When individual students are not making progress, we observe those students throughout their day. Is the instruction consistent? Is the classroom teacher using the same, consistent language as the intervention teacher? If a student is in special education, is there consistency between the classroom instruction and special education instruction? By our observations and feedback, teachers determine what is effective, what is getting results, and what changes need to be made. The data allows our observations to have more purpose and greater meaning. Our observations and feedback allow teachers the opportunity to have a greater impact on their students' learning.

## A Focus on Learning

By implementing a strong data system, we guide our teachers to take the focus off teaching and place it on *learning*. The dialogue changes from, "Did we teach it?" to "Did the students learn it?" If they did not, then what are we going to do in response? One consistent comment that I heard prior to changing this focus was, "I taught that." Teachers are correct when they say that sentence. They did teach it. They taught the lesson, taught the content. The question needs to be, "Did the students learn it?" If the students did not learn the way we taught, then what will our response be? What actions will we take in response? This empowers teachers to see that they are truly the change agent in the classroom. Students learn and master content due to the teachers' instruction. When teachers use the data to determine their effectiveness, it is a game changer for their students' growth.

## Put Data on Display

Once we have a strong data system, we must find a way to make the data have significance each week. It must be part of our school culture and the way we do business each day. We were able to do that by creating a data room. We had charts, growth tables, goal posters, weekly student progress monitoring charts, and more displayed in the data room. We met in that room surrounded by our data. Teachers began to plan in that room with their coworkers. Conversations between teachers became focused on data, and the results they were, or were not, getting. Staff members could not opt out of this process. We had to accept and own the numbers surrounding us. Low numbers can be hard to accept. It is tough to work hard and not get the results you are hoping for.

Visibly seeing the data each day helps everyone involved in the process with the ownership piece. Acceptance is a necessary component in the work with data. When a leader develops a strong data system and puts the data on display, it changes the dialogue in a school.

For the data to ensure success for all, then the results must be shared with *all*. We must inform all stakeholders of our successes and struggles. Everyone should know the results, the growth, and why the school is getting those results. If we know why, then we can continue to grow. It enables every staff member to feel like they are part of a team. The successes are shared by all. The challenges are shared by all. By doing this, we learn that a low score is an opportunity for growth. Data meetings are problem-solving sessions. Low numbers don't have to scare us, because we know what to do. When this is a system, then the work is a continuous cycle. The work never stops, and the data drive the work. Once a goal is reached, then a new goal is set. Every single day has a purpose. Teachers can answer the questions, Where are we? Where are we going? and How close are we to reaching our goal? This leads to collective efficacy, which has an effect size of 1.34 (Hattie, 2023)! Data-based decision making empowers our teachers and sets them up for more growth and a greater impact than they have ever had.

It must be emphasized that it is the leader who creates and sustains this system. We establish this and sustain it in our buildings or districts, or we fail to do so. It really is that simple. This is a responsibility, and I feel an obligation, that we owe to our teachers and students. I cannot imagine doing school or leadership without data. It simply isn't possible. Data drive what we do each day and the decisions we make. We empower all staff members and students by creating a strong data system. There is a structure to this work, and it is possible!

### *It's Possible* When Leaders Believe That:

- When we look deeper at our data, at the individual student level, we can make a difference in the lives of every single learner.

- Questioning why students make or do not make progress allows teachers to examine which strategies work and which do not for each student and then plan how to close the gap.

- Data discussions are powerful and empowering for staff members. Through data, teachers can take control and ownership of their instruction and planning.

- Data tell us exactly where we need to be as leaders and what we need to spend our time observing during the school day.

- By implementing a strong data system, we guide our teachers to take the focus off teaching and place it on student learning.

- When data are celebrated and visible to the entire school community, successes as well as challenges are shared by all.

As you begin to think about establishing a thorough data analysis system in your school, it may be helpful to revisit chapter 3 (page 57) on assessments and chapter 4 (page 83) regarding interventions. Both assessments and intervention practices are highly intertwined with data analysis, and one cannot be done without the other.

On my first visit to Matthews Elementary, when I asked Angie to show me what she was collecting for data, she presented four 6-inch binders of data. She was dutiful in her efforts to ensure teachers were providing the correct assessments, looking at the reports that the assessments offered, and even routinely checking the various assessment results throughout the year, hoping that students' reading ability would improve. After all, everyone was doing the absolute best that they knew how. But they weren't sure what the data were telling them, didn't know how to change instruction based on that data, and were instead hoping that students' reading would improve. Unfortunately, hope is not a school improvement strategy we can count on! I would even say that Matthews Elementary was a step ahead of most schools, since they were measuring students' foundational skills routinely and Angie had collected data. They just didn't know what to do with that data.

Research suggests that effective principals make use of data not only to make good decisions and address schools' needs but also to inspire action (Hitt, Woodruff, Meyers, & Zhu, 2018). Unfortunately, in many schools, if there is a data analysis system, then it typically begins with how students are doing when performing on grade-level standards. Grade-level standards are essential and necessary. However, if a student is not able to read at grade level, analyzing their data on a grade-level standard does not tell the whole story, nor will it provide any instructional strategy to fix a struggling reader's problem.

Though we strongly advocate for teaching *all* students grade-level standards and ensuring all students have access to those standards, we have to differentiate two big ideas in reading instruction. Those ideas include the following.

1. The process of learning to read—how students' skills are growing in learning to read, or the foundational standards.

2. The outcomes of what we read—how students apply their ability to read and to analyze what they are reading.

In a science of reading–aligned approach, it is best to design your data analysis system on the process of learning to read, not the outcomes of how students are reading. See table 5.1 (page 116) for a comparative list of effective and ineffective data analysis practices.

In a balanced literacy approach to reading, observing for students' struggles is an often used strategy. In the book, *How to Reach and Teach All Students Through Balanced Literacy*, Rief and Heimburge (2007) note, "It is important for teachers to observe students with a 'diagnostic' eye, identifying their learning strengths, weaknesses, and developmental stages" (p. 221). In a structured literacy approach, valid and reliable assessments like CBMs are used to determine students' strengths and areas of deficit. In a balanced literacy approach, when examining data, there is an emphasis on comprehension skills such as author's purpose,

**TABLE 5.1:** Ineffective Versus Effective Data Analysis Practices

| Practices to Move Away From | Practices That Ensure *It's Possible* |
| --- | --- |
| Observation of student reading behaviors | Analysis of regularly scheduled progress monitoring |
| Reading inventories | Valid and reliable foundational reading assessments, such as CBMs |
| Teacher created formative assessments | Standards benchmark assessments in grades 3 and up |
| Comprehension skills based on grade-level standards K–6 | Analysis of outcomes on measures such as MAZE, retell, background knowledge, and vocabulary |

finding evidence, and making connections, to name a few. Comprehension skills are an example of the outcome of how a student reads.

In the overview of the science of reading in appendix A (page 253), we highlighted two constructs of how students learn to read based on a preponderance of scientific evidence. In grades K–2, we must solidify word recognition skills before reading comprehension. Simply put, students aren't able to comprehend what they cannot read. Solidifying word recognition is the process of how students are reading. Therefore, in the earlier grades, we focus our instructional efforts and data analysis on decoding or word recognition, which also align with the foundational standards within state standards. Further, in third grade and beyond, we must not only analyze how students are performing on state standards, but also ensure that students have no phonological processing issues. Closing the gaps on phonological issues will ensure students will continue to grow in their reading ability throughout their educational career. Ultimately, "any instruction that improves the word recognition ability of a student will result in greater gains in reading comprehension if that student has stronger rather than weaker language comprehension skills" (Hoover & Tunmer, 2020, p. 30). Over 80 percent of struggling readers in fourth grade and beyond have phonological processing problems (Reed & Vaughan, 2010).

This chapter walks school leaders through a data analysis system for grades K–6 that ensures they know how every student is doing. We include grades 3 through 6 as well, because for those students who may enter school as a struggling reader in the upper grades or who are a struggling reader because of instructional gaps in their earlier education, we must have a way to identify those students and ensure their growth. It is certainly possible, as we have seen many times, for struggling readers in the upper grades to become grade-level readers as well. This chapter focuses on the following.

- Understanding the components of foundational reading assessments
- Setting up a data analysis system
- How to analyze benchmark data from an assessment system that measures the foundational skills of reading

- Progress monitoring data from that system
- Suggestions for instructional strategies and interventions based on the data
- Various intervention tracking systems

# An Understanding of the Data Analysis System

There are numerous ways to dissect and analyze data in schools. In many schools, however, we find that educators readily know what the data say, they just don't know what to do with the data to effectuate change. It is the next steps that are elusive, taking the data and creating actionable instructional strategies.

The domain of data-based decision making is found at the end of this chapter on page 143. This domain features the systems we have found that, once solidly established, create a seamless, ongoing structure for data analysis. Examine the criteria and think about where you are on each. On which area of data analysis would you like to begin working?

## Time to Meet

The most basic of criteria in a strong data analysis system is ensuring teachers have the opportunity to meet on a regular basis. It is the collaboration around data analysis that is so powerful. When teachers analyze the data together in collegial settings, they begin to ask questions like, If your students are 80 percent proficient in letter naming and my students are only 50 percent proficient in letter naming, what are you doing that I am not? It is this sharing of ideas around a common goal that makes data analysis so powerful! If your school has done work regarding professional learning communities (PLCs), then you know the three big ideas of the Professional Learning Community at Work® process are: (1) A focus on learning, (2) a collaborative culture, and (3) a results orientation (DuFour et al., 2024). These three ideas remain constant in our data analysis system as well. We also agree with recommendations for the frequency of teacher collaboration as expressed in *Taking Action: A Handbook for RTI at Work* (Mattos et al., 2025), which states that teachers should meet in collaborative teams weekly. We will share the frequency of analyzing each type of data set—benchmarking or progress monitoring—as we discuss the process for each.

The opportunity for teachers to meet relies on a quality master schedule. A master schedule is the linchpin for a schools' success, and, as such, how to develop a master schedule is discussed in depth in chapter 6 (page 145). Regarding data analysis, we believe teachers need at least forty-five minutes weekly to have quality discussion regarding data analysis and instructional next steps.

## Data Collection System

If teachers are to analyze data, then there must be a manner for them to access the data in an efficient way. Many schools and districts have a data warehouse system, such as that found within Illuminate Education®, for example. Though we recommend such warehouse systems, they can be expensive, and if teachers and administrators are not trained in using them, or if there is no structure in place to ensure teachers are using them, they become a waste of valuable resources. If there is no structure in place to analyze these reports, we find that teachers do not typically access them, even though there is a wealth of valuable information found within these reports. Once a structure for data analysis is in place, understanding and interpreting the data will become much more intuitive for teachers. If schools do not have the resources to purchase a data warehouse system, we have found that the procedures outlined in this chapter and the next will more than adequately suffice. Any data collection system should have the ability to incorporate progress monitoring data. A data analysis system is not complete unless you are analyzing both benchmark assessments and progress monitoring data. We will begin with how to dissect benchmark data analysis.

# Benchmark Data Analysis

The first step in analyzing reading data is examining the benchmark assessment or interim assessment outcomes. Remembering back to chapter 3 (page 57), benchmark assessments are given three times per year: at the beginning, middle, and end of the year. A study by Bulkley and coauthors found that analyzing the data from interim assessments can build instructional coherence (Bulkley, Oláh, & Blanc, 2010). Analyzing the benchmark assessments is our first look regarding how our students are doing in learning to read. To adequately understand how to interpret benchmark data, we must understand three critical factors as they relate to foundational reading assessments. These three factors are: (1) composite scores, (2) percentiles, and (3) norm-referenced tests.

1. **Composite scores:** On foundational reading assessments, composite scores are a calculated score based on various subskills in reading for each corresponding grade level. Each grade level has cut-off scores for the overall composite of the assessment that indicates what instructional level a student is performing toward the acquisition of reading. It should also be noted that the largest band range is found at the lowest instructional level. In other words, and as an example, a kindergarten student may need to grow 205 points to move from the red instructional level to the yellow instructional level, but only 21 points to move from the yellow instructional level to the green instructional level.

2. **Percentile ranks:** A percentile rank indicates how well a student performed compared to how other students in the same norm group performed in the same grade and subject. A student's percentile rank indicates that the student scored as well as, or better than, that percentage of students in the norm group.

3. **Norm-referenced:** A norm-referenced test compares one student's performance to others in a national peer group on the same assessment.

The outcome from benchmark assessments is generally based on a composite score. Each foundational reading assessment has criteria that they believe adequately describe what students should know in each grade level to be good readers. These criteria are the subskills that make up the battery of tests given to students at each grade level and align with the components of the acquisition of reading (refer to table 3.2, page 64). To receive a composite score, each of the subskills are weighted. Some subskills are more important in acquiring reading ability than others. These more important subskills have a heavier weight in figuring out composites. Further, the weight of the subskill may change over the course of different grade levels. There are multiple subskills in each composite score depending on the grade level, and each of the subskills may have a different weight at each of the grade levels. The number of questions a student answers multiplied by the weighted score of that subskill creates the composite score. An example of the weighted scores for DIBELS 8 in kindergarten and first grade is shown in figure 5.1.

| Grade | Subtest Score | Weight |
|---|---|---|
| Kindergarten | Letter Naming Fluency (LNF) BOY | 35.44 |
| | Letter Naming Fluency (LNF) MOY/EOY | 8.86 |
| | Phoneme Segmentation Fluency (PSF) | 4.13 |
| | Nonsense Word Fluency (NWF)-Correct Letter-Sound (CLS) | 14.93 |
| | Nonsense Word Fluency (NWF)-Whole words Read Correct (WRC) | 3.56 |
| | Word Reading Fluency (WRF) | 5.62 |
| First | Letter Naming Fluency (LNF) | 10.72 |
| | Phoneme Segmentation Fluency (PSF) | 2.13 |
| | Nonsense Word Fluency (NWF)-Correct Letter-Sound (CLS) | 23.13 |
| | Nonsense Word Fluency (NWF)-Whole words Read Correct (WRC) | 7.79 |
| | Word Reading Fluency (WRF) | 13.51 |
| | Oral Reading Fluency (ORF)-Whole words Read Correct (WRC) | 25.36 |
| | Oral Reading Fluency (ORF)-Accuracy (ACC) | 0.25 |

**FIGURE 5.1:** Example weighted scores for DIBELS 8 in kindergarten and first grade.

You can think of the composite score much like bowling. You receive a score for each of the ten frames that you bowl in one game, yet all the frames are calculated together to give you an overall score on your game. Each subtest in a reading assessment is a different score, yet all of them calculate together to provide you with an overall score in the assessment.

The assessment developers have determined what comprises instructional levels based on the outcome of the composite scores. (These are often referred to as green, yellow, or red or Tier 1, 2, or 3.) Composite scores are grouped based on percentiles which create the instructional levels for that assessment. When foundational reading assessments were originally published, each of the instructional levels were meant to demonstrate a student's level of risk regarding being able to read at grade level.

Table 5.2 indicates students' percentile rank and their instructional level associated with that rank for most assessments. Because educators readily understand the three tiers of instruction, many assessments continue to use these three instructional bands when providing information about instructional levels and typically combine the students in the average and above average categories to create the instructional level of Tier 1 or at grade level or benchmark.

**TABLE 5.2:** Percentile Ranks

| Well Below Average | 1st–10th percentiles | Tier 3 |
|---|---|---|
| Below Average | 11th–25th percentiles | Tier 2 |
| Average | 26th–74th percentiles | Tier 1 |
| Above Average | 75th–89th percentiles | |
| Well Above Average | 90th–99th percentiles | |

Taking the bowling analogy one step further, let's suppose I am a novice bowler. I want to know how my bowling compares to other bowlers in my local league. Let's assume that there are 100 bowlers in my league. I am an average bowler; forty-nine of my fellow bowlers score higher than I do, and fifty of my fellow bowlers regularly score lower than I do. That would place me in the 50th percentile based on local norms.

Most foundational assessments provide two ways to set benchmark norms. They can be set on local norms, meaning students are measured by how they are doing in comparison to other students in their same district or at the same school level. Let's go back to my bowling analogy. When I compare myself to other bowlers in my own league, I am in the 50th percentile based on local norms—comparing myself to the other ninety-nine people in my league. But perhaps I am interested in becoming a professional bowler. Suddenly, my expectations need to be higher, and I need to check to see where I am when I compare myself to bowlers nationally. Suddenly, my 50th percentile rank on local norms may now be in the 10th percentile when compared to bowlers across the United States.

Much like in the bowling example, norms on reading assessments can also be set at the national level or at the local level. When norms are set at the national level, the school compares how their students are doing on that assessment to how other students are doing at the national level. Schools and districts do have the ability to set their reading assessment norms at the local level by comparing their students to other students within the district. We advise against this. When you are in a low-performing school or district and most of your students have gaps in their learning because of inadequate reading instruction, comparing your students to other students in your district sets a very low bar for your students.

If we want our students to read at an appropriate level when compared to all students in the United States, it becomes crystal clear why we must set our expectations for our students at nationally normed levels. We believe that you must use national norms for your reading assessments to adequately measure how your students are doing. National norms represent how a student's score compares with how the reference group of students in the same grade were tested on the same content during the same time frame of the school year. Using national norms ensures that students will be measured against all students within the national norming sample, not just students within their district.

And yet, there is one more tricky knot to untangle when we begin to look at our bench-mark assessments. If we again look back at table 5.2, we see that, for most foundational reading assessments, a student can score as low as the 26th percentile and still be considered at benchmark—on national norms! Once again, dusting off our memory from our educational assessment class, we have to think where the 26th percentile lies within a standard deviation framework. Figure 5.2 may help to illustrate the big ideas when thinking about the benchmark assessment.

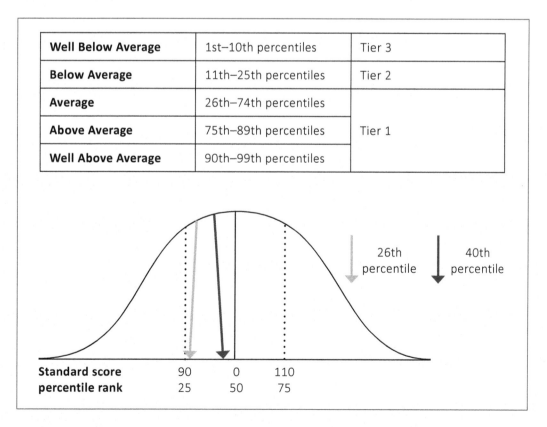

| Well Below Average | 1st–10th percentiles | Tier 3 |
| Below Average | 11th–25th percentiles | Tier 2 |
| Average | 26th–74th percentiles | |
| Above Average | 75th–89th percentiles | Tier 1 |
| Well Above Average | 90th–99th percentiles | |

**FIGURE 5.2:** Example of standard deviations.

Combining the information from figure 5.2, if we assume that the students who score "average" or at benchmark on most reading assessments are truly at grade level, note that the lowest range is the 26th percentile. When you overlay the 26th percentile with the graph on standard deviations (light gray arrow in the graph), you can see that this is just a notch above the below average range. If a student is in the 26th percentile in third grade on a foundational reading assessment and is offered no intervention, then most likely the student will have reading struggles as text becomes more difficult. Further, knowing that the grade-level expectation is the 40th percentile on most state summative assessments (the dark gray arrow on the graph), you can see that the student scoring at the 26th percentile, has a minimal chance of being proficient on state summative assessments.

As you can see in figure 5.2, a student scoring in the 26th percentile is actually a low average reader and very close to a below average reader. As David A. Kilpatrick (2015) outlines in *Essentials of Assessing, Preventing, and Overcoming Reading Difficulties*, the 25th percentile (or 26th) is within the range of the population of students who display weak reading skills.

Further, most state summative assessments measure benchmark, or grade-level proficiency, at the 40th percentile and above. No wonder we often hear school administrators saying, "the results of our reading assessments don't align to our state tests." The reason for that is exactly what we have outlined. For half of the students scoring in the benchmark range on most foundational reading assessments, the outcomes are below the 40th percentile. When analyzing reading data at the benchmark level, we suggest that you think of grade-level readers as those students who are scoring at the 40th percentile as a minimum mark. To put it in a nutshell, composite scores give us a rough overall view of how each grade level is progressing in their ability to acquire reading skills. To find out what is really going on with how students are progressing, you must dig further.

That said, information from benchmark assessments is not all for naught. Again, it's an overall view of how our students are doing as far as reading at grade level, how are they doing in acquiring that skill as they move through the school year, and whether our teachers need professional development in helping students learn to read more effectively—more on that in chapter 7 (page 185). As you analyze your benchmark assessments, we have developed a protocol that will help to steer you to the next steps of the data analysis process. Since benchmark assessments are given three times per year, the guiding questions have been nuanced from one benchmark to the next. We explore this protocol and guiding questions in the following sections. It is important to keep in mind the following prevailing thoughts for data analysis meetings.

- Data analysis should never be considered a "gotcha." The purpose of data analysis is to discuss openly what it is our students and teachers need to ensure that all students are reading at grade level.

- Since the process of data analysis is open and transparent, it is important that teachers and administrators conduct these procedures outlined in this chapter together.

- Using the protocols provided in this resource, benchmark data analysis meetings should take no longer than one hour to complete.

- Analyzing benchmark data should be completed as quickly as grade-level assessments have been completed—within the next week. The more efficient we are in analyzing data, the more quickly teachers and students can receive the help they need and deserve.

- For the data to make a difference and for teachers to know what to do with the data, it is important that all members of the grade level attend the data meetings about the benchmark information. Further, we strongly believe that special education personnel who serve that grade level should attend, as well as any multilingual teachers or providers.

- Can-do principals have high expectations and promote challenging goals for all (Hattie, 2023). It is therefore imperative that the building administrators attend these meetings as well and, ideally, lead them. If not the leader, then who? It is not the instructional coach's responsibility to inspire teachers through data; rather, it is the principal's role to get this done.

# Beginning of the Year Benchmark Analysis

We suggest analyzing benchmark data as quickly as possible. A nice time frame is to have these discussions the week after the benchmark assessments are complete. Because benchmarks provide a general overview of how students are learning to read at each grade level, we also analyze the data with three big ideas in mind: (1) class impact, (2) available interventions, and (3) grade-level goals.

## Class Impact

Is there one classroom that has more students reading below grade level than another? This is often the case in kindergarten, because for most schools, the initial student assessments start after school has begun. Kindergarten classrooms are divided based on numbers of student enrollment. This factor can create impacted classes, with some having a majority of students entering with early reading skills well below grade level while other classes may have the majority of students with early reading skills substantially higher.

This division of classes containing the haves and have-nots can put a tremendous strain on teachers. To compound the problem, in many schools, paraprofessional help or teacher assistant time is often dispersed equally to the adults. In other words, many schools in America provide teacher assistant time to all classrooms, or K–2 classrooms, equally. This is "fair" from an adult perspective—all teachers get the same amount of help. But if we truly want to ensure all students are reading at grade level, and one classroom has fifteen students with intensive needs and another classroom has six students with intensive needs, is ensuring these two teachers have the same amount of assistance going to move the needle regarding raising reading skills? We suggest that the teacher who has students with more intensive needs at the beginning of the year needs more help in moving students to grade level.

## Available Interventions

In chapter 4 (page 83), we discussed the importance of ensuring every student who needs an intervention receives an intervention. We also discussed the notion that, to meet the recommendations of intensive interventions, interventions need to be provided in addition to regular, universal, classroom instruction. Again, if students are receiving grade-level instruction five days per week (and they should), then intensive interventions also need to be provided five days per week.

By analyzing your grade-level benchmark data and using the intervention calculator introduced in chapter 4, you can readily see if every student who needs an intervention will receive an intervention. If it appears that there is not enough intervention time, then we must devise a plan.

## Grade-Level Goals

Too often in schools, we create schoolwide goals for reading that are seldom attainable; they remain the same year after year, are not progress monitored throughout the year, and are not communicated with teachers. In fact, most schoolwide reading goals are generally only found on the school's school-improvement plan that is submitted to the state or district. Yet goals are critical. New York City school leaders who worked collaboratively with teachers on establishing measurable goals, assisted the staff with monitoring and adjusting the goals throughout the year, and provided feedback to teachers on adjusting instructional strategies to meet their goals were associated with improved student outcomes on standardized assessments (Sun & Van Ryzin, 2014).

In chapter 8 (p. 232), we discuss and provide an example of how to set goals (targets) by grade level. You will note in the beginning of the year protocol that goals for each grade level need to be set when analyzing benchmark data. Figure 5.3 is a protocol to use when analyzing beginning of the year benchmark data.

| School: |
| Grade Level: |

**Section A**

Complete the following information by grade level, not by classroom.

1. List the percentage and number of students at benchmark:

   Grade level and above: _____% _____N (number of students)

2. List the percentage and number of students needing strategic interventions or who are below benchmark:

   Below benchmark: _____% _____N (number of students)

3. List the percentage and number of students needing intensive interventions or who are well below benchmark:

   Well below benchmark: _____% _____N (number of students)

4. List the goal for the end of the year: _____% (at benchmark and above) _____% (at well below benchmark)

**Section B**

If there are multiple sections of the grade level, is there one classroom where students are more impacted? If so, identify that classroom here:




If there is one classroom that is more impacted, is there a plan for resources such as paraprofessionals, teacher assistants, special education, professional development, push-in, and so on? Provide details for support here:




**Section C**

Regarding students in need of intensive interventions, are there enough intervention sections available so every student who needs an intervention will receive an intervention? (Refer to the intervention calculator from figure 4.2, page 100.): **Yes No**

Are students able to receive intensive interventions five days per week? **Yes No**

If any questions above were answered "No," what is the plan to correct the situation? Please list below:




**FIGURE 5.3:** Beginning of the year benchmark data analysis protocol.

*Visit **go.SolutionTree.com/literacy** for a free reproducible version of this figure.*

# Middle of the Year Benchmark Analysis

As indicated earlier, benchmark data analysis is a first look as to how students are doing. There is not enough information when dissecting the data at this level to truly determine individual growth of students, but by the middle of the year we can start to see what classrooms might be making gains. When making a midyear analysis, the two most productive foci are class impact and grade-level goals.

## Class Impact

When analyzing your middle of the year data, you should see more students moving into the benchmark instructional level. Further, if one class was more impacted than other classes, and you made adjustments such as providing extra paraprofessional time or special education support, this is a good time to ensure that is working. To do so, consider the following steps.

1. Ask yourself, "Are there fewer students now in the lowest tier of instruction?"

2. If not, analyze the composite score of each student in the lowest tier. At minimum, if you have devoted additional resources, students may not have moved one tier of instruction but they certainly should have substantially increased in their composite score.

## Grade-Level Goals

At the middle of the year, the percentage of students who are at benchmark should be halfway to your goal. For example, if the grade level was at 20 percent to start the year, with an end-of-year goal of 40 percent, your middle-of-the-year benchmark is 30 percent. This is critical to analyze, and once again, you will want to refer to your grade-level goal-setting sheet to see if you are there. If you are not, plans need to be put into place regarding how teachers and students can get the help they need. You may want to ask the following.

1. Are students getting a full literacy block of instruction?

2. Are all components of literacy being taught?

3. Are students reading text at the appropriate level on a daily basis and for an adequate amount of time?

4. Is there a structure in place for small-group instruction?

5. Are students receiving differentiated instruction in small groups?

6. Are students who are at grade level being adequately challenged?

Figure 5.4 is a protocol to use when analyzing middle of the year benchmark data.

| **School:** |
| --- |
| **Grade Level:** |

**Section A**

Complete the following information by grade level, not by classroom.

1. List the percentage and number of students at benchmark:

   Grade level and above: _____% _____N (number of students)

2. What was your goal for percentage of students at grade level and above for the end of the year? _____% _____N (number of students)

3. Regarding question 2, are you halfway to your goal? **Yes   No**

4. If not, were there particular classrooms that made the goal, while others did not? **Yes   No**

5. What was your goal for the percentage of students in the lowest instructional level at the end of the year? _____%

6. Regarding question 5, are you halfway to the goal? **Yes   No**

**Section B**

If there are multiple sections of the grade level, is there one classroom that has a significant number of students who have moved from below or well below benchmark into the benchmark instructional level? If so, identify that classroom here:

To what can you attribute success? Is there professional development or instructional strategies that need to be shared in other classrooms? If yes, identify here:

If there are multiple sections in the grade level, is there one classroom that has a significant number of students who have moved into below or well below benchmark instructional level? If so, identify that classroom here:

Is there a plan for resources such as paraprofessionals, teacher assistants, special education, professional development, push-in, and so on for those classrooms. Provide details for support here:

**FIGURE 5.4:** Middle-of-the-year benchmark data analysis protocol.

*continued* →

| Section C |
| --- |

1. Are both boys and girls making adequate progress in reading? **Yes No**

2. Are special education students making adequate progress or the same rate of progress as peers? **Yes No**

   If not, what adjustments can be made? List here:

3. Are English learners making adequate or the same rate of progress as peers? **Yes No**

   If not, what adjustments can be made? List here:

4. Are all minority/majority subgroups making adequate or the same rate of progress as peers? **Yes No**

   If not, what subgroup is not making adequate progress? List here:

   What adjustments can be made? List here:

*Visit **go.SolutionTree.com/literacy** for a free reproducible version of this figure.*

# End of the Year Benchmark Data Analysis

It is our end of year data that truly indicate what our instructional impact has been on students. In fact, it is at this time of year that we can sort out what and who were the drivers in making a difference in student achievement, whether good or bad. As you review the end of year data with teachers, it is important to keep in mind, again, that data analysis is not a "gotcha." If we want to inspire our teachers through data analysis, then we need to use the data to find out what some teachers are doing that makes a difference for students and ensure that the others are doing it, too!

## Class Impact

As you complete the end of year data protocol, pay particular attention to the number or percentage of students who have moved out of the lowest instructional level. If you have a highly effective intervention structure established, as described in chapter 4 (page 83), you will see a dramatic reduction in the number of students still in Tier 3. If you are just beginning this journey, your interventions are not effective, and your universal instruction is not where it needs to be, it is likely students may have remained stagnant from the beginning of the year or your data have worsened. This is cause for alarm!

## Grade-Level Goals

We have found that teachers or grade levels hitting their end of year goals is a great cause for celebration. Make a big deal out of this. Remember, effective principals inspire their teachers by using data (Grissom et al., 2021). The celebration of this occasion only enhances that inspiration. Reaching goals at Angie's school became such a commonplace occurrence that they often had to increase the goal by the middle of the year! Success really does breed success, and the more teachers and students reach their goals and are recognized for their achievement, the more achievement occurs.

## Planning for Next Year

It is your end of year benchmark or interim data that will establish where you begin the following year. Increasing reading achievement is an ongoing journey until 100 percent of students are reading at grade level, and it's possible when we continue to analyze our data, make adjustments where necessary, and continue the cyclical journey of teach, analyze, refine, and begin again. It is here, after each grade-level benchmark assessment has been analyzed, that you will again use the intervention calculator introduced in chapter 4 (page 83) to begin to plan for who needs interventions for next year.

Figure 5.5 is a data protocol that can be used to analyze end of year benchmark data.

| |
|---|
| **School:** |
| **Grade Level:** |
| **Section A** |
| Complete the following information by grade level, not classroom. <br><br> 1. List the percentage and number of students at benchmark: <br><br>    Grade level and above: _____% _____N (number of students) <br><br> 2. What was your goal for percentage of students on grade level and above for the end of the year? <br>    _____% _____N (number of students) <br><br> 3. Regarding question 2, did you make the goal for students at grade level? **Yes No** <br><br> 4. If not, were there particular classrooms that made the goal while others did not? **Yes No** <br><br> 5. What was your goal for the percentage of students in the lowest instructional level at the end of the year? <br>    _____% <br><br> 6. Did you make the goal? **Yes No** |
| **Section B** |
| If there are multiple sections of the grade level, is there one classroom that has a significant number of students who moved from below or well below benchmark into the benchmark instructional level? If so, identify that classroom here: |

**FIGURE 5.5:** End of year benchmark data analysis protocol.

*continued →*

To what can that success be attributed? Are there professional development or instructional strategies that need to be shared in other classrooms? If yes, identify those here:

If there are multiple sections in the grade level, is there one classroom that has a significant number of students who moved into below or well below benchmark instructional level? If so, identify that classroom here:

Is there a plan for resources such as paraprofessionals, teacher assistants, special education, professional development, push-in, and so on for those classrooms? Provide details for support here:

**Section C**

Using end of year data, complete the intervention calculator in figure 4.2 (page 100) to determine the number of sections of intervention required for next year.

Will all students who need an intervention be able to receive the intervention? **Yes No**

If no, what is the plan for adjustment? Please describe here:

*Visit **go.SolutionTree.com/literacy** for a free reproducible version of this figure.*

As you continue this journey and implement our suggestions, you will see that, every year, fewer and fewer sections of interventions are required, and more and more students are reading at grade level. Keep in mind that this is a three- to five-year journey. Analyzing and refining will happen continuously, but *it's possible*!

# Considerations When Analyzing Benchmark Data

Analysis of grade-level data is not the principal's job, nor is it the teacher's job. Rather, the analysis of benchmark and grade-level data should be a collaborative process that includes the thinking of all educators. Ensuring that all students are at grade level is a schoolwide effort that requires an "all means all" attitude, which in turn means that how students are doing throughout the year is the responsibility of all involved.

We believe that not only should grade-level teams analyze benchmark data, but leadership teams should also analyze benchmark data. By analyzing data during leadership meetings, all team members are aware of how the reading initiative is progressing, and the leadership team can develop opportunities for professional development, consider a reallocation of human resources if necessary, learn from one another, and of course, celebrate the improvement in reading achievement! The focus of chapter 8 (page 215) is to ensure that a quality structure for collaboration is in place. We will walk you through creating a leadership team as well as the roles of the leadership team. You will begin to see the importance they play when analyzing benchmark data and establishing goals for the school.

Aside from the concepts that are a part of each of the grade-level protocols discussed earlier, there are a few other ideas to keep in mind as you analyze each grade level's benchmark or interim assessment data. Most foundational reading assessment data can be disaggregated through filters that include trends of subgroups of students. When disaggregating data, the big ideas should include the following.

1. Are both boys and girls making adequate progress in reading?

2. Are special education students making adequate progress or the same rate of progress as peers?

3. Are English learners making adequate or the same rate of progress as peers?

4. Are all minority and majority subgroups making adequate or the same rate of progress as peers?

# Making Instructional Decisions Through Data Analysis

Analyzing benchmark data is just the first indicator of how students are doing. The information contained within composite scores is not granular enough to determine what students really need to make growth. Further, we sometimes find some of the subskills within the individual foundational assessments are not quality indicators of how students learn to read as other subskills. As an example, in some foundational reading assessments, sight word reading is tested in kindergarten. Students are just learning letter sounds and the ability to blend CVC words; therefore, sight word reading is not a critical skill by the end of the year and may be an example of teachers teaching students to memorize words rather than to decode words. Another example is the subskill of retelling. A test on the retelling of a passage has two flaws based on the way the test is administered: the scoring of how a student has retold the story is subjective and biased to what the assessor thinks is the correct answer, and further, retelling tests have only a moderate correlation ($r = 0.46$) when compared to other measures of comprehension such as cloze reading tests or MAZE tasks (Cao & Kim, 2021). Since the process of reading consists of many parts and pieces, we must analyze how students are doing on each of the most important parts and pieces as they progress through the grades.

In chapter 3, we discussed the subskills found within each of the foundational assessments at each of the respective grade levels (see table 3.2, page 64). This information becomes critical when we analyze not only how students are doing in this progression, but also in making instructional decisions to propel students' learning. These subskills (or a variety thereof) are found within every quality foundational reading assessment.

If we revisit the bowling example one more time, to meet my goal to become a professional bowler, it does me little good to say I must increase the points in my overall bowling game—though this is true—unless I have analyzed how I have done on each individual frame. Does my attempt at a straight ball result in a hook to the right? Does my hook throw finish too early? Do I have too many splits, and if so, why? I can't find out what I need to do to increase the overall points I am trying to obtain without analyzing these subskills.

This same analogy can be used for foundational reading assessments. Again, simply looking at the composite score tells us little regarding how to increase a student's overall score. But analyzing each of the subskills (bowling frames) gives a great deal of information regarding what we (a student and the teacher) need to do to improve overall reading ability.

There are many ideas regarding how to best analyze data when working in a collaborative team. Some promote the notion that teachers bring forward a number of students whom they might be worried about and analyze only their data, while some suggest looking at percentages of students who met the standard and who didn't and analyze the why or what to do differently. We hold fast to the notion, and suggest you do too, that to ensure *it's possible* that all students read at grade level, you must analyze the subskills of reading, those parts and pieces that go into the big idea of how students learn to read. And you must do so on a regular basis!

We have found that the following eight guiding principles ensure effective meeting processes, institutionalize data analysis, and make the process intuitive for all. These principles are:

1. Meetings take no more than forty-five minutes.

2. There is assurance that all students who are below grade level are being progress monitored as required.

3. There is awareness of which students are making progress and which students are not are being identified.

4. The area of individual student need is evident and matches the instructional grouping or strategy they are receiving.

5. An alert is built in when a student isn't making progress.

6. When students are showing a trend of not making progress, instructional changes are discussed immediately.

7. Principals and instructional leaders are able to readily see trends regarding classrooms and intervention rooms that are improving outcomes for students as part of the school culture and not in a punitive fashion.

8. Schools readily know how students are growing on an ongoing basis throughout the year.

In Angie's scenario, she repeatedly asked her teachers to consider, "Where are we? Where are we going? How are we doing?" These are excellent questions to keep in mind as you march forward on your road to ensuring *it's possible* that all students read at grade level (Hattie, 2023).

As stated earlier, and as Angie points out, a great number of schools are analyzing data, but in too many schools, it is to no avail. Richard DuFour and colleagues' (2024) original questions in PLC work are exactly the right questions: (1) What do we want our students to know? (2) How do we know we have gotten there? (3) What do we do when they struggle? and (4) How do we extend the learning for those that are already there?

# Sample Data Analysis System

The information and systems we highlight here align with the guiding principles of data analysis we have previously identified. Our system can be used in two methods. One is an old-fashioned card system that many schools still find incredibly powerful, and the other is an electronic data analysis spreadsheet that other schools find equally powerful. The choice of which system to use is simply based on which will work best for your school. The data analysis system described here ensures students master the critical subskills of reading.

This data analysis system is based on the progress monitoring data of all students not reading at grade level. In this system, students' data are tracked by the trends identified in each of the subskills in which the student is struggling. When you are considering data analysis, every part of successful reading acquisition is reliant on a mastery of previous subskills. These subskills are not lockstep, meaning we must master all of one skill before progressing to the next, but rather they are stepping stones, and there is a hierarchy to the skills (see figure 5.6, page 134), although one should not assume that to master one skill you must have mastered the previous skill. Full reading development is dependent on the many subskills involved in reading. These subskills are not developed in isolation, but rather, as they develop, they lead into acquiring the ability to further integrate the next phase of reading. Any knowledge of a new subskill is reliant on how well learned the previous subskill has been, though what level of mastery needed at each level is still not determined by research. Students who struggle with a lower skill will certainly struggle with mastering a skill at a higher level (Hoover & Tunmer, 2020). The subskills do overlap in their acquisition. A student who knows only five consonants and a vowel and their associated sounds might very well be able to put those corresponding letters and sounds together to decode a word. As we have discussed, in early reading acquisition, one skill builds on the next, so for students to read at grade level, the more fluent or adroit they are at the subskills appropriate for that grade level and those prior to that grade level, the more readily they will acquire the new skill. In other words, if students do not master these subskills, they will not be able to master the next subskill to which the previous is linked to and will continue to struggle.

Figures 5.7 (page 134) and 5.8 (page 135) show examples of both methods of data analysis. Each card or spreadsheet contains every pertinent subskill that relates to reading for each grade level. Both systems should be organized by grade level. As an example, the dot cards shown in figure 5.7 are for first grade. The example contained within the spreadsheet in figure 5.8 is also for first grade.

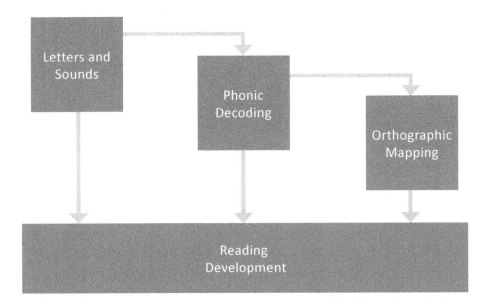

**FIGURE 5.6:** Three levels of reading development.

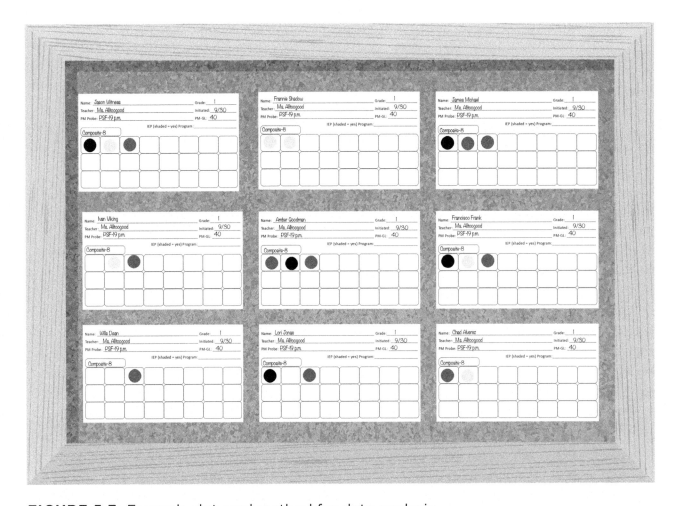

**FIGURE 5.7:** Example dot card method for data analysis.

| PSF Phoneme Segmentation Fluency Goal 40 (BOY) | | | | | | | | | |
|---|---|---|---|---|---|---|---|---|---|
| Student | BOY | BOY-PSF | 9/30 | 10/7 | 10/14 | 10/21 | 10/28 | 11/4 | 11/11 |
| Colonel Mustard | 103 | 33 | 35 | | 38 | | 40 | | 40 |
| James Michael | 112 | 26 | 26 | | 30 | | 33 | | 35 |
| Melanie Myers | 105 | 32 | 34 | | 34 | | 36 | | 39 |
| Abraham Burnett | 99 | 38 | 38 | | 40 | | 40 | | |
| Ivan Viking | 78 | 23 | 26 | 28 | 30 | 33 | 35 | 36 | 39 |
| Amber Goodman | 63 | 21 | 23 | 25 | 25 | 28 | 31 | 30 | 35 |
| Francisco Frank | 92 | 22 | 22 | 27 | 29 | 31 | 26 | 33 | 33 |
| Jason Witness | 88 | 19 | 19 | 20 | 19 | 18 | 19 | 18 | 20 |
| Frannie Shadow | 66 | 22 | 27 | 30 | 33 | 35 | 38 | 39 | 40 |
| Erin York | 52 | 25 | 27 | 27 | 30 | 32 | 32 | 36 | 38 |
| Wills Dean | 97 | 16 | 17 | 17 | 20 | 21 | 23 | 23 | 25 |

| < > First Grade PSF | First Grade LNF | First Grade NWF (CLS) | First Grade NWF (WWR) |
|---|---|---|---|
| First Grade ORF (WC) | First Grade ORF Accuracy | | |

*Source: © 2024 by Quest Academy. Used with permission.*

**FIGURE 5.8:** Example spreadsheet method for data analysis.

Looking at the spreadsheet for first grade, you will see along the bottom are the tabs for each of the subskills to be measured in first grade. Each tab has the names of students who are being progress monitored in that subskill. This school is using Acadience as the foundational reading assessment, and the subskills for each student to master are: phoneme segmentation fluency (PSF), letter naming fluency (LNF), nonsense word fluency (NWF) correct letter sound (CLS) and NWF whole words read (WWR), and oral reading fluency (ORF) words correct (WC) and ORF accuracy. A student is not likely to be progress monitored in all these subskills. Instead, we want to first teach both letter naming fluency and phonemic segmentation to the students who haven't mastered those skills. Since we are teaching skills to students who have not yet mastered the skills, we want to ensure that our help is helping and therefore progress monitor those skills. (It is also important to remember that, while we are progress monitoring each skill separately, we are not teaching students only one skill at a time.) Once letter naming fluency and phoneme segmentation are mastered, the student should be taught blending through nonsense words and decodable text. It is at that time that the student would move to the next hierarchy of progress monitoring.

As you look at these examples, you most likely notice the various colors on the dot cards or on the spreadsheet. It is important to note, this is not an indicator of instructional level; rather, it identifies trends within the student's instruction. A green cell or dot ●, whether on the card or spreadsheet, indicates nice growth from the last progress monitoring to the most current, a yellow cell or dot ● indicates no growth since the last progress monitoring, and a red cell or dot ● indicates the student is going backward and not making the necessary gains. This color-coding system gives a visual alert to the instructional leaders and teachers that what we are doing may not be working. When two consecutive red dots are on a card, a discussion needs to ensue.

This color-coding system also ensures that the school leadership can readily see what students are struggling with. In this system, we focus only on struggling students, devoting our full attention to those who need it most urgently. In public school settings, particularly in those schools where the vast number of students are reading below grade level, we must focus on those most in need.

Additionally, the dates for the week of the progress monitoring are either found on the dot itself or on the column of the spreadsheet for the subskill being monitored. This also serves as an alert to the instructional leadership as to whether or not progress monitoring is being completed as necessary.

To understand how both the spreadsheet and the dot card work, let's take a look at one particular student, Jason Witness (see figures 5.9 and 5.10). On September 17, Jason was administered the Acadience benchmark assessment. The following eight steps recount the process of assessing Jason's progress using the dot card and spreadsheet methods.

1. His overall composite score is 88, and his name is highlighted in red ●, indicating that he is at the lowest instructional level.

2. His score on the very important subskill of phoneme segmentation fluency is 19.

3. Since Jason is well below his expected ability to segment phonemes, he will receive progress monitoring assessments every week. He will also receive instruction that will increase his ability to learn to segment phonemes.

4. Jason's first progress monitoring probe was administered on September 30, and he received a score of 19. Since Jason made no progress, nor did he go backward, we would say his growth was stagnant and he received a dot of yellow ●, or his cell was shaded yellow.

5. The following week, Jason received a score of 20. This was progress for Jason, and his dot or cell was shaded green ●.

6. The following week, Jason did not progress and instead went backward. His dot was highlighted red ● to indicate his regression. The following week, he did not make progress and again his dot was highlighted red. The following week, Jason went back to 19. He did make progress, and his dot was highlighted in green ●. Unfortunately, the following week, he went backward again, and his score was highlighted red. But, as is often the case, students with low subskills are often slow to take off but can make gains with consistent instruction and many opportunities to practice—repetition.

7. On November 11, Jason received his weekly probe and scored 20. From that week forward, Jason continued to make progress each week. His dots and cells were green ●.

8. Once Jason makes the benchmark goal of forty, his cell will be shaded in blue ○, as indicated in Frannie Shadow's progress monitoring cells (see figure 5.9). To ensure that his score of forty is solid, he will be progress monitored the next week as well to make sure his phonemic segmentation skills are still at benchmark. Once we know that is secure, Jason will no longer receive progress monitoring in this subskill.

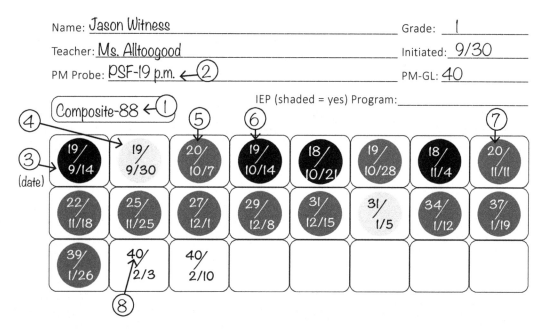

**FIGURE 5.9:** First-grade student example spreadsheet.

**FIGURE 5.10:** First-grade student example dot card.

*Visit go.SolutionTree.com/literacy for a free reproducible version of this figure.*

At many collaborative team meetings, we can become mired in the data. However, with a color-coding system, and stepping back so all the dot cards or dot cells are looked at globally, the group of educators can readily see who is struggling. Where are the red dots or cells ●? If students are progressing with green dots or cells ●, then what they are receiving is working. We don't need to spend time on those students. Instead, we only need to spend time on the students who are struggling—the sea of red. This greatly reduces the amount of time doing data analysis and instead allows us to focus on the necessary instructional strategies needed to increase outcomes for *all* students.

On the spreadsheet in figure 5.9, note that every other column at the top is shaded in. This allows for students who are receiving services from another provider other than the classroom teacher to progress monitor the student on off weeks. If a progress monitoring probe results appear in a shaded column, this indicates it was administered by a service provider other than the classroom teacher. When all educators progress monitor the students they service, all educators own all students' progress. Also note that the students who are in the strategic instructional level—those whose names are highlighted in yellow —are progress monitored every other week or every ten days; therefore, when using the spreadsheet method, there is typically a blank cell after each progress monitoring probe.

This system for data analysis may seem complicated. Once you get the hang of it, you will see that it is actually quite simple and efficient and makes your data analysis system intuitive, productive, and student driven. The dot card, as well as a template for the subskill spreadsheet and the steps to complete each, can be found online (visit **www.itspossible .schoolscubed.com**).

## Kindergarten Data Analysis

There are several critical subskills that we need to analyze in kindergarten. It is a realistic goal for students to master the alphabetic principle as well as basic phonemic awareness and the ability to link phonemes to their corresponding grapheme/letter name and sound along with letter writing or letter formation. It should therefore be assumed that the preponderance of focus on assessments in these grades will focus on these skills. Students who have an assessment result that indicates they are behind will need to be taught these skills and therefore should receive progress monitoring. Overall, these subskills include the following.

- Letter naming
- Phoneme segmentation fluency
- Letter sounds
- Nonsense word fluency

Many practitioners have come to believe that instruction should follow a sequence from larger to smaller phonological elements such as instruction of identification of syllable sound prior to instruction in individual phonemes. Research has now concluded that instruction in phoneme awareness does not need to be delayed until students master larger phonological skills such as syllable segmentation (International Dyslexia Association, 2022).

Though some foundational reading assessments do contain evidence of students' ability to recognize these larger subskills of phonological awareness such as sentence segmentation, rhyming, and onset-rime, we support beginning instruction at the phonemic awareness level coupled with letter knowledge. Directly teaching and linking speech sounds with the corresponding grapheme leads to more rapid reading acquisition.

## First-Grade Data Analysis

By the end of first grade, it is a realistic goal for students to master phoneme awareness in more complex syllables such as those containing two phoneme blends. Many foundational reading assessments begin to measure blending skills and phonics by testing nonsense word fluency typically beginning in kindergarten and through at least the beginning of first grade. Beth A. Harn, Mike Stoolmiller, and David J. Chard (2008) find that proficiency in nonsense word reading in the fall and winter of first grade is associated with better oral reading fluency in spring of first grade. Likewise, in most foundational reading assessments, the following subskills of reading will be found.

- Nonsense word fluency
- Whole words read
- Oral reading fluency

It should be noted that some students may still not have mastered the goal of blending and segmenting of simple syllables. These students will need further instruction or intervention in this skill. Looking back at the spreadsheet for first grade, you will notice that these subskills are still found within the data analysis process.

In other words, even though the foundational reading assessment is not testing that subskill, it will continue needing to be progress monitored and taught until the student is proficient in order for students to acquire more difficult reading levels.

## Second-Grade-and-Up Data Analysis

Beginning in second grade, the most crucial skill for reading is oral reading fluency (ORF). Many educators question why we do not recommend analyzing comprehension. In fact, to fully assess comprehension, we would have to provide students with multiple comprehension assessments. Reading comprehension is not easily quantified, and it can be difficult to separate out the factors that contribute to reading comprehension; teachers should have an understanding of the various components of comprehension (Kilpatrick, Joshi, & Wagner, 2019). Areas where students may struggle include language skills, comprehension monitoring, inferencing, and background knowledge, to name just a few.

Fortunately, we do know that when students are fluent in their reading without having to make a conscious effort to decode words on a page, then there is immediate access to the meaning of the words. This allows a student to integrate all the processes of reading and allocate mental resources toward understanding or comprehending the text.

Various studies have found there is a significant correlation of ORF to comprehension (White, Sabatini, Park, et al., 2021). In a study that Fuchs and colleagues (2001) refer to, the correlation of ORF to comprehension was 0.91 as compared to tests of question answering, recall measures, and cloze measures of reading. In other words, using an ORF probe is the best proxy to determine whether a student can comprehend text.

Using your foundational reading assessment, we recommend data analysis of ORF. It is necessary to analyze both accuracy and fluency separately. Accuracy must be at 98 percent, or reading is considered a struggle for students. Fluency should be at the rate indicated on the given reading assessment.

In creating your data analysis cards or spreadsheet, remember that students in second grade may still be struggling with first-grade prerequisite skills and therefore must receive intervention and progress monitoring in those areas.

As we discussed in chapter 3 (page 57), particularly in grades 3 and up, many students who are reading below grade level will have a great deal of difficulty reading the fluency passages at their grade level. For ORF, the optimal progress monitoring material is the highest level of material where the student reads with at least 90 percent accuracy and has an ORF words correct score above 20 in first-grade material, 40 in second-grade material, or 50 in third- through sixth-grade materials (Acadience Learning, 2020).

On your data analysis cards or spreadsheet beginning in third grade, instead of having a variety of subskills students are working on, you will now have students being tested on oral reading fluency at their grade level or at one or two grade levels below where they are currently placed. When a student is being progress monitored below their grade level, we recommend two consecutive weeks of the grade level at which they are performing and the third week at grade level. This two-off and one-on grade-level routine will show if the student is indeed making progress at their appropriate grade level.

Here are two off-level testing scenarios:

1. **Student A** is a struggling second-grade student who has not yet met benchmark on the prior years' subskills of phoneme segmentation or nonsense word fluency. Grade-level expectation for this student is that they are being assessed for ORF on second-grade passages, yet their intervention is working on phoneme-grapheme mapping, blending nonsense words, and reading decodable text to further practice the skill of blending. Our instruction during intervention is exactly on what the student needs based on their performance on their foundational reading assessment. To ensure that our instruction is indicating they are progressing in the areas of phoneme segmentation and nonsense word fluency, we assess this student on those two subskills every week until they are at benchmark on those corresponding assessments. Every third week of instruction, we want to see if our instruction is also getting this student to better read grade-level passages, so we progress monitor them on an ORF passage at their grade level.

2. **Student B** is a fourth-grade student who is reading at approximately a second-grade level. Their assessment results indicate that they are below grade in both accuracy and fluency. They receive an intervention focused on increasing their phonological processing skills. This intervention should increase their ability to accurately decode words that, in time, will lead to an increase in their fluency rate. Every week, they receive a progress monitoring probe in ORF at the third-grade level; this is above their actual reading level but below their actual grade level. Passages at this level will indicate if their accuracy is increasing at an appropriate level. Every third week, they receive a progress monitoring probe at the fourth-grade level to see if their accuracy and fluency rate are also increasing on a grade-level passage.

# School Spotlight

## Chippewa Valley Schools, Clinton Township, Michigan

In our district, we have been practicing MTSS for more than ten years. When we first began, we reviewed benchmark data three times per year to determine which students would benefit from extra support. Then, we provided a variety of interventions that our teachers and paraeducators could choose from to use as interventions for the students who were below a certain benchmark percentile. By offering different interventions at certain grade levels, we believed we were differentiating, yet we found ourselves identifying the same students for intervention each year, because the interventions did not show student growth or close a gap. Most of our students in need of Tier 3 MTSS intervention were identified again each year. For some, their entire elementary school experience consisted of being pulled out of their classrooms for intervention that did not match their needs or close the gaps in their skill deficits.

In the last few years, we began to use FastBridge as our benchmark system. We found that we could more clearly identify students' skill deficits and better identify what we thought were more targeted interventions. However, we realized that many of our intervention staff still tended to provide interventions based on their personal comfort with the intervention rather than it matching a student's perceived skill deficit. The cycle continued, and we could never truly determine if students were receiving the right intervention or even if the intervention seemed to be working. Benchmark scores never changed much, and our students were stuck in a cycle of pullout interventions that largely did not meet their individual needs.

Then, we began to analyze FastBridge data better to identify the specific skill deficits students had with much more accuracy. By using FastBridge data for its intended purpose, to capture a picture of a student's progress, we were able to identify what students needed and how we were going to provide that support in a systematic and consistent manner. We now use FastBridge data to help us identify who has decoding and accuracy deficits. We utilize that information to place students into intervention groups. Providers who deliver the instruction are responsible for progress monitoring their group of students. All students are progress monitored no matter their academic level. Through this process, we identify which students are not making progress and need to go to be assessed on a lower grade-level reading passage or foundational subskill level. We assess them at this level while also doing a probe on grade-level passages or skills. We use the information from their accuracy scores to determine the level at which to progress monitor and instruct. Areas of individual needs are evident from this process and match the instructional grouping they are receiving. When they are not making progress, changes are talked about as a team immediately so that we are not wasting time on the wrong intervention plan.

By using the data and consistently monitoring student progress, our staff members can make informed instructional decisions to ensure student progress. Our students are making progress in reading like we have never seen before.

---

*Niyoka Wright, Coordinator of Assessment and Data Analysis*
*Karen Langlands, Executive Director of Innovation and Learning*
*Marina Licari, Executive Director for Elementary Education*

# Summary

We've described that a good data analysis system should be based on the many complexities and components of how students learn to read and not on comprehension skills or grade-level standards. These components include skills such as letter naming, phoneme segmentation, nonsense word fluency, and oral reading fluency.

Data analysis begins with benchmark or screening data, and there are protocols provided to guide you through analyzation of benchmark data. Ensuring instructional strategies effectuate change in reading outcomes can only be guaranteed through the analysis of progress monitoring data. Since progress monitoring data are at the core of reading improvements, school leaders must ensure that their staff are progress monitoring students on the appropriate subskills of reading.

We have outlined eight guiding principles for data analysis. We believe these eight guiding principles, when used in a comprehensive system, will ensure schools can immediately use the information gleaned from the data to effectuate change. Further, these guiding principles will create a sustainable structure for your school or district's data analysis that ensures all students move toward grade-level reading attainment.

In chapter 6, we will take a broad look at the instructional strategies that should be used that align to the subskills in which students are receiving interventions.

# Data Analysis

A formal system for analyzing literacy data is in place. The staff meets regularly to discuss literacy outcomes, and the discussions lead to any necessary changes in instructional strategies and improved outcomes for students.

| Big Idea | Basic (1) | Effective (2) | Proficient (3) | Exemplar (4) |
|---|---|---|---|---|
| **The school understands the importance of professional collaboration and has created adequate time (like forty-five minutes weekly) for such in the master schedule.** | Team members sometimes meet together. | There is an opportunity for teams to collaborate throughout the year. | There is an effective master schedule that ensures all teams meet with regular consistency. | Members of each team value collaborative time. The time leads to increased outcomes for students and professional growth for educators. |
| **There is a data collection system in place that makes the access of literacy data readily available to staff.** | One person generally knows how to access data for all teachers. | There is a data system in place that staff know how to locate and use. | Teachers know and are able to use the various data reports available to them and feel comfortable accessing them. | Teachers regularly examine the data on their own, bringing insights and suggestions to meetings. |
| **There are common understandings regarding data analysis that are found within a data protocol. This protocol guides instructional adjustments, if necessary, as indicated through the analysis of the data.** | The school has a common data protocol. | The common data protocol is used on a regularly scheduled basis. | All teachers understand the use of the protocol and have suggestions for instructional adjustments based on data analysis. | As a result of data conversations, instructional adjustments are seen in the classroom. |
| **Throughout the scheduled benchmark assessments, the school leadership is aware of the literacy outcomes in each grade level. Support is provided where and when necessary to ensure *all* students are reading at grade level.** | School leadership is aware that some grade levels do better than others in increasing reading outcomes for students. | The school leadership reviews benchmark and screening data and is aware how each grade level is doing based on that assessment. | The school leadership has a pulse on the outcomes in literacy in each class and grade level and ensures professional development is aligned to needs. | The school leadership ensures teacher evaluations, instructional feedback, and job-embedded professional development are aligned and effectuate change for student learning and teacher knowledge. |

*Page 1 of 2*

| Big Idea | Basic (1) | Effective (2) | Proficient (3) | Exemplar (4) |
|---|---|---|---|---|
| **All grade levels create end of year goals for increased literacy outcomes. The goals are routinely analyzed and adjusted to ensure the goal is met.** | Yearly, the school creates a schoolwide reading goal. | The school leadership creates goals for each grade level at the beginning of the year. | Each grade level has input and works collaboratively toward meeting their literacy goals. | The grade levels have literacy goals for increasing the percentage or number of students who are at benchmark and decreasing the number of students well below benchmark. |
| **The instructional teams or grade levels regularly analyze data and understand the importance of improving outcomes for students.** | All members of the team know and bring the correct data to be analyzed. | The team members understand the different levels and subskills within the data and know which will substantiate change. | There is follow through by team members, and students regularly improve through a continued cycle of data analysis. | Teams have an intent to focus on the outcomes of students as they analyze data. |
| **The school leadership is focused on increasing literacy outcomes for students and, therefore, makes data analysis meetings a priority.** | The principal attends meetings when able. | The school leaders regularly attend data meetings and find resolutions to conflicts for attendance whenever able. | The school leaders or principals understand the data analysis process and contribute to instructional adjustments. | The staff value the input of the school leaders. The school leaders can readily provide instructional suggestions, and a shared voice in creating action steps for students is readily apparent in meetings. |
| **All student groups are analyzed during data analysis meetings, which includes a disaggregation by student trends in subgroups and individual students.** | Generally, schoolwide data are analyzed. | Data are analyzed by grade level and subskills found within the data. | A focus in data meetings is toward students who are *not* making adequate progress in the subskills of literacy. | Instructional adjustments for all students not making growth are created and committed to during data analysis meetings. |
| **The regular analysis of literacy data is a part of the school culture. The data substantiates the sense of urgency to ensure all students are reading at grade level.** | The data are analyzed by teachers. | The data are interpreted at the subskill level, and instructional strategies are created. | Instructional strategies to increase literacy are reevaluated to ensure student improvement was attained. | Routinely, instructional strategies that are implemented lead to literacy improvement for students. |

*Source: © 2024 by Schools Cubed (https://itspossible.schoolscubed.com). Used with permission.*

**It's Possible!** © 2025 Solution Tree Press • SolutionTree.com
Visit **go.SolutionTree.com/literacy** to download this free reproducible.

# Aligning Instructional Strategies With Data

## The Principal's Perspective

*By Angela Hanlin*

When we look deeper at our data at the individual student level, we can make a difference in the lives of every single learner. We have to make the best use of the data we are collecting. How do we do that? Results are based on the actual conversations that we have in data team meetings. Yes, we review the data. We determine who is making progress and who is not making progress. The next important step is determining what we are going to do in response to the data. What do we do when the data tells us that particular students are struggling? How will our classroom instruction change in response to the data? What interventions will we put into place?

### Use Data to Drive Change

At Matthews Elementary, the more discussions we had based on data, the better we got at answering those questions. As we became more adept at the literacy initiative, we noticed a fairly routine pattern to the order in which students became better readers. When we started the initiative, the majority of our students needed interventions in the area of decoding. A deficit of phonological awareness was evident for the majority of our struggling readers. As we intervened with decoding, no matter what the grade level, we noticed that students began to progress quite quickly. Having an intensive intervention in phonological processing became critical. In our data meetings, we could see from our dot cards that the intervention was working. For some students, it was having instructional gaps in their learning over the years. These students were able to quickly get to grade level in the accuracy subskill of reading. For others, even though they were making good, regular progress, it took them longer to get to grade-level accuracy, which meant a longer time was spent in the intervention for decoding.

We also noticed that once students were at grade-level accuracy, we could focus our efforts on fluency. It wasn't as though these students hadn't been working on fluency in their intervention; they indeed had. They would read appropriate decodables (students loved the decodables for older readers) or practice reading in authentic text that was right at or just slightly above their grade levels. They practiced fluency daily for at least twenty minutes, guided by the interventionist. We had dyad reading groups with a novel that had been chosen for the just right Lexile level. We did repeated readings of the core story from our core reading program, and students read to a partner. Inevitably, reading would soon be at grade level. At each data meeting, we could see by the dot cards that fluency rates were indeed getting better.

The majority of weaknesses in our younger students began with letter naming and letter-sound fluency. Students were not able to name the letter or sound in a reasonable amount of time. We had some students who only knew a few letters when they started school in kindergarten, so we began our interventions quickly. By reviewing data, we learned what letters students knew and did not know, and we developed an instructional plan for the classroom teacher and interventionist. We included a paraprofessional during small-group time to practice letters and sounds at another teaching table in the classroom. Some students needed additional pullout interventions because they needed a third dose of interventions. Some just needed more repetitions to master the skill required.

Results happened because of our conversations around the data and implementation of effective interventions in a timely manner. We trained staff members on intervention strategies that were effective. We came up with a master source of resources that teachers could use as additional instructional strategies during small-group time. We housed all these resources in the data room. This enabled teachers to gather in that room, around their data, especially the dot cards, and have a discussion with their fellow classroom and intervention teachers about what interventions should be used. Teachers would spend quality time each week reviewing data and creating an instructional plan based on their students' data. They would ask their fellow teachers what worked in their classrooms. They would ask, "What did you do to get those results?" These discussions led to a collective belief that we were making a difference. Teachers first developed self-efficacy when they changed their instruction based on data, and that change led to increased gains from the students. Teachers were able to see the connection between what they implemented and the response it had on student learning. As we grew more knowledgeable and made more progress as a team, teachers developed collective efficacy because they knew that, together, we were making a difference. They also knew that we would not stop until student learning increased.

Our designation rate for special education went from over 25 percent to 12 percent. When students were recognized and identified as being special education, they were not labeled. In other words, all interventionists—including special education teachers—were simply that, interventionists. Students received what they needed on their IEP, but students were not called "special education students."

There were data meetings where we could not quite determine exactly where a student was struggling and what intervention was needed. At those times, we administered a diagnostic assessment to drill down and determine exactly where students had skill gaps. We met to review the results of the diagnostic assessment and used that data to create an intervention plan. There were times that we had to reach out and get the help of an expert. I often called both Pati Montgomery and Jan Hasbrouck. One fact remained—we never left a data meeting without a plan for the upcoming instruction.

## Plan Instruction in Response to Data

As students developed into better readers, there were still some students struggling in the area of vocabulary. Then, we created intervention plans for our students who needed Tier 2 intervention. A lot of that work was done at the small-group table with the classroom teacher. We also knew, and our evidence supported it, that students struggling with vocabulary were also certainly struggling with various areas of comprehension, but it was difficult to pinpoint the exact area of need. At the data meetings, we asked ourselves, Was it just vocabulary that was interfering with comprehension? Teachers noted that many of these students also struggled with making inferences, and many seemed to lack the background knowledge necessary to have a good understanding of the story or passage that they were reading. We devised a plan.

Since deficits in comprehension can be terribly hard to tease out, we came up with a strategy to do a bit of front-loading of the story and then continue on our intervention in small-group instruction as the week went on and the students were reading the core stories in their program. Typically, on the day prior to the students reading their anchor text in their reading block, the students who were struggling in comprehension met at the teacher-led table, and the teacher directly taught the vocabulary words the students would encounter in the story. She intentionally tied the vocabulary words to words she knew they had previously learned or knew themselves. She always made sure to use a picture when providing students with direct instruction. This helped the students visualize the words as they came to them.

On the day the whole class had the "first read" of the story, the teacher built the background knowledge in small-group intervention. She found out what they knew about the topic that the story was based on—ensuring that there were no misperceptions about what they knew. To extend their background knowledge, she often showed a five-minute video that helped the students build background knowledge even more. Though at the time, virtual glasses were not available, I now think how much better it would be for each student to be able to experience and grow their background knowledge with the technology now available through virtual glasses. Can you imagine how much more exciting a story about Paris would be for students who had never stepped out of their hometowns, to put on a pair of glasses and visit the Louvre or see the inside of Notre Dame? The story would come alive!

On the third day of comprehension intervention, the teacher focused the time on providing students strategies to help with their inferencing skills. She taught students how to analyze the text to find clues for an inference, or she gave students a fact about the text and asked them to prove if it was right or wrong. This made the students analyze the text further and begin to find their own clues. By the fourth day of intervention on comprehension, the teacher and the students quickly summarized what they had read the previous days, ensuring that the students used the vocabulary words in her discussion. On this day, the teacher had preselected certain paragraphs she thought were important to the understanding or comprehending of the text. She asked the students to read these passages again and summarize what made them critical to the meaning of the story.

Despite the teacher's best efforts, there were days when the students still weren't sure what was critical about certain passages. When this occurred, the teacher got out sticky notes for all the students, and they put phrases on the sticky notes as they reread critical paragraphs. Once numerous paragraphs had been summarized, she had the students summarize the passage by putting together all of the sticky notes. This process became a routine, and soon the students were able to use this strategy themselves when they were reading the story during universal instruction. The teacher knew that repairing comprehension was not an easy fix and would probably be the reading component that took the most time to correct. The teacher also knew that before they could remediate comprehension, a great deal of work had to be done to correct the lower subskills of reading.

## Discuss Data With Urgency

A typical data discussion went something like this. We would review our latest data and share the celebrations we had. Next, we identified which students were not making progress and why. We compared their data to the end of year goal to determine how far they were below grade level. We reviewed other data to drill down and determine the exact point where a student needed intervention to begin. Then, we developed a plan for classroom instruction, intervention instruction, and special education instruction if it was applicable. We determined the length of time for each intervention and put it into place. Then, we met weekly to determine the student's response to intervention.

We were unsure and unsteady in the beginning. We relied on the expertise of specific staff members and learned from one another. We searched for resources that were proven effective for different literacy skills. We made those resources readily available to all staff members. We established an area where teachers could come together to brainstorm and create intervention ideas and discuss whether students were making progress. No matter what the data looked like, we owned it and focused on the plan that we would implement. We encouraged one another, took advice from others, and did everything with a sense of urgency. We firmly believed that our students could reach proficiency and read at grade level. They just were not there yet. By relying on the data and having rich discussions around instruction and interventions, we were able to accomplish literacy for all our students.

### *It's Possible* When Leaders Believe That:

- Results happen when we discuss data and implement effective interventions with urgency.
- Staff members should be trained on intervention strategies that are effective.

- Data help teachers plan differentiated instruction.
- We should never leave a data meeting without a plan for the upcoming instruction.
- All students can learn and make progress.
- We must accept our data. We can reach our goals. We simply aren't there yet.

Many books have been written regarding instructional strategies that align with the various components required in a structured literacy approach. Students struggling to acquire reading skills need to have a careful analysis of their strengths and weaknesses. We have outlined the system that should be used to analyze how each student is progressing. But what do we do when the data tells us particular students are struggling? It is this next step that is so critical—knowing what instructional strategies to use during interventions to ensure students reach grade-level proficiency.

You will not find an exhaustive list of strategies here—rather, we will outline the big ideas of the critical reading skills in each grade level, what the research says regarding instruction, and what we have found works best to facilitate effective interventions or differentiation in specific areas. They are not meant to be suggestive instructional strategies but rather ideas for school leaders to have a keen idea of what should be going on in classrooms and during interventions. Finally, we include a list of resources that can be used to find specific instructional strategies for each of these reading skills.

We suggest creating a compendium of quality resources and storing them in a common area—typically in the room where data are discussed. We have seen many a grade-level team begin to pore over these resources together. When this occurs, a belief that *it's possible* begins to develop much more quickly. Collaborative conversations begin to take place regarding what teachers can do next to increase literacy outcomes, and a feeling of building a proactive community—and a sense of urgency—develops.

# An Understanding of the Importance of the Subskills of Reading

Remember, all students should receive quality universal instruction, and lessons should be designed with a logical instructional hierarchy where one skill feeds into the next. The components we highlight here should be a part of the whole-group lessons for that grade level. However, some students will need more repetitions, as discussed, to achieve mastery. The intent here is that the instructional strategies outlined should be delivered in a small-group setting. Why do we say these instructional strategies are best delivered during small-group instruction?

Small-group instruction is where differentiation occurs. Students reading below grade level will need more repetitions, or a chance to fill in the gaps, where and when poor instruction or learning has occurred. When that is the case, students will need more practice with these skills in small-group instruction. For those students still behind, another dose—a third dose—may be required. Since some students may need three doses of the same prescription, to keep students engaged, more variances of how to teach that skill will go a long way. Further, Tier 2 instruction should be aligned with the core, universal instruction being taught in the general classroom. The implication is that no extra or additional resource should need to be used for Tier 2 instruction. Instead, differentiation of the skill delivered in a small-group setting should do the trick.

Students in Tier 3—our most struggling readers—should receive additional time beyond the regular classroom for intensive interventions, and they should receive these on a daily basis. Further, though a student who has a Tier 3 designation should not receive Tier 2 instruction that is aligned with the core, they should receive additional, differentiated time in small group to have additional practice in the skills they are receiving in their intensive Tier 3 intervention.

In chapter 4 (page 96), we suggested that interventions for Tier 2 should align with instruction in Tier 1. In this section, we will demonstrate how this bears out. To repeat, students who need Tier 2 intervention should be able to master the content from Tier 1 instruction with more practice and more repetitions. If we add yet another program, students get a little of this and a little of that and never have the opportunity to master any of it.

Philip Gough and William Tunmer's (1986) simple view of reading proposes two skills that comprise one's ability to read words: (1) cipher knowledge and (2) word-specific knowledge. *Cipher knowledge* refers to the ability to use the code of written English to pronounce words. There are several factors associated with the development of decoding (cipher) skills. As discussed, they include phonemic awareness, letter-sound correspondence, and the ability to blend phonemes. *Word-specific knowledge* refers to the knowledge about words in a given language.

Linnea Ehri (2005) outlines four phases of word recognition that we can use to frame our thinking regarding word reading and reading difficulties. We can use these phases as a framework for knowing and understanding what reading skills students should be acquiring and mastering at each grade level.

These four phases of word recognition skills include:

1. **Pre-alphabetic phase:** In this phase, students know little about the alphabetic system. They are memorizing visual representations of words—pretend reading. As an example, they may remember the word *look* by connecting it with two eyeballs in the middle, they may read the word *target* when they see the bullseye-looking, red-and-white sign containing the word Target. This phase is not real word reading but rather "reading" using visual cues. Early foundational reading assessments would indicate students are in this phase when they have no knowledge of letters and phonemes.

2. **Partial alphabetic phase:** In this phase, students begin to learn the names and sounds of letters and may link sounds to their corresponding letters. Typically,

students make connections between the first and last sounds prior to connecting the medial sounds and letters—vowels.

3. **Full alphabetic phase:** Students in this phase have mastered most letter-sound correspondence, can segment words, are gaining more fluent reading skills, and are mastering spelling of words. At this phase, readers are able to use decoding skills when they encounter unknown words.

- **Consolidated phase:** As students acquire a larger sight word memory in the full alphabetic phase, and as they become more familiar with letter patterns in words, whole words and word parts are stored as units, and they become quick and efficient readers.

Many of the foundational reading assessments contain subtests that aren't as relevant to these phases or the acquisition of reading skills. With that in mind, we use only the subtests that measure these critical skills as we analyze where to intervene.

As we discussed in the previous chapter, every part of successful reading acquisition is reliant on previous subskills. As previously stated, these subskills are not lockstep, meaning we do not have to master all of one skill before progressing to the next; rather, they are stepping stones, and there is a hierarchy to the skills, although you should not assume that to master one, you must have mastered the previous. Any knowledge of a new subskill is reliant on how well learned the previous subskill has been, though what level of mastery at each level is still not determined by research. Students who struggle with a lower skill will certainly struggle with mastering a skill at a higher level (Hoover & Tunmer, 2020). The subskills do overlap in their acquisition. A student who knows only five consonants and a vowel and their associated sounds might very well be able to put those corresponding letters and sounds together to decode a word. As students become more adept in the area of phonemic awareness and are provided explicit instruction with phoneme-grapheme associations, they become more efficient readers.

# School Spotlight

## Fox Elementary, Macomb, Michigan

For many years, we have been analyzing our data three times per year by gathering around a table, staring at our SMART Board, and looking at benchmark data from a local assessment. Each student would have their percentile listed next to their name, and we would also have some data from a few various interventions we did. Truth be told, we were equipped with more intervention programs than we knew what to do with. In fact, as hard as we worked, we really didn't know what to do with them or with whom to effectively use them. We moved students the best we knew how with the very best of intentions, hoping for a different result and an improved outcome. We were working hard, really hard, but we weren't focusing on the right things. We had benchmark data, a temperature check, but nothing more, and nothing told us what specific skills the student was truly missing. We also progress monitored, but it was not all hands on deck. Some did it more than others, and we had no consistency.

We did the best we could with what we knew at the time. But as the old saying goes, when you know better, you do better. At Fox Elementary, what we have learned over the past couple years has allowed me to totally transform the way I lead as a principal so I can work with our team in our efforts to improve literacy for all students. We now look at the data to ensure that our revised practices and strategies in core instruction, small group, or MTSS interventions are working for each student.

Through a new system of data analysis, our team can accurately determine how students are growing. Utilizing our local assessment as both a benchmarking and progress monitoring tool, we now have all grade-level teachers and paraeducators progress monitoring students in windows, based on the needs of the student. For example, our students in most need of support, Tier 3, are progress monitored on a weekly basis. Students who need Tier 2 intervention are progress monitored bi-weekly, and our students at or above grade level are also progress monitored but on a less frequent basis, such as every four weeks. All progress monitoring data for all grade levels go into a progress monitoring tracker that all teachers and support staff utilize to both input and analyze their student's progress. In addition to progress monitoring data, benchmark data from fall, winter, and spring is also charted in the same document.

Additionally, we also utilize a data tracker for two of our main interventions, SIPPS and Sound Partners. These data trackers give us crucial information directly relating to our interventions that various students are in. We are able to track what level students are at in each program, who their intervention provider is, and who their classroom teacher is. All data are utilized throughout the year on a frequent basis.

Rather than meeting three times per year, our school truly is a professional learning community now. Our teachers, administrator, and reading interventionist have regularly scheduled meetings with our collaborative teams so that we can review progress monitoring data to make in the moment data-based decisions on our students and our instructional practices. During our collaborative teams, our teachers are able to review which students are improving and which students are not. We now look for patterns, ask tough questions, and hold each other accountable for all students. No longer is it "my students from my class," but "our students from our grade level" and "students from our school."

All grade levels have an MTSS intervention template created by our reading interventionist in which all students are grouped strategically in interventions that match the subskills they show deficits in. The same type of grouping by subskills is also utilized for small-group instruction. Knowing exactly what subskills our students are struggling in and improving in has been an absolute game changer. It has allowed us to know what we should be doing instead of what we think we should be doing. Once students demonstrate the necessary skills and show consistent improvement or lack thereof, we are able to move students in and out of intervention and truly direct our small-group and core instruction in ways that will impact our students.

To say that our school has changed our systems, structures, and practices surrounding literacy would be an understatement. The work we have done has been challenging but truly transformational. Now that we know better, we are able to do better for the good of our students. *All* our students.

*Frank Bellemo, Principal*
*AngeLee Conrad, Instructional Coach*

# Instruction in Kindergarten

As stated, instruction in kindergarten should not be delayed until students have a mastery of phonological sensitivity. In fact, a realistic goal for students in kindergarten is that they master phoneme awareness in simple syllables along with connecting the phoneme to the represented letter names. The practice of letter writing along with the practice of grapheme-phoneme connections acts to solidify the letter-sound correspondence (International Dyslexia Association, 2022).

Many students will enter kindergarten in the partial-alphabetic phase of reading and some, regrettably, will enter at the pre-alphabetic phase. The importance of differentiation for these students is clear. Students not knowing any letters and sounds will need much more time with a teacher intervening than those entering at the partial alphabetic phase. In most foundational reading assessments, these components align to a variation of the subtests in table 6.1.

**TABLE 6.1:** Kindergarten Goals and Subtests

| Goals for Mastery |
| --- |
| Letter names |
| Basic phonemic awareness (including segmenting and blending) in simple syllables |
| **Foundational Reading Assessment Subtests** |
| Letter naming |
| First sound fluency |
| Phoneme segmentation fluency |
| Letter sounds |
| Nonsense word fluency (an indication of phonemic blending and decoding) |

Letter naming on some foundational reading assessments is used as a proxy for rapid, automatic naming and therefore may not have a letter naming progress monitoring probe. We highly recommend that letter naming is progress monitored with the same level of frequency of other progress monitoring that we have outlined in this chapter. If your reading assessment does not have a progress monitoring probe for the assessment, a helpful resource is *Next STEPS in Literacy Instruction, Second Edition* by Susan M. Smartt and Deborah R. Glaser (2024), which contains a letter naming probe as well as suggestions for teaching letter naming fluency.

## The Research on Teaching Letter Names and Sounds

Correlational studies suggest that alphabetic knowledge and phonological awareness are reciprocally related, and combining alphabet and phonological awareness instruction may be advantageous for phonemic awareness and reading outcomes (Cabell et al., 2023). We strongly support this and have seen tremendous success for students when letter names and sounds are learned simultaneously. We do add the following caution: various graphemes in English may be represented by more than one phoneme (for example, *c* can be pronounced as a /k/ as in *cap* or /s/ as in *cider*). When this is the case, we recommend only teaching one phoneme at a time. We typically begin with the hard /c/ as in *cat* and the hard /g/ as in *goat*.

If readers have fast, accurate rate recognition of individual letters, then they can identify and learn familiar letter sequences (Birsch & Carreker, 2018). A key word is *fast*! Students must have automaticity with naming all letters within the alphabet, both upper and lower case. Letter naming subskills are often only found on foundational reading assessments through the beginning of first grade. Because of this, many teachers stop teaching letter names and assume, like with mathematic facts, that some students just won't learn them. *This couldn't be further from the truth*! Except for students with severe cognitive impairments, all students can learn letter names and sounds (Lyon, 2002a). Some students just need more practice and repetition. Virginia W. Berninger (2000) found that students identified with dyslexia needed more than twenty times the practice than students without dyslexia to learn letter sequencing (Birsh & Carreker, 2018).

In quality comprehensive core reading programs, there is a logical scope and sequence to how letters and sounds are taught. Tier 2 or small-group instruction should be aligned to what students are receiving in their quality Tier 1 or universal instruction. Students who need Tier 3 intervention will likely require more repetitions or fewer items (letters and sounds) to learn at one time to master the letters and sounds. (See chapter 2, page 27, for a refresher on the frequency of repetitions for students to master.)

## How to Facilitate Interventions and Differentiation on Letter Naming and Sounds

We have found that students enter kindergarten with a wide range of ability in knowing letter names and sounds, yet this is a critical skill for reading acquisition. In order to move students on to word recognition, a great deal of differentiation in this subskill is required.

- Begin with what students know. This can be discovered by looking at the results of the benchmark assessment. If students have done poorly on this assessment or if the indication is that a student knows very few letters and sounds, we suggest beginning with the letters in the students' names.

- Teach five to seven letters at a time.

- Some students can learn both uppercase and lowercase letters at the same time. For struggling students, begin with teaching uppercase letters.

- Teaching the formation of letters should be a part of instruction in learning letter names and sounds. Have students repeat the letter name and the sound it makes as they are writing the letter name.

- When having students learn letter formation, make sure students have appropriate materials. This includes whiteboards or paper with appropriately sized lines. This also includes dry erase markers that are working as well as appropriately sharpened pencils.

- Small-group instruction or interventions in learning letter names and sounds should last approximately fifteen to twenty minutes. We recommend the layout shown in table 6.2 for this time slot.

**TABLE 6.2:** Letter Names and Sounds Small-Group Instruction

| Letter Names and Sounds | |
|---|---|
| **Duration (15–20 minutes total)** | **Small-Group Activity** |
| 3–4 minutes | Designated letter naming and sounds via flash cards |
| 3–5 minutes | Letter formation direct instruction and practice |
| 9–11 minutes | Various hands-on activities with alphabet strips, arcs, plastic letters or multidimensional letters, or letter cards |

## The Research on Teaching Phonemic Awareness

It seems the terms phonemic awareness and phonological awareness can create much confusion to educators regarding literacy instruction. Each are important and we will differentiate here.

*Phonological awareness* is a broad term that refers to the conscious awareness and ability to discern sound components in spoken words. These include spoken words, syllables, rhymes, and individual phonemes—sounds that letters make.

*Phonological sensitivity* refers to an awareness of and ability to manipulate the larger units of sound in words (rimes and syllables) and the term phoneme awareness refers to the segmenting and blending of the individual phonemes in words (Smartt & Glaser, 2024).

The National Reading Panel identified the importance of the teaching of phonemic awareness in 2000 and indicated it as one of the five critical components of reading instruction. It was assumed for many years by practitioners, and often taught in professional development courses, that phonological awareness should be taught in a hierarchy and each component mastered—beginning with the ability to identify words in a sentence, syllables in a word, or the beginning sound (onset) and remaining sound (rime)—prior to the instruction of phonemic awareness.

Multiple research studies have indicated that delaying the instruction of phoneme awareness to ensure the mastery of phonological sensitivity does not enhance a student's ability to decode but rather delays the acquisition of reading development.

Lucy H. Paulson (2018) writes, "In kindergarten, students learn to segment phonemes in simple CVC words" (p. 219). Regarding our data analysis, virtually every quality foundational reading assessment contains a subtest in phonemic segmentation fluency. This subtest demonstrates a student's ability to segment the phonemes into words. Phoneme segmentation assessments begin in kindergarten and generally continue through first grade. Students will not benefit from phonics instruction until they have developed some basic level of phonemic awareness skills (Birsh & Carreker, 2018).

Blending is the activity of joining individual sounds, syllables, or words into meaningful units. For example, saying /p/ /ǎ/ /t/ as *pat*, or saying "cow" and "boy" as *cowboy*. Phonemic blending is an easier skill than segmenting, but both are crucial in the development of word recognition. The most common subtest of a student's ability to blend words is nonsense word fluency. Nonsense word fluency is typically assessed in kindergarten and first grade. However, struggling students beyond first grade who have not readily acquired the subskill of blending and are receiving intervention directed toward mastering blending skills should still be progress monitored in their ability to blend pseudowords through the assessment of nonsense word fluency.

## How to Facilitate Interventions and Differentiation on Phonemic Awareness

The following are suggestions related to the big ideas for differentiation in small-group instruction for students who have not yet mastered the critical skill of phonemic awareness.

- Students do not need to have mastery of all phonemic awareness skills before they have phonics instruction. Research has indicated that teaching phonemic awareness in combination with phonics has proven to be the most effective instructional approach in helping students learn to read (Kilpatrick, 2015).

- Phonemic awareness itself has a range of difficulty. Segmenting each sound in CVC words is much easier than deleting, substituting, or manipulating phonemes. Be sure that the level of difficulty is appropriate for the group of students at hand.

- Phonemic blending is equally important as segmenting, but in general, it is an easier skill in phonemic awareness. When having students segment words, it is critically important that students blend the word back together to activate the possible meaning of the word.

- Explicitly teaching phonemic awareness requires modeling of the task (I do), followed by guided practice (we do), and finally independent practice with a teacher observing (you do).

- When using Elkonin boxes instead of including manipulatives, such as blocks and discs, use actual letters to enhance grapheme-phoneme connections.

- Incorporate the teaching of handwriting into the teaching of phoneme-grapheme mapping.

- Begin teaching phoneme awareness with simple syllables first, such as bat, top, nip.

- When introducing a decodable text in early phonemic awareness, ensure students already have an awareness of the sound and letter correspondence contained within the decodable text being used.

When we described our data analysis system in the previous chapter (page 111), we described a system that ensured that every student who was struggling in some aspect of reading would be monitored, and our data discussions should be based on how each student was doing. We have highlighted in this section what a student's dot card and spreadsheet might look like if they are struggling in letter naming and receiving interventions. Figure 6.1 features a dot card for a kindergarten student, and figure 6.2 (page 158) shows the spreadsheet method for this same student and several of her peers. The critical factors of reading skills are listed in each tab.

In the spreadsheet in figure 6.2, I am alerted to two students, Penny Picker and Janell Jumper. Penny Picker's name is highlighted in red ●, which indicates she is in the well below instructional level. Her subskill score in letter naming fluency was a 12, which is well below expectations for kindergarten. It is also shaded in red. Her teacher, Ms. Doingmybest, began progress monitoring her and giving her intensive interventions in letter naming and other subskills with which she may also need help. From this kindergarten spreadsheet, you can see that each subskill we have discussed here is part of the data.

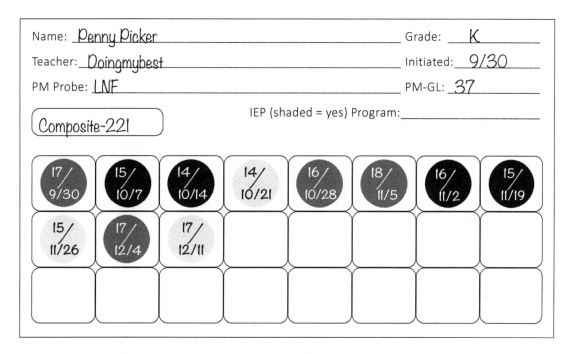

**FIGURE 6.1:** Kindergarten student example dot card.

**Goals: Fall: 25; Winter: 37; Spring: 42**

| Name | Teacher | Fall Window — Fall Benchmark Composite | Subskill Letter Naming Fluency — BOY LNF Score | Date: 9/30 LNF | Date: 10/7 LNF | Date: 10/14 LNF | Date: 10/21 LNF | Date: 10/28 LNF | Date: 11/5 LNF | Date: 11/12 LNF | Date: 11/19 LNF | Date: 11/26 LNF | Date: 12/4 LNF | Date: 12/11 LNF |
|---|---|---|---|---|---|---|---|---|---|---|---|---|---|---|
| Marsha Witness | Alltoogood | 329 | 18 | 20 | 26 | 28 | 32 | 32 | 36 | 37 | 40 | | | |
| Blanche Smirk | Alltoogood | 308 | 23 | 26 | 28 | 28 | 30 | 33 | 35 | 37 | 41 | | | |
| Austin Noisey | Gettingbetter | 289 | 17 | 22 | 22 | 25 | 28 | 28 | 30 | 33 | 36 | 37 | 38 | |
| Brandon Scuffy | Doingmybest | 280 | 22 | 22 | 22 | 22 | 24 | 30 | 33 | 36 | 37 | 38 | | |
| Aleta Moves | Gettingbetter | 298 | 24 | 26 | 24 | 26 | 26 | 32 | 36 | 37 | 39 | | | |
| Penny Picker | Doingmybest | 221 | 12 | 17 | 15 | 14 | 14 | 16 | 18 | 16 | 15 | 15 | 17 | 17 |
| Carrisa Cares | Doingmybest | 212 | 12 | 12 | 14 | 17 | 21 | 24 | 26 | 28 | 32 | 35 | 37 | 38 |
| Mark Mustgo | Gettingbetter | 276 | 16 | 18 | 20 | 23 | 27 | 29 | 32 | 34 | 34 | 36 | 38 | 38 |
| Janell Jumper | Alltoogood | 203 | 10 | 12 | 10 | 12 | 10 | 9 | 9 | 12 | 12 | 11 | 12 | |
| Alan Gored | Gettingbetter | 248 | 13 | 13 | 15 | 18 | 21 | 24 | 28 | 32 | 34 | 36 | 38 | 39 |
| Jill Jiggles | Alltoogood | 207 | 14 | 17 | 19 | 22 | 24 | 27 | 30 | 32 | 38 | 38 | | |

K Grade—Letter Naming Fluency (LNF)

Kindergarten PSF | Kindergarten LNF | Kindergarten NWF (CLS) | Kindergarten NWF (WWR)

Key: PSF = Phoneme Segmentation Fluency, LNF = Letter Naming Fluency, NWF = Nonsense Word Fluency, CLS = Correct Letter Sounds, WWR = Whole Words Read

**FIGURE 6.2:** Kindergarten data spreadsheet.

Penny's first progress monitor was administered on September 30. On this progress monitor, she received a score of 17. Since this was an improvement, her dot card or dot cell is highlighted in green ●. On her next two progress monitoring probes in letter naming frequency her score was lower and is indicated by the red cells or dots ●. On her October 21 probe, she made no growth. On the next two probes on October 28 and November 15, she made some progress. However, when looking at all her cells or dots, she is overall making little progress. In fact, after eleven probes, she has made no growth since the first progress monitoring probe. At the data team meetings, how to change her intervention in letter naming should certainly be discussed.

Janell Jumper is also struggling with letter naming fluency. She initially improved slightly but then regressed and remained stagnant, and after six weeks of intervention in letter naming, she is not making the adequate progress needed. A change in Janell's intervention should also be a part of the conversation at the data meeting.

Again, as we look at the spreadsheet or the colors on the dot cards, we should focus our attention on students who are not making progress. Using this method allows us to have conversations focused on the students who need the most help. Also note the following.

- The columns for each of the scores in the beginning of the year, middle of the year, and end of the year can be hidden for easier use.

- Students are not aiming to meet the benchmark from the beginning of the year but instead must meet the benchmark for the middle of the year.

- The spreadsheet can also be sorted by teacher name so that a principal is able to see how students in particular classrooms might be growing.

- Intervention teachers can also be added to the spreadsheet, and progress in particular intervention teacher's rooms can also be examined.

# Instruction in Late Kindergarten and First Grade

In late kindergarten and through first grade, students typically move from the partial-alphabetic phase of learning letters and sounds to their corresponding sound to the full alphabetic phase of reading. In this phase and by the end of first grade, we can expect students to have mastered most letter-sound correspondence; they can segment words, are gaining more fluent reading skills, and are mastering spelling of words. Decoding is the process of sounding out unfamiliar words (or nonsense words) via a letter-sound conversion process combined with phonemic blending. Scarborough's reading rope is a quick reminder of the importance of reading decoding since it comprises half of the rope! The inability to decode directly relates to the inability to comprehend (Gough & Tunmer, 1986). It is therefore critical that students who are below grade level in decoding skills have adequate interventions to bring them up to grade level.

Fluent word recognition should be the goal for the end of first grade. Decoding requires not only the phonemic awareness subskills previously discussed, but it also includes the ability to isolate and then blend the sounds of a word back together to activate the word read.

Foundational reading assessments typically measure decoding through a variety of subtests. These tests typically appear with the names in table 6.3.

**TABLE 6.3:** Late Kindergarten and First Grade Goals and Subtests

| Goals for Mastery |
| --- |
| Awareness of phonemes in simple syllables (end of kindergarten) |
| Awareness of phonemes in complex syllables (end of first grade) |
| Awareness of phonics and decoding (end of first grade) |
| **Foundational Reading Assessment Subtests** |
| Nonsense word fluency |
| Correct letter sounds and whole words read, or words read correctly and completely (WRC) |

Intervention in both kindergarten and the first semester of first grade should be based on grade-level data in these subskills. Referring back to our chapter on intervention, kindergarten and first-grade students have not had a significant amount of instruction. All instruction, including interventions, should therefore be based on the core components taught in the general curriculum. When quality universal instruction is in place, a canned intervention program should not need to be provided until the second semester of first grade. This does not mean interventions are not being provided; it simply means that interventions are not a separate program but instead are directly aligned to the data of the needs of the students. Interventions should be further repetition of the content the student was previously taught and the data shows they have not yet mastered.

## The Research on Teaching Phonics

Students are in the full-alphabetic phase when they know the major grapheme-phoneme connections (Ehri, 2005). The more efficient they become in their letter-sound correspondence, the more readily they store words that they can recognize by sight.

Systematic and explicit phonics instruction is more effective than nonsystematic instruction (Kilpatrick et al., 2019). Nonsystematic instruction can be described as "as the need arises," which is neither a complete scope and sequence nor teaching to mastery. Regarding intervention, students who are struggling in phonic decoding must have a clear and systematic scope and sequence where one skill is a subset of the next skill. In interventions, that includes establishing instructional routines within the framework of instruction.

For students to master decoding, they must know how the sounds of the letters in the words are pronounced, and they must blend those sounds together and pronounce the word that is blended together. Simply put, they must have grapheme-phoneme (letter-sound)

correspondence of every letter in the word and the ability to blend the sounds together to form the word. Grapheme-phoneme connections provide glue for sight word storage (Kilpatrick et al., 2019).

## How to Facilitate Interventions and Differentiation of Phonics

The following suggestions are the big ideas for differentiation in small-group instruction for students who have not yet mastered phonic decoding.

- Systematic and explicit phonics instruction is particularly beneficial for students who are having difficulty learning to read and who are at risk for developing future reading difficulties (Kilpatrick et al., 2019).

- A quality scope and sequence should be used in the teaching of phonics.

- Phoneme-grapheme mapping is a critical prerequisite skill to being able to blend words.

  ⇨ Have students use Elkonin boxes and letter tiles to map the grapheme to the phoneme represented.

- Students must learn to blend the sounds of letters together to create words; therefore, the teaching of blending is critical.

  ⇨ To teach blending as part of an intervention routine, use flip books or blending boards.

  ⇨ A downloadable blending board can be found on Reading Rockets (www.readingrockets.org/resources/literacy-apps /blending-board). These are highly effective when used in small-group settings.

  ⇨ The words practiced during phonics instruction should align with the decodable text being used in the lesson.

The most effective means we have found for ensuring students have efficient word recognition is using decodable text. Decodable texts are books that are based on the phonetic elements being taught. Usually, books progress from texts with CVC words to books with vowel pairs, digraphs, trigraphs, and so on. The repeated reading of decodable text further secures those concepts in memory. A second benefit of decodable text is that it develops independence in dealing with new words. Students learn that they can sound out most unfamiliar words while reading (Birsh & Carreker, 2018).

We recognize a failure in the structured literacy format of reading is teaching skills without students in connected text, even though research bears out the necessity of teaching the skills and then using a practical application of reading in either connected text to the skills just taught or as students

**List of Quality Decodable Readers**

Our organization has vetted a list of over three dozen decodable readers (visit https://schoolscubed.com/download/approved-list-of-decodable-readers-2023). We find the decodables here align closely with the suggested scope and sequence as outlined in figure 4.2 (page 100).

progress in authentic text. We use the term *connected text* to mean students reading in text that aligns with the skills they are being taught. In lower grades, this could be decodable text, but in upper grades, this could be typical grade-level text or even novels. As an example, students who are being taught CVC words with short /a/ should, within the lesson, read a book with the same phonetic element of short /a/. In *Handbook on the Science of Early Literacy*, Barbara R. Foorman (2023) notes that the What Works Clearinghouse practice guide provides four recommendations for teaching reading in the primary grades. One of these recommendations is to ensure that each student reads connected text every day to support reading accuracy, fluency, and comprehension (Foorman, 2023). As a beginning reader, explicit and systematic instruction should include the practice of the sound-spelling pattern being taught in not only word lists but also in connected text. For most students, particularly those struggling with the application of decoding, nothing fits this bill as well as decodable text.

Small-group instruction with a duration of fifteen to twenty-five minutes for students struggling (Tier 2 learners) with nonsense word fluency in first grade may go something like shown in table 6.4.

**TABLE 6.4:** Nonsense Word Fluency Small Group Instruction

| Nonsense Word Fluency (Tier 2 Intervention in First Grade) | |
| --- | --- |
| **Duration (15–25 minutes total)** | **Small-Group Activity** |
| 3–5 minutes | Direct instruction/review in the phonetic element being taught in the whole-group lesson |
| 3–6 minutes | Reading word lists containing the phonetic element or use of blending board |
| 4–6 minutes | Direct instruction in reading a decodable text aligned with the phonetic element |
| 5–8 minutes | Repeated reading of the decodable text to establish fluency |

For students with more intensive needs, Tier 3 or small-group instruction in the same duration of time might look something like table 6.5.

Figure 6.3 is is a decodable text reading routine that we have found to be highly effective.

**TABLE 6.5:** Nonsense Word Fluency Tier 3 Small-Group Instruction

| Nonsense Word Fluency (Tier 3 Intervention in First Grade) | |
|---|---|
| **Duration (15–25 minutes total)** | **Small-Group Activity** |
| 5–7 minutes | Direct instruction/review in the phonetic element that data indicates the student needs (Note: at Tier 3, instruction may not be aligned with whole-group instruction) |
| 3–5 minutes | Direct instruction and practice in phoneme-graphene mapping in the same phonetic element taught above |
| 3–5 minutes | Writing words that contain the same phonetic element being taught |
| 4–8 minutes | Reading a short passage and one or two sentences of the phonetic element being taught using the same decodable routine |

| Duration (14 minutes total) | Reading Routine |
|---|---|
| **Decodable Words:** (2 minutes) | Practice reading decodable words students will see in the text using a focus board |
| **High-Frequency Words:** (2 minutes) | High-frequency words from the text written on a focus board<br>Three words students know and two new words to learn |
| **Read the Text:** (10 minutes) | **First read:** Teacher will model fluent reading of the text as students follow along with their pointer finger.<br>**Second read:** Teacher and students read the text together.<br>**Third read:** Students chorally read without teacher support.<br>**Fourth read:** Students partner to read the story.<br>**Fifth read:** Students independently read the story while the teacher is listening and supporting as needed. |

**FIGURE 6.3:** Decodable reading routine.

*Visit **go.SolutionTree.com/literacy** for a free reproducible version of this figure.*

Figure 6.4 (page 164) is a snapshot of our data analysis spreadsheet for first grade. Notice the tabs along the bottom align with the instructional strategies previously highlighted. Data analysis and instructional strategies for oral reading fluency will be discussed in the next section.

| PSF Phoneme Segmentation Fluency Goal 40 (BOY) | | | | | | | | | |
|---|---|---|---|---|---|---|---|---|---|
| Student | BOY | BOY-PSF | 9/30 | 10/7 | 10/14 | 10/21 | 10/28 | 11/4 | 11/11 |
| Colonel Mustard | 103 | 33 | 35 | | 38 | | 40 | | 40 |
| James Michael | 112 | 26 | 26 | | 30 | | 33 | | 35 |
| Melanie Myers | 105 | 32 | 34 | | 34 | | 36 | | 39 |
| Abraham Burnett | 99 | 38 | 38 | | 40 | | 40 | | |
| Ivan Viking | 78 | 23 | 26 | 28 | 30 | 33 | 35 | 36 | 39 |
| Amber Goodman | 63 | 21 | 23 | 25 | 25 | 28 | 31 | 30 | 35 |
| Francisco Frank | 92 | 22 | 22 | 27 | 29 | 31 | 26 | 33 | 33 |
| Jason Witness | 88 | 19 | 19 | 20 | 19 | 18 | 19 | 18 | 20 |
| Frannie Shadow | 66 | 22 | 27 | 30 | 33 | 35 | 38 | 39 | 40 |
| Erin York | 52 | 25 | 27 | 27 | 30 | 32 | 32 | 36 | 38 |
| Wills Dean | 97 | 16 | 17 | 17 | 20 | 21 | 23 | 23 | 25 |

| First Grade LNF | First Grade PSF | First Grade NWF (CLS) | First Grade NWF (WWR) |
|---|---|---|---|
| First Grade ORF (WC) | First Grade ORF Accuracy | | |

Key: LNF = Letter Naming Fluency, PSF = Phoneme Segmentation Fluency, NWF = Nonsense Word Fluency, CLS = Correct Letter Sounds, WWR = Whole Words Read, ORF = Oral Reading Fluency, WC = Words Correct

**FIGURE 6.4:** Important subskills in reading assessment for first grade.

# Instruction in Second Grade

As students have multiple encounters and practice with sound-symbol correspondence and, in turn, the reading of real words, they begin to store the spelling patterns found within those words. This process is called *orthographic mapping*. With repeated opportunities for practicing, the reader builds an orthographic memory so that, eventually, the student instantly recognizes the word without having to sound it out. Instant word recognition is achieved by these repeated encounters with words and by overlearning the orthographic and phonological patterns of the language (Birsh & Carreker, 2018). Solid orthographic mapping ensures a reader knows the regular and irregular patterns found within words. This rapid identification of spelling patterns ensures word recognition leads to being a fluent reader.

To establish an orthographic memory for words, students must first have phonemic awareness, letter-sound correspondence, and the ability to apply a solid decoding or phonics strategy. Further, knowing the meaning of words acts as one more connection for immediate activation of the sight word. This is precisely the reason that up to this point, our interventions and data analysis system is so reliant on these three components. Visualizing students in classrooms in third grade and up who encounter words and are using their fingers to tap them out are perfect examples of students who are lacking instant word recognition—although their strategy is on the right track!

Foundational reading assessments that measure orthographic mapping are not blatantly stated. There are a variety of subtests that one could use to substantiate that a student has instant word recognition, such as those in table 6.6.

**TABLE 6.6:** Second-Grade Goals and Subtests

| Goals for Mastery |
| --- |
| Orthographic mapping |
| Reading fluency |
| **Foundational Reading Assessment Subtests** |
| Nonsense word reading (as a prerequisite skill) |
| Whole words read |
| Oral reading fluency |

This is to assume that prior to analyzing nonsense word fluency, whole words read, and oral reading fluency, a student was fairly proficient with phonemic awareness as indicated on a phonemic segmentation assessment.

There are some foundational reading assessments that measure sight words, beginning as early as kindergarten. These are typically words from the Dolch or Fry word lists that comprise the most frequently encountered words. Many of the words found on these lists are simply high-frequency words as determined by either Edward Dolch in 1936 or Edward Fry in 1980. Though a timed assessment on a word list may indicate a student's ability or disability in sight word reading, drawing a true conclusion of a student's ability with their sight word reading would be dependent on also checking to ensure phonemic awareness was intact, as well as the ability to decode on a nonsense word assessment. For this reason, we seldom use a sight word reading test solely as an indicator of solidified orthographic mapping.

## The Research on Teaching for Orthographic Mapping

As students acquire basic sound-symbol correspondences, they build their knowledge of orthographic patterns in the language and begin to generalize this knowledge to new and novel words they come upon. This is known as the self-teaching hypothesis (Share, 1995). This orthographic mapping must also include learning to instantly recognize irregularly spelled words as well. Think of those words that do not have an entire direct letter-sound correspondence—such as *have*, *said*, and so on. In her book *Speech to Print*, Louisa Moats (2020a) points out the following.

- 50 percent of English words are spelled accurately by sound-symbol correspondence rule alone.

- 36 percent more are spelled with only one error.

- 10 percent more are spelled accurately if word meaning, origin, and morphology are considered.

- Fewer than 4 percent are true oddities.

To succinctly state, even most irregular words have properties that are decodable. Ensuring sound-symbol knowledge and directly teaching the component that is irregular, along with frequently practicing and overlearning, such as reading of irregular words, will aid students in becoming proficient readers of all words.

There is scant research on the use of decodable text in early reading development. However, after working with thousands of students, we have found that the logical pattern for developing rapid word recognition is by first practicing the words being directly taught in sound-symbol lessons, or phonic decoding, in books that repeat those same patterns—decodable readers. Once students have become more proficient in the instant word recognition of simple sound-symbol patterns, they can progress to reading connected text with less of a predictable pattern and move on to authentic text such as those found typically in the anchor text of comprehensive core reading programs. Regrettably, many quality core reading programs offer one or two selections of reading decodable text. Yet to overlearn or acquire an adequate memory, many students will need opportunities to read more than what the core program offers, which is why we suggest all classrooms have a sufficient library of decodable text.

## How to Facilitate Interventions and Differentiation in Orthographic Mapping

The following suggestions are the big ideas for differentiation in small-group instruction for students who have not yet mastered fluent word recognition.

- Orthographic mapping will occur if a student has prerequisite skills of phonemic awareness including segmenting and blending, major letter-sound correspondence and the ability to apply a decoding strategy (Bell, 2023).

- Teach to the point of what seems to be overlearning. By repeated encounters with words, particularly in text (first decodable and then moving to authentic), students begin to recognize the patterns found within words.

- Direct instruction in structured analysis will help unitizing portions of words.

- While a student reads, the word's pronunciation, spelling, and meaning all influence one another during the sight word reading process (Bell, 2023).

We have found that, by second grade, students who need Tier 2 intervention and who demonstrate relatively high accuracy rates (96 percent or higher) but have slow reading rates are struggling with the instantaneous ability to recognize words. We translate that as needing more miles on the page. Remembering that Tier 2 instruction should be aligned with Tier 1 instruction, we have found that a valuable teaching strategy is the repeated reading of the core story students are reading in whole-group instruction. This opportunity to repeat the same passage being read in whole group gives students the opportunity to solidify those frequent patterns in the words they are seeing.

If you have a quality core reading program, the core story should align or include the phonetic elements being taught in whole-group instruction. Small-group instruction for students who need Tier 2 intervention in a fifteen- to twenty-minute time frame who have solid decoding and phonemic awareness skills would look something like table 6.7.

**TABLE 6.7:** Securing Orthographic Mapping Small-Group Instruction

| Securing Orthographic Mapping (Students who need Tier 2 intervention with high accuracy but low fluency rates) | |
| --- | --- |
| **Duration (15–20 minutes total)** | **Small-Group Activity** |
| 3–5 minutes | Direct instruction and reviewing the core phonetic element being taught in whole-group instruction |
| 12–15 minutes | Oral rereading of the passage read during whole-group instruction with a focus on fluent reading |

By rereading the passage being taught during whole-group instruction instead of using a supplemental passage reading program, we believe and have seen proof that giving students multiple exposures to the same patterns in words more rapidly solidifies instant word recognition. Words read correctly in practiced passages that are not mapped to permanent memory will not likely be instantly recognized when encountered in an unpracticed passage (Kilpatrick, 2015).

The need for a highly accurate decoding ability cannot be overstated. The more accurately students read, the more efficient and fluent the reading process is, and students are better able to comprehend what they are reading. In the book *Multisensory Teaching of Basic Language Skills,* Judith R. Birsh and Suzanne Carreker (2018) provide clarity on the accuracy rate as it aligns with instruction. It is as follows.

- 97 to 100 percent word accuracy (not more than 3/100 inaccurate) roughly corresponds to an independent level

- 90 to 96 percent word accuracy (4/100–10/100 inaccurate) corresponds to an instructional level

- Below 90 percent accuracy (more than 10/100) corresponds to a frustration level

Students who have accuracy rates below 96 percent should be receiving interventions in a phonological decoding program, such as SIPPS (Systematic Instruction in Phonological Awareness, Phonics, and Sight Words). (See the recommendations for students with phonological decoding issues on page 94 in chapter 4.) This intensive intervention typically happens outside regular classroom instruction. Back in the main classroom, small-group instruction for students who need Tier 3 intervention should align with the intervention focus from their Tier 3 instruction. See table 6.8 (page 168).

**TABLE 6.8:** The Content Alignment of Small-Group Instruction

| If . . . | Then . . . |
|---|---|
| Students are in Tier 2 small groups in the classroom | Small group should be aligned with classroom instruction |
| Students are in Tier 3 intensive intervention | Small group should be aligned with intervention instruction |

Highly effective intervention programs such as SIPPS provide students with connected reading in text, typically via a decodable text. As we have stated earlier, we have found that providing students with added opportunity to read another decodable text with an emphasis on the same phonetic element being taught in their intervention provides students with more practice in recognizing and seeing the same word patterns, thus solidifying their orthographic mapping skills.

Differentiation and intervention in small-group instruction for students who have low accuracy rates or are not proficient on nonsense word fluency subtests should look like table 6.9.

**TABLE 6.9:** Phonics/Decoding Tier 3 Small-Group Instruction

| Phonics/Decoding (Students who need Tier 3 intervention with low accuracy and nonsense word fluency rates) | |
|---|---|
| **Duration (15–20 minutes total)** | **Small-Group Activity** |
| 3–5 minutes | Direct instruction in the phonetic element being taught in interventions |
| 12–15 minutes | Oral reading practice of decodable text that aligns with interventions |

This scenario is designed for small-group instruction in the regular classroom and is not intended as a pullout program. Instead, it is another dose based on student data that will help accelerate student learning. For this to be successful, coordination between the interventionist and the general classroom teacher is imperative. There must be communication and a system built so that both the interventionist and the classroom teacher understand what is being taught.

Figure 6.5 is a sample data spreadsheet for second grade. In this case, students are being progress monitored on oral reading fluency. As you can see from the tabs along the bottom, students in second grade may still be struggling and receiving interventions geared toward increasing nonsense word fluency as well.

As you can quickly see, we worry immediately about two students on the spreadsheet: Stacey Johnlun and Niyoka Wrung. After six weeks of instruction, neither student has made gains in their intervention for oral reading fluency. Since both students, and the majority

Second Grade—Grade Level—Oral Reading Fluency and Accuracy

* For any student who is being progress monitored "Off Level" using ORF lower grade-level passages or lower foundational skills, please capitalize their first and last name.

| Name | Teacher | Fall Bench-mark Com-posite | Fall Bench-mark ORF | Fall Bench-mark Accuracy | 9/30 ORF | 9/30 Accuracy | 10/7 ORF | 10/7 Accuracy | 10/14 ORF | 10/14 Accuracy | 10/21 ORF | 10/21 Accuracy | 10/28 ORF | 10/28 Accuracy | 11/6 ORF | 11/6 Accuracy |
|---|---|---|---|---|---|---|---|---|---|---|---|---|---|---|---|---|
| Loren Huff | Betterbe | 330 | 46 | 98 | 50 | 98 | 56 | 97 | 58 | 98 | 63 | 98 | 72 | 98 | 78 | 97 |
| Jacob Hafey | Sogood | 329 | 47 | 97 | 52 | 98 | 58 | 98 | 62 | 97 | 68 | 98 | 76 | 97 | 80 | 98 |
| Melissa Jostka | O'Wiley | 317 | 42 | 86 | 48 | 90 | 52 | 92 | 56 | 94 | 60 | 96 | 70 | 96 | 76 | 97 |
| Peggy Greenbow | Betterbe | 319 | 39 | 86 | 44 | 88 | 48 | 90 | 52 | 93 | 55 | 95 | 63 | 96 | 68 | 98 |
| Taylor Tutz | Sogood | 324 | 47 | 88 | 50 | 90 | 52 | 90 | 54 | 94 | 59 | 94 | 64 | 95 | 68 | 96 |
| AngeeLee Conroy | Betterbe | 270 | 26 | 72 | 40 | 74 | 40 | 76 | 44 | 80 | 44 | 86 | 52 | 89 | 66 | 92 |
| Frank Bellarus | Betterbe | 312 | 20 | 78 | 28 | 80 | 36 | 84 | 42 | 86 | 52 | 90 | 54 | 94 | 60 | 96 |
| Karen Langsea | Sogood | 314 | 27 | 82 | 36 | 82 | 36 | 80 | 34 | 80 | 36 | 86 | 42 | 90 | 47 | 94 |
| Marina Lucci | O'Wiley | 227 | 24 | 68 | 28 | 72 | 32 | 76 | 36 | 79 | 38 | 82 | 44 | 86 | 48 | 90 |
| Stacey Johnlun | O'Wiley | 296 | 28 | 77 | 30 | 76 | 30 | 76 | 30 | 76 | 30 | 76 | 32 | 78 | 36 | 78 |
| Niyoka Wrung | Sogood | 298 | 28 | 80 | 32 | 80 | 32 | 78 | 30 | 78 | 30 | 74 | 28 | 74 | 28 | 72 |

Second Grade NWF-WRC  Second Grade NWF-CLS  Second Grade ORF and Accuracy

Key: NWF = Nonsense Word Fluency, WRC = Words Read Correctly, CLS = Correct Letter Sounds, ORF = Oral Reading Fluency

**FIGURE 6.5:** Second-grade intervention tracking.

of students on this list, have accuracy issues, they should be receiving an intervention in phonological processing to help with their oral reading fluency. At the next data meeting, both Stacey and Niyoka should be on the top of the list regarding changes to intervention services.

The dot card for Niyoka Wrung (figure 6.6) shows her same struggles in her intervention as the spreadsheet. No matter what system you use, a sea of red ● or yellow ○ stagnant scores should issue a call to arms for the students, and an immediate discussion regarding how to change the instructional strategies and interventions should take place.

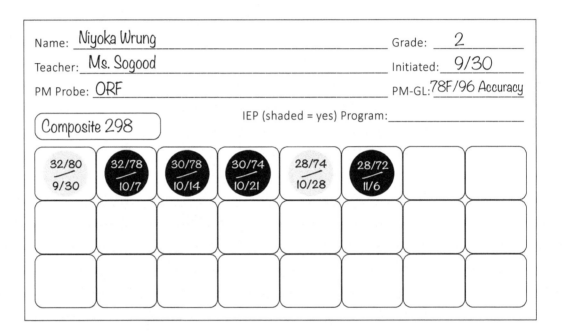

**FIGURE 6.6:** Second-grade student example dot card.

Also note the two students at the top of the spreadsheet, Loren Huff and Jacob Hafey. Both students were at benchmark on their composite score at the beginning of the year on their DIBELS 8 Benchmark Assessment. Though they were at benchmark, both students were below in their fluency rate but at grade level in their accuracy rate. Had the school in this scenario only examined their composite score, these students may not have received the intervention needed for fluency. As you can see from the progress monitoring tracking, after several weeks of receiving fluency work, both of these students are now at grade level.

# Instruction in Third Grade and Up

As outlined previously, if students reading below grade level are identified and provided quality reading interventions that align with their deficits based on the assessment data, *it's possible* to have them achieve grade-level reading expectations. The consequences of delaying identification and intervention are ominous. As Sally Shaywitz (2003) reported, at least 70 percent of students who do not learn to read by age 9 will never catch up to their typically developing peers (Birsh & Carreker, 2018). For students in third grade and up who are still struggling readers, these students can still learn to read at grade level (Lovett, Lacerenza, De Palma, & Frijters, 2012).

We have noticed that many educational settings mistakenly believe literacy struggles can only be detected in kindergarten through second grade. Instead of using an assessment that measures any of the foundational skills, they make the switch to assessing students on grade-level standards. There are a variety of reasons, however, that a student may not be able perform proficiently on these assessments; the number one issue is likely the inability to read at grade level. When assessments are used in third grade and up that only measure standards, there are no data to determine what might be getting in the way. We strongly recommend all schools with students in third through sixth grade have a way to measure foundational reading skills.

Common foundational reading assessments in third grade and up can sound the alarm for potential reading issues. The subtest used to identify basic reading proficiency is found in table 6.10.

**TABLE 6.10:** Third-Grade Goals and Subtests

| Goals for Mastery |
| --- |
| Reading fluency |
| Text comprehension |
| **Foundational Reading Assessment Subtests** |
| Oral reading fluency |

Assessments of oral reading fluency (ORF) consist of two measures—accuracy and fluency. A fluency score includes a number rate for the number of words read in, typically, one minute, along with a percentage of the accuracy with which the words were read. This accuracy percentage is based on how many words a student was able to accurately decode in the passage read. If a student has a low percentage of words they can accurately read, it will not only impact the fluency in which they can read but also their reading comprehension. If student data indicate that a student has deficits in either of these two areas, these should be the area of focus for small-group differentiation or intervention depending on the severity of need. However, it is critically important to discern between the two!

Students who are not accurate in their word reading are often so because of phonological processing deficits, as inaccurate reading is due to poor phonic decoding skills. Students whose assessments indicate that they have a significantly low accuracy rate (95 percent or lower) are typically flagged in foundational reading assessments. These students should immediately receive a placement test to see if they qualify for an intensive intervention into a systematic phonics program. We will discuss the procedure for students identified having fluency issues due to a low rate in following sections.

## The Research on Teaching Fluency

Students who read aloud with appropriate speed, accuracy, and expression (these are students who have oral reading fluency) are more likely to comprehend connected text because they are able to conserve cognitive resources that can be applied to the comprehension of meaning (Perfetti, 2007; Sabatini, Wang, & O'Reilly, 2019). Thus, oral reading fluency is a reliable and easily accessible indicator of overall reading competence—and a strong marker of progress in learning to read (Fuchs et al., 2001)—and its assessment has become one of the primary means of determining which elementary school students are on track toward meeting state reading standards and which students would benefit from additional services and intervention (McGlinchey & Hixson, 2004; Reschly, Busch, Betts, Deno, & Long, 2009; White, Sabatini, Park, et al., 2021).

Students with a range of reading disabilities who do not establish foundational skills by early in third grade can develop accurate word recognition and can increase reading fluency when they are provided intensive intervention focused on both areas (Birsh & Carreker, 2018; Torgesen, Rashotte, Alexander, Alexander, & MacPhee, 2003)

In general, the best candidates for fluency interventions are students with slow, accurate reading (Spear-Swerling, 2022). When accuracy dips below 95 percent performance on reading tasks, reading comprehension suffers (Hasbrouck & Glaser, 2018; National Assessment of Educational Progress, 2018). Students who frequently misread words are likely to have difficulty understanding the text because the words are likely content words that are important for comprehension, not function words (for example, *the*, *and*, and *on*; McGlinchey & Hixson, 2004; Reschly et al., 2009; White, Sabatini, Park, et al., 2021).

## How to Facilitate Interventions and Differentiation in Reading Fluency

The following suggestions are the big ideas for differentiation in small-group instruction for students who may need additional intervention with fluency difficulties.

- Fluency is two-pronged and encompasses both accuracy and rate.
- Students with low accuracy rates—those at 95 percent and below—will not improve their fluency with intervention in repeated reading.
- Low accuracy rates indicate a need for phonological decoding interventions.
  - ⇨ In addition, phonological decoding is regarded by almost all reading researchers as a critical prerequisite for the development of skilled, fluent reading and reading comprehension (Castles, Rastle, & Nation, 2018; Share, 1995).
- To have fluent readers, we must first remediate accuracy and then intervene on fluency.
- Paired reading of students who are slightly below their grade-level fluency rate can make excellent growth in fluency by rereading the passages from the core story during teacher-led small-group instruction.
- Incorporate the use of dyad reading during small-group instruction. See the following page for a description.

When considering the implications for interventions, students who are slow *but accurate* readers should receive an intervention for becoming more fluent readers. On foundational reading assessments, these students may be indicated as Tier 3 or Tier 2 in fluency. The level of instructional need is not the main concern with remediating fluency issues, but rather how to remediate.

As with the remediation of orthographic mapping, we have found that students who do display a profile of accurate but slow reading need more "miles on the page." In other words, they need more practice at reading at their appropriate level, thus solidifying orthographic mapping or instant word recognition. There are several intervention strategies we have found to be appropriate. A Lexile level is a measure that provides both the readability level of a text as well as its complexity. In using any of the following techniques, you will need to acquire the Lexile levels for the students. A conversion to a student's Lexile level can now typically be found in most foundational reading assessments.

The first technique we have found for effectively increasing fluency rate is dyad reading. Dyad reading was developed by Dennie Butterfield and J. Lloyd Eldredge in 1986. We have found dyad reading to be one of the most cost-effective methods for increasing reading fluency that is available to schools. In essence, a strong reader is paired with a weaker reader who sits side by side reading the same book aloud simultaneously. The idea is to have the weaker reader read at the same natural speed as the stronger reader. When all assessments were considered, assisted readers reading texts two grade levels above their instructional levels showed the most robust gains in oral reading fluency and comprehension. Lead readers also benefit from dyad reading and continue their respective reading developmental trajectories across measures (Brown, Mohr, Wilcox, & Barrett, 2018).

Instead of using grade-level equivalency, we have found pairing students with an approximate Lexile level range difference of 200 to 300 to be most effective. The Lexile level chosen should be the starting Lexile of the stronger reader. Dyad reading is an excellent activity to do during small-group instruction and is one that can be used in independent stations while the teacher is working with other groups of students. Our procedure for dyad reading can be found in the following list.

1. **Pairing students:** Begin by ranking students by high to low based on Lexile level. Once Lexile levels are known for each student, begin to pair students. Paired students should be 200 to 300 points apart; 250 Lexile levels is ideal.

2. **Text selection:** Select a book based on the higher students' Lexile level. For students near grade level, you can use current textbooks students are reading in class. This could include the following:

   ⇨ Grade-level science or social studies text

   ⇨ Any grade-level text that has a copy for each student

3. **Student procedure:**

   ⇨ Each student has the same text

   ⇨ Sit side by side

   ⇨ Two voices (choral reading)

⇨ Eyes on words

⇨ Not too fast, not too slow

⇨ Students read for five to ten uninterrupted minutes

4. **Teacher procedure:**

⇨ Cruise the room and monitor

⇨ Listen to students' reading

Another method for increasing reading rate for students who are accurate in reading fluency but have a slower rate is simply the rereading of passages from classroom text. Text for rereading can be from any content including social studies, science, or English language arts. We find it particularly helpful to use the rereading of passages from their core reading program. Align passages selected from the core reading program whenever possible (Hasbrouck & Glaser, 2019).

The third technique we have found to be particularly helpful for those students who have recently reached grade-level accuracy through an intensive intervention based on phonics is to have them partner read controlled text, ensuring an encounter with multisyllabic words while the predominant focus is to build text stamina for students. We have found the *Amber Guardian Series* from Phonicbooks.com fits this bill perfectly. It is a series of ten books that includes multisyllabic words with a higher ratio of text to illustration. This series bridges the gap between decodable text and authentic text and is appropriate for older students in fourth grade and above.

## How to Facilitate Interventions and Differentiation for Accuracy

As stated, when ORF data indicates a student has a reading accuracy level of 95 percent or lower, they should be receiving a phonological processing intervention. Accuracy rates of 95 percent or lower indicate that a student is struggling with phonic decoding. Yet we can accelerate the ability for student growth if we provide additional instruction aligned to the intervention. As an example, in a systematic phonics program, there is a specific scope and sequence of phonetic elements that are taught. In a quality phonological program, there is controlled text that aligns with the skills being taught, typically via decodable text. We have found that if students have the opportunity to practice in another decodable text with the same focus of phonetic element, students have more opportunity to practice in text what is being taught. Consequently, the outcomes for students becoming grade-level proficient in accuracy are much more rapid.

An example of small-group instruction in the general classroom setting for students receiving intensive interventions in a systematic phonological intervention in grades 3 and up should look like table 6.11.

**TABLE 6.11:** Accuracy in Small-Group Instruction

| Accuracy (Tier 3 interventions in third grade and up) | |
| --- | --- |
| **Duration (15–20 minutes total)** | **Small-Group Activity** |
| 5–7 minutes | Teacher review and direct instruction of the phonetic element the students are receiving in intervention |
| 10–13 minutes | Oral reading in a decodable text aligned with the phonetic element |

Figures 6.7 and 6.8 (page 176) illustrate how tracking the intervention for struggling readers might look in third grade.

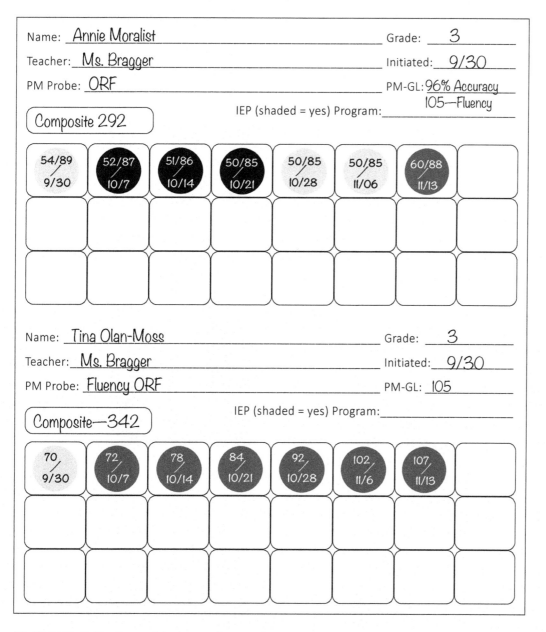

Name: _Annie Moralist_    Grade: ___3___

Teacher: _Ms. Bragger_    Initiated: _9/30_

PM Probe: _ORF_    PM-GL: _96% Accuracy_

IEP (shaded = yes) Program: _105—Fluency_

Composite 292

| 54/89 9/30 | 52/87 10/7 | 51/86 10/14 | 50/85 10/21 | 50/85 10/28 | 50/85 11/06 | 60/88 11/13 | |

Name: _Tina Olan-Moss_    Grade: ___3___

Teacher: _Ms. Bragger_    Initiated: _9/30_

PM Probe: _Fluency ORF_    PM-GL: _105_

IEP (shaded = yes) Program: _____

Composite—342

| 70 9/30 | 72 10/7 | 78 10/14 | 84 10/21 | 92 10/28 | 102 11/6 | 107 11/13 | |

**FIGURE 6.7:** Two third-grade student example dot cards.

| Name | Teacher | Fall Benchmark Composite | Fall Benchmark ORF Words Correct | Fall Benchmark Accuracy | 9/30 ORF | 9/30 Accuracy | 10/7 ORF | 10/7 Accuracy | 10/14 ORF | 10/14 Accuracy | 10/21ORF | 10/21 Accuracy | 10/28 ORF | 10/28 Accuracy | 11/06 ORF | 11/06 Accuracy | 11/13 ORF | 11/13 Accuracy |
|---|---|---|---|---|---|---|---|---|---|---|---|---|---|---|---|---|---|---|
| Tina Olan-Moss | Bragger | 342 | 70 | 96 | 70 | 96 | 72 | 96 | 78 | 97 | 84 | 98 | 92 | 92 | 101 | 98 | 102 | 98 |
| Karen Salvage | Thronsen | 336 | 68 | 96 | 70 | 96 | 74 | 96 | 89 | 98 | 94 | 99 | 101 | 101 | 106 | 99 | 110 | 99 |
| Michael Mostt | Bragger | 331 | 68 | 91 | 72 | 94 | 76 | 94 | 78 | 96 | 84 | 97 | 92 | 92 | 98 | 97 | 105 | 97 |
| Jan Dimee | Smyth | 317 | 66 | 91 | 70 | 93 | 74 | 95 | 76 | 95 | 80 | 96 | 88 | 88 | 94 | 99 | 99 | 99 |
| Candice Julian | Mussel | 323 | 70 | 92 | 74 | 94 | 76 | 95 | 82 | 96 | 86 | 97 | 94 | 94 | 100 | 97 | 104 | 96 |
| Julie Spital | Bragger | 329 | 72 | 93 | 76 | 95 | 80 | 96 | 86 | 96 | 90 | 97 | 98 | 98 | 103 | 99 | 107 | 99 |
| Annie Moralist | Bragger | 292 | 54 | 89 | 54 | 89 | 52 | 87 | 51 | 86 | 50 | 85 | 50 | 85 | 50 | 85 | 60 | 88 |
| Jade Barlow | Mussel | 306 | 54 | 90 | 52 | 90 | 54 | 88 | 52 | 89 | 52 | 88 | 54 | 88 | 54 | 86 | 62 | 86 |
| Belinda Krock | Thronsen | 312 | 46 | 91 | 48 | 93 | 52 | 95 | 57 | 95 | 64 | 97 | 76 | 98 | 80 | 98 | 88 | 98 |
| Craig Belgrain | Bragger | 289 | 48 | 78 | 48 | 80 | 54 | 84 | 58 | 86 | 63 | 88 | 70 | 90 | 76 | 94 | 85 | 94 |
| Kristen Boyle | Mussel | 294 | 44 | 76 | 46 | 78 | 52 | 82 | 56 | 86 | 60 | 88 | 74 | 90 | 80 | 92 | 88 | 95 |

Third Grade—Grade Level—Oral Reading Fluency and Accuracy

*For any student who is being progress monitored "Off Level" using ORF lower grade-level passages or lower foundational skills

Fall Window: —

Fall Goal: 73 ORF, 96% Accuracy

Third Grade NWF-CLS • Third Grade NWF-WRC • Third Grade ORF and Accuracy

**FIGURE 6.8:** Data analysis spreadsheet for third grade.

Key: NWF = Nonsense Word Fluency, CLS = Correct Letter Sounds, WRC = Words Read Correctly, ORF = Oral Reading

*Visit go.SolutionTree.com/literacy for a free reproducible version of this figure.*

As with the other dot card and corresponding cell dots, you can quickly see who is struggling and who isn't. In this case, using Dibels8, if we take a deeper dive into Annie Moralist (on her dot card, in figure 6.7, page 175), you can see that she has never made growth. She started out with a red dot cell ●. Her first progress monitoring was the same as it was for her benchmark assessment. She was stagnant. Her scores are then yellow . We hope that she was placed in an intervention, but as you can see, her cells are red ● for the next three progress monitoring probes. She continued to make no progress. Although her next progress monitoring probes are yellow dots, it isn't because of progress, it's in fact because she hasn't progressed.

Based on Annie's benchmark scores, which indicate she has low accuracy, one would wonder if she instead was placed on an intervention focusing on fluency rate. This would do nothing to increase her accuracy and instead would cause this perpetual stagnation. Annie does begin to get better by her last progress monitoring probe. One has to wonder, was she removed from the intervention that was focusing on fluency and instead placed in an intervention that would resolve her accuracy issues, such as one focusing on phonics?

Let's also take a look at Tina Olan-Moss. This is a student who appears to be on grade level. Her composite score is at benchmark. If we look a bit further, her fluency is just below expectations. Her accuracy is at grade level. If we simply looked at her composite score, we wouldn't know that a bit of extra fluency work could ensure this student remained at grade level. Tina should receive fluency interventions. Since we are focusing on fluency, her dot on her card is based on growth on her fluency score. After six weeks of extra help in fluency, we can see that she, too, is now at grade level.

# Instruction in Vocabulary and Comprehension

A frequent criticism of a structured literacy approach is the absence of a focus in the areas of vocabulary and comprehension. This common misplaced critique is largely due to the lack of understanding of two reading concepts: (1) students cannot put meaning to words that they simply cannot read (that is, decode), and (2) to comprehend, students must have a fluent and reliable resource from which they can recognize words.

We can highlight this by considering that the vast majority of students come to school with the ability to comprehend language. As an example, if you say to a kindergarten student on the first day of school, "Please place your pencil in your desk," few would struggle with the understanding of what you were asking of them. But if you asked a kindergarten student on the first day of school to *read* the request, "Please place your pencil in your desk," most students would not be able to complete the task. All students must first learn the code before they are able to read. The more they do learn the code, the more they are able to comprehend text they read.

If something interferes with the underlying processes necessary for reading, the student will struggle with comprehending any text. If there are reading deficits in decoding or accurate word reading, we must remediate that before intervening with explicit vocabulary or comprehension instruction. An improved understanding of vocabulary cannot come into play in reading comprehension until their word recognition skills have become more automatic (Hoover & Tunmer, 2020).

If we have remediated phonological processing issues, and a student has solid word recognition, as evidenced by fluent reading, we begin our work with intervening with vocabulary and comprehension. This is not to say that intervention instruction is void of developing vocabulary or comprehension—absolutely not! Remember, students progress faster when teachers focus. Our focus should first be on automatic word recognition.

As students progress through the grades, text and the vocabulary included within that text becomes increasingly more difficult. The ability to comprehend becomes more apparent as the text becomes more complex (Spear-Swerling, 2016).

## Assessments for Vocabulary and Comprehension

Some foundational reading assessments contain two subtests often associated or assumed to be associated with comprehension. These two measures are the retell component of ORF in Acadience and the MAZE subtest in aimswebPlus, Acadience, and DIBELS 8. Retelling of a passage read is an indicator of a student's comprehension ability, but it is a subjective test. The student retells the passage read, and the teacher counts the number of related words the student uses. We find teachers often overrate students' responses and therefore unintentionally elevate student outcomes on the measurement. Additionally, there is only a moderate relation between retell and reading comprehension (Cao & Kim, 2021). Thus, in our data analysis, we do not recommend using the retell subtest as an adequate measure of a student's ability in reading comprehension.

The MAZE subtest measures students' ability to select the appropriate word from a choice of three words to complete a passage or sentence. The MAZE subtest is known as a cloze procedure. Cloze procedures require students to select the correct word that fits into a passage or sentence. Though a cloze test measures comprehension, the question becomes, What part of comprehension is it really measuring? Based on the layout of the assessment, it very well may be measuring vocabulary, but if a student does not have the background knowledge for the passage, the student's issue may be inferencing from a limited understanding of the topic, not a problem with vocabulary.

Reading comprehension is not easily quantified, and it can be difficult to separate out the factors that contribute to reading comprehension (Farrall, 2012). Areas where students may struggle include language skills, comprehension monitoring, inferencing, and background knowledge, to name just a few. This is not to say that foundational reading assessments are not a good barometer of reading comprehension. Since a focus on intervention in the areas of vocabulary and comprehension begins after students are at benchmark in phonological processing, most of the students with issues in these areas should appear as strategic learners, or Tier 2 learners, on the foundational reading assessments.

Fortunately, we do know that when students are fluent in their reading without having to make a conscious effort to decode words on a page, then there is immediate access to the meaning of the words. This allows a student to integrate all the processes of reading and allocate mental resources for understanding or comprehending the text.

In a study that Fuchs and colleagues (2001) refer to, the correlation of ORF to comprehension was 0.91 as compared to tests of question answering, recall measures, and cloze measures of reading. In other words, using an ORF probe is the best proxy to determine whether a student can comprehend text.

Foundational reading assessments are also scant when it comes to assessing vocabulary. Apart from aimswebPlus, which has a valid and reliable vocabulary subtest, all others have a limited scope in vocabulary. In fact, most lack any vocabulary assessment at all. Again, time is precious in elementary schools, particularly when we are discussing struggling readers. Every minute counts, but all is not lost when it comes to detecting comprehension and vocabulary problems. If you recall back to chapter 3 (page 57), we urged the use of your core programs' unit assessments. This is especially critical in grades 3 and up, when we want to reveal vocabulary and comprehension issues.

Beginning with grade 3, we should begin to measure how students are doing on standards. These unit assessments in a quality core reading program typically offer an assessment that is not only aligned to the standards but also has sections that broadly align with the foundational skills. Typically, these assessments have a vocabulary portion tested as well as a question-and-answer section. If used regularly after each unit, they can act as a screener for those students struggling with vocabulary and comprehension.

Unfortunately, they do not meet the rigor of a valid and reliable measure of comprehension or vocabulary, but they do indicate when a student may be struggling with vocabulary and answering questions about a text.

## The Research on Teaching Vocabulary and Comprehension

It is self-evident how vocabulary knowledge affects outcomes for comprehension. But vocabulary is not the only enabler of comprehension. Other major factors that can also impede reading comprehension beyond vocabulary are background knowledge, inferencing, and comprehension monitoring. Comprehension monitoring is the process where a student checks their understanding as they are reading a text or passage—being aware as to whether the text makes sense. In fact, there are so many pieces that combine to ensure a student can comprehend text, our attempt here is not to parse each out but rather look at the overall findings from the research and provide broad examples of what should be happening for differentiation for students during small-group instruction that can ultimately improve comprehension.

It is important to keep in mind that because comprehension is multidimensional, differentiation, under most circumstances, should not focus on only one area but rather interweave them while intervening as well. One study found that, in typically developing readers, the various strands of reading comprehension, such as vocabulary, grammatical knowledge, knowledge of story structure, inferencing, and comprehension monitoring, all contributed to the unique variance of reading comprehension (Fletcher et al., 2019). Students must integrate the many parts of the text to adequately comprehend, which is where interventions can be particularly helpful. Consider the following as you begin to create a system for intervening on vocabulary.

## Resources for Specific Strategies

Countless books have been written on instructional strategies for the various subskills. The following are our recommended invaluable resources.

For instructional strategies on the teaching of letter names and sounds, phonological awareness including segmenting and blending, and phonic decoding:

- *Multisensory Teaching of Basic Language Skills* (Birsh & Carreker, 2018)
- *Next STEPS in Literacy Instruction, Second Edition* (Smartt & Glaser, 2024)
- *Reading Teachers Source Book*
- Reading Rockets
  - ⇨ www.readingrockets.com
- Florida Center for Reading Research
  - ⇨ https://fcrr.org

For support with understanding and supporting vocabulary:

- *Creating Robust Vocabulary* (Beck, McKeown, & Kucan, 2008)
- *Teaching Basic, Advanced, and Academic Vocabulary* (Marzano, 2020)
- *Multisensory Teaching of Basic Language Skills* (Birsh & Carreker, 2018)

For support with understanding and supporting reading comprehension:

- *Understanding and Teaching Reading Comprehension* (Oakhill et al., 2015)
- *The Reading Comprehension Blueprint* (Hennessy, 2021)
- *Multisensory Teaching of Basic Language Skills* (Birsh & Carreker, 2018)

For instructional recommendations in all areas of literacy:

- *Seven Mighty Moves: Research-Backed, Classroom-Tested Strategies to Ensure K-to-3 Reading Success* (Kemeny, 2023)

- Do not limit students' reading because of a low vocabulary. Most new vocabulary is learned through reading, not from being directly taught word meanings (Kilpatrick et al., 2019).

- When providing intervention on comprehension and specifically vocabulary, students should not only learn word definitions but also how unfamiliar words relate to one another (Oakhill, Cain, & Elbro, 2015).

- Provide prereading activities with key words students will encounter. Discuss what has or is being learned about these words during the reading of the passage (Oakhill et al., 2015).

Interventions should not focus on only one area or the other, but rather fuse the components while providing interventions. Keeping the aforementioned items in mind will ensure a holistic approach as you design your intervention.

## How to Facilitate Interventions and Differentiation for Vocabulary

Prior to intervening, it is assumed that the general education classroom setting has provided direct and appropriate instruction in vocabulary and the other components of comprehension that have been discussed earlier. If students are still struggling, consider ensuring that small-group instruction for students includes the following.

- Preteach vocabulary words for upcoming reading passages prior to students reading the text.

- Incorporate and use vocabulary words while building background knowledge prior to reading a text.

- Have students discuss the vocabulary words, how words relate to one another, what they know about the topic, and other words that are similar during small-group instruction and while building background knowledge.

- Give students struggling with vocabulary acquisition more instruction in the depth of word knowledge beyond learning definitions and meanings of words in whole-group instruction.

- Ensure students are making note of other words in the passage with meanings they do not know when they are working in teacher-led small-group instruction and reading the text.

- Have students work in pairs during independent small-group time to categorize words and later explain why they categorized the words as they did. This strategy, having no right answer necessarily, facilitates students' deep thinking about words.

- Include specific instruction in morphology.

- Incorporate the use of teaching antonyms and synonyms.

When you begin to create a system for intervening on background knowledge, remember that background knowledge in a topic is critical to comprehending the text. However, most comprehensive core reading programs have limited direction in how to build background knowledge. Because many teachers do not understand the importance of background knowledge, often even if a core program does have a component on building background knowledge, it is pushed to the wayside.

Gaps in background knowledge, along with weak vocabulary development, can have a significant effect on comprehending text (Hirsch, 2003, 2006; Beck, McKeown & Gromoll, 1989; Stahl, 1991; Willingham, 2007). Students who lack background knowledge during a reading comprehension task will struggle with the task (Hoover & Tunmer, 2020). Further, as explored next, "even very simple inferences cannot be made if the reader does not have the requisite background knowledge" (Kilpatrick et al., 2019, p. 95).

## How to Facilitate Interventions and Differentiation for Background Knowledge and Inferencing

To accurately comprehend, students must learn to gather a lot of information from the written text in which much information is implied and not explicitly stated. Further, students who were able to remember more details in a passage made a greater number of inferences. Vocabulary knowledge and background knowledge related to the topic of the text being read also appear to enhance the ability to accurately make inferences. Poor memory impedes a student's ability to make inferences; therefore, longer text passages are more difficult for inference making for students with memory issues (Oakhill et al., 2015). The following are methods for facilitating interventions and differentiation for activating background knowledge.

- Prior to students reading the text, activate background knowledge with students using Know, Want to Know, and Learned (KWL) charts.

- Prior to students reading the text, teach background knowledge and vocabulary together. Often, the vocabulary words are a part of the background knowledge students need.

- Engage in discourse and discussion with students regarding what they know about the story, facts, or information within the text.

- Use pictures, realia (authentic items), and video clips to pictorially provide visual information to students related to the text they are reading.

- Consider other recently read texts that may be of similar content and help students make connections.

- Incorporate virtual headsets into small-group instruction, utilizing virtual tours to different places and events.

Children who were better at recalling explicitly stated facts in a text made a greater number of inferences. When you begin to create a system for intervening on inferencing, consider the following recommendations.

- Teach students how to analyze text for clues by finding key words.

- Break text into smaller segments and help students make inferences as they go along.

- Use graphic organizers to support identifying inferences.

- Make predictions of what might happen and discuss students' reasoning, then go back to check why it was right or wrong.

- Use "wh" questions of who, what, when, and where. Answers in the text may not be explicit, and the students analyze the text to answer the questions.

### How to Facilitate and Differentiate Interventions for Comprehension Monitoring

As good readers read, they are continually checking in with themselves to ensure what they are reading is making sense and that they are understanding the content. This meta-cognitive task is called *comprehension monitoring*. Good readers regularly check their own understanding and have strategies to use when something doesn't make sense, such as going back and rereading a portion of the text or breaking a word apart into its morphological pieces to help understand its meaning. The following is a list of methods for facilitating interventions for comprehension monitoring.

- Provide students with sticky notes to list key words containing main ideas about the paragraphs. Have students exchange their ideas regarding what the paragraphs were about.

- Have students visualize what they have read after reading a paragraph. Invite discourse and comparison of students' visualization.

- Ask students specific questions such as, Does that make sense? Why did they do that?

- Have students reread paragraphs, ask questions aloud about the part of the text that confused them, read ahead, and read captions.

# Key Considerations and Common Pitfalls

All the examples indicated previously are by no means quick fixes. Accelerating students' growth in reading can be achieved by examining the data, providing interventions that align to that data, and giving students as many opportunities for practice as is possible. Using the strategies outlined requires keen attention to the progress monitoring of students. Because growth is to be expected, staff must be nimble as reading groups will change— and should change—as students become more proficient and move into the next level of reading intervention.

In too many schools we visit, we see a hodgepodge of interventions, many from paid-access websites for teacher materials, being provided to groups of students based on the instructional level and not the subskill level derived from a foundational reading assessment.

Teachers are not analyzing the data to understand what it is students need—what is the subskill interfering with the growth of students? To compound the situation further, rarely is the reading of text taking place and, even more seldom, are students being progress monitored to ensure that the help is indeed helping. Is it a surprise that the outcomes for such promising initiatives as either RTI or MTSS are failing (Fletcher et al., 2019; Reynolds & Shawitz, 2009)?

For the majority of children with word reading deficits, we have found that placing them in an intervention program and ensuring the following elements leads to success.

- Mastery of letter-sound correspondence and phonemic awareness

- Teaching a systematic approach to phonics and decoding

- Providing opportunities for reading connected text

Our own work and research bears this out—we would add with an ardent eye and monitoring of student data. When these elements are part of a systemic data analysis and intervention structure, *it's possible* for all students to succeed.

## Supplemental Phonics Reading Programs

If the core reading program you are using is poor or void of any letter-sound instruction, phonemic awareness instruction, or phonics, it is advisable to bring in a separate phonological awareness program. We have a strong caveat when choosing to have a supplemental phonological awareness program. If a program you are using has *some* phonological awareness, but you believe it is not adequately robust—it is explicit in instruction, does not include a logical scope and sequence, or does not provide enough repetitions—but teachers are still using it, be cautious. Students who are five and six years old and learn a few skills from their core reading program before going to an intervention or differentiated small-group instruction and learning a few more different skills have a slim chance of being able to master any of the skills. Instead, we recommend either beefing up the robustness of the phonological awareness program in your core program by including more examples, more repetition, and more explicit instruction, or omitting it entirely and supplementing with a phonological program. The message here is that teaching struggling readers with more time in a supplemental phonological awareness program while continuing to teach the phonological component of a core reading program will bring confusion instead of mastery.

If you have decided that a supplemental program will be beneficial, we suggest the following programs.

- 95 Percent Group
  - ⇨ www.95percentgroup.com
- Enhanced Core Reading Instruction
  - ⇨ https://ctlmarketplace.uoregon.edu/product/enhanced-core -reading-instruction
- UFLI Foundations
  - ⇨ https://ufli.education.ufl.edu/foundations

For a specific intervention to enhance reading comprehension, we recommend the following.

- 95 Comprehension, Grades 3–6 (95 Percent Group)
    ⇨ www.95percentgroup.com/products/95-comprehension-grades-3-through-6

# Summary

Interventions for students should align with the subtests and subskills students have not yet mastered that are found in the foundational reading assessment. Students should not simply receive interventions based on the instructional level of the foundational reading assessment.

Students cannot just be remediated in skills. They must also have the opportunity to use those skills reading connected and authentic text. This is one of the biggest mistakes we see schools making—students are not reading. Ensure your intervention time contains time in text daily.

Many of the foundational reading assessments provide subtests that are not necessarily the most important for learning to read. We have outlined a framework for the subskills found within reading assessments to be used at each grade level that is based on phases of reading acquisition.

Whole-group instruction should align to grade-level standards and expectations. All students should be a part of whole-group instruction. Small-group instruction is where student differentiation occurs. Research has found that small-group instruction is more effective if it is targeted to a specific skill rather than as part of a comprehensive intervention program that addressed multiple skills. Targeted small-group instruction had an effect size as high as 0.64 when provided to students in the elementary years (Hall & Burns, 2018).

As Wesley A. Hoover and William E. Tunmer (2020) point out, it is simply not possible to teach each student individually. A partial solution is to understand individual needs and then to address those through the best mechanisms available—heterogeneous small groups of students when they can learn from each other and homogeneous small groups of students who share the same learning needs and can benefit from the same instruction. We believe this chapter outlines the processes to create such a situation.

Teachers and staff will need ongoing professional development to understand the intricacies and nuances of effective intervention as well as other portions of your literacy initiative. Chapter 7 will provide you with these suggestions.

# Prioritizing Ongoing Professional Development for Educators

## The Principal's Perspective

*By Angela Hanlin*

When I first became a principal, I felt that I had a good idea of the classroom instruction going on in the building, because I had been the instructional coach for the district for several years. I soon learned, however, that not all the professional development that had been provided had been implemented. To leave our focus school status, we would have to implement the research-based, evidence-based professional development that had been provided regarding instruction. The teachers were also going to need ongoing professional development and specific coaching. This would need to be a layered approach, because the teachers were still in need of several different professional development concepts, especially if we planned to exit focus school status in a timely manner and make significant gains in student performance. I created a comprehensive school-improvement plan, and one section of the plan was to provide specific professional development sessions on necessary topics, deliver on-the-job coaching and support, and develop a mindset for a continuous cycle of improvement all while instilling an attitude that this was possible. No easy task, but it is possible!

### A New Approach to Implementation

First, we needed a mindset change. I began by establishing the mindset that, as educators, we are all lifelong learners who are continuously perfecting our craft. We never master it! We are always striving to be better and to know more. When we learn of new research, then that information must be studied and implemented effectively. We talked a lot about progress instead of perfection. We were going to continuously be *striving* for perfection so that our instruction had an impact on student learning.

Teachers also needed to be told that a lot of information would be shared with them in a short span of time. We would need to find every spare minute and use it efficiently. We did not have any professional development days scheduled throughout the remaining days of our school calendar, so the professional development we needed would have to be provided outside of the school day or during the school day. We had to develop the mindset that striving to make growth and trying new things would mean that we would require feedback to improve our practices. Teachers then saw all feedback as necessary information for their continued growth. They began to live within the continuous cycle of professional growth. It was never going to be a one-and-done culture. This is a mindset that must be developed in our schools if we want to promote teacher growth, develop collective efficacy, and change academic results.

## Observe and Support Implementation

The next mindset change was that once we gained knowledge from professional development, it would need to be *implemented*. I cannot stress enough the importance of setting an expectation for implementation. When teachers leave a professional development session without a specific plan for how to best implement the information in their own classroom, I do not believe they have truly been professionally developed. Merely talking about a topic does not go deep enough to produce real change in our classrooms. Teachers were given the promise and commitment that only research-based ideas would be shared with them and specific implementation steps would be provided. Trainings would include what this information would look and sound like in their classrooms. Once these were provided, new learning would need to be implemented immediately in their classrooms. It was the only way we could make significant gains in a timely manner. Teachers were told the implementation might not always go smoothly, but we still had to implement. We adopted the mindset that errors are welcomed in our school culture because it is proof that we are trying new things. I then began providing teachers with the professional development that they needed on explicit instruction and research-based instructional practices.

As a building leader, it is so important to provide teachers with exactly what they need for professional development. For example, I saw through classroom walkthroughs and observations that the instruction provided in the area of literacy was not explicit and that the vocabulary instruction was not direct, explicit, or systematic, so that is where we began. I provided specific professional development on explicit instruction. What did that look like in the classroom? What did that sound like in the classroom? What did the teachers need to say to their students to make the instruction explicit? Professional development and training on these topics were provided to all teachers and staff members. They readily accepted the new information, because they saw that it was what they needed to implement in their classrooms to make an impact on student learning. They made the connection between where their instruction was at, the professional development provided, and how these changes, if made, could directly impact their students' learning. They received exactly what they needed to make gains in learning.

One way to know what professional development our teachers need is to be in the classrooms observing instruction. We can see through classroom walkthroughs what teachers need and where teachers are struggling. We can also look to our school data to see if there are areas where teachers need specific training. Once the cycle of professional development is in place and teachers see that their new learning impacts instruction, teachers will start requesting specific training on key topics and ideas.

All new learning was backed up with coaching and support so that we would have a successful implementation. Teachers were expected to implement the new learning, and they knew that I would be in their classrooms providing modeling and coaching whenever and wherever they needed it. I would support them throughout the implementation phase. This support was crucial. It helped teachers find the courage to step out and take on the new learning and implement it in their classrooms. A safety net had been provided. I would catch them if and when they stumbled. This was coaching and support, not evaluation. We made this very clear. I was not entering their classrooms to evaluate them or to catch them not doing something. Instead, I was entering to see *how* they were doing with the *implementation* of the new learning. I modeled when necessary, team taught with a teacher when they wanted it, helped develop lesson plans, and did whatever was needed to help the teachers implement what they had just learned through professional development.

It is important to note that I had to be as engaged in the implementation of the professional development as the teachers were. I was learning right along with them. I provided a lot of the professional development, and when I did, I explained to the staff that I was still learning along with them. This was collaboration at its best, because we were all learning with one another and from one another. We built in time to reflect on the professional development and how the implementation was going. Again, during all these conversations, I was coaching and never evaluating.

Whenever someone became effective at implementing a strategy or instructional practice, we all took turns watching that teacher provide the instruction and implement the new practice. We videoed lessons and watched them as a group. I would model in a classroom, have some teachers sit in to watch, and video the lesson so that all staff members could watch it, too. We focused on strengths. We celebrated any and all growth. We talked about what was working well instead of focusing on the struggles. We always brought our discussion back to student learning. Remember, the emphasis must be on the learning instead of on the teaching. Was the professional development being implemented correctly? Was it having an impact on student learning? If not, what would we change about our implementation? When learning is the focus, when students are the focus, it takes the focus off the teacher. They stop seeing it as something they are not doing well. It isn't personal. It is, instead, something that we are doing or changing to have a greater impact on student learning.

## Connect Data and Feedback to Professional Growth

To know if our implementation of professional development was having an impact on student learning, we had to steadily review our data. During our data meetings, we would look for evidence that our instructional practices were making a difference in the lives of the students and having an impact on their learning. If it was having an impact, then we would continue our practices. If our instruction was not having an impact on student learning, then we would make changes to our instruction. During these meetings, I learned the power of teacher collaboration on data and the mighty impact it can have on student learning. This was where the magic happened! We would come together to collaborate and review data, we would discuss why we were getting these results, and we would find the correlation and connection to our professional development.

Teachers saw that, when they implemented a research-based instructional practice with a high effect size effectively, it changed their student data. Their instruction made a difference in their students' learning. Their implementation had made an impact. Seeing their "Aha!" moments was exhilarating! Data meetings became their own kind of professional development. Teachers began to learn from their fellow teachers. We set aside time for purposeful reflection. In the beginning, I facilitated these discussions. Eventually, someone would ask the question, "What did you do in your classroom to get that result?" Others would comment on how large the growth was and ask, "How did you do that?" I knew we were onto something incredibly special when teachers started asking to go watch another teacher teach in their classrooms after seeing growth in that teachers' student data! All of this led to the development of first self-efficacy and then collective efficacy.

Another step to ensuring that there is ongoing professional development for teachers is providing effective feedback. Since we were a small school with limited staff members, I often had to be both principal and instructional coach. I enlisted one of our classroom teachers who was having great success with implementing effective practices to coach her fellow teachers. The two of us worked with teachers on a regular basis. We used the information from John Hattie's (2012) book *Visible Learning for Teachers* to ensure our feedback was intentional and purposeful. We provided feedback on the instructional practices we were focused on at the time. When we were working on posting and sharing clear learning objectives, that was the area we provided feedback on. We told teachers their next step in the teaching cycle to make a greater impact on learning. We would then watch the students' data, especially progress monitoring scores, to see if our feedback was having an impact on the teachers' instruction, which would then impact student learning. Providing feedback on the implementation of professional development throughout the implementation is necessary, and teacher growth is not possible without it. Teachers must know what they are doing well, where they can make improvements, and how they are doing regarding the goal. They must know what their next step is for improving their instruction.

We then took our new mindset about professional growth and connected it to the evaluation system. Teachers had previously seen the evaluation cycle as something that was done to them and not *with* them. Through discussion and reflection on walk-throughs, teachers chose an area of growth they wanted to focus on. My purpose was to provide them with specific feedback to help them make that professional growth. We all took this very seriously, and if their instruction was not improving, then I did not feel that I was successful. Their growth was proof of my impact. Their lack of growth was evidence that I needed to provide them with more information. I strongly believe that the overwhelming majority of struggling teachers, or below average teachers, can become effective teachers with the right development and support.

As leaders, we need to look at the teacher evaluation system as a tool for teacher growth and instructional improvement and not as something done strictly out of mere compliance. It can actually be a tool for professional development. Popping into a classroom three times a year, watching a lesson for thirty minutes, and then completing an evaluation form will never change classroom instruction or impact learning. For real change and growth, it needs to be a collaborative conversation around a clear, common goal.

Having this focus completely changed the way all of us looked at the teacher evaluation cycle. It changed teachers' perceptions and beliefs about an evaluation and helped teachers make significant growth in their instruction and impact on student learning.

## Build Time for Staff Training

Another aspect of professional development that received dramatic changes was our orientation program for new teachers. The further we got into the science of reading and research-based instructional practices, the more information our new teachers needed. The more our staff learned, the more information new teachers would need to learn. We expanded our new teacher orientation to a week instead of a morning session or one full day, as it had been in previous years. During that week, we spent time on the areas that would provide the teachers with the best information for them to go into their new classrooms and have an impact on student learning. A few of the practices we focused on were explicit instruction, engagement, feedback, and developing assessment-capable learners. For example, after implementing a new reading series, we realized that all new teachers would need training on those programs because they missed the original training sessions. This is something we must be aware of and develop an intentional plan for. We then expanded our mentor program and took the most effective teachers and instructional coaches and had them mentor new staff members. Again, this was an intentional plan. Professionally developing new teachers is one of our main priorities as building and district leaders. I always say that this happens due to our leadership or this fails to happen due to our leadership. It is intentional either way.

Finally, I want to discuss scheduling professional development. As educators, we know that our enemy is time; there is never enough of it. Someone could have looked at our daily, monthly, and yearly schedules and said we did not have time for any additional professional development. I probably would have agreed with them, but our data said we had to find the time, so that is exactly what we did. We used common planning time to provide teachers with professional development. We would provide teachers coverage in their classrooms so they could attend a professional development session. We planned sessions before school, after school, during staff meetings, and even on a few Saturday mornings. I share this to say that no matter what, we must provide teachers with the professional development they need so their instruction can have an impact on student learning. We must find the time. I learned that often the best time was right through the school day when the students were learning. The job-embedded professional development had a huge impact on teacher growth and student achievement. Throughout the school year, we used every spare moment we could find for professional development, because we knew it would make the difference in our instruction and student learning.

As building and district leaders, we must never forget that we are the instructional leaders. We lead the growth that happens in our schools and districts. I felt like I earned my teachers' respect by having the knowledge base to walk into their rooms and model effective instruction and provide them with feedback that helped them make gains. When I look back on the role of principal, I readily admit it was one of the hardest jobs I've ever had, but in the very next breath, I always add it was by far the most rewarding work of my career! Success truly is possible for all of us, and professional development is one of the drivers that helps us achieve success for all!

*It's Possible* **When Leaders Believe That:**

- Teachers must leave a professional development session with a specific plan for how to best implement the information in their own classroom.

- The only way to know what professional development our teachers need is to be in their classrooms observing instruction.

- Classroom observations are a time for coaching and support, not evaluation. Observation is for the purpose of seeing how teachers are implementing their new learning.

- Feedback should be intentional, purposeful, and focused on specific instructional practices.

- The teacher evaluation system is a professional development tool for growth and instructional improvement.

- The building and district leader is also the instructional leader who leads the growth that happens in their schools and districts.

Angie understood the importance of professional development—after all, she had been the district's instructional coach for several years before she became a principal. But Angie, prior to becoming a principal, did what so many other principals do (including myself): They assume that because teachers were provided with quality professional development, they will go forth and implement. It wasn't until she became a principal, and long after I became a principal, that we both came to understand that providing professional development is simply the first step.

## An Understanding of the Importance of Ongoing Professional Learning

Throughout this book, we have discussed how moving from one sort of literacy instruction to another is a dramatic shift in more than just teachers' philosophy or the types of professional development you provide to your staff. As I am hoping we have demonstrated, it is a transformation in how the school operates daily. Overall, in a school devoted to 100 percent of students reading at grade level utilizing a structured literacy approach, systemic practices shift. In a structured literacy environment, the system is devoted to data and how every student is progressing toward grade level. Professional learning becomes a part of the fabric of the school. Typically, in bygone years, professional development was determined by the district or school principal and delivered at the beginning of the year in what we describe as a stand-and-deliver model that utilized perhaps a full day or even a two-hour professional development on the intended topic. It was then surmised that the teaching staff would go forth and deliver.

Thankfully, we now know so much more about the best practices that effectuate change within the classroom and that ultimately lead to increased student outcomes. At the same time, teachers and principals are leaving the profession at a faster rate than ever before (Diliberti & Schwartz, 2023). It may feel that as soon as you have a group of educators trained, they leave, find another profession, or go to another school. This creates a huge burden on our system.

Many schools today have instructional coaches in their buildings. An additional person beyond the school leader to assist teachers in shifting practices provides a tremendous advantage as they try to implement literacy change. It also provides teachers with a partner to help them in their teaching skills. For those schools who do not have a coach, it lies on the shoulders of principals to get the job done. When we discuss this principle with district and school leaders, however, we often hear that principals don't coach, they provide feedback. However, instructional interactions with teachers, including feedback, are one of the most powerful instruments a principal can use (Grissom et al., 2021). Not only must the person providing the professional development have a deep knowledge about structured literacy, but they should also be familiar with different types of coaching, particularly those that more rapidly enhance a change of the teaching system. Table 7.1 compares some commonly found ineffective coaching practices to practices that are informed by evidence.

**TABLE 7.1:** Ineffective Versus Effective Coaching Practices

| Practices to Move Away From | Practices That Ensure *It's Possible* |
| --- | --- |
| Coaching is based on teacher reflection. | Coaching is based on student data. |
| Coaching cycles are extended. | Coaching cycles are shorter with defined expectations. |
| Coaching is based on what the teacher would like to do. | Coaching is based on student data. |
| Professional development is based on a menu of teacher choices. | Professional development is based on schoolwide student data and observational trends. |

As you begin or are enhancing a literacy initiative in your school or district, there are four overarching considerations that you must take into account and incorporate into a system of ongoing professional development. The system you set out to create will have limited endurance unless these considerations are a part of your planning.

1. The need for teachers to truly understand how students learn to read

2. The process of implementing effective reading practices in the classroom

3. The ongoing concern of teacher turnover

4. The current lack of knowledge in the area of literacy instruction provided to teachers from universities

As we go forward, we use the terms *professional development* and *professional learning* interchangeably and strongly believe both must be utilized for a system of professional growth to succeed. Although we will use the terms interchangeably here, it is important to note we do believe that it is wise to know the distinction between the two. Your school or district, and what we describe in our definition, relies on both—professional development and professional learning—as being a part of the educators' work setting. A nice distinction of each is provided in *Student Focused Coaching* by Jan Hasbrouck and Daryl Michel (2022). We have taken their distinctive identification and included them in table 7.2.

**TABLE 7.2:** Professional Development Versus Professional Learning

| Professional Development | Professional Learning |
|---|---|
| Specialized training | "Ownership" over "compliance" |
| Formal education | Conversation over transmission |
| Team development | Deep understanding over rules and routines |
| Intended to help educators improve their professional knowledge | Goal-directed over content coverage |

*Source: Hasbrouck & Michel, 2022.*

# Criteria for Creating a System of Ongoing Professional Development

When we support schools and districts in creating a system of ongoing professional development, we define it as the following: *Professional development* is an embedded part of the school or district culture and includes many avenues to increase educator effectiveness, such as workshops, courses, book studies, evaluation, peer mentoring, feedback, and coaching, which ultimately improve literacy achievement. Professional development is aligned to evidence-based principles and instructional practices.

As we work with schools to ensure a quality structure for professional development for their teachers is in place, we guide them by using the criteria found in the domain on professional development at the end of this chapter (page 212). Examine the criteria and think about where you are on each to determine on which area you would like to begin working.

To move the dial in literacy, your long-term professional development plan needs to align with the literacy initiative. There need to be various avenues to accomplish your goals for your literacy outcomes. We have outlined below how to implement the criteria and meet the definition for professional development.

## Establish a Long-Term Vision for Literacy Instruction

Frankly, it isn't enough to say we want to move to a structured literacy approach or embed the findings from the science of reading. The science of reading is a body of research about reading and writing. (Refer to the overview of the science of reading in appendix A, page 253, for a full definition.) Research is ever evolving, and if we are to commit to embracing this body of research and its findings, we must be committed as a school to evolve with the intended outcome of improving literacy gains through evidence-based practices that include prevention and intervention so no student struggles to learn to read. If a school's mission or vision is not to increase literacy outcomes for all students, moving to a structured literacy approach will be to no avail.

In creating a literacy vision, a school must work with their staff to answer questions such as the following.

- Do we believe *all* students can learn to read at grade level?
- If so, how will we get there?
- When will we get there?
- Who will we engage as partners?
- What does reading instruction look like for our varying degrees of learners?
- How do we engage our parents?
- How will we engage our community?
- How will we adapt our plan to ensure no student is left out?

Any system that wants to ensure that all students learn to read must ensure all teachers know how students learn to read. Unfortunately, as of this writing, our universities are woefully unprepared for this task. The NCTQ's (2023a) *Teacher Prep Review* evaluates elementary teacher preparation programs against seven research-based standards that are proven to have the greatest impact on teacher effectiveness and student learning outcomes. One critical standard measured is how universities and colleges across the United States teach reading foundations in their teacher preparedness programs. From 2018 to 2022, the NCTQ analyzed 693 courses from colleges and universities in all fifty states on how reading instruction was taught to future teachers, specifically determining whether incoming teachers were learning to incorporate the five components of literacy instruction as outlined from the science of reading. Discouraging results prevailed. Outcomes of the analysis include the following.

- Only 25 percent of programs adequately address all five core components of reading instruction.
- Over 40 percent of programs are still teaching multiple practices contrary to the research.
- Phonemic awareness receives the least attention across programs.
- One in three programs do not provide any practice opportunities connected to the core components (NCTQ, 2023a).

## Suggested Professional Development Courses for Structured Literacy

- Keys to Literacy
  - ⇨ https://keystoliteracy.com
- Top 10 Tools™ by 95 Percent Group
  - ⇨ www.95percentgroup.com/products/top-10-tools
- LETRS
  - ⇨ www.lexialearning.com/letrs
- Reading Rockets, Reading 101 Learning Modules
  - ⇨ www.readingrockets.org/reading-101/reading-101-learning-modules
- The Reading League Online Academy
  - ⇨ www.thereadingleague.org/online-academy

This indication that colleges and universities are not preparing incoming teachers with the necessary knowledge in how students learn to read implies that the schools and districts must be self-reliant on ensuring that teachers and principals have the adequate professional development on how students learn to read. Fortunately, many states are now requiring that teachers in at least grades K–3 must demonstrate this knowledge and are mandating districts provide this professional development; in some cases, states are providing it themselves.

Numerous programs are now available that provide teachers with this information. The level of complexity in these courses varies, and schools or districts should gauge what depth of knowledge they want their teachers to have. We have found that all teachers do not need to be reading specialists, although some should exist within the building. Some of these programs do just that. When determining who needs the most knowledge, we focus our efforts on ensuring K–2 teachers, instructional coaches, and special education teachers or interventionists have the strongest knowledge. We also suggest that the most expensive is not necessarily the best. When looking at coursework for teachers, we believe you should also consider how attainable it is for all teachers, the collaborative experiences that might be provided through the professional development, and the direct applicability to the classroom setting. See the sidebar for a list of some suggested professional development courses in how students learn to read.

Although these professional development opportunities teach professionals how students learn to read, it is important to note they do not teach teachers or principals how to implement this coursework in their classrooms. The coursework in these programs will provide teachers with the knowledge of how students learn to read, but teachers must still learn how to implement this effectively in their classrooms. (See chapter 2, page 27, on universal instruction.)

The remainder of this chapter will provide you with the big ideas we have found to be highly effective when it comes to deepening the professional learning of all teachers and truly ensuring *it's possible* for all students read on grade level.

## Involve Inexperienced Staff in the Teaching and Learning Culture

As we have discussed, teacher turnover even prior to the pandemic was a vital concern for schools. In a study from 2012–2013, federal statisticians estimated that 8 percent of teachers leave the profession annually and another 8 percent move between schools (Goldring, Taie, & Riddles, 2014). In the RAND Corporation's American School District Panel survey conducted in 2022, researchers found that teacher turnover increased to 10 percent nationally at the end of the 2021–2022 school year. Principal turnover increased too, reaching 16 percent nationally going into the 2022–2023 school year (Diliberti & Schwartz, 2023).

A literacy initiative, or even moving to a structured literacy approach to teaching, is not a one and done event. To ensure 100 percent of students read at grade level, the initiative must also be able to be sustained. This cannot be reliant on one principal or a group of teachers. Understanding the reality of teacher turnover, quality school settings will ensure there is a system in place that provides new teachers in the building, not necessarily just those new to teaching, with structures that ensure they have the skills necessary to get the job done.

Today, it is common practice for most schools and districts to offer mentorships, orientation programs, and teacher teams. Some districts offer everything on this menu. We have found in such situations the robustness of the menu offerings for professional development rarely lead to enhanced teaching skills.

The interview process in schools can be thoughtful, well enacted, and aligned with a structured literacy approach—and still, once hired, the candidates we hoped would form our future dream team may not necessarily hit academic home runs! In our experiences walking into thousands of classrooms, we have found the vast majority of teachers can become above-average educators. Many have simply not had the proper professional learning.

The only way to ensure a new teacher in your building has adequate skills is by observing their teaching. Principals often assume that their new hires have learned the new curriculum by getting support from the teachers down the hall, or by figuring it out themselves. What we see actually happening in most situations is that new teachers are reluctant to ask for help. They don't want to feel like they don't know how to do something, so they use the curriculum or analyze the data as best as they can.

I was once in a school very much steeped in a structured literacy approach. They had two new hires from a local university very much steeped in a balanced literacy approach. Though the instructional coach had provided both teachers with lesson plan templates, reviewed the curriculum, and was assured by the teachers they had it, nine weeks into the school year—as we observed instruction—the kindergarten teacher was leaving out the phonemic awareness and phonics components of the lesson! Though she had been given guidance on what to do, because her training was not in structured literacy, she had no idea of the importance of both the phonics and phonemic awareness components and was simply too embarrassed to say she didn't understand. The students had not had either phonics or phonemic awareness instruction for nine weeks of the school year because the principal or the instructional coach had not taken the time to make ten-minute observations to determine that she had indeed understood.

During the first week of school, the primary job of the principal is to soothe the crying souls of woeful kindergartners and *be present in every classroom*, guaranteeing that the work is getting done! If you are fortunate enough to have an assistant principal or instructional coach, the observations can be divided among you. The clear communication should be that these observations are not evaluative but are to determine who needs help and emphasize we are here to support you. Further, as early in the year as possible, the message from the school leadership should be to convey a message that, in this school, we pride ourselves in reaching a high level of teaching performance so our students thrive. Creating a culture where educators feel free to ask for help is just as important as being able to provide help!

## Base Professional Development on Research, Data, and Teacher Input

If the intent of our professional development offerings and learnings are to change professional practices—as it should be—then we must give our educators the opportunity to practice what they are developing. In a landmark study by TNTP, they found in the districts they analyzed that an average of $18,000 was spent per teacher per year on professional development efforts (Jacob & McGovern, 2015). There is no doubt that districts focus an exorbitant amount of money on increasing teachers' effectiveness. We can assume that with such a vast shift in focus in literacy instruction throughout the United States, a large amount of district moneys earmarked for professional development are geared toward literacy, yet still, only 36 percent of our fourth-grade students are reading at grade level. It should also be noted that, based on that study by TNTP, "the teacher development efforts in the districts we studied are falling short. Most teachers' performance does not appear to improve substantially from year to year, especially after their first few years in the classroom" (Jacob & McGovern, 2015, p. 12). With so much on the line regarding the literacy outcomes for our students, one would hope past professional development practices might adapt to processes more readily aligned to the current research in the area of professional learning and development.

If we are to make serious inroads into how educators teach literacy, then substantially more thought beyond simply providing professional development in structured literacy practices must be used. To make the point even more clear, teacher content knowledge—knowing *how* students learn to read—has an effect size of $d = 0.13$. Yet the craft of how one teaches can have an effect size as large as $d = 0.63$ (Hattie, 2023). By simply taking that content knowledge further and incorporating the research on effective professional development, one can quickly see that *it's possible* all students are learning to read at grade level. They are being taught by highly effective teachers.

The professional development provided to teachers in workshops, courses, and so on is the first step toward effectiveness, but quality professional learning that effectuates student achievement has many more critical elements. A report published by Learning Policy Institute (Darling-Hammond, Hyler, & Gardner, 2017) identifies the following seven characteristics of effective professional development.

1. Is content focused
2. Incorporates active learning utilizing adult learning theory
3. Supports collaboration, typically in job-embedded contexts
4. Uses models and modeling of effective practice
5. Provides coaching and expert support
6. Offers opportunities for feedback and reflection
7. Is of sustained duration

Reflecting on these findings, providing professional development in the content of how students learn to read is simply one of the key characteristics of quality professional development. To be effective, we must also give consideration to ensuring professional development provides teachers with real hands-on opportunities, using their own data to learn about instructional strategies that will enhance the outcomes for the students in their classrooms. It's also advantageous for educators to see what it "looks" like, to see strategies modeled or to watch a video showing a demonstration.

Though we believe it a luxury to have an instructional coach, pairing teachers and watching fellow teachers who have been using a strategy longer or who have developed a quicker knack for a strategy is an excellent way to provide feedback and support. Teachers can't be expected to be experts overnight. They need the opportunity to become good at teaching the content before a school moves onto the next big thing.

Examining students' literacy achievement data can expose a great deal of information regarding how their teachers are teaching and provide trends that lead to the sorts of professional development they may need. Let's use the example in figure 7.2 to illustrate.

| Kindergarten Teacher | Beginning of the Year Outcomes for Letter Naming Fluency | Middle of the Year Outcomes for Letter-Naming Fluency |
|---|---|---|
| Mrs. Wright | 22% proficient | 26% proficient |
| Ms. Dowright | 19% proficient | 32% proficient |
| Mrs. Alwaysdowright | 17% proficient | 52% proficient |

**FIGURE 7.2:** Linking professional development to student's literacy outcomes.

Assuming that the characteristics in this group of three classrooms are similar, one can see that Mrs. Alwaysdowright's students are performing much stronger in letter naming than the other two classrooms. These data should prompt teachers during their professional development team meetings to collaboratively discuss what Mrs. Alwaysdowright is doing differently. Early in the initiative, the desire would be for one of the instructional leaders in the school to facilitate the conversation. The teachers wouldn't be getting such drastically different results if they were all teaching letter naming like Mrs. Alwaysdowright, so obviously, they are not aware. The instructional leader would also set up peer observations, videoing lessons, or modeling lessons, depending on what the teachers thought might be the best next step. Data discussions given the information gleaned from chapter 6 (page 145) can help guide the discussions.

As the literacy initiative progresses and teachers have had the opportunity to participate in conversations with their peers led by their instructional leaders regarding their data, professional learning communities become robust. Before too long, teachers can lead these conversations themselves.

This job-embedded professional development is simply one way to use the data to determine the needs of teachers. Data can also help us to notice grade-level or even schoolwide trends that may need addressing. Another example might be:

> The school leadership team has noticed that, for the past three years, very little gains have been made from beginning of year data to end of year data on oral reading fluency. They decide to take a deeper dive and look at the subskills associated with each. They notice that students are not making growth in phonemic segmentation in grades K–1, nonsense word fluency is stagnant in first and second grades, and accuracy rates actually drop from third to fourth grades with no improvement in fifth grade. They have discovered

*that they have a phonological processing issue schoolwide! They immediately make a plan to ensure there is a schoolwide professional development on the components of teaching phonological processing through the grades and how that varies from grade level to grade level.*

Further, teachers need to have a say within those practices regarding how they feel they are doing and what they need more assistance in developing. In his book *Unmistakable Impact*, Jim Knight (2011) describes that to make an impact, everyone in the school must have a clear understanding of the goal and how to get there. We've taken this one step further and established with schools the idea of creating an *instructional focus* and sharing with the staff. This one-page paper should be laminated and provided to all staff members so they understand what it is they are expected to do. Figure 7.3 is an example of an instructional focus sheet from one of our partner schools in Colorado.

| Sunset Elementary Instructional Focus |
|---|
| **Universal Instruction** |
| **By using the Wonders Program and utilizing the instructional coach, ensure that:** |
| • Teachers demonstrate an understanding that literacy instruction includes both knowledge and skill based procedures. |
| • Balance of knowledge and skill based procedures is based on program requirements and student needs based on data. |
| • Literacy is taught daily in both differentiated whole-group and small-group formats based on students' needs. |
| • Whole-group instruction is taught with fidelity to the core program, and small-group instruction is regularly adjusted (both concept and materials) based on student growth. |
| • Lesson objectives are clear, transferable, and communicated to students in a manner that is understandable. |
| • The student understands and is able to reflect on lesson objectives and demonstrate understanding or mastery. |
| • Technology is used to support or accelerate student learning and is aligned with the instructional focus. |
| • Diagnostic data are used to adjust technology focus. |
| **Data-Based Decision Making** |
| **Strengthen our data dialogues with the help and support of our ELG consultant** |
| • The student understands and is able to reflect on lesson objectives and demonstrate understanding or mastery. |
| • Teacher communicates the lesson objective to the students throughout the lesson. When asked what they are doing and why, the student can readily respond and demonstrate their learning. |

**FIGURE 7.3:** Instructional focus sheet example.

We then utilize our instructional focus to create a survey for teachers, soliciting their input on what they feel they need help with to accomplish the instructional focus so they have a voice in their own professional learning. If a preponderance of teachers need help with the same thing, schoolwide professional development is called for. If only a couple of teachers choose a particular topic, job-embedded professional development is offered to those teachers.

## Provide a Variety of Professional Development Avenues

Using a system such as providing teachers with a survey that aligns with the school's instructional focus honors teachers' professionalism while at the same time keeping the instructional focus focused!

Although we strongly value teachers having a say in their professional learning, steering too far away from your literacy initiative and randomly having topics of learning for teachers will not move the literacy work forward. In that same study examining professional development for teachers, the largest district the authors studied offered more than 1,000 professional learning courses during the 2013–2014 school year (Jacob & McGovern, 2015). Though commendable for their efforts in attempting to provide as much choice as possible, such a process might move the dial on individual teacher skills, but it would not increase the literacy outcomes for a school as a whole.

When schools build a culture around high expectations for professional learning and provide multiple avenues in which to receive professional development, an environment of professional inquiry also begins to permeate throughout the school. Teachers get excited about their own learning. There have been many times in my years as a principal when teachers would excitedly find a professional learning opportunity linked to our instructional focus and meet me in the hall with the information saying, "Can I go to this?" or "Have you read this?" Most often the answer was, "Yes," and I usually went along, too, or read it along with them!

As we think about various avenues for professional development, the last item that may come to mind is that of teacher evaluations. The teacher evaluation system, however, should actually be a driver for professional development. In studies of professional development, the one factor that consistently showed a relationship to teacher growth was an alignment between teachers' perceptions of their own instructional effectiveness and their formal evaluation (Jacob & McGovern, 2015). In other words, when teachers received an evaluation that they felt accurately portrayed their own effectiveness, they were more likely to apply the feedback received in their evaluation to their classroom practices.

There have been multiple studies that demonstrate students benefit academically from sophisticated teacher evaluation structures. Such structures can lead to an increase in reading achievement of gains of 0.10 standard deviations (Steinberg & Sartain, 2015). To effectively evaluate any teacher on their practice of literacy instruction, principals need to have an intense dialogue with faculty members about what constitutes good teaching of literacy. As a result of that dialogue, there should be a shared understanding of what is good practice in literacy instruction. When teachers feel like they belong to a community of continued learning and professional inquiry, quality feedback from the principal both before and after teacher observation becomes innate.

Regrettably, many systems of evaluation in our schools and districts have not caught up with the notion of a structured literacy approach. For the most part, evaluation rubrics still analyze teaching based on a discovery or constructivist approach to learning. When teachers are evaluated on their literacy practices, they need to know exactly what literacy practices their evaluator will be observing for. If the evaluation system does not match the instructional vision of the school, teachers, rightly so, will see their own evaluation as not relevant. It is incumbent on school leaders to make the connections clear for teachers so the evaluation becomes a powerful source of feedback for teachers.

Regardless of your evaluation rubric, the following areas typically contain language that aligns with the teacher effectiveness rubric. To assure alignment to your literacy initiative, focus on the following.

1. Assessment

2. Data-based decision making

3. Engagement strategies

4. Opportunities for practice

5. Differentiation

## Encourage Teachers to Improve Literacy Instruction Through Frequent Observations and Feedback

We all know that principals are overworked, overburdened, over-everything! It's the hardest job I (Pati) ever had, but it was by far the most rewarding! I will also be frank—I hated the work in the office. I came up with every excuse to get in the classroom. If we were low on subs, I was the first one to raise my hand to fill in; if teachers wanted something modeled, I volunteered. I was roaming the halls to ensure all was secure and everyone was in their place. I had a million reasons *not* to be in the office. But that was me. My area of expertise is not completing forms on time, dealing with cranky parents, or arranging the picture schedule! In fact, the more I was in the office, the more I hated my job. My profound distaste for sitting in an office was exactly what propelled me to create systems and structures that kept the school going when I was not in the office.

Today, I see principals who have a hundred reasons not to be in the classroom. It has become particularly glaring since the pandemic. Behavioral issues of students seem to be the most frequent reason for staying in the office. I don't deny that the pandemic created social and emotional issues for our students like we have never seen. The National Center for Education Statistics (2022a) reports that 87 percent of public school leaders agree or strongly agree the pandemic has negatively impacted student social emotional development, and 56 percent of respondents identify classroom disruptions from student misconduct as increasing the most, while another 49 percent of respondents note an increase in acts of disrespect toward teachers and staff. The violence in our society is out of control, but all these concerns are even more of a reason to be in the classrooms! Students feel safer seeing the person in charge out and about. Further, when students know that at any time the principal is going to show up, they behave!

I believe there is another reason principals are glued to their offices. As we shift to a more technical approach to the teaching of literacy—a structured literacy format—principals, who are often the last to be trained in the science of reading, may feel inadequate. Even the principals who have completed coursework in the science of reading can feel inadequate if they don't have the opportunity to apply their new knowledge regularly. Principals everywhere live in fear of a phoneme!

I strongly advocate that principals have solid knowledge in how to teach reading, because fear of a phoneme cannot prevent classroom observations and feedback. In fact, thinking back to what we know about instruction, content knowledge—that knowledge of how students learn to read—has an effect size of $d = 0.09$, while the craft of how we teach can have an effect size as high as 0.63. Further professional development to teachers in how students learn to read does not entail the pedagogical practices of effectively teaching that content; that's implementation (Cunningham, Firestone, & Zegers, 2023)! School leaders should focus on instruction while observing, especially if they feel less confident in the details of the pedagogical practices.

There is strong evidence to indicate that teachers who have observations four or more times per year report a more positive view of their evaluation system, compared to those teachers who are observed less often (NCTQ, 2023a).

## Block Out Time for Classroom Observations

The more well-established systems and structures a school has in place, the more time a principal has for classroom observations. Here are a few tips for finding time in the day to observe in classrooms.

- Ensure you have a systematic, quality, schoolwide behavioral plan in place and that it is adhered to consistently and with fidelity.

- Purchase a large desk calendar and block out a variety of two-hour spots each day on the calendar. Train the front office personnel that during these two-hour spots, you are in classrooms and not to be interrupted unless the superintendent calls or a student is bleeding. Vary the times of the two-hour block each day so that you can observe at different times of the day and see all aspects of teaching and learning.

- If you have an assistant principal, use the same system as in the preceding bullet, but block out different times for each of you.

- Keep a log of the times that you are in particular teachers' classrooms so you can ensure you are seeing all teachers at their high points and low points of their interactions with students. Be sure to visit all classrooms regularly.

- Create a staff committee to organize highly effective systems for yearly and daily operations such as picture day, field day, eye exams, dismissal, and so on. Including staff members ensures various perspectives are heard and generally creates a better system. Once the event is over, take notes immediately for improvement for next year and file them for future reference.

### Recommended Behavior Management Resources

- IRIS Center
  - ⇨ https://iris.peabody.vanderbilt.edu
- Center on PBIS
  - ⇨ https://www.pbis.org
- SEL in the School (CASEL)
  - ⇨ https://casel.org/systemic-implementation/sel-in-the-school
- *Reducing Behavior Problems in the Elementary School Classroom* (Epstein, Atkins, Cullinan, Kutash, & Weaver, 2008)
  - ⇨ https://ies.ed.gov/ncee/wwc/Docs/PracticeGuide/behavior_pg_092308.pdf
- *Seven Steps for Developing a Proactive Schoolwide Discipline Plan, Second Edition* by Geoff Colvin and George Sugai (2018)

- Sit in the front office area and observe the office at off hours—9:30 a.m., 1:15 p.m., and so on. Check the times and people that appear idle and consider reassignments.

- Reduce staff meeting times to once per month by creating a weekly newsletter that communicates administrivia such as duties, instructional tips, assessment updates, meeting times, and so on.

- Develop specific times of the day to return emails. Choosing times prior to teachers and students beginning the day and again after teachers and students have gone for the day can be effective.

When principal observations become part of the norm and provide quality, action-oriented feedback, the observations seem and feel more like coaching and less like evaluation. When teachers respect the knowledge of their instructional leaders, they appreciate the feedback. It bolsters feelings of instructional leadership even further when principals provide the feedback and see it in action on the next observation.

## Provide Ongoing, Job-Embedded Professional Development on Instructional Materials

As we visit schools and observe in classrooms, one of the first glaring inconsistencies we see is the lack of use of quality materials. Even when schools have a quality core program, it often is not being used consistently. In fact, researchers at Harvard University's Center for Education Policy Research found that 89 percent of elementary teachers use their own materials at least once a week (Kane, Owens, Marinell, Thal, & Staiger, 2016). We find this to be a low estimate, and regrettably, many of those materials are selected from Teachers Pay Teachers or Pinterest and are of low quality.

As schools continue to move away from balanced literacy systems and implement new, research-based core reading programs and interventions, there is consideration given to training on that curriculum. But what happens after year one of the new curriculum? Who is responsible for training teachers new to the building or new to using the curriculum after year one? To teach a core curriculum correctly, it's important to remember all incoming teachers will need training in the programs they have been instructed to use. Regrettably, new teachers are most often left to their own devices to figure it out, which creates a huge snowball effect. If teachers attempt to train themselves, and they are not trained in the science of reading, they are likely to leave out critical pieces of instruction. The same is true of the school's intervention program. If we have not established a system for ongoing curriculum training, and 16 percent of our teaching staff turns over yearly, how can we assume our teachers are teaching the curriculum to fidelity? Yet fidelity is critical! Research suggests that teachers' implementation fidelity is a critical lever for improving students' literacy outcomes (Kim & Mosher, 2023). Once teachers have been trained in the use of their curriculum materials, the opportunity for collaborative planning on those materials will heighten their ability for usage. When teachers new to a curriculum were provided with scaffolds and the opportunity to collaborate with their peers for the development of lesson planning, there was an increase in student learning, compared to the teachers who were simply provided the curriculum (Kleickmann, Tröbst, Jonen, Vehmeyer, & Möller, 2016).

Many publishers create core reading programs that may be adapted to either a balanced reading approach or a structured literacy approach, depending on the preference of the teacher. These core reading programs, when following the structured literacy approach, can be more than adequate if a teacher understands what parts of the program they should be teaching and when to enhance the lessons. Using a lesson plan template, such as the one included in chapter 2 (page 27), along with providing teachers with the opportunity for collaborative deep planning time with that template, can create highly effective lessons. The templates become, in essence, a script for what needs to be taught, with teacher input. This system can be a great alternative for teachers who prefer not to use a scripted program. The lesson plan template is the script, while teachers have the autonomy to develop the lesson using both the template and the core program materials.

## Make Professional Development Evident in Classroom Practices and Student Outcomes

The end result of our efforts to increase the professional development of teachers is, of course, the goal that all students are able to read at grade level. It takes time for this to happen. Teachers cannot hone their craft and become experts overnight.

Thinking back to my (Pati's) own experience while a middle school principal, I remember once giving my staff a book to read on engaging student strategies that they could use in their classroom. I had observed many times, in many classrooms, and knew from my observations that students were not engaged in learning. Teachers were lecturing to students. My expectation was for them to read the book and each month select one strategy that they would use. The results were disastrous! Rarely did I see any use of any of the strategies. I was heartbroken, the students were left with a lecture format, and I felt like a failure as a principal. What was missing was my deep understanding of what it takes for professional development to create a change in instructional practices.

A much better line of attack would have been for each department to pick one strategy they would like to try. The instructional coach or myself would model the strategy, teachers would try, and we would observe and give feedback. My teachers should have been given the opportunity to master one skill before moving onto the next. They needed feedback when they did try a strategy. They needed to be able to collaborate with their peers regarding how others used the strategy. As teachers became more adept at both analyzing their data and thinking about the instructional strategies they already knew, this reflection would lead them to begin thinking about what they still might need in their instructional practices. Regardless, my hope of giving teachers a book to read and then thinking I would see engaging strategies across my building was shortsighted, indeed.

A 2007 study conducted by Kwang Suk Yoon, Teresa Duncan, Silvia Wen-Yu Lee, Beth Scarloss, and Kathy L. Shapley found that, to have an even moderate effect size on students' achievement, where $d = 0.54$, the average number of contact hours in professional development was forty-nine. Knowing this, the implications are huge for our schools. Though, as we have mentioned, professional development practices have certainly gotten better, far too often I am still seeing requests for daylong, six-hour, or half-day professional development with the expectation that teachers will learn the new, expected practice in that short time frame. Worse yet, sometimes teachers will receive a book to read and be told, "Pick a strategy and then go forth and use!" This is a great oversimplification of what really needs to happen for classroom practices to change. Professional development takes time and lots of opportunity for practice, feedback, reflection, and collaboration in order for teaching practices—and, therefore, student achievement—to change.

## Align the School's Improvement Plan With Current Data and Professional Development Decisions

In a continual effort of improvement, many states or districts require schools to submit a school-improvement plan indicating the areas within their school in need of improvement, goals the school creates from one year to the next to improve the school, and the improvement strategies they commit to following. In most cases, these improvement plans focus on the areas of mathematics or literacy. It should be a worthwhile effort. Unfortunately, in too many cases, the school does not communicate to their teachers what the goals are within the school-improvement plan or the instructional strategies that need to be used to meet the goal.

Let's suppose instead that the school leadership team works with the principal to create a school-improvement plan that is truly based on the needs of the students and teachers. The teachers have input on what their goals might be, look at the evidence that indicates what areas need to be strengthened, and devise the ways to realize the goal.

If we go back to our instructional focus in figure 7.2 (page 197), after observing all classrooms, the principal in that school could see her teachers were either focusing on comprehension (the knowledge strand of reading) for the majority of the lesson, or phonics (the skills strand of reading) for the majority of the lesson. She knew that for all students to read at grade level, the teachers must fully understand that comprehensive literacy instruction includes both strands of reading at all grade levels. To increase literacy outcomes for her students, she knew she'd have to place a great deal of focus on ensuring her teachers knew this distinction, could apply it in their lessons, and routinely check the data to see if students were advancing in both areas of instruction.

She devised a plan that through the year, or until substantive changes as evidenced through data were apparent in the school, the professional development would be focused on all educators in the school understanding and instructing that specific principle of literacy instruction—that comprehensive literacy instruction includes both the strand of language comprehension and the strand of decoding. You can see from the following graphic that every point of professional learning was aligned with this goal. Figure 7.4 displays the significance of ensuring our efforts are all focused on the same professional learning.

We have talked at depth about focusing our efforts and ensuring our practices are aligned with our goals. That is what it takes for all students to read at grade level. It is the alignment of all our initiatives that ensures *it's possible* for all students to read at grade level.

**FIGURE 7.4:** The impact of an instructional focus.

# The Principal as Instructional Leader

Any discussion regarding professional learning in schools would be remiss if we assumed all schools have an instructional coach or know what to do when they have a coach. It is difficult to track exactly how many schools have someone assigned as an instructional coach, even on a part-time basis. For a variety of reasons, coaches have various titles, and a national data bank estimating the number of schools with access to an instructional coach simply doesn't exist.

When schools do have an instructional coach, it can vastly alleviate a large strain on the principal. Regardless, the principal always remains the instructional leader. The coach supports the facilitation of the instructional leader in accomplishing the instructional vision for the school. It should be noted, "coaches have no power and no authority" (Hasbrouck & Michel, 2022, p. 8).

## Distinguishing the Roles of Coach and Principal

Many of the roles between a coach and principal can become murky, particularly if the separation of the two has not been carefully thought out by each person in those roles. Table 7.3 is a starting point to help a school in clarifying the respective roles of the instructional coach and principal.

**TABLE 7.3:** Defining the Role of Principal and Coach

| Principals | Coaches | Both Principals and Coaches |
|---|---|---|
| • Evaluate teachers on instructional practices<br><br>• Provide action-oriented next steps for instructional practices<br><br>• Know and can model good instructional practices<br><br>• Create systems of support for data-based decision making<br><br>• Lead and participate in data-based decision-making conversations<br><br>• Create school leadership teams<br><br>• Have ready access to all curriculum materials<br><br>• Understand administrators' reports in curriculum and assessments<br><br>• Know and understand the lesson block framework<br><br>• Suggest possible teacher study groups<br><br>• Attend instructional coaches' workshops<br><br>• Contact family for instructional concerns<br><br>• Identify and address grade-level, department, or schoolwide concerns<br><br>• Refer teachers to the coach<br><br>• Work with staff to develop the instructional vision of the school | • Support teachers in instructional practices<br><br>• Provide coaching cycles<br><br>• Model and co-teach instructional practices<br><br>• Collaboratively create next steps for instructional practices<br><br>• Support in the creation of systems for data-based decision making<br><br>• Participate in data-based decision-making conversations<br><br>• Are members of school leadership teams<br><br>• Are authorities on curriculum materials<br><br>• Help teachers organize and manage curriculum materials<br><br>• Help teachers with logins, understanding reports and resources in assessment and curriculum<br><br>• Facilitate and assist teachers in lesson planning<br><br>• Facilitate teacher study groups<br><br>• Provide workshops on instructional strategies<br><br>• Build relationships with teachers to induce further coaching work<br><br>• Organize assessments | • Support teachers in instructional practices<br><br>• Observe classrooms<br><br>• Provide instructional feedback<br><br>• Develop and plan professional development opportunities for various teacher teams<br><br>• Develop a culture of trust and collaboration<br><br>• Know and can model good instructional practices<br><br>• Know the research and reasoning on instructional decisions<br><br>• Know and interpret assessment information<br><br>• Fill in for a substitute as a last resort<br><br>• Are aware of local, state, and federal rules, regulations, and policies<br><br>• Facilitate the instructional vision of the school |

Frankly, the roles of both instructional coach and principal are tremendous. We hope this comparison will help teachers understand to whom they should go for what, and that it will help all parties.

# School Spotlight
## Davis School District, Farmington, Utah

In our work revamping literacy, we have realized that coaching benefits our district at every level. None of us are experts in every area of instruction. Teacher assistants can benefit from guidance on interventions they are providing students. Teachers can be coached in scientifically researched teaching practices for specific subject areas. School leaders can learn how to provide more useful and helpful feedback to all their teachers. Even as district leaders, charged with managing a major shift across our large, suburban district, we have benefited from having a coach who has been in our shoes making similar changes. The guidance we have received has helped us focus on the factors that matter the most in shifting our literacy practices: (1) universal instruction, (2) interventions, (3) assessment, (4) school leadership, (5) professional development, and (6) data-based decision making. Had we not sought coaching from someone who had led this type of change in a school/district, it would have taken us many years to narrow down the areas on which we needed to focus our efforts.

Early on, we focused our professional development on the literacy coaches who were in our sixty-three elementary schools; and we believed that by educating the literacy coaches, we would be growing each school's practice around the science of reading. However, the outcomes in schools did not change! Literacy coaches did not have the supervisory influence to expect and inspect the changes required from educators. Though providing professional development to principals on the science of reading is not new in our district, we now ensure their monthly professional development is tailored specifically to what they should be observing in classrooms. We also provide associated principal support materials, such as planning guides. School leaders receive monthly assignments around their learning that we check in on at the subsequent month's training. Literacy coaches are then taught what the principals learned and the upcoming assignment so they can support their administrators in their own growth in becoming science of reading instructional leaders. Our strongest efforts are now placed on building administrators, with literacy coaches in a supporting role.

The next major change around professional development was shifting the focus of literacy coaches to Tier 1 instruction, as historically our coaches focused on the intervention space, which had not led to increased proficiency or growth in our district. From Joyce and Showers (2002), we know the likelihood that an educator will put something into practice without ongoing coaching and administrator support is close to 0 percent, but with the coach and administrator's support, the likelihood of implementation is 95 percent. Not seeing a literacy coach as a catch-all type of position is still hard for many. Becoming coaches who link arms with educators to do the hard thinking together, rather than cheerleaders, friends, or teacher's assistants, has proved challenging for administrators, coaches, and teachers. The rewards, however, have been tenfold. Many coaches who were unsure of their abilities in a grade level are now courageously jumping into the unknown with teachers. Teachers who believed coaching was only for educators on a plan have opened themselves up to coaching with the understanding that coaching is the best professional development they have ever received. Together with coaches, school leaders, and district leaders, we have built science of reading knowledge and competency, we have built teaching capacity, and, finally, we have built confidence.

*Belinda Kuck, Director of Teaching and Learning*
*Julie Barlow, Humanities Section Director*
*Angie Morales, English Language Arts Coordinator*

## Providing Action-Oriented Feedback

Many schools simply do not have an instructional coach. Prior to being the principal, Angie had been the district's instructional coach, meaning each school received her services for one day a week. When Angie began her principalship, she quickly realized that for her teachers to make gains, and for all students to read at grade level, she had to provide feedback and coach her teachers every day. She couldn't wait for the arrival of the district's instructional coach one day per week.

Principals have a grand opportunity to provide instructional feedback to teachers in the following situations.

- After observations
- With feedback and coaching
- During data-driven instructional PLCs
- In informal conversations
- Through evaluations

Remember, no principal should fear a phoneme. To help principals hone their skills, we have created table 7.4, which outlines the topic for feedback and resources principals can access to hone their skills in these areas to be a true instructional leader!

Many principals who have no experience in the teaching of reading have become excellent instructional leaders. Good instruction is good instruction. *It's possible* that all students read at grade level when all teachers are providing high-quality instruction because of ongoing feedback and coaching. Teachers respect principals who are instructional leaders.

As we mentioned earlier, it is often the teachers performing below average who do not want coaching. When teachers are reluctant to improve their skills, and data and observations indicate that students are not making gains, the principal must step up to the plate and provide action-oriented feedback after observations.

Figure 7.5 (page 210) is an example of an email from a principal to a teacher following a casual observation. This teacher had refused to work with the coach when directed and was in a school that offered multiple avenues for professional learning. The principal had met with the teacher numerous times to talk about her expectations for using the core reading program and aligned materials.

**TABLE 7.4:** Helpful Resources for Principals and District Leaders

| To Provide Feedback, It's Important to . . . | Suggested Resources and Ideas |
| --- | --- |
| • Understand the components of reading across grade levels<br>• Understand implications for universal instruction and interventions | • Literacy Professional Development—Keys to Literacy (https://keystoliteracy.com)<br>• Top 10 Tools for Teachers On-Demand Webinar: Top 10 Tools (www.95percent group.com/on-demand-improving-instructional -practices-with-top-10-tools)<br>• Reading Rockets Reading 101: Self-Paced Learning Modules \| Reading Rockets (www.readingrockets.org/reading-101 /reading-101-learning-modules)<br>• The Reading League Online Academy—The Reading League (www.thereadingleague.org/online-academy) |
| • Understand the layout of a quality literacy block | • Instructional hierarchy of skills<br>• Alignment of skills<br>• Length of time for each skill based on grade levels<br>• The layout and components of the curriculum are being used<br>• Following the scope and sequence of the designated curriculum<br>• Teaching the critical components<br>• Logins to teacher resources<br>• Lesson plan templates<br>• Core programs pacing guide<br>• See chapter 2 (page 27) for a further description of each of these elements; use as a framework when you are making observation |
| • Understand explicit and systematic instruction | • The explicit instruction observation sheet provided in chapter 2 (page 47) |
| • Be able to dissect and analyze teacher literacy data and possible next steps | • Technical manual of the assessment being used in chapter 6 (page 145) |

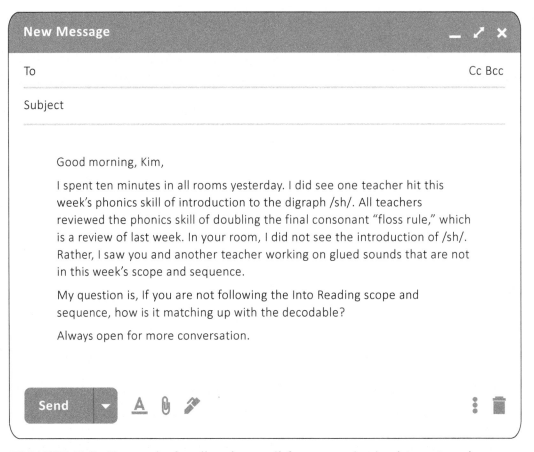

**New Message**

To                                                                              Cc Bcc

Subject

Good morning, Kim,

I spent ten minutes in all rooms yesterday. I did see one teacher hit this week's phonics skill of introduction to the digraph /sh/. All teachers reviewed the phonics skill of doubling the final consonant "floss rule," which is a review of last week. In your room, I did not see the introduction of /sh/. Rather, I saw you and another teacher working on glued sounds that are not in this week's scope and sequence.

My question is, If you are not following the Into Reading scope and sequence, how is it matching up with the decodable?

Always open for more conversation.

Send

**FIGURE 7.5:** Example feedback email from a principal to a teacher.

## Suggested Resources on the Topic of Professional Learning

- *The Art of Coaching: Effective Strategies for School Transformation* by Elena Aguilar (2013)

- *Student Focused Coaching: The Instructional Coach's Guide to Supporting Student Success Through Teacher Collaboration* by Jan Hasbrouck and Daryl Michel (2022)

- *Taking the Lead: New Roles for Teachers and School-Based Coaches, Second Edition* by Joellen Killion and Cindy Harrison (2017)

- *The Impact Cycle: What Instructional Coaches Should Do to Foster Powerful Improvements in Teaching* by Jim Knight (2018)

- Learning Forward, https://learningforward.org

This email is able to convey several messages. Clearly this principal is an instructional leader who knows the curriculum and understands what teachers should be teaching. (It's actually a first-year principal who received leadership coaching for just three months!) It also supports the school's initiative of increased literacy outcomes for all students, as well as the expectations of high-quality instruction by all.

If you are a building principal who has never had coaching experience, the following are some big ideas to get you started.

- Follow up with a feedback conversation the day of observing or the following day.

- Try to keep your tone informal.

- Ask follow-up questions so teachers may share more information and reflect on their lesson.

- Based on the situation, offer:

  ⇨ Praise

  ⇨ Reinforcement

  ⇨ Suggestions—not criticism

# Summary

Currently, teacher preparation programs in our universities are failing to address the research on how students learn to read. Districts must therefore create a system of ongoing professional development to assure teachers and administrators receive this knowledge. It is estimated that up to 16 percent of teachers leave their schools each year. The prevalence of ongoing professional learning to enhance teacher skills and therefore student outcomes must be a built-in part of the instructional system. Professional impact will make an undeniable difference when there is an aligned system of professional learning. Student data, school achievement trend data, observational data, teacher preference, and evaluation should all point in the same direction. Principals observing classrooms and providing feedback to teachers is a critical step in altering the teaching practices of all teachers. Principals should always be the instructional leaders of their school, whether a coach exists or not. It is the role of the instructional leader to work with the staff to create a literacy vision for students where all means all.

It is important teachers feel that a literacy initiative is not being done *to* them, but rather being done *with* them. In chapter 8, we lay out the systems and structures that will ensure the teachers—those doing the work in the classroom—have a say in the initiative. We also include the domain of collaboration, which describes the systems and structures necessary to create a collaborative school culture.

# Professional Development

Professional development is an embedded part of the school or district culture that includes many avenues to increase educator effectiveness, such as workshops, courses, book studies, evaluation, peer mentoring, feedback, and coaching, which increase literacy achievement. Professional development is aligned to evidence-based principles and instructional practices.

| Big Idea | Basic (1) | Effective (2) | Proficient (3) | Exemplar (4) |
|---|---|---|---|---|
| A long-term vision for literacy instruction is in place for the school or district. | Professional development has been provided to educators regarding how students learn to read. | The professional development provided to teachers is aligned with the literacy vision and increased student outcomes. | The literacy vision is regularly reviewed and updated to reflect the current situation that is based on student data. | The systems and structures for sustaining the literacy vision are in place, and revisions to the structures are ongoing and reflective of current needs. |
| There is a structure in place that ensures inexperienced staff are equipped to become a part of the teaching and learning culture. | New staff receive orientation from the school/district and ask for help from colleagues when needed. | School leadership (may include the coach) are able to identify who is needing more support and time and make sure both are allocated sufficiently. | There is consistent follow-up with new educators to the building, and support is provided to ensure there is fidelity to intended implementation. | There is ongoing communication in place between school leadership and educators' support (such as IC) so that a continual cycle exists to determine growth and needs of inexperienced staff. |
| Decisions for professional development are based on research and data and are made with a collaborative, representative process through the work of the school leadership team. | Professional development decisions are made by the school administrators using data but may not address the root cause of underachievement. | The school leadership team (SLT) has a role in selecting professional development, using data to determine the needs of staff and students. | The SLT recommends professional development based on feedback from grade level teams. Data and trends are used to determine professional development. | Professional development is aligned to research and data, is sustained until professional mastery is attained, and is aligned to grade-level or school goals. |
| A variety of professional development avenues exist to meet the needs of staff and ensure sustainability of the literacy vision. | All educators receive the same professional development on a topic relevant to the school. | Job-embedded professional development is provided that is student centered and based on the needs of the instructor and students. | There are options for professional development that meet the needs of staff based on their data, interest, and observational trends. | Professional learning is continuously analyzed, aligns with the teacher evaluation system, and is collaborative in nature. |

*Page 1 of 2*

| Big Idea | Basic (1) | Effective (2) | Proficient (3) | Exemplar (4) |
|----------|-----------|---------------|----------------|--------------|
| **School leaders regularly encourage teachers to improve instruction regarding literacy after observing frequently and providing specific feedback.** | School leaders have a strong understanding of good literacy instruction. | School leaders observe literacy instruction regularly and provide timely feedback. | Feedback and professional next steps are aligned to teacher and school goals and teacher evaluation. | Leadership routinely observes to ensure feedback and continual instructional improvement is effectuating classroom change. |
| **Teachers receive ongoing, job-embedded professional development on the instructional materials used for all three tiers of instruction as relevant to each teacher's usage.** | Initial training is provided for all instructional materials to relevant staff. | Follow-up support is provided as needed, and every year, new teachers are trained on materials by a highly qualified person. | Implementation is strengthened throughout the school year. Strategies learned are observed in classroom instruction. | Teachers are fluent with the use of programming and materials and know how to embed evidence-based instructional strategies into the program as needed. |
| **Professional development is evident in classroom practices and student outcomes.** | Classroom practices and data are considered when selecting professional development. | Teachers are able to master newly acquired skills and strategies before new professional development is provided. | Teachers use student data to reflect and to determine their own professional development. | Teachers are able to self-reflect on implementation of practices and adjust instructional practices as needed. |
| **The school's improvement plan reflects current data and professional development decisions are aligned.** | The school's improvement is generic in nature regarding improved literacy outcomes. | Professional development is aligned to the goals outlined in the school's improvement plan. | The school's improvement plan goals are shared with the staff, and the staff understand the improvement vision. | Professional development leads to increased student outcomes as indicated in the school-improvement plan. |
| **Structures are in place for providing ongoing, job-embedded professional development for inexperienced staff members.** | Inexperienced staff members receive initial orientation to school and school structures. | Support staff are able to identify teachers needing the most support (that is, new teachers) and allocate their time appropriately based on teacher needs. | Consistent coaching and follow-up are provided to ensure fidelity of implementation. | A collaborative process is developed where teacher and coach/administrator are consistently able to work together to determine growth and needs. |

*Page 2 of 2*

# Collaborating Through Shared Leadership

## The Principal's Perspective

*By Angela Hanlin*

As educators and school leaders, we do not have to have all the answers to every single problem. Collaboration becomes the best way to solve problems and direct the work of the school. Collaboration is key! Collaboration is more than just coming together, however. It is about coming together to do the right work in the best way to live out the mission of the school. In this book, we are discussing the mission of ensuring that *all* students read at grade level, and to do that, there must be a strong system of collaboration throughout the building and a strong sense of teamwork.

To ensure that all students are reading at grade level, all team members must be committed to the work and be willing to do whatever it takes to ensure reading growth for all. That does not happen overnight, and it takes intentional planning and focus to build a culture where the work can be done. Through establishing collaboration and team structures, we as school leaders have the greatest opportunity to build trust and set the foundation for the work to be built on.

When I began my journey as an elementary principal, I quickly realized that there was a lack of trust in the building, which is often the case in low-performing schools. Teachers trusted neither the school nor district leaders nor each other. If we were going to be able to embrace the reality of where we were and work together to create change, then we would have to trust one another. Teachers cannot experience true collaboration if they do not trust their fellow staff members, so developing trust was the foundation of our work. To do that, we had to change a lot of the existing practices. We had to create a safe environment where teachers could express their weaknesses, celebrate their growths, and problem solve to find ways to reach every single learner.

## A Mindset for Collaboration

Staff members first had to be able to trust me as their leader. I began by being open and honest about the work. It was not going to be easy, but we could reach our goals if we all worked together. I was honest about the data and where we were as a team. The data were hard to accept and were a painful realization, but we had to accept the data to make gains and change the number of students who were reading at grade level. I had to be transparent. I informed them of the data, the growth, the expectations, the accountability, the celebrations, the vision, the mission, the next steps, and the purpose for everything that we did. In an effort to be transparent, all information was shared with all staff members. I had to be reliable. They had to know that they could count on me when they needed me. With time, I was able to earn their trust.

Trust is so important in this work. Our teams must see us as leaders who will do whatever it takes to help students reach their goals and help teachers become the most effective they have ever been. Our teams must see us as instructional leaders—leaders who have the vision and goals to help the team get where they need to be and who are deeply committed to the work. Leaders who have the courage to hold everyone accountable to the work. Leaders who will have the difficult discussions when problems arise. When teachers see us in that light, they develop trust in us and our leadership, and they, too, become committed to the work.

The teachers also needed to be able to trust one another. If they could not trust each other, then they would never feel safe enough to share their struggles or ask others for guidance. We had to be open and honest about the past and what had led us to this point. Part of their lack of trust was from not working as a united team on a common goal. The teachers had been in separate silos and did not collaborate around a common plan and collective goal, and teachers had viewed some previous collaboration efforts as a waste of time. I made the promise and commitment that our collaboration would have a purpose and make a difference, and that I would hold everyone accountable to do the work.

Teachers' mindset around collaboration had to be changed, too. Yes, they needed to see it as useful and a way to solve problems, but they also needed to see it as something other than a griping session or blaming zone. Some staff members saw data meetings as a time when they would be blamed for failing to meet the needs of their students. We simply could not have that belief and mindset if we were going to reach all students, so I developed a motto for our staff, wrote it on poster board, and displayed it in the data room. Our motto was, "It doesn't matter about the PAST! What matters is NOW! No blaming! Only fixing! This is URGENT!" I began every meeting by saying that motto and often had to gently remind staff members of it in the beginning of our work together. Our environment had to become an area of no blaming and no shaming. It needed to be a safe zone where all staff members could express their feelings and receive the help they needed to reach their students. And with our data the way they were, we absolutely had to develop a sense of urgency!

## Assemble a Team to Lead the Work

There was absolutely no way that I, as the building leader, could do this work by myself. We needed a team of people to collaborate with and help guide the work.

Our first process was to develop a school leadership team and establish professional norms for our meetings. We chose teachers who were seen as building leaders from each department or grade band to serve on the school leadership team. For example, we chose one teacher from grades K–2, one from grades 3–5, a special education representative, someone to represent interventions, and the building principal. We chose individuals who were honest, open, trustworthy, and committed to the work. The team met monthly to solve problems within the building, set goals, determine next steps, and constantly evaluate where we were regarding reaching our goals. We worked as a team to set professional norms and meeting norms. We asked ourselves, How we would like to be treated in a meeting? What would we need to do to best work together as a team? We took the answers to those questions and used them to create norms for each meeting.

The first thing our school leadership team did was set a schedule for all meetings for the entire year and share that with all staff members. By doing that, people could plan ahead and ensure they could be present for the meeting. We assigned roles for the meetings. We chose a facilitator, a timekeeper, a note taker, and a snack provider, and we chose to hold all meetings in the data room so we could easily review our data and progress on a regular basis. We developed an agenda that would be used for each meeting. The norms were placed at the top of each agenda. The agenda was shared with team members and all staff members prior to the meeting so people could share ideas for agenda items. The final agenda would be approved prior to the meeting, and the facilitator brought copies to the meeting. In the beginning of our process, I was the main person who added items to the school agenda because I had developed the comprehensive school-improvement plan and was working with Pati to lead the work. After several months, and once teachers really began to understand and trust this process, they began to submit items for the agenda.

It took some work to fully develop the meeting process. We had a lot of work to do in a short amount of time, so we had to be prompt and decisive. Having a timekeeper definitely helped our meetings stay focused and keep us on topic. School leadership team members quickly realized that they were making decisions for the good of the entire school, and that would mean that they would not always get their way. Having a voice in the process did not mean the same thing as having ultimate control. We had to learn how to disagree respectfully and make a decision that was best for the entire school. We had to remind ourselves often of the goal and that every decision we made was to help us reach proficiency for all. We chose to vote on meeting ideas using thumbs-up or thumbs-down. Once a decision was made, we had to not only support that decision but also share it with the rest of the staff members.

Minutes were taken during each meeting and were then shared with building staff members within twenty-four hours of the meeting. Ideas that were developed in the school leadership team meetings were shared with all staff members during the monthly staff meeting. The beauty of this process is that ideas were shared by members of the team to members of the faculty. The information was presented by their peers and not by me, the building principal. The school leadership team members were bold in their decisions and were strong leaders when they shared the decisions with the rest of the faculty members. We were a united front with a common goal and were dedicated to the work we were doing.

I grew to love this team and the process so much! I cannot imagine leading a building without a school leadership team. Developing teams for collaboration made the work structured and systematic. Each month, we repeated the exact same process. It put all of us on the same page. When a problem came up, it was placed on the agenda for the next month's meeting. The team became a strong, reliable force to solve problems and direct the work. I was not in this process alone! I had the support of a team that would do whatever it took to get the job done. They would also strongly show their support for initiatives and speak with staff members who were not completely bought in at first. Our teamwork changed the dialogue in the building! Teachers began discussing problems as opportunities for growth. Meetings became problem-solving sessions. The team helped establish trust between everyone in the whole building. This was not a team of the principal's favorites or a private club that met after school. This was a team of people who would work diligently to help our building reach the goal we were striving daily to achieve, and that was reading success for all. The presence of a school leadership team builds trust and promotes growth for all!

School leadership teams also grow great leaders! In the beginning, I facilitated most meetings. Once the team members fully understood the process, different members of the team facilitated different items or sections of the agenda. Eventually, we got to a place where a member of the team could completely facilitate the meeting, and where one of the team members was able to develop the agenda and send it out to staff members. With this team, we were able to grow our own school leaders. When I left Matthews Elementary to take on a superintendent position in another school district, a member of the team became the next principal. Honestly, any member of that team could have stepped into the role of building principal, because they all had all the necessary components to be a successful school leader.

## Collaborate on Schoolwide Goals and Initiatives

We used the school leadership team to consistently review our data and set goals for the building and each grade level. Setting goals was intimidating work in the beginning. We had no idea what we were capable of achieving by the end of the school year, because we simply had not done this work before. Our mindset was that goals needed to be set high and needed to be challenging, but Pati pointed out that goals also needed to be attainable. In all honesty, we felt like we were just taking our best guess at middle of year and end of year goals in the beginning. After doing this work for a few years, we learned more about goal setting and what was reasonably acceptable growth from one benchmark to another. The goals were then shared with everyone and displayed throughout the building for all to see. Our process was to review beginning of year benchmark data and use it to set middle of year and end of year goals. We would review our progress monitoring data on a regular basis to see if we were on pace to reach our goals. We would ask ourselves these questions when reviewing the data: Which students made growth? Why? Which students did not make growth? Why? How close are we to reaching our goal? What are we going to do in response to the data? Goals were shared with everyone in the building. We revisited the goals during each time of collaboration.

In addition to setting building goals, the school leadership team took on many other tasks to improve the school. One of the biggest, most important tasks we worked on was developing the master schedule. It had many flaws, so it was a major undertaking. Again, I am so thankful; multiple heads are better than one, and I did not have to solve this problem by myself. I was shocked to learn that building teachers had never been involved in the process of developing the master schedule. They had never had the opportunity to provide suggestions or tweak their schedule. I thought this was odd, because it was their schedule, and surely, they had ideas to make it run most efficiently and effectively. The schedule was not efficient or effective in the beginning, and this was a serious problem. We were losing instructional minutes in several spots throughout each school day. When added together, it was staggering to see the number of instructional minutes lost in a week, month, and school year. Our mission was to maximize instructional minutes, and that was the mindset we had throughout our work on the master schedule. We were constantly reflecting on our work and practices and made whatever changes were necessary to reach the highest level of success. Each improvement made us stronger. The school began to run like a well-oiled machine! I will never forget the day when I stood in the hallway and observed every single person in the building being where they were supposed to be and doing exactly what they were supposed to be doing! I immediately called Pati to celebrate.

There were other opportunities for collaboration in addition to the school leadership team. Teachers had common planning periods where they met to review data and plan lessons and upcoming instruction. Data meetings became a great time for collaboration. Weekly progress monitoring meetings turned into problem-solving sessions for our struggling learners. We would brainstorm ways to address each learner who was not making progress. Each meeting had a purpose, a plan, an expectation, and an agenda.

During all this work, I learned the power of collaboration and the impact it can have on our school data. First, we cannot truly collaborate without reviewing data. We must come together to review data to know where we are, how our students are performing, and how close we are to reaching our goals. We cannot successfully analyze data and plan instruction and interventions to reach every single learner without collaboration. To reach every learner and develop every learner into a proficient reader, we must have opportunities for collaboration and ensure that the time spent collaborating makes an impact on student learning. All of this is set up by the building and district leaders. We must look for and schedule times for collaboration throughout the building and school district. We must set a purpose for the collaboration, and teachers must leave that time together with something they will take into their classroom to impact their students' learning. This is continuous work that never stops. Collaboration is necessary, powerful, and can be one of the systems that enables all students to read at grade level.

## *It's Possible* When Leaders Believe That:

- To ensure that all students read at grade level, there must be a strong system of collaboration throughout the building and a strong sense of teamwork.

- Trust must be the foundation of true collaboration.

- Developing a school leadership team for collaboration makes the work structured and systematic.

- The presence of a school leadership team builds trust and promotes growth for all.

- Every decision made is to help achieve the goal of reaching proficiency for all.

A change in literacy practices can be mandated by a building leader, a district, or even a state or province. But, if your intent truly is to ensure all students read at grade level, then all teachers in the building must be on board.

Angie was a stellar principal, but when she started at Matthews Elementary, her teachers had been left without guidance for many years. They didn't even know they were a designated focus school! They were outraged. *They* believed that every student could read at grade level, and further, they wanted everyone to know they were not a focus school staff. Even under those circumstances, however, not all staff members fervently bought in.

To ensure that all students are reading at grade level, all teachers must be willing to do what it takes to get them there. There must be a schoolwide sense of urgency. Eventually, by year three of Angie's mission, parents from other nearby towns and other school districts were driving their students to Matthews Elementary School to enroll. Parents want their students to be in schools where every student counts and where the staff will do whatever it takes to ensure their student is receiving the best education. Word got out fast that Matthews Elementary was that school.

# An Understanding of Collaboration

No one single teacher nor one single principal can move 100 percent of students to read at grade level, but a collective group of teachers and a principal can. Colleagues collaborating is key! Without collaboration, urgency means nothing. In fact, in his report *What Works Best in Education: The Politics of Collaborative Expertise*, John Hattie (2015) states, "the greatest influence on student progression in learning is having highly expert, inspired, and passionate teachers and school leaders working together to maximize the effect of their teaching on all students in their care" (p. 2).

We hear school leaders talking about collaboration as if it's common practice. Indeed, many, many schools have professional learning communities where teachers do spend time together collaborating. But the collaboration is often on the wrong thing. Collaborating on the wrong work and engaging with the wrong student information will not have a positive impact on student achievement (DuFour & Marzano, 2011). When 36 percent of students are reading at grade level, collaborating on the wrong work is a waste of teacher time and only prolongs students not reading at grade level.

Schools create teams of collaboration, or professional learning communities, and tell the teams, Good luck, make haste, and improve our students' achievement through your collaboration! Yet many professional learning communities are left to their own devices and don't necessarily know what to collaborate on or about. Individual teachers can indeed raise the literacy outcomes for students in their own classrooms, but the intent is to raise the outcomes for all students. Therefore, "[To] ensure all students learn at high levels, *educators must work collaboratively and take collective responsibility for the success of each student*" (DuFour, DuFour, Eaker, Many, & Mattos, 2016, p. 11). We define *collaboration* as:

> *Teachers and grade-level teams have time to discuss and analyze student data, plan lessons, and engage in professional collaborative dialogue. Shared*

*leadership is in place by an active school leadership team, with the result of establishing a positive organizational climate and shared decision making. The school leadership team serves the purpose of leading the school's efforts to increase student achievement, determine professional development, and discuss building resources and practices of improvement. Representation consists of various grade levels and departments and an administrator.*

After working with hundreds of schools and reading countless books and research on collaboration, we have identified four key factors to collaboration. When combined with the outcome of moving all students to reading at grade level, in a structured literacy approach, these factors seem to be the key. We call them the four Ts of collaboration: (1) teams, (2) targets, (3) trust, and (4) time.

Both trust and time are significant factors in building a culture of collaboration, and we elaborate on each of these further in this chapter. The domain rubric on collaboration, found at the end of this chapter, ensures that schools are using efficient and effective practices in the area of teams and targets.

As indicated in the domain of collaboration located at the end of this chapter (page 244), school success is highly dependent on teachers working together. In schools, collaboration is often done through various teams and committees. The following discusses why teams are so critical and how they might be enhanced to support increased literacy outcomes.

# Teams

I have provided many a professional development to school leaders and routinely ask them to write down the number of committees or teams they have going on in their school. I have learned not to be shocked when school leaders come up with a list of committees in the double digits, often as high as twenty! How can you focus and lead with that many committees and teams going on? How can you possibly know what that many committees or teams are getting done? Are all twenty teams working toward the vision the school leadership has set out? Or, are most of those twenty teams simply there because of tradition? We've had that team, so we just keep having that team.

School committees and teams are much like classroom curricula. Teachers have their favorite literacy unit to teach—like *Charlotte's Web*—so they keep teaching it. Teachers and school leaders also have their favorite committees to attend. They plan the same school activities year after year. We suggest that, unless a committee or team is working toward progressing the goal—in this case, literacy—the committee or team should be abandoned. We've talked about precious time in schools. No teacher or building administrator has time to serve on a committee or team unless it is moving the ball forward. Each grade level in your school should have a data team, or a PLC collaborative team, devoted to data analysis. The school leadership team is the other committee that is essential for a literacy initiative.

## Efficient Team Practices

We couldn't agree more with Richard DuFour, Rebecca DuFour, Robert Eaker, Thomas W. Many, and Mike Mattos (2016) when they write that "the fundamental purpose of the school is to ensure that all students learn at high levels" (p. 11). If you have not, we strongly suggest reading the book, *Learning by Doing: A Handbook for Professional Learning Communities at Work, Fourth Edition* (DuFour et al., 2024). The authors note that, beyond the tremendous number of teams that many schools have, another barrier to efficient teams is the avoidance of productive conflict (DuFour et al., 2016). We have been in many schools where staff and even the principal say, "We have this committee because we have been doing it this way forever, but it isn't the most productive." As DuFour and colleagues (2016) state, "Dysfunctional teams prefer artificial harmony to insightful inquiry and advocacy" (p. 71). Leaders help teams become more efficient and productive by setting the stage and modeling vulnerability with meaningful disagreements, articulations of public commitments, a willingness to confront those who honor the decisions of the school teams, and an unrelenting focus on and accountability for results (DuFour et al., 2024).

As we have stated, there is not enough time in schools for any of it to be wasted. Educators are professionals who have families and obligations outside of the school, and their time needs to be respected, too. Therefore, if we want teachers to take the time to be on committees, we need to honor their time during committees.

School leadership teams or data team meetings should be scheduled at the beginning of the year, placed on the school calendar, and held sacred unless there is an emergency. The time and place of the meetings should also be determined and shared with all members at the beginning of each school year. This simple task allows educators to know what their obligations are and when their obligations will take place so they can make personal arrangements if their attendance is after or before work time. Scheduling all meetings at the beginning of the year sets a sense of urgency and importance so no one is left guessing and tracking down where the meeting is, watching the clock for fear they need to pick up their own children, or any other task that will prevent them from being mindfully present during the meeting.

To run efficiently, all teams need to utilize agendas or protocols. Explicit protocols for collaboration allow the collaborative work to be more systematic and increase teams' effectiveness (Gallimore, Ermeling, Saunders, & Goldenberg, 2009). I particularly like the idea of a common and consistent protocol for each, as I view a protocol as a treaty of sorts. A protocol should serve as a common view among all parties that is written down and used to hold all members of the team accountable. In chapter 6 (page 145), we went into depth regarding what data a data team should be looking for at each of the grade levels as well as a common protocol for data team or grade-level team meetings after benchmarking. We will focus our efforts here on collaboration through shared decision making. Specifically, we will focus on the school leadership team.

## School Leadership Team

Recognize that finding solutions to complex problems requires the intelligence and talents of everyone. "Create a task team (school leadership team) that is small but representative of the layers of the organization to strategize a plan and provide leadership" (Fullan & Quinn, 2016, p. 22). As a leader, the best thing you can do is recognize you don't have to be the keeper of all knowledge. Multiple heads are better than one! This couldn't be more important than when you are shifting from a balanced literacy approach to a structured literacy approach. We need a team of people to guide the coalition. DuFour and colleagues (2016) refer to this team as a guiding coalition, because "no one person will have the energy, expertise, and influence to lead a complex change process until it becomes anchored in the organization's culture without first gaining the support of key staff members" (p. 27). I clearly remember about midyear after Angie had put together her school leadership team saying to me, "I feel like the weight of the world has been removed from my shoulders. I have other people to think things through with me." A school leadership team makes the following possible.

- Makes it so no one person has all the answers all the time

- Allows for transparency and open dialogue regarding decision making

- Creates teacher leaders (and future school leaders)

- Creates an investment and ownership of the school and grade-level goals

- Creates an interdependency to realizing the goal

A quality school leadership team begins with ensuring that the right people are at the table. The group selected for this team needs to be doggedly committed to the mission of 100 percent of students reading at grade level. The commitments (adapted from DuFour et al., 2016, 2024) should include the following.

- Initiate, support, and implement the structures and systems to foster qualities and characteristics consistent with learning-centered schools. These include the systems and structures outlined in this book, which include universal instruction, interventions, assessment, data-based decision making, professional development, and the leadership team.

- Create processes to monitor the goals. These are the reading goals that are determined by and for each grade level.

- Reallocate resources, which include human, material, and time resources, to support the proclaimed literacy initiative.

- Pose the right questions regarding the progress toward all students reading at grade level. Are students reading at grade level? Which students are not reading at grade level? What will we do when a student is not reading at grade level? What will we do for our students who can exceed reading at grade level?

- Model what is valued and being asked of all teaching staff. The members of the school leadership team should demonstrate that they value the instructional mission, that all students will read at grade level, and that they can model quality instruction in their classrooms.

- Celebrate progress with the entire staff. When teachers at the various grade levels are moving students significantly in reading—and they will—celebrations are in order and should be genuine.

- Confront violations of commitments.

I believe that it is critical to note that "leaders who are unwilling to promote and defend improvement initiatives put those initiatives at risk" (DuFour et al., 2016, p. 37). Principals who cannot confront those staff members who know teachers are continuing to act against the initiatives that the school leadership team puts forth cannot expect to ensure *it's possible* that all students will read at grade level. Leadership takes courage, and you must be able to confront those who do not have the student's best interests at heart by continuing to instruct in a manner that is not based on research. It's that simple. As DuFour and colleagues so aptly state, "A leader of the PLC process cannot verbally commit to a school mission of learning for all but then allow individuals within the organization to act in ways that are counterproductive to this commitment" (DuFour et al., 2016, p. 37).

We recommend the school leadership team is comprised of no more than ten to twelve members. In a small school, a team of four to six may be sufficient. This limited membership helps keep decision making manageable. We believe that representation from the following groups is critical.

- Each department or grade configuration; this could be kindergarten and first or kindergarten through second grades, third and fourth or third through fifth, or any combination thereof. The purpose is to ensure the staff feel like they are represented without the team being overloaded.

- Interventionists; this includes a representation of personnel providing interventions to students. It may be Title I, paraprofessionals, and so on.

- A special education representative; in this case, we are referring to the person who provides educational services.

- A person who provides social-emotional learning support for the school; this may include a social worker, school psychologist, and so on.

- A building administrator and assistant principal, if there is one

- Instructional coaches

We find that efficient meetings can be held monthly for approximately one and a half hours. Additionally, we have found it is extremely helpful to have a half-day retreat either prior to the start of the school year or after the school year has ended to ensure all systems and structures and their modifications are in place for the following school year.

## Agenda Setting

It's important that a school leadership team, or guiding coalition, does not become confused as the principal's team or the complaint team. Either of those can easily happen. When all teachers have a voice in the agenda, when minutes of the agenda are shared, and even opening meeting attendance to all members of the staff, it quickly becomes clear what the purpose is—to create a shared decision-making process with the motive of moving the mission forward.

As Megan Tschannen-Moran (2014) states, "When principals extend trust to teachers through shared control, they elicit greater trust from teachers" (p. 90). Building that trust takes time. As you begin using a shared decision-making process, many teachers are reluctant to suggest agenda items. For the first agenda, it is likely the principal will have to create many of the agenda items themself. Once school leadership team members realize and can see the meeting is not the *principal's* meeting but rather the *school's* meeting and have built trust with the principal, folks will gradually share suggested topics, and soon, the principal will rarely have to add agenda items.

We find that using the following steps to create an agenda meets the goal of ensuring all voices are heard in the creation of the agenda.

1.  Agenda suggestions or possible topics are sent out to all members two weeks ahead by the administrator. (Remember, the principal will likely have to provide items for the first couple of meetings.)

2.  Representatives of the team speak with their constituents to determine whether anyone has anything to add to the agenda beyond what was sent as suggested topics.

3.  New ideas are sent back via reply all so all members of the school leadership team can see what other grade levels or team members are considering. All new topic ideas need to be received by the principal one week prior to the meeting.

4.  Whenever possible, data should be used to show the agenda item is a high priority.

5.  The principal resends the new agenda no later than one week before the meeting.

6.  School leadership team members share the new agenda with constituents for input into agenda topics.

7.  The meeting is held with the new agenda.

Remembering our discussion on building trust, minutes from the meeting need to be publicly shared once the meeting is complete and all members have agreed on the accuracy of the minutes. To ensure this is a quick turnaround, we suggest projecting the minutes as the meeting is occurring. Any corrections to the meeting minutes can be made immediately.

## Agenda Items Based on Data

To ensure school leadership teams stay productive and focused and prevent them from becoming an arena where one lodges their complaints about what is going on within the school, there needs to be a basis for agenda items. We suggest linking them to data whenever possible.

A plausible agenda item based on data might include: The incoming third-grade class has a high percentage (62 percent) of students who need Tier 3 intervention requiring progress monitoring. Would it be possible to train paraprofessionals on administering the DIBELS 8 assessment so they can assist with the progress monitoring?

A nonplausible agenda item not based on data might include: The kindergarten teachers feel they need more paraprofessional help in their classrooms because their students seem so impacted. The beginning of the year benchmark data have not yet been obtained.

There should be a consistent agenda protocol. We believe it contains the following information.

- Date of meeting
- Members in attendance
- Topic
- Data to support topic
- Necessary action steps required
  - ⇨ Who is responsible
  - ⇨ When it should be completed
- Follow through

Figure 8.1 offers a template for school leadership team agendas.

| **School Leadership Team**<br>Date: _____ | | | | |
|---|---|---|---|---|
| Presenting Topic: | Evidence: | Action Plan:<br><br>Activity:<br><br>Who Is Responsible:<br><br>Timeline:<br><br>Resources: | Follow-up: | Time: |
| Presenting Topic: | Evidence: | Action Plan:<br><br>Activity:<br><br>Who Is Responsible:<br><br>Timeline:<br><br>Resources: | Follow-up: | Time: |
| Presenting Topic: | Evidence: | Action Plan:<br><br>Activity:<br><br>Who Is Responsible:<br><br>Timeline:<br><br>Resources: | Follow-up: | Time: |

**FIGURE 8.1:** School leadership team agenda.

*Visit **go.SolutionTree.com/literacy** for a free reproducible version of this figure.*

## Team Member Roles

For meetings to run efficiently, there need to be clearly defined roles on the school leadership team, and each person who commits to the role should be devoted to what they are supposed to do. We have tried rotating roles at each meeting but find the meetings become more effective if less change is made at each meeting. The following roles and a description of each follow.

- **Facilitator:** This is *not* the principal. To build trust and ensure it truly is a school leadership team, the principal cannot be at the helm. The facilitator is another member like everyone else and has the same equal say as the other members of the team. The facilitator leads the meetings and works with the principal when creating the agenda. The facilitator ensures team practices, such as norms of operation and consensus building, are being utilized as intended.

- **Timekeeper:** This is one of the most critical roles. As you will see, each item on the agenda has a time frame for discussion. It is the role of the timekeeper to give a warning when the time is about to expire. The timekeeper cannot be timid and occasionally will have to cut folks off to honor the work of the team.

- **Note taker:** This is another critical role. This person must be able to attend the meeting and accurately capture the voices of the discussion and outcomes as the committee intended. As mentioned, it is helpful if notes are projected as the discussion takes place so that any member can dispute a recap if necessary. There should be consensus, as well, that the notes are accurately capturing what was said. This is a key role that will help cement the culture of trust during and after the meetings.

- **Snack provider:** Typically, school leadership team meetings are held after school, and folks are hungry. Providing snacks is a nice gesture and is one that adds to collegiality. It gives the members an opportunity to relax and enjoy the company of their teammates. This is the one role that we rotated at each meeting.

- **Room keeper:** This is an interesting concept for someone's role, but it is important. The room where the meeting is held should be clean, set up for the meeting with the projector, have an area for snacks, and be comfortable in general. Initially, we tried rotating this room but found it difficult to be ready on time. There was a nice conference room in our school, and we continued to hold the meetings there for years. As part of her duties, the school secretary always ensured the meeting was set up and ready to go.

## Norms of Operation

Norms of operation, if they are adhered to—and they must be, for teams to be successful—are a support for building trust. They are not rules of behavior, but rather, they are ground rules or habits that govern the group. They are collective commitments that each member of the group must make. Therefore, they should be stated as commitments to act or behave in certain ways rather than as beliefs. To establish these habits, norms should be reviewed at the beginning and end of each meeting for at least six months and must be put into practice faithfully until they are part of the routine.

The leadership team should formally evaluate their effectiveness at least twice a year. To steer the discussion in the right direction, ask the following questions.

- Are we adhering to our norms?
- Do we need to establish a new norm to address a problem occurring on our team?
- Are all members of the team contributing to its work?
- Are we working interdependently to achieve our team goals? (DuFour et al., 2024)

Norms can generally be developed by what we refer to as the sticky note method. Two questions are placed onto two large pieces of plain white chart paper. At the top of one piece of paper is the question, How do I want to be treated? On the other is the question, How would I like the meetings to function? Each member of the team receives two different colored sticky notes. One color of sticky note should be designated for one question and the other color for the other question. Members of the team are asked to answer the questions independently and place their answers on the corresponding large sheet of paper.

Members sit back and analyze the responses. Through the facilitator and working with the group, duplicates are removed, or some may be combined if necessary. The remaining become the norms of operation. Typically, they will have to be word-smithed to everyone's satisfaction. Norms of operation are not intended to be written as a tome. Usually, six to eight norms are adequate. It's helpful to keep them visual as a reminder of the collective commitment to the norms of operation (Robbins & Judge, 2018). A sample of norms of operation can be seen in figure 8.2.

---

**Norms of Operation**

1. We will start and stop our meetings on time.
2. We will value the opinions of others.
3. We will keep an open mind.
4. We will represent the desires of our fellow teachers.
5. We will keep our students' success at the forefront.
6. We will respect and honor the final decisions.

---

**FIGURE 8.2:** Sample norms of operation.

## The Meeting Process

Prior to the meeting, but once all agenda items have been suggested, the facilitator and the principal meet to discuss the agenda and ensure the agenda items are appropriate, for example, determining if a meeting item is based on data, whether it is a plausible discussion, or if it has already been an agenda item with consensus reached on it.

When these issues come up, it is imperative that the principal meet with the team who brought up the nonplausible action item and talk to the team about why it will not be an agenda item. Say, for example, as in our earlier sidebar (page 225), the kindergarten team places on the preliminary agenda that kindergarten needs more paraprofessional time because their classes are significantly impacted, but no assessments have yet been given to determine how impacted this class is. It may indeed be very true, but until there is clear evidence that kindergarten is more impacted than other classrooms, it should not be a part of the agenda. This is a discussion for the principal and the kindergarten team to have. Perhaps, once benchmarking has been completed and there is evidence that a large portion of students are highly impacted, it should be an agenda item.

Meetings should always start promptly and on time. If school leadership team meetings start after school, think about the logistics of dismissal, getting students out the door and so forth. Ensure all members agree to starting on time. The discussion of the crisis of the day should not be what starts the agenda; the agenda starts the agenda.

All participants review the agenda. Items that had a follow-up are reviewed as a group to ensure that the follow-up happened. The facilitator begins the process of asking for time on each agenda item. Typically, the person who brought the agenda item to the meeting—or the team they are representing that brought the agenda item—should say what they believe will be the length of time for an adequate discussion of the meeting item. All members agree if this suggested time is correct. Time for each item is then documented on the agenda by the timekeeper.

The meeting begins with a clock running for each item. The timekeeper gives a check approximately two minutes prior to the clock running out. If the item discussion is nearly completed, no more time is needed. If it appears that more time is needed, the timekeeper gives the two-minute warning and asks the group if more time is needed. If the consensus is that more time is needed, again, the person who brought the item to the agenda says how much more time is needed. Consensus again must be reached for additional time on the clock. In some cases, it is apparent that much more time is needed. It is at this point that the facilitator asks the group if the discussion should be tabled for the next agenda or if the group believes they can come to a consensus on the topic. In some cases, more information is needed by the group, and in that case, the person who brought the item should have further discussion with their constituents and report back at the next meeting.

A note of caution here. As the previous paragraph illustrates, team members who bring an agenda item to the meeting should be fully versed and know the entire perspective of their constituents. Agenda items should not be about half-knowns or schoolwide complaints. The school leadership team is a way to have all voices heard and to make sure the school is running smoothly. All the routines do take a bit of practice, but if there is a true collective commitment, success will ensue!

## Team Consensus

The ultimate goal of the school leadership team is to ensure the mission—100 percent of students reading at grade level—is moving forward. Many decisions will have to be made regarding this work. Some may be quite contentious. There needs to be a system in place for coming to consensus. Building-leadership team members need to be committed to the school's mission being actualized. The team should always seek to understand what is collectively best for the school. A group has arrived at consensus when all points of view have not been merely heard but have been actively solicited (DuFour et al., 2024).

We have found two effective methods to determine consensus: (1) fist to five and (2) thumbs-up. Once it is time to decide, teams need to know that there is consensus regarding the decision.

1.  **Fist to five:** Each person votes by holding up zero, one, two, three, four, or five fingers. The facilitator (or vote caller) looks around the room and quickly tallies the votes. The votes break down like this.

    ⇨ *Zero fingers (a fist)*—No way, terrible choice, I will not go along with it, regardless of the will of the group.

    ⇨ *One finger*—I am opposed to this proposal.

    ⇨ *Two fingers*—I have some reservations and am not yet ready to support this proposal.

    ⇨ *Three fingers*—It's OK. I will support the idea.

    ⇨ *Four fingers*—I strongly agree, sounds good.

    ⇨ *Five fingers*—Absolutely, best idea ever! I'll champion it.

2.  **Thumbs-up:** Each person votes by holding up a thumb. The facilitator looks around the room and quickly tallies the votes. The votes break down like this.

    ⇨ *Thumbs-down*—I am opposed to this proposal.

    ⇨ *Thumb sideways*—I have some reservations and am not yet ready to support this proposal.

    ⇨ *Thumbs-up*—Absolutely, best idea ever! I'll champion it.

Once a decision has been made, the school leadership team must display a sense of stick-togetherness. It should be clear that the team is working together, and all members support the decisions. The will of the group should be obvious, even for those who opposed the decision to begin with. As the building principal, I used to gloat that I didn't vote during the meetings (which was true), and that I simply facilitated the decisions the school leadership team made.

Many principals struggle with what may feel like "handing control of the school over to the teachers." I, like Angie, found it a bit freeing. There is still much the principal must do that demonstrates they are in charge while at the same time creating a culture of trust. During meetings, it is up to the principal to demonstrate enthusiasm for meaningful exploration of disagreements and to model vulnerability when their idea is not the one accepted by the group. As the facilitator of the decisions being made, the principal should be quick to model or articulate those decisions (DuFour et al., 2024). They must be willing to confront those who fail to honor the decisions made by the team, and they must have an unrelenting focus on accountability for results, never forgetting that *it's possible* for all students to read at grade level!

## Decision-Making Items

There are two main objectives of the school leadership team when it comes to the literacy initiative. The first objective is to create and monitor the progress of both the schoolwide literacy goals and the grade-level goals. If all grade levels are not working toward meeting their own goals, the schoolwide literacy goals will not be met. The second objective is to facilitate dialogue regarding teaching and learning. Typically, that dialogue comes after each schoolwide benchmark assessment on the foundational skills of reading. Please refer to the benchmark protocol in chapter 5 (page 125) as a tool to examine benchmark data.

Other items that should be a part of the school leadership decision-making topics that align with the literacy initiative include the following.

- **Master schedule:** When will literacy and other subjects be taught across the school day? How will ancillary personnel align their time to the master schedule? When and how will paraprofessional time be allocated?

- **Core curriculum:** What is the core curriculum? How are we using our core curriculum? Is the core curriculum adequate? Do we need a new core curriculum? Who will be a part of the decision if a new core curriculum is needed?

- **Supplemental materials:** What supplemental materials do we all agree should be used for literacy instruction? When should they be used for literacy instruction? Who should be using them? Have appropriate folks been trained on how to use the supplemental materials? Are there specific grade levels that should be using the supplemental materials?

- **Professional development decisions**: What topics do the data indicate staff need professional development on? When should the professional development be provided? Who should provide the professional development? In what sort of format should the professional development be delivered?

- **Interventions:** Are all students who need an intervention receiving an intervention? What sort of interventions do students need? Who provides the intervention? How will the interventionists be trained?

- **Intervention schedule:** Is the intervention schedule maximized? Are there enough intervention slots available so all students who need an intervention are receiving an intervention? Does the intervention schedule ensure no child is removed from whole-group instruction? Do we have adequate resources to cover the intervention schedule?

- **Paraprofessional schedule:** Are we maximizing the use of our paraprofessionals? Who makes the paraprofessional schedule? Does the paraprofessional schedule prioritize so both the teachers and students who need the most help get help? Does everyone have access to the paraprofessional schedule?

- **Ancillary personnel schedule:** Who creates the schedule for the ancillary personnel? Is it maximized so the students who are needing service receive service? Has it been coordinated with the master schedule so that students are receiving services at the appropriate times?

- **Assessment calendar:** Who creates the assessment calendar? Has it been coordinated with the appropriate personnel? Is it on the instructional calendar?

# Targets

I vividly remember walking into a school with the Chief Academic Officer of a large school district in March of one year. We looked at the school's goals, very visibly displayed on a bulletin board in the front hall as we entered. As I looked at them, she leaned over and whispered in my ear, "That bulletin board has been up since September, and not once have they looked at their data."

Regrettably, this is quite often the case when it comes to school goals for increasing literacy. Too often, the goal is set by the principal at the beginning of the year, based on either the state summative assessment from the previous year or the results of the beginning of the year foundational reading assessment. Regardless, too often, it isn't reexamined, checked against how each grade level is doing, and given consideration as to what to do to meet the goal. It seems to just hang on the bulletin board.

School goals need to be alive. Each grade level should contribute to the school goal, and each teacher should have a voice in what those goals are. We believe and have seen that when grade-level teams have a goal to work toward, it creates a sense of camaraderie and enhances collaboration. Grade-level goals should be realistic, attainable, and they should constantly be revisited. The school above created a goal at the beginning of the year but never revisited it. If the goals aren't kept alive, the teachers' enthusiasm for achieving the goal will wane over time as the year goes on.

We believe that goals should ensure the school is making progress every year, in every grade level. We ask for, and schools nearly always achieve, goals in which each grade level increases literacy outcomes by a minimum of 10 percent more than the year before or 10 percent higher for that group of students. We also believe that the number of students in the lowest instructional range should be reduced by 25 percent. In grades K–2, we measure these goals on the foundational reading assessment used by the school. In the third through fifth or sixth grade, we measure this by the results of the state summative assessment. Some find only increasing the goal by 10 percent each year seems not to be rigorous enough. What we find is that it is very realistic, the teachers readily buy into it, and often, in the middle of the year, when the goal has already been met, the teachers decide to raise the goal even higher. In kindergarten, because there were no students in that grade level previously, we push teachers to make a goal that 95 percent of students are at grade level by the end of the year. Figure 8.3 is an example of what these goals might look like.

| Grade level | Percent in year 1 in 2023 | Percent in year 1 in 2023 | Percent in year 2 for that grade level this school year (2024) | Percent in year 2 for that grade level this school year (2024) | Goal for students in year 2 in 2024 | Goal for students in year 2 in 2024 |
|---|---|---|---|---|---|---|
| First Grade | 18% | 69% | 12% | 73% | 9% | 80% |
| Second Grade | 14% | 72% | 18% | 76% | 13% | 76% |

**FIGURE 8.3:** Establishing goals for first- and second-grade students

In first grade, at the end of the year, there were 18 percent of students in Tier 3, and 69 percent in Tier 1. Those students are now in second grade, and we want to ensure that at least 10 percent more students are at benchmark than last year, but we also want to ensure that each year, every grade level is better than the year before. In second grade last year, 72 percent of students were at benchmark at the end of the year. If we increase our current second grade students by 10 percent more than they ended last year, their goal would be 76 percent of students at grade level. Again, considering that we want each grade level to grow each year, 76 percent of students at grade level is indeed higher than the group of second graders last year, and it ensures the current group of students has increased by 10 percent. You can access from our website a grades K–5 worksheet that calculates the goals for you (visit **https://itspossible.schoolscubed.com**). Figure 8.4 (page 234) illustrates a condensed K–2 version of the worksheet.

Regardless of how your school decides to determine goals, we have seen that schools without a set system for doing so are more likely to flounder and never achieve dramatic results. Instead, a few teachers doing good things will continue, whereas a schoolwide effort collaboratively working together to achieve their goals will realize many gains.

# Trust

Teachers cannot collaborate unless they trust one another. Trust seems to be the bedrock of collaboration. In schools where there is greater trust, there tends to be more collaboration. When trust is absent, people are more reluctant to work closely together, and collaboration is more difficult (Tschannen-Moran, 2014).

For a school to be able to reach a goal of all students reading at grade level, it requires interdependence on your teammates and an assurance and trust that we are all doing what is right and what we have collectively agreed to. We find that teachers and educators can often be resistant to change. They believe that, in their school, things are going OK. Everyone seems happy.

However, as schools become more transparent with their data, and staff begin to realize that most students aren't reading at grade level, a fear of the unknown begins to surface. The staff take this information personally, and rightly so. They feel responsible. The forthcoming necessary change to instructional practices becomes apparent, and they resist the unknown because they are afraid of the unknown. When teachers trust one another, however, and when they trust their principal, they are more likely to accept the necessary changes. Trustworthy leaders form the heart of productive schools (Tschannen-Moran, 2014).

## TABLE 1

| Grade Measures | Previous Year Percentage of Proficient or Benchmark and Above or Advanced Students | Previous Year Percentage of Proficient or Benchmark and Above or Advanced Students Plus 10 Percent |
|---|---|---|
| | Column 1 | Column 2 |
| Kindergarten Composite | | |
| First-Grade Composite | | |
| Second-Grade Composite | | |

## TABLE 2

| Measure | A<br>Percent of advanced students | B<br>Percent of students at benchmark | C<br>Percent of students below benchmark | D<br>Columns A + B + one-half of C | E<br>Percent of students well below benchmark | F<br>Half of students from column E | G<br>Number from table 1, column 2 | H<br>Choose the higher number of column D or column G |
|---|---|---|---|---|---|---|---|---|
| Kindergarten Composite | | | | | | | | |
| First-Grade Composite | | | | | | | | |
| Second-Grade Composite | | | | | | | | |

*Source: © 2024 by Schools Cubed (https://itspossible.schoolscubed.com). Used with permission.*

**FIGURE 8.4:** Example goal calculator worksheet for grades K–2.

To have change stick and to ensure teachers are letting principals lead the way, principals must develop trust with their teachers.

In Tschannen-Moran's (2014) book, *Trust Matters: Leadership for Successful Schools,* she describes the facets of trust that people rely on in making trust judgments regarding other people. The following are the facets she outlines, as well as how a principal may display these facets.

- **Benevolence:** Showing of consideration of the staff, sensitivity for employees' needs and interests, acting in a way that protects employees' rights, appreciating the hard work of staff, publicly thanking them for their hard work, having a willingness to listen, and displaying genuine goodwill and concern for teachers' well-being in their personal realm.

- **Honesty:** Being honest and upfront about situations, not hiding facts such as the percentage of students reading at grade level or outcomes on state summative assessments, accepting responsibility for one's actions, no passing the buck, no pointing fingers at others, owning up to mistakes, and treating people with respect.

- **Openness:** Having accurate and forthcoming communications; providing adequate explanations of decisions that are made; giving timely feedback on observations; disclosing facts, intentions, and judgments; exchanging thoughts and ideas freely with teachers regarding school improvement; and maintaining strict standards of confidentiality. Principals who display openness tend to have teachers warn them of potential problems on the horizon so problems can be resolved quickly.

- **Reliability:** Doing what is expected on a regular and consistent basis, following through with what has been committed, being dependable so they can be counted on in times of need, and stepping up to the plate in predictable and sometimes extraordinary ways.

- **Competence:** The ability to perform a task as expected, solving problems, pressing for results, resolving conflicts, working hard, setting an example, holding teachers accountable in a fair and reasonable manner, not letting problems get out of hand, acting as a buffer for teachers during tricky situations, calming down a parent, and discreetly handling problems among the staff (Tschannen-Moran, 2014).

When a trusting culture exists, schools are more open to sharing their data with colleagues. They understand that any signs of students not making gains is an opportunity for problem solving and learning with colleagues and school leadership. It is not about blame and consequences.

Being a stellar principal does not require being high in every facet of trust. Personally, I worked hard at being benevolent. When I was busy—like principals are—I didn't always take the time to thank my staff like I should have. I would have to write myself reminders to make a stop in a teacher's room when there was a personal issue going on. It is wise to know where your strengths and weaknesses lie within the five facets. To do so, we have created a fun, non-scientific quiz you can take to see what areas you may need to bolster. The self-quiz on the five facets of trust can be found in figure 8.5 (page 236).

**Directions for completing the survey:** Please rate yourself on the following statements, 1 being least like you and 5 being most like you.

1. I routinely show my appreciation by saying "thank you" in some fashion after teachers have spent an extra-long time at school.

    ① ② ③ ④ ⑤

2. I am typically on time or early for work and generally am the last one to leave.

    ① ② ③ ④ ⑤

3. When I find out later I was mistaken, I always let the other person know.

    ① ② ③ ④ ⑤

4. I provide my teachers feedback within forty-eight hours of a classroom observation.

    ① ② ③ ④ ⑤

5. I walk the halls daily, enter classrooms, and make myself visible throughout the school to head off any potential problems.

    ① ② ③ ④ ⑤

6. I never ask my teachers to do anything I wouldn't or couldn't do myself unless it was outside my field of expertise.

    ① ② ③ ④ ⑤

7. Despite the demands of my job, I always make time for a teacher or staff member when they need me.

    ① ② ③ ④ ⑤

8. If our scores on state summative assessments are less than what I had hoped, I take responsibility for the disappointment and ask teachers how I can offer my help.

    ① ② ③ ④ ⑤

9. If I must leave the school early, I let the staff know where and why I am going.

    ① ② ③ ④ ⑤

10. Instead of acting like I know the answer to something I may not, I readily say I can help the teacher find an answer.

    ① ② ③ ④ ⑤

11. I always ask permission first before speaking about something someone has told me in confidence.

    ① ② ③ ④ ⑤

12. Despite the demands of my job, I always get back to a staff member promptly regarding a question or concern they may have about a school matter.

①      ②      ③      ④      ⑤

13. If a new initiative in our school fails, I seldom blame others for the failures.

①      ②      ③      ④      ⑤

14. If an event at school is unsuccessful because a teacher did not follow through on their part, I keep it between myself and the teacher.

①      ②      ③      ④      ⑤

15. During difficult situations, I act as a buffer for teachers. As an example, If I know a teacher may have a difficult conference with a parent, I readily volunteer to be available or accompany the teacher at the conference.

①      ②      ③      ④      ⑤

16. I routinely and appropriately check in on a staff member whom I know may be having a personal issue.

①      ②      ③      ④      ⑤

17. I make sure that all important dates of the school year, including field trips, fire drills, evacuation drills, assessments, and progress monitoring, are laid out and communicated to all at the beginning of the year.

①      ②      ③      ④      ⑤

18. If a teacher is routinely late for school, I do not hesitate to confront the teacher about their tardiness.

①      ②      ③      ④      ⑤

19. There is an active decision-making body where most major decisions regarding day-to-day operations are made.

①      ②      ③      ④      ⑤

20. A schoolwide behavior management system is in place that minimizes classroom disruptions.

①      ②      ③      ④      ⑤

21. Before acting on a new school initiative, I check in with my staff for their input.

①      ②      ③      ④      ⑤

22. I make sure that nothing interferes with the activities planned on the important dates of the school year.

①      ②      ③      ④      ⑤

**FIGURE 8.5:** Five facets of trust principal self-reflection survey. *continued* →

23. If our school has an initiative, I always ensure we see it through.

① ② ③ ④ ⑤

24. I rarely have to be reminded of an upcoming deadline or commitment.

① ② ③ ④ ⑤

25. There is a level of communication in my building that enables teachers and staff members to know what is to be expected on a daily, weekly, and monthly basis.

① ② ③ ④ ⑤

26. Teachers and staff readily know that I am the first line of defense with difficult parents, community members, and others.

① ② ③ ④ ⑤

Benevolence: Add responses to questions, 1, 6, 11, 16, and 21. Divide by 5. Score: _____

Reliability: Add responses to questions 2, 7, 12, 17, 22 and 24. Divide by 6. Score: _____

Honesty: Add responses to questions 3, 8, 13, 18, and 23. Divide by 5. Score: _____

Openness: Add responses to questions 4, 9, 14, 19, and 25. Divide by 5. Score: _____

Competence: Add responses to questions 5, 10, 15, 20, 26. Divide by 5. Score: _____

*Visit **go.SolutionTree.com/literacy** for a free reproducible version of this figure.*

Though often intuitive, it is helpful to know how much your staff trust one another. If you are interested, there are several trust surveys available. We recommend the survey found in the appendix of *Trust Matters: Leadership for Successful Schools* (Tschannen-Moran, 2014), or, for working together in teams, "The Trust on Our Team Survey" found in *Taking Action: A Handbook for RTI at Work* (Mattos et al. 2025).

# Time

If trust is the bedrock for collaborative cultures, time is the linchpin! The more efficient your schedule is, the slicker your entire system is. Schools are very busy places, there is no denying that. There are countless tasks, responsibilities, and worries placed on schools today. Time is such a scarcity in schools that there isn't enough time to get everything done as well as one should. We must prioritize, and we must prioritize first meeting the needs of all students and the teaching and planning demands that accompany that. That requires a master(ful) school schedule! When I say *masterful*, I am not kidding. A quality master schedule is indeed the linchpin for school success. A schedule becomes masterful when it includes the following:

- Every student who is reading below grade level receives appropriate intervention. *Every one*!

- There is collaborative planning time for teachers to plan together and have time for PLCs.

- There is an efficient schedule for ancillary personnel, such as paraprofessionals and special education staff.

Incorporating common planning time into your master schedule is important not only for collaboration; it also has a measurable effect on student achievement. Elementary schools in which grade-level teams were allotted common planning time saw higher achievement growth, particularly in reading (Grissom et al., 2021). Prior to creating your schedule, consider the following dos and don'ts in table 8.1.

**TABLE 8.1:** Master Schedule Dos and Don'ts

| Master Schedule Dos | Master Schedule Don'ts |
| --- | --- |
| Create in a collaborative process, such as with the school leadership team. | Allow individual teachers to say when they will teach what. |
| Ensure literacy blocks are staggered throughout the day. | Have literacy at one time of the day, schoolwide. |
| Create a schedule for paraprofessionals and ancillary staff that aligns with the master schedule. | Allow teachers to create a schedule for their paraprofessionals. It needs to be a collaborative process as with the school leadership team. |
| Consider transportation and lunch times first. | Allow lunch to dominate your schedule. |
| Have thoughtful recess times. | Permit grade levels to take recess whenever they want. |

Perhaps you do have a quality master schedule, but you still feel there isn't enough time for adequate literacy instruction across the grade levels. Think about the classrooms in which this is occurring. You may want to give some of the following considerations.

- Is classroom management adequate?

- Are teachers and students ready with the curriculum and materials?

- Are there quality classroom routines, such as settling in chairs, transitions, and dismissals?

- Are engaging instructional strategies being utilized?

- Are all students expected to participate in active learning?

Also think about ways to maximize literacy time schoolwide by incorporating the following practices.

- Consider having a specific set time for announcements—such as five minutes after the morning bell rings or five minutes prior to the afternoon dismissal bell. These are often when classrooms are settling in or getting ready to leave.

- Meetings, such as IEP meetings or other pertinent meetings for teachers to attend, should not be set during literacy time.

- Rotate assemblies throughout the school day during the year. If the October assembly was at 9 a.m., then hold the next assembly at 1 p.m.

- A field trip is a wonderful way to learn, but be sure to think about the value added when it disrupts learning.

- Certainly, students need to go to the restroom, but taking whole-class bathroom breaks and then a water break wastes a tremendous amount of time. Consider classroom routines that allow students to go to the bathroom or get drinks with the least amount of disruption to learning as possible.

- Minimize transition times to the lunchroom. Think about having a student helper call the rooms to come to the lunchroom when the lunchroom is ready. This solves an abundance of issues, such as students gathering in the halls, scuffling with one another as they pass each other for recess, and so on.

## Time for Tiers of Instruction

In chapter 2 (page 27) we recommended that Tier 1 or universal instruction consists of both whole-group and small-group instruction and must be at least 90 minutes; 120 minutes is ideal. Whole-group instruction is generally fifty to sixty minutes, while small-group instruction is typically an additional forty to sixty minutes. All students should receive both whole-group and small-group instruction.

Students who need Tier 2 intervention can receive instruction during small-group time, but some jurisdictions do consider Tier 2 to be in addition to the 90 to 120 minutes of whole-group and small-group instruction. Ensure you know what your state or district mandates for Tier 2 intervention time. Students testing in the instructional level of Tier 2 should receive instruction that aligns to Tier 1 instruction.

Tier 3 is in addition to Tier 1. Tier 3 instruction and intervention should vary across grade levels. Students in kindergarten do not need and should not receive the same amount of Tier 3 intervention time as a fifth-grade student. In kindergarten, twenty-five minutes of Tier 3 intervention is more than adequate—when done properly—to see students to grade level by the end of the year. Beginning in third grade and up, students should receive forty to forty-five minutes of quality Tier 3 intervention time. To help you plan for the adequate sections of Tier 3 intervention, refer to the intervention calculator in chapter 4 (page 99).

## Schedule Creation

To create a masterful school schedule, there must be a coordination of human resources. The resources we are referring to include special education personnel, paraprofessionals, and any interventionists, such as Title I. When teachers randomly determine for themselves when they will be teaching literacy, it is impossible to make the best use of resources across the school. Schedules need to be developed in a coordinated manner with many voices in the room. We believe the school leadership team—who represents their constituents—is the best way to develop the school's schedule.

In the early 2000s, there was a trend in schools to have a schoolwide literacy block. Typically, it was first thing in the morning and lasted two hours. The logic behind this thinking was that students are at their best first thing in the morning. For two hours, the school would focus on literacy. All human resources would flood in to support literacy instruction. Though I greatly appreciate a focus on literacy, and that literacy is critically important and should be delivered when students are at their prime, the disadvantages far outweigh advantages in such a model.

Schools need to have a staggered schedule in place when teaching reading. The advantages are many. Schools have tremendously limited resources. If schools utilize all their human resources during that two-hour block, what are the resources doing the rest of the day? A better utilization of resources is to spread them out so that they can be used more efficiently throughout the day. Spreading out the literacy block is much more efficient for observing instruction, allowing the principal to visit more classrooms throughout the day and ensure that instruction is being delivered consistently schoolwide.

We find there are three good systems to create a masterful school schedule. The first is to use a scheduling board with magnetic strips designed specifically for creating schedules. You can purchase an effective one for less than $200. The second system is simply to use four large sheets of white poster paper and sticky notes. The advantage to this type of system is that you can overlay paraprofessionals and ancillary assistance over the sticky notes for literacy and create their schedules, as well, at the same time. The third is to use the schedule builder found on the Schools Cubed free resources webpage (**https://schoolscubed .com/free-resources**).

Schedules are best built thinking about them diagonally, typically beginning with literacy instruction earliest in the day for first grade and kindergarten just afterward. We suggest first grade first as we find kindergarten takes a bit longer to establish morning routines, such as getting into school without tears, tying shoelaces, putting away coats, and so on. If each grade level's literacy block starts approximately thirty minutes after the next, human resources can flood into each small-group time, thus having two adults to provide small-group instruction.

When building your schedule, the following steps may be helpful.

1. Plan lunch times first.

2. Schedule art, music, and physical education next—typically, these will become planning times for classroom teachers.

3. Plan literacy next, beginning with earliest grades first—see note above about first grade rather than kindergarten starting first.

4. Use 90 to 120 minutes for literacy instruction—in as large a block as possible.

5. Complete with other subjects.

## Suggested Resources for Leading Collaboration

- *Learning by Doing: A Handbook for Professional Learning Communities at Work, Fourth Edition* by Richard DuFour, Rebecca DuFour, Robert Eaker, Thomas W. Many, Mike Mattos, and Anthony Muhammad (2024)

- *Taking Action: A Handbook for RTI at Work, Second Edition* by Mike Mattos, Austin Buffum, Janet Malone, Luis F. Cruz, Nicole Dimich, and Sarah Schuhl (2025)

- *Trust Matters: Leadership for Successful Schools, Second Edition* by Megan Tschannen-Moran (2014)

There is much talk about an uninterrupted literacy block. It is always helpful if a literacy block can be continuous so as not to interrupt students' thinking. However, we have created endless schedules in schools, and we have found that in a typical school day of six hours and twenty minutes, one or two grade levels have a block that must be interrupted with lunch or specials. We have found placing this in the upper grades seems to be the least disruptive.

We have provided two samples of masterful schedules that both allow for common teacher (visit **go.SolutionTree.com/literacy** for free reproducibles). One has a designated two-hour block for literacy, and the other has only a six hour and fifteen minute school day with a ninety-minute literacy block. We can't iterate enough that a two-hour time block is much better to get the job done, but this district, with a limited schedule, was superb in ensuring no time was wasted. They would have loved to have had more time in the day!

## School Spotlight

### Sunset Elementary School, Sunset, Utah

At the time my school began participating in intensive literacy support, we had nearly 60 percent of our students not reading at grade level. I had been at Sunset Elementary for a few years, doing what I thought was the right work with teacher and students, with little to no net gain.

As we embarked on the work of improving literacy at our school, one of the first things we did was create a master schedule. I had been using a master schedule for a few years, but my thinking around it this time was greatly challenged. I didn't understand the why behind what I was being asked to change, and it wasn't until year two in the work that the light turned on, and I more fully understood the why. A master schedule is a critical piece to put in place to ensure that the right amount of time is given to literacy instruction. In addition, as you stagger literacy blocks on your schedule, you as the instructional leader can get into classes to see that instruction in action.

We are starting to have intentional conversations around literacy. We have created common times in our days or weeks to discuss literacy data. Teachers are learning to dive deep into their student data to find the holes in learning that need to be addressed. The work of changing literacy instruction should not be done in isolation, for school leaders or teachers. Collaboration is where our best work happens and our greatest outcomes are started.

Our hard work as a school staff is starting to pay off. Teachers have been trained in the science of reading and are implementing those best practices into their teaching. We continue to make small adjustments to our literacy efforts to continue to do what is best for students. In the 2023–2024 school year, we have seen a 10 percent increase in reading proficiency, and 71 percent of our students are growing the way they should in their reading. This work matters and makes a difference.

As an instructional leader, I have gained knowledge about the science of reading through professional development and can more eloquently speak to literacy with all stakeholders. This added knowledge and understanding has allowed me to create a culture of intentionality in our building around planning, teaching, and assessing literacy efforts.

*Jodi Rees, Principal*

# Summary

There are four Ts of collaboration, and they are teams, targets, trust, and time. Ensuring that these Ts are in place will ensure the school culture collaborates to meet the mission of all students reading at grade level. For teachers to work toward a mission of 100 percent of students reading at grade level, each teacher must trust their fellow teachers will do what is necessary to get the job done. A masterful schedule should include time for all students who are reading below grade level to receive an intervention, common planning time for teachers, and ancillary personnel to efficiently maximize human resources. For efficiency and better management of human resources and instructional feedback, literacy blocks should be staggered throughout the day instead of all students having literacy at one time during the day. Teams and committees in schools should be designed to meet the mission of the school—increased literacy achievement. Many schools have committees or teams that are not focused on improving the outcomes of the school. Leadership takes courage, and you must be able to confront those who do not have the student's best interests at heart by continuing to instruct in a manner that is not based on research. The school leadership team must have efficient meeting practices in place along with norms of operation. Grade levels should have goals that are realistic and attainable. Goals should be monitored toward progress throughout the school year.

# Collaboration

Various aspects of collaboration are evident. Teachers and grade-level teams have time to discuss and analyze student data, plan lessons, and engage in professional dialogue. Shared leadership is in place by an active school leadership team with the result of establishing a positive organizational climate and shared decision making. The school leadership team (SLT) serves the purpose of leading the school's efforts to increase student achievement, determine professional development, and discuss building resources and practices of improvement. Representation consists of various grade levels/departments and an administrator.

| Big Idea | Basic (1) | Effective (2) | Proficient (3) | Exemplar (4) |
|---|---|---|---|---|
| **The agenda for the SLT is communicated, all participants have input and action steps, and due dates and responsibilities are followed through.** | School leadership creates the agenda, and team members receive the agenda when they arrive at the meeting. | Team members have input into the agenda items prior to the start of the meeting. | The agenda is created in a timely fashion so all members of the school have input into agenda items. | Prior to the meeting, the agenda has been discussed with stakeholders, and representatives know the viewpoint of their constituents. |
| **All school team meetings, including data meetings and SLTs, follow effective meeting practices such as prompt start times, established agenda, norms of operations, time management, check in of prior meeting's to-do lists, and established action items.** | School leadership leads the meetings, sets agendas, and establishes meeting protocols. | A good organizational structure is in place for both grade-level data meetings and SLTs; this includes an agenda, protocol, time on task, norms of operation, note taking, and a decision-making process. | Meetings— whether data meetings or SLTs—are efficient, follow a specific protocol, and have established norms. Members and participants have equal voices and feel heard. | Representatives from the grade levels or SLT members facilitate the meetings. Each member is clear on their roles and how to enact the outcomes from the meetings. |
| **Both grade-level and school leadership teams have common, well-defined, and attainable goals.** | The school has a schoolwide goal for increasing literacy achievement. | Each grade level has literacy goals that are measurable and attainable. The team(s) can articulate the achievement goals. | Attainable grade-level goals include both plans for reducing students at the lowest tiers of instruction and increasing students at the grade level and advanced bands of instruction. | The SLT and grade-level teams have input into the measurable and attainable goals and evaluate progress toward goals at regular intervals throughout the year. |

| Big Idea | Basic (1) | Effective (2) | Proficient (3) | Exemplar (4) |
|----------|-----------|---------------|----------------|--------------|
| **Grade-level data team meetings focus on instruction and are results oriented.** | Dialogue of data team meetings may be focused on instruction but may not be results oriented. | Data team dialogue is consistently focused on instruction and progress toward the grade-level goals. | There is a protocol in place that ensures any student not making progress is identified. | Instructional strategies are discussed, and plans are put into place to ensure all students are making progress. |
| **The collaborative learning culture of the school environment ensures new learnings and understandings regarding the instruction and mastery of literacy.** | Staff members look at their own data during data team meetings. | Protocols and professional learning norms are in place that allow for learning around data analysis. | Data analysis is used to create action steps. Team members understand that dialogue is about improvement. | Team members openly share instructional strategies and problem solving, and they collaboratively work together to reach their goals. |
| **The grade-level data teams are focused, proactive, and concentrating on data and future planning; little time is spent on reacting to current crises or needs that do not relate to the team.** | Focus is scattered, and time is spent during data teams pulling data reports. | The grade-level data are prepared prior to the meeting, and the agenda is results oriented. | Teachers readily know how to access the data and are ready when the meeting starts. All team members understand its use. | All members of the grade-level team are aware of their data and have a sense of urgency regarding improvement. |
| **SLT members review data after each benchmark to determine whether subgroups of students are or are not making the expected progress. Further action statements are developed.** | The SLT looks at grade-level proficiency data for each of the grade levels. | When analyzing benchmark data, subgroups are broken down and examined for proficiency levels. | Next steps are developed based on data analysis. The appropriate subskill and subgroup data analysis is routine. | Professional development aligns to subgroup trends. Data indicate that achievement gaps are closing based on action steps. |
| **The members of the school leadership team regard increasing student achievement as their highest priority.** | Team members participate in the SLT as part of the school's duty rotation as assigned by the building leadership. | Team members are eager or volunteer to participate on the school leadership team and take responsibility for the school's success. | Commitment to the school's success is clear. SLT members are passionate about student success. | There is a common vision that *all* students will read at grade level and *all* staff share in the success of the school. |
| **The school leadership team analyzes end of year assessment data and creates improvement strategies for the following year.** | School leadership analyzes end of year data. | School leadership and grade-level teams analyze end of year data. | School leadership and grade-level teams use a common protocol to analyze end of year literacy data. | The school leadership reviews all end of year data protocols and ensures action items have been completed for ongoing continual improvement. |

*Page 2 of 2*

# It's Possible

*By Angela Hanlin*

The first chapter began with the question, What would you do if anything were possible? When I first began the initiative to transform literacy scores in our school, as principal, my answer to that question was, "Ensure that all students could read at or above grade level." That is still my answer today, because I now know and have seen that *it's possible*! Things do not have to stay the way they are right now in our schools. Literacy for all does not need to feel like a hope, wish, or dream. It can become a reality for all schools. It is our moral obligation to make literacy possible for all our students, and it *is* possible.

Let's have a real, honest discussion. Now that you have read this book, you have a decision to make. What will you do now? What will be your next step? Will the words in this book inspire change? If so, what will that change look like? Let's take our final few pages to discuss what those next steps could, and should, look like.

## The Path Forward

Our first step is to acknowledge that we are going to commit to literacy reform in our district, school, or classroom. We look at where we are and what changes need to be made. We reflect on what we are currently doing that supports the science of reading and what can be an area of growth. We determine our next steps and work on one initiative at a time. We give ourselves time to get better and make improvements before moving on to the next initiative.

The starting point is systems change. Low-performing schools lack well-established, successful systems. We, as leaders, must commit to building those systems in our schools. We need to establish systems to collect and review data, collaborate with others, and provide the most effective, evidence-based instruction in our classrooms. As superintendents and building leaders, this is the work we must do in our schools so all students achieve academic success. There must be a sense of urgency about this work to make sure it happens in a timely manner. Systems and structures are built as a result of our leadership.

# Universal Instruction

What does the instruction in our classrooms look like? Do our teachers know the most effective instructional practices? If not, we must make sure that they do! Their instruction must be explicit and systematic. If only a few teachers are implementing effective practices, then we will only have pockets of success in our buildings and school districts. We must ensure that *all* teachers are providing explicit instruction. No one can opt out of this work. When discussing instruction, we need to take the emphasis off teaching and place it on the *learning*. We need to move away from discussing whether we have taught the information or covered the material to instead asking whether or not our students have *learned* the information. Is our instruction having an impact on student learning? If it is not, then what will we do about it? By first looking at Tier 1 or universal instruction, and making improvements there, we can quickly begin to have an impact on student learning.

In addition to knowing how to teach effectively, our teachers must know *what* to teach. We have to ensure all teachers are trained in the science of reading and that they understand *how* students learn to read. To teach students how to read effectively, teachers need high-quality reading materials to use in their classrooms. We now know that for all students to learn to read, they must receive instruction that is explicit and systematic, especially in the foundational literacy concepts such as phonemic awareness, phonological awareness, and phonics. We need to allocate funds to purchase resources that are founded in the science of reading and stop spending money on programs that are proven to be ineffective. Our teachers deserve better. Our students deserve better.

# Comprehensive Assessment Plan

All districts need a districtwide assessment plan. The only way to know which students are struggling is to have a data system where we administer benchmark assessments to all students three times a year. We review the benchmark data after each benchmarking period during data team meetings. Teachers leave those meetings with an instructional plan for how to teach the students who are not reading at grade level. Intervention teachers leave those meetings with an intervention plan for what skill gaps they will be addressing during their intervention lessons. Then, after about six weeks of instruction, we come together to review the students' progress monitoring data. We review the data to see if the students are learning and making progress. Is our instruction having an impact? We ask ourselves these questions: Which students are making gains? Why? Which students are not making gains? Why? What will we do in response to the data?

We use the beginning of year benchmark data to set goals for the middle and end of the school year. We share those goals with all staff members, students, parents, and school board members. We post the goals so that all can see and revisit them during our team meetings and staff meetings. This helps hold all team members accountable for the work. We consistently review weekly progress monitoring data to determine whether we are on track to meet our goals. When students are not making progress, we do whatever it takes to help them make progress. Often, a diagnostic assessment is needed to determine exactly where the student is struggling and what intervention is needed.

# Intervention

We must teach teachers what to do when their students struggle to learn to read. Every student can learn to read, but they may not all learn at the same pace. We must intervene as quickly as possible with these students, and there must be a sense of urgency. Schools also need intervention resources that are based on the science of reading—programs that *explicitly* provide instruction in the areas where the students have gaps in their knowledge. We need to train our intervention teachers on a systematic approach to help close the reading gaps in our struggling readers. This cannot be a one-size-fits-all approach. Instead, it strategically and explicitly provides the student with the exact instruction they need to help them close the gap in their learning.

As building leaders, we must observe intervention lessons to determine whether the interventions are being provided with fidelity and if the instruction is having an impact on student learning. Is the instruction explicit? Is the instruction systematic? Is the instruction provided at a brisk pace? Are the students responding?

# Data Analysis

There must be a radical acceptance of our data, no matter what it looks like, and where we are currently performing. We must own it! Fearlessly, courageously own it! This is where we are. We simply aren't where we want to be *yet*. I have sat in data meetings that were uncomfortable because our students were not making progress. It was hard to look at and accept some of our data. It was extremely hard not to take it personally, but we had to own it, embrace it, and make changes to our instruction. We must do so to experience change in our schools.

The review of data needs to be thorough. We need to deeply analyze the data not just to identify which students are not reading at grade level but also to identify where their struggles are and what interventions they need. We review the data student by student to determine what each student needs to reach grade level. We use the data to set goals for the school and each classroom or grade level. Is our instruction having an impact and getting us closer to the goal? If not, then what are we going to do about it? Once we meet a goal, then we celebrate that growth and set the next goal. It is a continuous cycle of improvement.

# Ongoing Professional Development

We should provide our teachers with ongoing professional development that is based on data. What does the data show our teachers need to improve their students' academic success? We need to be in classrooms and use the observations from our classroom walk-throughs to assess where teachers' instruction is lacking and what professional development is needed for those teachers to have an impact on student learning. We bring teachers into the discussion and planning and ask them in what areas they would like to experience growth. We should acknowledge that teachers need encouragement, support, coaching, and feedback. They will not make gains without receiving feedback, and we cannot provide teachers with effective feedback if we are not in their classrooms watching their instruction.

Our presence in the classrooms is to identify what the teacher is doing well, what their areas of growth are, and what their next steps should be. Teachers need to feel safe to try new instructional practices and take risks. That means we create an environment where we welcome error. Mistakes are proof that we are trying something new. We can learn from those mistakes and improve and grow. Teachers need to feel they are being supported by the building administrator and instructional coaches and that our presence in their classrooms will make them more effective teachers.

As leaders, we must first and foremost be the instructional leaders of our schools. We need to have instructional conversations with our teachers and engage in dialogue that will make them better teachers. We should constantly reflect on and assess our leadership. Is our leadership making a difference in our teachers? Is their instruction improving? Has our feedback improved their instruction? Are we enabling them to have a greater impact on their students' learning?

# Collaboration

It is important to provide teachers with time to collaborate and to establish a structure for their collaboration. We do not simply put teachers together for the sake of conversation. We establish a *purpose* for their collaboration. We create a system of collaboration and establish school leadership teams that lead and guide the work of the school. These teams are made up of the leaders within the school and help develop our teachers and grow great leaders. Our teams also impact the lives of our students as we make the best decisions for the schools, teachers, and students.

It is also important to embrace the stakeholders of the school and bring them along on the literacy journey. It is important to educate the parents and be transparent in the literacy work that we are doing as a school and specifically with their student. We should notify the parents of struggling readers and honestly let them know where their student is on their literacy journey, where they are proficient, and the areas where they need an intervention. We share the intervention plan and goals that have been set for their student. We keep parents updated throughout the year on how their student is doing and whether or not they are making progress. We should embrace our community members and let them know where we are and what we are doing in our schools. We share our goals and vision for the school with all stakeholders. We also need to bring our school board members along on the journey. They need to know where we are with our current data, what goals have been set, and how close we are to reaching those goals. It takes everyone working together to truly make a difference and have the greatest impact on student achievement. Teachers working together and learning from one another to improve student learning is the truest form of collaboration.

# This Is Life-Changing Work

Throughout this journey, we have to remind ourselves that this is important work. Life-changing work. Our students depend on us. Students can reach literacy proficiency because of the work we do in our schools. I have often said that being a building principal was by far the hardest job I've ever had, but it was also the most rewarding work I've ever done! When times get tough, and they definitely will, we need to remember our students. Everything we do is because of those individuals who are counting on us. There is nothing more rewarding than witnessing a student learn to read. It is powerful! My favorite memories of being a principal are celebrating the reading goals and milestones with students. Celebrating when students reached grade level and no longer needed interventions. Celebrating when students were able to read with 100 percent accuracy. Celebrating one goal at a time on the progression to literacy for all. Literacy empowers students. I have watched students go from being anxious, discouraged, and feeling they just could not do it to seeing them transform, walking straighter and taller, holding their heads up, maintaining eye contact, and being empowered because they have learned to read. It's possible for all students to experience that feeling. That is the work we are called to do.

## Compliance Versus Commitment

As educators, we often do things because those things need to be done. We do the work and make a check mark when the work is done. We stay in compliance. Changing the literacy trajectory in a school and district is not merely compliance work. There has to be a true commitment from everyone involved that we are going to make a change in our literacy practices and we are going to have a greater impact on the lives of our students. Compliance may help us establish the routines, procedures, and protocols, but true commitment leads to literacy for *all*.

## All Means All

We hope that this book changes the lives of students, teachers, and leaders. Literacy for all is more than just a hope, however. It's possible, but we need to wrap our minds around the word *all*. All students deserve to learn to read. All students deserve a teacher who knows how students learn to read. All teachers deserve a leader who will ensure they gain the knowledge of the science of reading and work in an environment where the work is done on a daily basis. All can learn. All can make progress. All can learn to read. All schools can experience literacy for all. We must embrace that all really means *all*. Do you believe that? Are you ready to make that happen in your school?

# Literacy for All Is Possible

Currently, about one-third of the students in the United States read at grade level. Research tells us that 95 percent of students can read at grade level. We, as the authors of the book, firmly believe that this is possible! We have seen it, lived it, and desperately want all schools to achieve this with their students. We readily admit that it is hard work, but it is possible. However, the right thing to do is rarely easy. If this was easy, then all schools in the United States would already be highly performing.

We can change our current reality. We can become the instructional leaders who create environments that make learning possible for all students. We can create schools where all students are welcomed, all can learn, and all feel safe to grow, make mistakes, and reach their highest potential. We can create schools where all teachers come together to grow, master their craft, and teach explicitly. Every student deserves to learn to read, and they deserve to have a teacher who fully understands how a student learns to read. All students and teachers deserve a leader who will be an instructional leader and who believes all students can be successful and learn to read.

Let's join together and take on the challenge of literacy for *all*. Let's change lives. Educators have the opportunity to make a difference and change lives every single day. Teaching a student to read changes their life forever. It opens opportunities for them and puts them on a different path. To do that, we simply have to start the work. Lead from wherever you are currently. That is exactly how my journey began. I was a classroom teacher who had just received training on the science of reading. When I learned that there was over forty years of research about what worked and what students needed for instruction to learn to read, I thought, "Why don't we just do that?" So, I began the work in my classroom. I changed what I taught and how I taught. I went into my classroom and started teaching my students and providing effective literacy instruction using research-based instructional practices. It began with one teacher. The students' data began to change. Teachers paid attention. One teacher became two teachers, then four teachers, a grade level, a school, and so on.

Where are you on your literacy journey? What does your data look like? What improvements would you like to make? What would you like to begin in your school after reading this book? And finally, what would you do if anything were possible?

With our leadership, we can build the systems and structures that make this work *possible* for *all*. The beauty of the work is that it can be replicated in all schools. We can all become practitioners who put the research of effective schools into place. We can enable teams to work together to solve problems and achieve goals. We can empower teachers and show them how to effectively impact their students' learning. We can create these schools! We can do this work and make literacy possible for all! We owe it to our students. We owe it to our staff members. We owe it to our families and communities. It is a great responsibility, but it is also a great opportunity. This is what we are called to do, and it is our moral obligation. Our students are depending on us. Let's begin the work, stay the course, and make the possible become a reality. The time is now. Let's lead and prove to everyone that *it's possible*!

# *Appendix A*

# Science of Reading Overview

We understand that school leaders find themselves in the principalship with a variety of experiences and backgrounds. If you perhaps are a secondary person who has just stepped into the elementary world, or have little background in the science of reading, the following is a brief overview.

Across the United States, within school districts, schools, and even within classrooms, there are various approaches to how students are taught to read. For the most part, they come under names such as *whole language, balanced literacy*, or the *science of reading*. There is a preponderance of research that supports how students learn to read. In the education world, it has become known as the science of reading. To ensure that schools are relying on this research, many states have passed legislation that ensures students receive the best reading instruction.

The Reading League (2021) published the following definition of the science of reading in *Science of Reading: Defining Guide*:

> The *science of reading* is a vast, interdisciplinary body of *scientifically based** research about reading and issues related to reading and writing.
>
> This research has been conducted over the last five decades across the world, and it is derived from thousands of studies conducted in multiple languages. The science of reading has culminated in a preponderance of evidence to inform how proficient reading and writing develop; why some have difficulty; and how we can most effectively assess and teach and, therefore, improve student outcomes through prevention of and intervention for reading difficulties. (p. 6)

There are two well-established constructs of how students learn to read that are based on this preponderance of scientific evidence: the simple view of reading (see figure A.1, page 254) and Scarborough's rope (www.azed.gov/scienceofreading/scarbreadingrope).

These models highlight the various complexities of reading. Both constructs illustrate that, to arrive at the end result of comprehension, there are many strands, factors, and components that must be in place to succeed. Both of these constructs of how students learn to read are based on the final outcome of comprehending what is read. Both constructs also illustrate that, to arrive at the end result of comprehension, there are many factors that must be in place to succeed. In other words, learning to read is a *process.* Describing or answering questions about what we read is the *outcome* or *product* of reading.

*The Simple View of Reading* is a formula that was developed in 1986 by Philip B. Gough and William E. Tunmer. Gough and Tunmer (1986) observed that early reading has two components: (1) print knowledge and (2) comprehension. Beginning readers can already comprehend spoken language. They will be able to read if they can just gain access to language from print (Seidenberg, 2017). Mark Seidenberg (2017) goes on to interpret Gough and Tunmer's understanding by explaining that written words must be recognized and understood efficiently, requiring basic skills. Basic skills and comprehension are not independent; both are tied to spoken language, and they shape each other over the course of learning to read (Seidenberg, 2017).

The simple view formula, orignially presented by Gough and Tunmer in 1986, can be observed in figure A.1.

*Source: The Reading League, 2021, p. 17.*

**FIGURE A.1:** The simple view of reading.

*Scarborough's Reading Rope* was developed by Hollis Scarborough in 2001, and it depicts skilled reading as a rope consisting of lower and upper strands. Word recognition strands include the skills of phonological awareness, decoding, and sight word recognition. The language comprehension strands include background knowledge, vocabulary, language structure, verbal reasoning, and literacy knowledge. Both strands must be woven together to create a skilled reader, or a reader who comprehends.

In educational settings, this science of reading approach can sometimes be called a structured literacy approach. This approach relies on the five components of reading. These five components include (1) phonemic awareness, (2) phonics, (3) fluency, (4) vocabulary, and (5) comprehension. In a structured literacy approach, it is typically best taught using a core reading program. This core reading program generally has a clear *scope* and *sequence* so that students learn to read in a hierarchy method. Simple skills such as letters and sounds are taught first, then progressing consonant-vowel-consonant words—commonly referred to as CVC words—long vowel letters, compound words, and then multisyllable words. This hierarchy of skills enables students to master a logical progression of learning to read—a structured approach to literacy.

In a structured literacy approach, students spend a great deal of time in kindergarten through second grade focusing on learning to master word recognition. This is generally taught using resources such as decodable text. A student in these grades becomes fluent and practices acquiring *fluency* by practicing the skills in *decodable text* as well as reading in authentic text that aligns to these skills. *Comprehension* at this age is best taught through listening comprehension, which the teacher may provide in a story being read to the students. Typically, in grades K–2, *vocabulary* is explicitly and implicitly taught while students are listening to a story and in daily classroom use.

To ensure that each student receives the reading instruction geared toward their needs, a literacy block is usually divided into two sections, *whole-group instruction* and *small-group instruction*. Whole-group instruction generally ranges in time from thirty-five to forty-five minutes, increasing in time by grade level. Small-group instruction, where students meet with their teacher to receive instruction aligned to their needs, usually lasts twenty to twenty-five minutes per group. Though there is no solid research to substantiate that a literacy block should be 120 minutes, in the hundreds of schools we have worked with, we have found this to be the ideal number of minutes needed to ensure all students receive quality literacy instruction. In some of our schools, where the contractual day is limited to six hours and fifteen minutes, ninety minutes had to work. In situations such as this, students reading at grade level or above were not seen for small-group instruction by the teacher five days per week. Instead, the teacher would check in with those students as needed, at a minimum of one to two times per week.

It is during the literacy block that classrooms should be using a core reading program and should be comprised of the five components of literacy. Understand that no core reading program is perfect in every component of literacy instruction; therefore, a school may select to *supplement* its core program.

It is important to keep in mind that, for a student to master reading skills, they need a great deal of practice. An opportunity to practice the skills they are learning is critical. If the supplemental programs the school is using do not align with the instruction they are being given, a student may become confused and, in fact, may not have the chance to master any of the skills. When schools select supplemental materials, it is critical they align with the scope and sequence and with the skills being taught in the core reading program.

When students enter grades K–3, they are administered a benchmark assessment. To assure that a student is progressing as needed, this benchmark assessment is administered three times per year. Most benchmark assessments can be provided four times per year. We find and recommend that administering a benchmark assessment three times per year is sufficient. This measure is also used to determine whether a student is on grade level, above grade level, below grade level, or well below grade level.

For a number of reasons, some schools or districts have decided that a variety of tests should be used once the mandatory assessments have been given. Many assessments outside

## Phonological Processing Interventions

Over 90 percent of struggling readers we have assessed over the past seven years have phonological processing issues. Rather than provide a diagnostic assessment for each of these students, we have found that using a phonological processing intervention that has a placement test, along with various entry points (instructional levels) into the intervention program, saves a great deal of time. Further, this streamlines the intervention process regarding oversight, management, training, and implementation.

of this list can be very subjective and are lengthy to administer. These can take away from valuable instructional time and are not recommended.

If a student is not scoring at benchmark (grade level) on the research-based assessment, the school should then put into process three actions:

1. Provide a diagnostic screening assessment to determine the appropriate interventions for the student.
2. Provide interventions for the student.
3. Progress monitor how the student is doing to attain grade-level literacy skills and proficiency.

Note: Students should be progress monitored on the same tool with which they are being benchmarked.

# Intervention

Extending the duration and time a student receives intervention is critical. If a student receives interventions five times, and that is aligned with the student's needs, the student has a much greater likelihood of reaching grade-level proficiency in reading level than if they had received the intervention three or even four times per week. It is therefore important that a student identified as at risk or reading below grade level receives interventions at an appropriate frequency with interventions proven to be effective (Fletcher, Lyon, Fuchs, & Barnes, 2019).

Some schools use multiple interventions. Again, if interventions are not aligned in all tiers of instruction, core, supplemental, and intervention programming (in other words, students receiving the same skill instruction throughout their day utilizing the same language and phrasing), then the student is apt to become confused and not able to master the intended skills. In other words, do not confuse the confused. We suggest that schools focus their interventions by aligning their instruction so students are more likely to achieve grade-level proficiency.

It is our hope that certified teachers provide interventions to students. In some cases, this is not possible, and schools may have dedicated paraprofessionals providing interventions. Paraprofessionals can be highly effective in providing interventions if they have been trained in the intervention in which they are providing instruction.

There are specific interventions that are recommended that the student should receive. These interventions have gone through an extensive vetting process and are proven to be effective. Some schools have decided to provide students with alternative interventions, but these interventions are not considered as effective and typically do not align with the science of reading.

# Data

A lot can be discovered regarding how a school is doing in the teaching of reading by simply looking at their reading data. There is a wide body of research that indicates 95 percent of all students can be at grade level by the end of third grade. Each school should be striving to meet this percentage.

The data detailing how your school district is doing can be found through the benchmark assessments provided to students. Outcomes of the state summative assessment in English language arts is also an indicator of how students are reading.

The fewer the students in the lowest instructional level, and the higher the reading level of students, we can surmise that the school or district is teaching reading with aligned materials rooted in the science of reading. Of course, it is also dependent on how many students enter the school at risk for reading difficulties.

It is imperative that all students who are reading below grade level, even those not on an intervention plan or with disabilities, are receiving evidence-based reading instructional programming. It is important that all students below grade level are able to receive interventions. Consideration should be given to who provides the intervention, the frequency of the intervention, and for what duration of time the intervention occurs.

# Instructional Practices and Programs

Since there are various understandings of the science of reading, we have created a list below of some commonly implemented instructional practices and programs in the area of literacy that we consider red flags. These should not be considered programs and strategies that align with the findings from the science of reading. These include:

- Balanced Literacy
- The Daily Five Café
- Fountas and Pinnell Guided Reading
- Four Block Literacy Model
- Leveled Literacy Intervention
- Literacy Footprints Next Steps
- Lucy Calkins' Units of Study
- Reading Recovery
- Workshop Model

# Resources

We have found that once most principals start to learn about the science of reading, they want to become even more knowledgeable. The following is a list of some of our favorite resources to get you going.

- *Language at the Speed of Sight* by Mark Seidenberg (2017)
- *Reading in the Brain: The New Science of How We Read* by Stanislas Dehaene (2009)
- *Speech to Print: Language Essentials for Teachers, Third Edition* by Louisa C. Moats (2020a)
- *Shifting the Balance: Six Ways to Bring the Science of Reading Into the Balanced Literacy Classroom* by Jan Burkins and Kari Yates (2021)
- *Proust and the Squid: The Story and Science of the Reading Brain* by Maryanne Wolf (2007)

# Lesson Plan Template

The following lesson plan is designed for whole-group instruction for grades 3 through 5.

# Generic Lesson Plan Template for Grades 3–5

| Weekly Lesson Plan |
| --- |
| Grades 3–5 |
| Unit_____ Week_____ |

| Preplanning Section |
| --- |
| Standards being taught: |
| Necessary background knowledge: |
| Phonics/word study focus: |
| Vocabulary words for unit: |
| Comprehension focus: |

| Day 1 (50–60 minutes) |
| --- |
| Phonics/word study objective: |
| Comprehension objective: |

| Vocabulary words: | |
|---|---|
| Standards taught: | |
| 15 minutes | Phonics/word study: |
| 10 minutes | Build background knowledge: |
| 15 minutes | Directly teach vocabulary: |
| 15–20 minutes | Comprehension: |

### Day 2 (50–60 minutes)

| Phonics/word study objective: | |
|---|---|
| Comprehension objective: | |
| Standards taught: | |
| 15 minutes | Phonics/word study: |

**It's Possible!** © 2025 Solution Tree Press • SolutionTree.com
Visit **go.SolutionTree.com/literacy** to download this free reproducible.

| | |
|---|---|
| 10 minutes | Directly teach vocabulary: |
| 5–10 minutes | Review previous day's reading and fluency model: |
| 20–30 minutes | Comprehension focus: |

## Day 3 (50–60 minutes)

**Phonics/word study objective:**

**Comprehension objective:**

**Standards taught:**

| | |
|---|---|
| 15 minutes | Phonics/word study: |
| 10 minutes | Vocabulary: |
| 5 minutes | Purpose for reading/fluency model: |
| 20–30 minutes | Comprehension focus: |

| Day 4 (50–60 minutes) | |
| --- | --- |
| **Phonics/word study objective:** | |
| **Comprehension objective:** | |
| **Standards taught:** | |
| 15 minutes | **Phonics/word study:** |
| 10 minutes | **Vocabulary:** |
| 5 minutes | **Review/discuss previous story/reading and fluency model:** |
| 20–30 minutes | **Comprehension focus:** |

| Day 5 (50–60 minutes) | |
| --- | --- |
| **Phonics/word study objective:** | |
| **Comprehension objective:** | |
| **Standards taught:** | |

| 15 minutes | **Phonics/word study:** Likely, a cumulative review of previous four days; it should include dictation, encoding, and so on. |
| --- | --- |
| 10 minutes | **Vocabulary:** Interactive activity using vocabulary taught throughout the unit. |
| 25–35 minutes | **Comprehension focus:** This should be a cumulative activity of stories/passages read including comparing and contrasting and/or analysis of the stories/passages. If writing has not been integrated with the unit—begin writing activity aligned with big ideas. |

*Source: © 2022 by Schools Cubed (https://itspossible.schoolscubed.com). Used with permission.*

*Appendix C*

# Performance Level Profiles With Small-Group Suggestions

Use the figures in this appendix in conjunction with the descriptions of how to intervene and differentiate in chapter 6 (page 145).

| Screening Performance Level Student Profiles for Kindergarten | Big Ideas For Small-Group Instruction | Instructional Routine/Intervention | Suggested Resources for Teachers | Progress Monitoring Probe | Frequency of Probe | Independent Work During Small Group |
|---|---|---|---|---|---|---|
| **Well below in subskill of letter naming fluency, letter-sound fluency** | Begin with letters in the student's names. Teach five to seven letters at a time. Begin with teaching uppercase letters. Include teaching formation of letters. Have students repeat the letter name and the sound it makes as they are writing the letter name. Ensure students have appropriate whiteboards or paper with appropriately sized lines. Duration—15 to 20 minutes | 2–3 minutes—Direct instruction in designated letter names and accompanying sounds via flash cards 2–4 minutes—Practicing letter formation on whiteboards 8–10 minutes—Various hands-on activities with alphabet strips, alphabet arcs or mats, letter cards | *Next STEPS in Literacy Instruction* (Smartt & Glaser, 2024) Reading Teachers Source Book Seven Mighty Moves: Research-Backed, Classroom-Tested Strategies to Ensure K-to-3 Reading Success (Kemeny, 2023) FCRR alphabetic principle lessons https://fcrr.org /student-center-activities /kindergarten -and-first-grade Reading Rockets: The Alphabetic Principle https://www .readingrockets.org /topics/phonics-and -decoding/articles /alphabetic-principle Climbing the Ladder of Reading and *Writing* (Young & Hasbrouck, 2024) | Measures of letter names and letter sounds or phoneme segmentation | Weekly | Matching pictures or objects to beginning sound or end sound • Practicing letters and sounds on computer program • Handwriting practice of focus letters • Paper with alphabet printed in circle, students clothes pin letters to correct letter on circle • Students pair lowercase letter to uppercase letter |
| **Below in subskill of letter-naming fluency, letter sounds** | Identify specifically the letters the student has not yet mastered that have been taught in core content. Begin with five to seven letters. Add all letters on occasion. Include teaching formation of letters. Have students repeat the letter name and the sound it makes as they are writing the letter name. | 2–3 minutes—Direct instruction in designated letter names and accompanying sounds via flash cards 2–3 minutes—Practicing letter formation on whiteboards 8–9 minutes—Various hands-on activities with alphabet strips, alphabet arcs or mats, letter cards | See above | See above | Every two weeks or monthly | See above |

| Performance level | | | | | | |
|---|---|---|---|---|---|---|
| **Below benchmark in phoneme segmentation and nonsense word fluency (generally tested the second semester of kindergarten)** | Ensure students have appropriate whiteboards or paper with appropriately sized lines. Duration—10 to 15 minutes. Reinforce with phoneme-grapheme mapping. Begin to introduce decodable text and passages. Use Elkonin boxes. Use Blending boards. Use letter tiles and plastic letters. | 5–7 minutes—Direct instruction and review in the phonetic element that data indicate the student needs; note: at Tier 3, instruction may not be aligned with whole-group instruction. 3–5 minutes—Direct instruction and practice in phoneme-graphing mapping in the same phonetic element taught above 4–5 minutes—Writing words that contain the same phonetic element being taught 4–7 minutes—Reading a short passage—one or two sentences of the phonetic element being taught using the same decodable routine | See above | Phoneme segmentation (if needed) and (or) nonsense word fluency | Weekly | Practice letter formation. Use flip books to create words; write words in reading journal. Incorporate writing, such as sentence writing. Practice reading decodables. |
| **On track with all subskill probes** | Begin to develop phoneme-grapheme mapping. Begin to introduce decodable text. Align all instruction with whole-group instruction. | 5 minutes—Phoneme-grapheme mapping with letters and sounds directly taught in whole-group lesson 2–3 minutes—Practice with blending board 2–3 minutes—Review of any irregular words taught 5–10 minutes—Reading the aligned text from core (if decodable) or read earliest decodable passage | See above and also include: Elkonin boxes Blending boards Letter tiles/plastic letters Entry-level decodable text | Use grade-level benchmark assessment as indicated on foundational reading assessment. | At benchmark unless a subskill is below grade-level expectation | Practice letter formation. Use flip books to create words—write words in reading journal. Incorporate writing such as sentence writing. Practice reading decodables. |
| **Above grade level on all subskill probes** | Depending on the reading level of students, they may start to explore novel sets at their appropriate level. | Discussion and comprehension focus on text being read. May meet with this group one to two times per week | *Climbing the Ladder of Reading and Writing* (Young & Hasbrouck, 2024) | Use grade-level benchmark assessment as indicated on foundational reading assessment. We suggest three times per year. | At scheduled benchmark assessment | |

**FIGURE C.1:** Kindergarten performance levels.

| Performance Level Student Profiles for First Grade | Big Ideas for Small-Group Instruction | Instructional Routine/Intervention | Suggested Resources for Teachers | Progress Monitoring Probe | Frequency of Probe | Independent Work During Small Group |
|---|---|---|---|---|---|---|
| **Well below benchmark in letter names and sounds** | Identify specifically the letters that the student has not yet mastered that have been taught in core content. Begin with 5–7 letters of above. Add all letters on occasion. Include teaching formation of letters. Have students repeat the letter name and the sound it makes as they are writing the letter name. Ensure students have appropriate whiteboards or paper with appropriately sized lines. Ensure lots of opportunity for multiple repetitions. | 2–3 minutes—Direct instruction in designated letter names and accompanying sounds via flash cards. 2–3 minutes—Practicing letter formation on whiteboards. 8–9 minutes—Various hands-on activities with alphabet strips, alphabet arcs or mats, letter cards. | *Next STEPS in Literacy Instruction* (Smartt & Glaser, 2024). Reading Teachers Source Book. *Seven Mighty Moves: Research-Backed, Classroom-Tested Strategies to Ensure K-to-3 Reading Success* (Kemeny, 2023). FCRR alphabetic principle lessons https://fcrr.org/student-center-activities/kindergarten-and-first-grade. Reading Rockets classroom strategy library www.readingrockets.org/classroom/classroom-strategies | Measures of letter names and letter sounds or phoneme segmentation | Weekly | Matching pictures or objects to beginning sound or end sound • Practicing letters and sounds on computer program • Handwriting practice of focus letters • Students pin matching upper- or lowercase corresponding letter on pin to mat. • Students pair lowercase letter to uppercase letter. |
| **Well below benchmark in phoneme segmentation and nonsense word fluency** | Reinforce with phoneme-grapheme mapping. Begin to introduce decodable text and passages. Use Elkonin boxes, blending boards, or letter tiles/plastic letters. | 5–7 minutes—Direct instruction/review in the phonetic element that data indicate the student needs (Note: at Tier 3, instruction may not be aligned with whole-group instruction). 3–5 minutes—Direct instruction and practice in phoneme-graphing mapping in the same phonetic element taught above. 4–5 minutes—Writing words that contain the same phonetic element being taught. 4–7 minutes—Reading a short passage, one or two sentences of the phonetic element being taught using the same decodable routine | See above | Phoneme segmentation (if needed) and nonsense word fluency | Weekly | Practice letter formation. Use flip books to create words—write words in reading journal. Incorporate writing such as sentence writing. Practice reading decodables. |

| Performance level | | | | | |
|---|---|---|---|---|---|
| **Below benchmark in phoneme segmentation and nonsense word fluency** | Should be aligned with the phonics and phonological skill that was taught in current or previous lessons in core or universal instruction. Reinforce with blending boards, Elkonin boxes. Reread portion of same passage/decodable as in whole-group/core instruction. | 5–7 minutes—Direct instruction/review in the phonetic element being taught in the whole-group lesson 3–5 minutes—Reading word lists containing the phonetic element or use of blending board 4–5 minutes—Direct instruction in reading a decodable text aligned with the phonetic element or with the decodable from the core story 5–7 minutes—Repeated reading of the decodable text to establish fluency | See above | Phoneme segmentation (if needed) and nonsense word fluency | Every ten days or monthly | Partner reading core text, partner reading decodable Letter formation Creating words from flip books and writing in reading journal Work on technology such as Lexia (no longer than twenty minutes) Irregular word practice Listening to recorded word lists and encoding independently |
| **Benchmark in all subskills** | Should be aligned to grade-level skills in any of the components. It should be tied to the core text. Teacher should analyze based on the needs of the group. Typically, for at grade level, students may need support in becoming more fluent readers using the core text. | 5–7 minutes—Direct instruction in the core component that the teacher is teaching 10–12 minutes—Working in the grade-level text and incorporating comprehension skills | See above | At benchmark unless there is a subskill that is below benchmark. That subskill should be progress monitored appropriately. | At scheduled benchmark assessments. For students just at benchmark, we recommend a monthly probe. | Reading appropriate level text with a partner Creating words from flip book and recording in reading journal |
| **Above benchmark in all Subskills** | May begin to explore novels, extended learning comparing the passage read to other books or passages read. This should include writing. | Discussion and comprehension focus on text being read. May meet with this group one or two times per week. | *Climbing the Ladder of Reading and Writing* (Young & Hasbrouck, 2024) | Use grade-level benchmark assessment as indicated on foundational reading assessment. We suggest three times per year. | At scheduled benchmark assessment | Novel reading Writing Extended work on computer that aligns with either core story or independent reading |

**FIGURE C.2:** First-grade performance levels.

| Screening Performance Level Student Profiles for Second Grade | Big Ideas for Small-Group Instruction | Instructional Routine/Intervention | Suggested Resources for Teachers and Students | Progress Monitoring Probe | Frequency of Probe | Independent Work During Small Group |
|---|---|---|---|---|---|---|
| **Well below benchmark on oral reading fluency—accuracy** | Lots of opportunity for multiple repetitions<br><br>Opportunities to read connected text frequently<br><br>Should also be receiving an intensive intervention in phonological processing | 3–5 minutes—Direct instruction in the phonetic element being taught in interventions<br><br>3–5 minutes—Practiced dictation of words with phonetic element being taught<br><br>10–13 minutes—Oral reading practice of decodable text that aligns with interventions | Decodable text<br><br>*Next STEPS in Literacy Instruction* (Smartt & Glaser, 2024)<br><br>*Reading Teachers Source Book*<br><br>*Seven Mighty Moves: Research-Backed, Classroom-Tested Strategies to Ensure K-to-3 Reading Success* (Kemeny, 2023)<br><br>Reading Rockets classroom strategy library www.readingrockets .org/classroom /classroom-strategies | Nonsense word fluency—CLS and WWR | Weekly | Repeated reading of previously taught decodable text<br><br>Partner reading of decodable text<br><br>Lexia training in phonics (limit to twenty minutes per day)<br><br>Practices with irregularly spelled words that have been previously taught<br><br>Spelling center of words aligned to Tier 3 intervention |
| **Below benchmark on word reading fluency** | Struggling with instantaneous recognition of words<br><br>Frequent opportunities to repeat reading of what is being taught or has been taught | 3–5 minutes—Direct instruction and reviewing the core phonetic element being taught in whole-group instruction<br><br>12–15 minutes—Oral rereading of the passage read during whole-group instruction with a focus on fluent reading | See above<br><br>Dyad reading routine<br><br>Repeated reading passages from core reading program<br><br>*Reading Fluency: Understand—Assess—Teach* (Hasbrouck & Glaser, 2019) | Oral reading fluency—examining progress in word rate | Every ten days or monthly | Partner reading of core story<br><br>Rereading of previously taught/read core story<br><br>Recording reading of story into computer for teacher to analyze later<br><br>Practice of irregularly spelled words<br><br>Vocabulary work<br><br>Writing work<br><br>Spelling practice |

| At benchmark on all subskills | Should be aligned to grade-level skills in any of the components. It should be tied to the core text. Teacher should analyze based on the needs of the group. Typically, for at grade level, students may need support in becoming more fluent readers using the core text. | 5–7 minutes—Direct instruction in the core component that the teacher is teaching 10–12 minutes—Working in the grade-level text and incorporating comprehension skills | *Next STEPS in Literacy Instruction* (Smartt & Glaser, 2024) Reading Teachers Source Book *Seven Mighty Moves: Research-Backed, Classroom-Tested Strategies to Ensure K-to-3 Reading Success* (Kemeny, 2023) Reading Rockets classroom strategy library www.readingrockets.org/classroom/classroom-strategies | At benchmark unless there is a subskill that is below benchmark. That subskill should be progress moniotred appropriately. | At scheduled benchmark assessments. For students just at benchmark, we recommend a monthly probe. | Vocabulary work Writing work Spelling practice Responding to text |
| Above benchmark on all subskills | May begin to explore novels, extended learning comparing the passage read to other books or passages read. Should include writing, responding to text, independent projects related to standards and core content. | Discussion and comprehension focus on text being read. May meet with this group one to two times per week. | *Climbing the Ladder of Reading and Writing* (Young & Hasbrouck, 2024) | Use grade-level benchmark assessment as indicated on foundational reading assessment. We suggest three times per year. | At scheduled benchmark assessment | Novel reading Writing Extended work on computer that aligns with either core story or independent reading |

**FIGURE C.3:** Second-grade performance levels.

| Screening Performance Level Student Profiles for Third | Big Ideas for Small-Group Instruction | Instructional Routine/Intervention | Suggested Resources for Teachers and Students | Progress Monitoring Probe | Frequency of Probe | Independent Work During Small Group |
|---|---|---|---|---|---|---|
| **Well below benchmark phonemic segmentation/nonsense word fluency** | Lots of opportunity for multiple repetitions<br><br>Opportunities to read connected text frequently<br><br>Should also be receiving an intensive intervention in phonological processing | 3–5 minutes—Direct instruction in the phonetic element being taught in interventions<br><br>12–15 minute—Oral reading practice of decodable text that aligns with interventions | Decodable text<br><br>Next STEPS in Literacy Instruction (Smartt & Glaser, 2024)<br><br>Reading Teachers Source Book<br><br>Seven Mighty Moves: Research-Backed, Classroom-Tested Strategies to Ensure K-to-3 Reading Success (Kemeny, 2023)<br><br>Reading Rockets classroom strategy library www.readingrockets.org/classroom/classroom-strategies | Oral reading fluency—examining progress in accuracy measure | Weekly | Repeated reading of previously taught decodable text<br><br>Partner reading of decodable text<br><br>Lexia training in phonics (limit to twenty minutes per day)<br><br>Practices with irregularly spelled words that have been previously taught<br><br>Spelling center of words aligned to Tier 3 intervention |
| **Below benchmark on word reading fluency** | Struggling with instantaneous recognition of words<br><br>Frequent opportunities to repeat reading of what is being taught or has been taught | 3–5 minutes—Reviewing the content previously read of the core story<br><br>10–15 minutes—Rereading or prereading core story with a target of fluency; teacher models, and students choral read, partner read, or read for prosody and expression. | See above<br><br>Dyad reading routine<br><br>Repeated reading passages from core reading program<br><br>Appropriate Lexile level stories read with partner or teacher<br><br>Reading Fluency: Understand—Assess—Teach (Hasbrouck & Glaser, 2018) | Oral reading fluency—examining progress in word rate | Every ten days or monthly | Partner reading of core story<br><br>Partner reading of Lexile-leveled book<br><br>Rereading of previously taught/read core story<br><br>Recording reading of story into computer for teacher to analyze later<br><br>Practice of irregularly spelled words<br><br>Vocabulary work<br><br>Writing work<br><br>Spelling practice |

| Profile | Description | Time/Grouping | Resources | Assessment | Schedule | Independent work |
|---|---|---|---|---|---|---|
| **At benchmark on all subskills** <br> **Profile: On track with all screening probes** | Should be aligned to grade-level skills in any of the components. It should be tied to the core text. Teacher should analyze based on the needs of the group. Typically, for at grade level, students may need support in becoming more fluent readers using the core text. | 5–7 minutes—Direct instruction in the core component that the teacher is teaching <br><br> 10–12 minutes—Working in the grade-level text and incorporating comprehension skills | *Next STEPS in Literacy Instruction* (Smartt & Glaser, 2024) <br><br> Reading Teachers Source Book <br><br> *Seven Mighty Moves: Research-Backed, Classroom-Tested Strategies to Ensure K-to-3 Reading Success* (Kemeny, 2023) <br><br> Reading Rockets classroom strategy library www.readingrockets.org/classroom/classroom-strategies | At benchmark unless there is a subskill that is below benchmark. That subskill should be progress monitored appropriately. | At scheduled benchmark assessments. For students just at benchmark, we recommend a monthly probe. | Vocabulary work <br> Writing work <br> Spelling practice <br> Responding to text |
| **Above benchmark on all subskills** | May begin to explore novels, extended learning comparing the passage read to other books or passages read. Should include writing, responding to text, independent projects related to standards and core content. | Discussion and comprehension focus on text being read. May meet with this group one to two times per week. | *Climbing the Ladder of Reading and Writing* (Young & Hasbrouck, 2024) | Use grade-level benchmark assessment as indicated on foundational reading assessment. We suggest three times per year. | At scheduled benchmark assessment | Novel reading <br> Writing <br> Extended work on computer that aligns with either core story or independent reading |

**FIGURE C.4:** Third-grade and up performance levels.

# References
and Resources

Aaron, P. G., Joshi, M., & Williams, K. A. (1999). Not all reading disabilities are alike. *Journal of Learning Disabilities, 32*(2), 120–137.

Acadience Learning. (2020, January 13). *Progress monitoring with Acadience Reading K–6.* Accessed at https://acadiencelearning.org/wp-content/uploads/2020/03/2020-02 _Progress_Monitoring _Guidelines_color.pdf on March 12, 2024.

Adams, G. L., & Engelmann, S. (1996). *Research on direct instruction: 25 years beyond DISTAR.* Seattle, WA: Educational Achievement Systems.

Agarwal, P. K., & Bain, P. M. (2019). *Powerful teaching: Unleash the science of learning.* San Francisco: Jossey-Bass.

Aguilar, E. (2013). *The art of coaching: Effective strategies for school transformation.* San Francisco: Jossey-Bass.

Al Otaiba, S., Connor, C. M., Foorman, B., Schatschneider, C., Greulich, L., & Sidler, J. F. (2009). Identifying and intervening with beginning readers who are at-risk for dyslexia. *Perspectives on Language and Literacy, 35*(4), 13–19.

Allor, J. H., Mathes, P. G., Roberts, J. K., Cheatham, J. P., & Al Otaiba, S. (2014). Is scientifically based reading instruction effective for students with below-average IQs? *Exceptional Children, 80*(3), 287–306.

Archer, A. L., & Hughes, C. A. (2011). *Explicit instruction: Effective and efficient teaching.* New York: Guilford Press.

Bambrick-Santoya, P. (2012). *Leverage leadership: A practical guide to building exceptional schools.* Hoboken, NJ: Jossey-Bass.

Beck, I. L., McKeown, M. G., & Gromoll, E. W. (1989). Learning from social studies texts. *Cognition and Instruction, 6*(2), 99–158.

Beck, I. L., McKeown, M. G., & Kucan, L. (2008). *Creating robust vocabulary: Frequently asked questions and extended examples.* New York: Guilford Press.

Bell, N. (2023). *A deep dive into phonemic proficiency.* Macquarie Park, NSW, Australia: Five from Five/MultiLit Pty Ltd. Accessed at https://fivefromfive.com.au/wp-content/uploads/2023/03/A-deep-dive-into-phonemic-proficiency_Mar2023.pdf on October 22, 2024.

Berninger, V. W. (2000). Development of language by hand and its connections with language by ear, mouth, and eye. *Topics in Language Disorders, 20*(4), 65–84.

Birsh, J. R., & Carreker, S. (Eds.). (2018). *Multisensory teaching of basic language skills* (4th ed.). Baltimore, MD: Brookes.

Blachman, B. A., Schatschneider, C., Fletcher, J. M., Francis, D. J., Clonan, S. M., Shaywitz, B. A., et al. (2004). Effects of intensive reading remediation for second and third graders and a 1-year follow-up. *Journal of Educational Psychology, 96*(3), 444–461.

Boyes, M. E., Tebbutt, B., Preece, K. A., & Badcock, N. A. (2018). Relationships between reading ability and student mental health: Moderating effects of self-esteem. *Australian Psychologist, 53*(2), 125–133.

Brown, L. T., Mohr, K. A. J., Wilcox, B. R., & Barrett, T. S. (2018). The effects of dyad reading and text difficulty on third-graders' reading achievement. *Journal of Educational Research, 111*(5), 541–553.

Buffum, A., Mattos, M., & Malone, J. (2018). *Taking action: A handbook for RTI at Work.* Bloomington, IN: Solution Tree Press.

Buffum, A., Mattos, M., & Weber, C. (2012). *Simplifying response to intervention: Four essential guiding principles.* Bloomington, IN: Solution Tree Press.

Bulkley, K. E., Oláh, L. N., & Blanc, S. (2010). Introduction to the special issue on benchmarks for success? Interim assessments as a strategy for educational improvement. *Peabody Journal of Education, 85*(2), 115–124.

Burkins, J., & Yates, K. (2021). *Shifting the balance: Six ways to bring the science of reading into the balanced literacy classroom.* Portsmouth, NH: Stenhouse.

Burt, J. S. (1996). Spelling in adults: Orthographic transparency, learning new letter strings and reading accuracy. *European Journal of Cognitive Psychology, 8*(1), 3–44.

Cabell, S. Q., Neuman, S. B., & Terry, N. P. (Eds.). (2023). *Handbook on the science of early literacy.* New York: Guilford Press.

Cao, Y., & Kim, Y.-S. G. (2021). Is retell a valid measure of reading comprehension? *Educational Research Review, 32*, Article 100375. https://doi.org/10.1016/j.edurev.2020.100375

Carnine, D. W., Silbert, J., Kame'enui, E. J., Slocum, T. A., & Travers, P. A. (2017). *Direct instruction reading* (6th ed.). Boston: Pearson.

Castles, A., Rastle, K., & Nation, K. (2018). Ending the reading wars: Reading acquisition from novice to expert. *Psychological Science in the Public Interest, 19*(1), 5–51.

Catts, H. W., & Hogan, T. P. (2003). Language basis of reading disabilities and implications for early identification and remediation. *Reading Psychology, 24*(3–4), 223–246.

Center for School Turnaround. (2017). *Four domains for rapid school improvement: A systems framework*. San Francisco, CA: WestEd. Accessed at https://csti.wested.org/wp-content /uploads/2024/09/CST_Four-Domains-Framework.pdf on February 18, 2024.

Cerino, E. S. (2014). Relationships between academic motivation, self-efficacy, and academic procrastination. *Psi Chi Journal of Psychological Research, 19*(4), 156–163.

Chang, H., Balfanz, R., & Byrnes, V. (2022, September 27). *Pandemic causes alarming increase in chronic absence and reveals need for better data* [Blog post]. Accessed at www .attendanceworks.org/pandemic-causes-alarming-increase-in-chronic-absence-and-reveals -need-for-better-data on March 15, 2024.

Ciurczak, E. (2016, December 17). *Looking at illiteracy: Consequences and solutions*. Accessed at www.hattiesburgamerican.com/story/news/education/2016/12/17/looking-illiteracy -consequences-and-solutions/94732880 on February 18, 2024.

Clay, M. M. (1987). Learning to be learning disabled. *New Zealand Journal of Educational Studies, 22*(2), 155–173.

Clay, M. M. (2017). *Running records for classroom teachers* (2nd ed.). Portsmouth, NH: Heinneman.

Colvin, G., & Sugai, G. (2018). *Seven steps for developing a proactive schoolwide discipline plan: A guide for principals and leadership teams* (2nd ed.). Thousand Oaks, CA: Corwin Press.

Cortiella, C., Gamm, S., Rinaldi, C., & Goodman, S. (n.d.). *RTI-based SLD identification toolkit: Criterion 2—Insufficient progress to adequate instruction*. Accessed at www.rtinetwork.org /getstarted/sld-identification-toolkit/ld-identification-toolkit-criterion-2 on March 13, 2024.

Cunningham, A. E., Firestone, A. R., & Zegers, M. (2023). Measuring and improving teachers' knowledge in early literacy. In S. Q. Cabell, S. B. Neuman, & N. P. Terry (Eds.), *Handbook on the science of early literacy* (pp. 211–223). New York: Guilford Press.

Cunningham, A. E., Perry, K. E., Stanovich, K. E., & Share, D. L. (2002). Orthographic learning during reading: Examining the role of self-teaching. *Journal of Experimental Student Psychology, 82*(3), 185–199.

The Danielson Group. (n.d.). *Our story*. Accessed at https://danielsongroup.org/our-story on February 17, 2024.

Darling-Hammond, L., Hyler, M. E., & Gardner, M. (2017, June). *Effective teacher professional development*. Palo Alto, CA: Learning Policy Institute. Accessed at https:// learningpolicyinstitute.org/media/478/download?inline&file=Effective_Teacher_Professional _Development_FACTSHEET.pdf on February 20, 2024.

Dehaene, S. (2009). *Reading in the brain: The new science of how we read*. New York: Viking.

Dehaene, S. (2020). *How we learn: Why brains learn better than any machine…for now*. New York: Viking.

Deno, S. L., Fuchs, L. S., Marston, D., & Shin, J. (2001). Using curriculum-based measurement to establish growth standards for students with learning disabilities. *School Psychology Review*, *30*(4), 507–524.

Denton, C. A., Foorman, B. R., & Mathses, P. G. (2003). Perspective: Schools that "beat the odds"—Implications for reading instruction. *Remedial and Special Education*, *24*(5), 258–261.

Diamond, L., & Thorsnes, B. J. (2018). *Assessing reading multiple measures* (2nd ed.). Novato, CA: Academic Therapy.

Diliberti, M. K., & Schwartz, H. L. (2023, February 16). *Educator turnover has markedly increased, but districts have taken actions to boost teacher ranks: Selected findings from the sixth American School District Panel survey*. Santa Monica, CA: RAND. Accessed at www.rand .org/pubs/research_reports/RRA956-14.html on March 13, 2024.

DoSomething.org. (n.d.). *11 facts about literacy in America*. Accessed at www.dosomething .org/us/facts/11-facts-about-literacy-america on March 13, 2024.

DuFour, R., and Marzano, R. J. (2011). *Leaders of learning: How district, school, and classroom leaders improve student achievement*. Bloomington, IN: Solution Tree Press.

DuFour, R., DuFour, R., Eaker, R., Many, T. W., & Mattos, M. (2016). *Learning by doing: A handbook for Professional Learning Communities at Work* (3rd ed.). Bloomington, IN: Solution Tree Press.

DuFour, R., DuFour, R., Eaker, R., Many, T. W., Mattos, M., & Muhammad, A. (2024). *Learning by doing: A handbook for Professional Learning Communities at Work* (4th ed.). Bloomington, IN: Solution Tree Press.

EdWeek Research Center. (2020). *Early reading instruction: Results of a national survey*. Bethesda, MD: Author. Accessed at https://epe.brightspotcdn.com/1b/80 /706eba6246599174b0199ac1f3b5/ed-week-reading-instruction-survey-report-final -1.24.20.pdf on February 17, 2024.

Ehri, L. C. (2005). Learning to read words: Theory, findings, and issues. *Scientific Studies of Reading*, *9*(2), 167–188. https://doi.org/10.1207/s1532799xssr0902_4

Elharake, J. A., Akbar, F., Malik, A. A., Gilliam, W., & Omer, S. B. (2023). Mental health impact of COVID-19 among students and college students: A systematic review. *Student Psychiatry and Human Development*, *54*(3), 913–925.

Ellis, C., Holston, S., Drake, G., Putman, H., Swisher, A., & Peske, H. (2023). *Teacher prep review: Strengthening elementary reading instruction.* Washington, DC: National Council on Teacher Quality. Accessed at www.nctq.org/dmsView/Teacher_Prep_Review _Strengthening_Elementary_Reading_Instruction on February 17, 2024.

Epstein, M., Atkins, M., Cullinan, D., Kutash, K., & Weaver, R. (2008). *Reducing behavior problems in the elementary school classroom: A practice guide.* Washington, DC: National Center for Education Evaluation and Regional Assistance. Accessed at https://ies.ed.gov /ncee/wwc/Docs/PracticeGuide/behavior_pg_092308.pdf on March 15, 2024.

Erbeli, F., Rice, M., Xu, Y., Bishop, M. E., & Goodrich, J. M. (2024). A meta-analysis on the optimal cumulative dosage of early phonemic awareness instruction. *Scientific Studies of Reading.* https://doi.org/10.1080/10888438.2024.2309386

Farrall, M. L. (2012). *Reading assessment: Linking language, literacy, and cognition.* Hoboken, NJ: Wiley.

Farrell, T. S. C. (2012). *Reflecting on teaching the four skills: 60 strategies for professional development.* Ann Arbor, MI: The University of Michigan Press.

Flesch, R. (1955). *Why Johnny can't read—and what you can do about it.* New York: Harper.

Fletcher, J. M., Lyon, G. R., Fuchs, L. S., & Barnes, M. A. (2019). *Learning disabilities: From identification to intervention* (2nd ed.). New York: Guilford Press.

Florida Center for Reading Research. (n.d.). *FCRR student activities.* Tallahassee, FL: Florida State University. Accessed at https://fcrr.org/student-center-activities on October 22, 2024.

Foorman, B. R. (2023). Learning the code. In S. Q. Cabell, S. B. Neuman, & N. P. Terry (Eds.), *Handbook on the science of early literacy* (pp. 73–82). New York: Guilford Press.

Foorman, B. R., & Al Otaiba, S. (2009). Reading remediation: State of the art. In K. Pugh & P. McCardle (Eds.), *How students learn to read: Current issues and new directions in the integration of cognition, neurobiology and genetics of reading and dyslexia research and practice* (pp. 257–274). New York: Psychology Press.

Frey, N., Hattie, J., & Fisher, D. (2018). *Developing assessment-capable visible learners, grades K–12: Maximizing skill, will, and thrill.* Thousand Oaks, CA: Corwin Press.

Fuchs, L. S., Fuchs, D., Hosp, M. K., & Jenkins, J. R. (2001). Oral reading fluency as an indicator of reading competence: A theoretical, empirical, and historical analysis. *Scientific Studies of Reading, 5*(3), 239–256.

Fullan, M., & Quinn, J. (2016). *Coherence: The right drivers in action for schools, districts, and systems.* Thousand Oaks, CA: Corwin Press.

Gallimore, R., Ermeling, B. A., Saunders, W. M., & Goldenberg, C. (2009). Moving the learning of teaching closer to practice: Teacher education implications of school-based inquiry teams. *The Elementary School Journal, 109*(5). https://doi.org/10.1086/597001

Goldberg, M., & Goldenberg, C. (2022). Lessons learned? Reading wars, Reading First, and a way forward. *The Reading Teacher, 75*(5), 621–630.

Goldring, R., Taie, S., & Riddles, M. (2014, September). *Teacher attrition and mobility: Results from the 2012–13 teacher follow-up survey—First look.* Washington, DC: U.S. Department of Education. Accessed at https://nces.ed.gov/pubs2014/2014077.pdf on February 20, 2024.

Good, R. H., & Kaminski, R. A. (2020). *Acadience Reading K–6 assessment manual.* Accessed at https://acadiencelearning.org/wp-content/uploads/2020/08/AcadienceReading_ALO_Assessment_Manual.pdf on February 18, 2024.

Gough, P. B., & Tunmer, W. E. (1986). Decoding, reading, and reading disability. *Remedial and Special Education, 7*(1), 6–10.

Governor's Early Literacy Foundation. (n.d.). *Early literacy connection to incarceration.* Accessed at https://governorsfoundation.org/gelf-articles/early-literacy-connection-to-incarceration on March 13, 2024.

Governor's Early Literacy Foundation. (2023). *Impact.* Accessed at https://governorsfoundation.org/impact on May 27, 2024.

Grissom, J. A., Egalite, A. J., & Lindsay, C. A. (2021). *How principals affect students and schools: A systematic synthesis of two decades of research.* New York: The Wallace Foundation. Accessed at https://wallacefoundation.org/sites/default/files/2023-09/How-Principals-Affect-Students-and-Schools.pdf on March 13, 2024.

Hall, M. S., & Burns, M. K. (2018). Meta-analysis of targeted small-group reading interventions. *Journal of School Psychology, 66,* 54–66.

Hall, T., & Vue, G. (2004). *Explicit instruction: Effective classroom practices report.* Wakefield, MA: National Center on Accessing the General Curriculum. Accessed at https://aem.cast.org/binaries/content/assets/common/publications/aem/ncac-explicit-instruction-2014-10.docx on March 13, 2024.

Hanford, E. (Host). (2022). *Sold a story* [Audio podcast]. *APM Reports.* Accessed at https://features.apmreports.org/sold-a-story on March 15, 2024.

Harn, B. A., Stoolmiller, M., & Chard, D. J. (2008). Measuring the dimensions of alphabetic principle on the reading development of first graders: The role of automaticity and unitization. *Journal of Learning Disabilities, 41*(2), 143–157.

Hasbrouck, J., & Glaser, D. (2018). *Reading fluently does not mean reading fast.* International Literacy Association. Accessed at www.literacyworldwide.org/docs/default-source/where-we-stand/ila-reading-fluently-does-not-mean-reading-fast.pdf on February 20, 2024.

Hasbrouck, J., & Glaser, D. (2019). *Reading fluency: Understand—assess—teach.* New Rochelle, NY: Benchmark Education.

Hasbrouck, J., & Michel, D. (2022). *Student-focused coaching: The instructional coach's guide to supporting student success through teacher collaboration*. Baltimore, MD: Brookes.

Hattie, J. (2012). *Visible learning for teachers: Maximizing impact on learning*. New York: Routledge.

Hattie, J. (2015). *What works best in education: The politics of collaborative expertise*. London: Pearson. Accessed at www.pearson.com/content/dam/corporate/global/pearson-dot-com /files/hattie/150526_ExpertiseWEB_V1.pdf on March 13, 2024.

Hattie, J. (2023). *Visible learning: The sequel—A synthesis of over 2,100 meta-analyses relating to achievement*. New York: Routledge.

Hempenstall, K. (2013). What is the place for national assessment in the prevention and resolution of reading difficulties? *Australian Journal of Learning Difficulties, 18*(2), 105–121.

Hennessy, N. L. (2021). *The reading comprehension blueprint: Helping students make meaning from text*. Baltimore, MD: Brookes.

Hernandez, D. J. (2011). *Double jeopardy: How third-grade reading skills and poverty influence high school graduation*. Baltimore, MD: Annie E. Casey Foundation. Accessed at https://files .eric.ed.gov/fulltext/ED518818.pdf on February 18, 2024.

Hirsch, E. D. (2003). *Reading comprehension requires knowledge—of words and the world: Scientific insights into the fourth-grade slump and the nation's stagnant comprehension scores.* Accessed at www.aft.org/sites/default/files/Hirsch.pdf on February 20, 2024.

Hirsch, E. D. (2006). *The knowledge deficit: Closing the shocking education gap for American students*. Boston: Houghton Mifflin.

Hitt, D. H., Woodruff, D., Meyers, C. V., & Zhu, G. (2018). Principal competencies that make a difference: Identifying a model for leaders of school turnaround. *Journal of School Leadership, 28*(1), 56–81.

Holston, S. (2024, January). *Five policy actions to strengthen implementation of the Science of Reading*. Washington, DC: National Council on Teacher Quality. Accessed at www.nctq.org /dmsView/Print-Ready_SOTS_2024_Five_policy_actions_for_reading on March 13, 2024.

Honig, B., Diamond, L., & Gutlohn, L. (2018). *Teaching reading sourcebook* (3rd ed.). Novato, CA: Academic Therapy.

Hoover, W. A., & Tunmer, W. E. (2020). *The cognitive functions of reading and its acquisition: A framework with applications connecting teaching and learning*. Cham, Switzerland: Springer.

Hudson, R. F., Lane, H. B., & Pullen, P. C. (2005). Reading fluency assessment and instruction: What, why, and how? *The Reading Teacher, 58*(8), 702–714.

International Dyslexia Association. (2022). *Building phoneme awareness: Know what matters*. Accessed at https://dyslexiaida.org/building-phoneme-awareness-know-what-matters on August 27, 2024.

Irwin, V., De La Rosa, J., Wang, K., Hein, S., Zhang, J., Burr, R., et al. (2022, May). *Report on the condition of education 2022*. Washington, DC: National Center for Education Statistics. Accessed at https://nces.ed.gov/pubs2022/2022144.pdf on February 20, 2024.

Jacob, A., & McGovern, K. (2015). *The mirage: Confronting the hard truth about our quest for teacher development*. New York: TNTP. Accessed at https://files.eric.ed.gov/fulltext/ED558206.pdf on March 14, 2024.

Joyce, B. R., & Showers, B. (2002). *Student achievement through staff development* (3rd ed.). Arlington, VA: ASCD.

Kane, T. J., Owens, A. M., Marinell, W. H., Thal, D. R. C., & Staiger, D. O. (2016, February). *Teaching higher: Educators' perspectives on Common Core implementation*. Cambridge, MA: Center for Education Policy Research. Accessed at https://cepr.harvard.edu/files/cepr/files/teaching-higher-report.pdf on March 14, 2024.

Kauffman, D. L., & Kauffman, M. D. (2021). *Systems 1: An introduction to systems thinking* (4th ed.). San Diego, CA: System Dynamics Society.

Keesey, S., Konrad, M., & Joseph, L. M. (2015). Word boxes improve phonemic awareness, letter–sound correspondences, and spelling skills of at-risk kindergartners. *Remedial and Special Education, 36*(3), 167–180.

Kemeny, L. (2023). *Seven mighty moves: Research-backed, classroom-tested strategies to ensure K-to-3 reading success*. New York: Scholastic.

Killion, J., & Harrison, C. (2017). *Taking the lead: New roles for teachers and school-based coaches* (2nd ed.). Oxford, OH: Learning Forward.

Kilpatrick, D. A. (2015). *Essentials of assessing, preventing, and overcoming reading difficulties*. Hoboken, NJ: Wiley.

Kilpatrick, D. A., Joshi, M. R., & Wagner, R. K. (Eds.). (2019). *Reading development and difficulties: Bridging the gap between research and practice*. Cham, Switzerland: Springer.

Kim, J. S., & Mosher, D. M. (2023). Structuring adaptations for scaling up evidence-based literacy interventions. In S. Q. Cabell, S. B. Neuman, & N. P. Terry (Eds.), *Handbook on the science of early literacy* (pp. 253–268). New York: Guilford Press.

Kleickmann, T., Tröbst, S., Jonen, A., Vehmeyer, J., & Möller, K. (2016). The effects of expert scaffolding in elementary science professional development on teachers' beliefs and motivations, instructional practices, and student achievement. *Journal of Educational Psychology, 108*(1), 21–42.

Knight, J. (2011). *Unmistakable impact: A partnership approach for dramatically improving instruction*. Thousand Oaks, CA: Corwin Press.

Knight, J. (2018). *The impact cycle: What instructional coaches should do to foster powerful improvements in teaching*. Thousand Oaks, CA: Corwin Press.

Korhonen, V. (2024). *Number of incidents where a gun is fired, brandished, or a bullet hits school property, regardless of the number of victims, time, day, or reason in K-12 schools in the United States from 1999 to July 22, 2024.* Accessed at www.statista.com/statistics/1463594 /number-of-k-12-school-shootings-us on October 13, 2024.

Kraft, M. A., Papay, J. P., & Chi, O. L. (2019). Teacher skill development: Evidence from performance ratings by principals. *Journal of Policy Analysis and Management, 39*(2), 315–347.

Leach, J. M., Scarborough, H. S., & Rescorla, L. (2003). Late-emerging reading disabilities. *Journal of Educational Psychology, 95*(2), 211–224.

Lemoine, H. E., Levy, B. A., & Hutchinson, A. (1993). Increasing the naming speed of poor readers: Representations formed across repetitions. *Journal of Experimental Student Psychology, 55*(3), 297–328.

Levin, S., Scott, C., Yang, M., Leung, M., & Bradley, K. (2020). *Supporting a strong, stable principal workforce: What matters and what can be done.* Accessed at www.nassp.org /wp-content/uploads/2020/08/LPI-and-NASSP-Research-Agenda-Final-Report.pdf on February 17, 2024.

Lezotte, L. W., & Snyder, K. M. (2011). *What effective schools do: Re-envisioning the correlates.* Bloomington, IN: Solution Tree Press.

Lovett, M. W., Lacerenza, L., De Palma, M., & Frijters, J. C. (2012). Evaluating the efficacy of remediation for struggling readers in high school. *Journal of Learning Disabilities, 45*(2), 151–169.

Lyon, G. R. (2002a). Reading development, reading difficulties, and reading instruction educational and public health issues. *Journal of School Psychology, 40*(1), 3–6.

Lyon, G. R. (2002b). *Testimonies to Congress: 1997–2002.* Covington, LA: Center for the Development of Learning. Accessed at https://files.eric.ed.gov/fulltext/ED475205.pdf on February 17, 2024.

Lyon, G. R., Fletcher, J. M., Fuchs, L. S., & Chhabra, V. (2006). Learning disabilities. In E. J. Mash & R. A. Barkley (Eds.), *Treatment of childhood disorders* (3rd ed., pp. 512–591). New York: Guilford Press.

Marken, S., & Agrawal, S. (2022, June 13). *K–12 workers have highest burnout rate in U.S.* Accessed at https://news.gallup.com/poll/393500/workers-highest-burnout-rate.aspx on February 17, 2024.

Marzano, R. J. (2019). *The handbook for the new art and science of teaching.* Bloomington, IN: Solution Tree Press.

Marzano, R. J. (2020). *Teaching basic, advanced, and academic vocabulary: A comprehensive framework for elementary instruction.* Bloomington, IN: Marzano Resources.

Mattos, M., Buffum, A., Malone, J., Cruz, L. F., Dimich, N., & Schuhl, S. (2025). *Taking action: A handbook for RTI at Work* (2nd ed.). Bloomington, IN: Solution Tree Press.

McArthur, G., Castles, A., Kohnen, S., & Banales, E. (2016). Low self-concept in poor readers: Prevalence, heterogeneity, and risk. *Peer Journal, 4*, Article e2669. https://doi.org/10.7717/peerj.2669

McGlinchey, M. T., & Hixson, M. D. (2004). Using curriculum-based measurement to predict performance on state assessments in reading. *School Psychology Review, 33*(2), 193–203.

Moats, L. (2018). *Knowledge and practice standards for teachers of reading—A new initiative by the International Reading Association.* Accessed at https://dyslexiaida.org/kps-for-teachers-of-reading/ on July 30, 2024.

Moats, L. C. (2020a). *Speech to print: Language essentials for teachers* (3rd ed.). Baltimore, MD: Brookes.

Moats, L. C. (2020b, Summer). Teaching reading *is* rocket science: What expert teachers of reading should know and be able to do. *American Educator.* Accessed at https://files.eric.ed.gov/fulltext/EJ1260264.pdf on March 14, 2024.

Moats, L., & Tolman, C. (2009). *Language Essentials for Teachers of Reading and Spelling (LETRS): The speech sounds of English: Phonetics, phonology, and phoneme awareness (Module 2).* Boston: Sopris West.

Montgomery, P., Ilk, M., & Moats, L. C. (2013). *A principal's primer for raising reading achievement.* Longmont, CO: Cambium Learning Group.

The Nation's Report Card. (n.d.). *Reading and mathematics scores decline during COVID-19 pandemic.* Accessed at www.nationsreportcard.gov/highlights/ltt/2022 on March 14, 2024.

The Nation's Report Card. (2022). *NAEP report card: Reading.* Accessed at www.nationsreportcard.gov/reading/nation/scores/?grade=4 on May 23, 2024.

National Association of Secondary School Principals. (2019). *Supporting a strong, stable principal workforce: What matters and what can be done.* Accessed at www.nassp.org/nassp-and-lpi-research-agenda/nassp-lpi-research-report on May 22, 2024.

National Center for Education Statistics. (2022a, July 6). *More than 80 percent of U.S. public schools report pandemic has negatively impacted student behavior and socio-emotional development.* Accessed at https://nces.ed.gov/whatsnew/press_releases/07_06_2022.asp on February 18, 2024.

National Center for Education Statistics. (2022b, March 3). *U.S. schools report increased teacher vacancies due to COVID-19 pandemic, new NCES data show.* Accessed at https://nces.ed.gov/whatsnew/press_releases/3_3_2022.asp on February 17, 2024.

National Center for Education Statistics. (2023, September). *Violent deaths at school and away from school, school shootings, and active shooter incidents.* Accessed at https://nces .ed.gov/programs/coe/indicator/a01/violent-deaths-and-shootings on February 17, 2024.

National Center for Education Statistics. (n.d.). *Long-term trends in reading and mathematics achievement.* Accessed at https://nces.ed.gov/fastfacts/display.asp?id=38 on February 17, 2024.

National Comprehensive Center for Teacher Quality. (2008, March). *Key issue: Identifying how highly effective leaders support teachers.* Washinton, DC: Author.

National Council on Teacher Quality. (2023a, June). *Teacher prep review: Strengthening elementary reading instruction.* Washington, DC: Author. Accessed at www.nctq.org /dmsView/Executive_Summary_Teacher_Prep_Review_Strengthening_Elementary _Reading_Instruction on February 18, 2024.

National Council on Teacher Quality. (2023b, September). *Teacher prep review standards: Reading foundations.* Accessed at www.nctq.org/review/standard/Reading-Foundations on May 21, 2024.

National Institute on Child Health and Human Development. (n.d.) *Reading and reading disorders research information.* Accessed at www.nichd.nih.gov/health/topics/reading /researchinfo on May 21, 2024.

National Reading Panel. (2000). *Teaching students to read: An evidence-based assessment of the scientific research literature on reading and its implications for reading instruction.* Bethesda, MD: Author.

Northern, A. M. (2023, November 30). *From the statehouse to the classroom: The effects of early literacy policies on student achievement.* Fordham Institute. Accessed at https:// fordhaminstitute.org/national/commentary/statehouse-classroom-effects-early-literacy -policies-student-achievement on May 25, 2024.

Oakhill, J., Cain, K., & Elbro, C. (2015). *Understanding and teaching reading comprehension: A handbook.* New York: Routledge.

Oakley, B., Rogowsky, B., & Sejnowski, T. (2021). *Uncommon sense teaching: Practical insights in brain science to help students learn.* New York: TarcherPerigee.

Olson, L. (2023, June). *The reading revolution: How states are scaling literacy reform.* Accessed at www.future-ed.org/wp-content/uploads/2023/06/The-Reading-Revolution.pdf on March 14, 2024.

Parker, A. (2024, March 8). *US literacy rates 2024: Statistics and trends.* Accessed at www .prosperity foramerica.org/literacy-statistics/ on March 14, 2024.

Paulson, L. H. (2018). Teaching phonemic awareness. In J. R. Birsh & S. Carreker (Eds.), *Multisensory teaching of basic language skills* (4th ed., pp. 205–254). Baltimore, MD: Brookes.

Perfetti, C. (2007). Reading ability: Lexical quality to comprehension. *Scientific Studies of Reading, 11*(4), 357–383.

The Reading League. (2021). *Science of reading: Defining guide.* Syracuse, NY: Author. Accessed at www.thereadingleague.org/wp-content/uploads/2022/01/Science_of _Reading_Defining_Guide_eBook.pdf?mc_cid=14cb92ae5e&mc_eid=fd33e621c7 on February 17, 2024.

The Reading League. (n.d.). *Policymakers and state education agencies.* Accessed at www .thereadingleague.org/compass/policymakers-and-state-education-agencies on February 8, 2024.

Reading Rockets. (n.d.). *Reading Rockets classroom strategy library.* Washington, DC: WETA. Accessed at https://www.readingrockets.org/classroom/classroom-strategies on October 22, 2024.

Reed, D., & Vaughn, S. (2010). Reading interventions for older students. In T. A. Glover & S. Vaughn (Eds.), *The promise of response to intervention: Evaluating current science and practice* (pp. 143–186). New York: Guilford Press.

Reschly, A. L., Busch, T. W., Betts, J., Deno, S. L., & Long, J. D. (2009). Curriculum-based measurement oral reading as an indicator of reading achievement: A meta-analysis of the correlational evidence. *Journal of School Psychology, 47*(6), 427–469.

Reynolds, C. R., & Shaywitz, S. E. (2009). Response to intervention: Ready or not? Or, from wait-to-fail to watch-them-fail. *School Psychology Quarterly, 24*(2), 130–145.

Richardson, J. (2009). *The next step in guided reading: Focused assessments and targeted lessons for helping every student become a better reader.* New York: Scholastic.

Rief, S. F., & Heimburge, J. A. (2007). *How to reach and teach all students through balanced literacy: User-friendly strategies, tools, activities, and ready-to-use materials.* San Francisco: Jossey-Bass.

Robbins, S. P., & Judge, T. A. (2018). *Essentials of organizational behavior* (14th ed.). Upper Saddle River, NJ: Pearson.

Sabatini, J., Wang, Z., & O'Reilly, T. (2019). Relating reading comprehension to oral reading performance in the NAEP fourth-grade special study of oral reading. *Reading Research Quarterly, 54*(2), 253–271.

Scanlon, D. M., Gelzheiser, L. M., Vellutino, F. R., Schatschneider, C., & Sweeney, J. M. (2008). Reducing the incidence of early reading difficulties: Professional development for classroom teachers versus direct interventions for students. *Learning and Individual Differences, 18*(3), 346–359.

Scanlon, D. M., Vellutino, F. R., Small, S. G., Fanuele, D. P., & Sweeney, J. M. (2005). Severe reading difficulties—Can they be prevented? A comparison of prevention and intervention approaches. *Exceptionality, 13*(4), 209–227.

Scarborough, H. S. (2001). Connecting early language and literacy to later reading (dis) abilities: Evidence, theory, and practice. In S. B. Neuman & D. K. Dickinson (Eds.), *Handbook of early literacy research* (pp. 97–110). New York: Guilford Press.

Schmoker, M. (2018). *Focus: Elevating the essentials to radically improve student learning* (2nd ed.). Alexandria, VA: ASCD.

Schwartz, S. (2022a, July 20). *Which states have passed 'science of reading' laws? What's in them?* EdWeek. Accessed at www.edweek.org/teaching-learning/which-states-have -passed -science-of-reading-laws-whats-in-them/2022/07 on February 22, 2024.

Schwartz, S. (2022b, July 20). Why putting the 'science of reading' into practice is so challenging. *EdWeek.* Accessed at www.edweek.org/teaching-learning/why-putting-the- science-of-reading-into-practice-is-so-challenging/2022/07 on March 14, 2024.

Schwartz, S. (2024, February 9). How much time should teachers spend on a foundational reading skill? Research offers clues. *EdWeek.* Accessed at www.edweek.org/teaching -learning/how-much-time-should-teachers-spend-on-a-foundational-reading-skill-research -offers-clues/2024/02 on February 18, 2024.

Seidenberg, M. (2017). *Language at the speed of sight: How we read, why so many can't, and what can be done about it.* New York: Basic Books.

Shankweiler, D., Lundquist, E., Katz, L., Stuebing, K. K., Fletcher, J. M., Brady, S., et al. (1999). Comprehension and decoding: Patterns of association in students with reading difficulties. *Scientific Studies of Reading, 3*(1), 69–94.

Share, D. L. (1995). Phonological recoding and self-teaching: Sine qua non of reading acquisition. *Cognition, 55*(2), 151–218.

Shaywitz, S. (2003). *Overcoming dyslexia: A new and complete science-based program for reading problems at any level.* New York: Knopf.

Shaywitz, S. E., Fletcher, J. M., Holahan, J. M., Shneider, A. E., Marchione, K. E., Stuebing, K. K., et al. (1999). Persistence of dyslexia: The Connecticut longitudinal study at adolescence. *Pediatrics, 104*(6), 1351–1359.

Smartt, S. M., & Glaser, D. R. (2024). *Next STEPS in literacy instruction: Connecting assessments to effective interventions* (2nd ed.). Baltimore, MD: Brookes.

Snow, C., Griffin, P., & Burns, M. S. (Eds.). (2005). *Knowledge to support the teaching of reading: Preparing teachers for a changing world.* San Francisco: Jossey-Bass.

Spear-Swerling, L. (2016). Common types of reading problems and how to help students who have them. *The Reading Teacher, 69*(5), 513–522.

Spear-Swerling, L. (Ed.). (2022). *Structured literacy interventions: Teaching students with reading difficulties, grades K–6.* New York: Guilford Press.

Stahl, S. A. (1991). Beyond the instrumentalist hypothesis: Some relationships between word meanings and comprehension. In P. J. Schwanenflugel (Ed.), *The psychology of word meanings* (pp. 157–186). Hillsdale, NJ: Erlbaum.

Steinberg, M. P., & Sartain, L. (2015). Does teacher evaluation improve school performance? Experimental evidence from Chicago's Excellence in Teaching Project. *Education Finance and Policy, 10*(4), 535–572.

Steiner, D. (2017, March). *Curriculum research: What we know and where we need to go.* Accessed at https://standardswork.org/wp-content/uploads/2017/03/sw-curriculum -research-report-fnl.pdf on March 14, 2024.

Sun, R., & Van Ryzin, G. G. (2014). Are performance management practices associated with better outcomes? Empirical evidence from New York Public Schools. *The American Review of Public Administration, 44*(3), 324–338.

Texas Education Agency. (n.d.). The alphabetic principle. *Reading Rockets.* Washington, DC: WETA. Accessed at https://www.readingrockets.org/topics/phonics-and-decoding/articles /alphabetic-principle on October 22, 2024.

Torgesen, J. K., Rashotte, C. A., Alexander, A., Alexander, J., and MacPhee, K. (2003). Progress toward understanding the instructional conditions necessary for remediating reading difficulties in older children. In B. R. Foreman (Ed.), *Interventions for children at risk for reading difficulties or identified with reading difficulties* (pp. 275–298). Timonium, MD: York Press.

Tschannen-Moran, M. (2014). *Trust matters: Leadership for successful schools* (2nd ed.). San Francisco: Jossey-Bass.

Underwood, S. (2018, January). *What is the evidence for an uninterrupted, 90-minute literacy instruction block?* Accessed at https://educationnorthwest.org/sites/default/files/resources /uninterrupted-literacy-block-brief.pdf on May 22, 2024.

United States Census Bureau. (2024). *New Madrid township, New Madrid County, Missouri - Census Bureau profile.* Accessed at https://data.census.gov/profile/New_Madrid_township, _New_Madrid_County,_Missouri?g=060XX00US2914352094 on May 21, 2024.

United States Department of Education. (2011). *Reading First Implementation Study, 2008– 09: Final report.* Washington, DC: Author. Accessed at www2.ed.gov/rschstat/eval/other /reading-first-implementation-study/report.pdf on February 18, 2024.

Vaughn, S., & Fletcher, J. M. (2021). Identifying and teaching students with significant reading problems. *American Educator, 44*(4), 4–11.

Vellutino, F. R., Scanlon, D. M., Sipay, E. R., Small, S. G., Pratt, A., Chen, R., et al. (1996). Cognitive profiles of difficult-to-remediate and readily remediated poor readers: Early intervention as a vehicle for distinguishing between cognitive and experiential deficits as basic causes of specific reading disability. *Journal of Educational Psychology, 88*(4), 601–638.

Vellutino, F. R., Scanlon, D. M., Small, S., & Fanuele, D. P. (2006). Response to intervention as a vehicle for distinguishing between students with and without reading disabilities: Evidence for the role of kindergarten and first-grade interventions. *Journal of Learning Disabilities, 39*(2), 157–169.

Vellutino, F. R., Scanlon, D. M., & Zhang, H. (2007). Identifying reading disability based on response to intervention: Evidence from early intervention research. In S. R. Jimerson, M. K. Burns, & A. M. VanDerHeyden (Eds.), *Handbook of response to intervention: The science and practice of assessment and intervention* (pp. 185–211). New York: Springer.

Wanzek, J., Vaughn, S., Scammacca, N., Gatlin, B., Walker, M. A., & Capin, P. (2016). Meta-analyses of the effects of tier 2 type reading interventions in grades K–3. *Educational Psychology Review, 28*(3), 551–576.

White, S., Sabatini, J., Park, B. J., Chen, J., Bernstein, J., & Li, M. (2021, April). *Highlights of the 2018 NAEP Oral Reading Fluency study.* Washington, DC: Institute of Education Sciences. Accessed at https://nces.ed.gov/nationsreportcard/subject/studies/orf /2021026_2018_orf_highlights.pdf on March 14, 2024.

White, T. G., Sabatini, J. P., & White, S. (2021). What does "below basic" mean on NAEP reading? *Educational Researcher, 50*(8), 570–573.

Willingham, D. T. (2007, Summer). *Critical thinking: Why is it so hard to teach?* American Educator. Accessed at www.aft.org/sites/default/files/media/2014/Crit_Thinking.pdf on February 20, 2024.

Wolf, M. (2007). *Proust and the squid: The story and science of the reading brain* (C. Stoodley, Illus.). New York: HarperCollins.

Yasir, W., Iqbal, M., Jamal, B., Taseer, N. A., Maqsood, A., & Kazmi, S. F. (2023). The role of dyslexia on self-esteem and aggression of primary and secondary school students. *Journal of Positive School Psychology, 7*(4), 477–489.

Yoon, K. S., Duncan, T., Lee, S. W.-Y., Scarloss, B., & Shapley, K. L. (2007, October). *Reviewing the evidence on how teacher professional development affects student achievement.* Washington, DC: U.S. Department of Education. Accessed at https://files.eric.ed.gov /fulltext/ED498548.pdf on February 20, 2024.

Young, N., & Hasbrouck, J. (Eds.). (2024). *Climbing the ladder of reading and writing: Meeting the needs of all learners.* New Rochelle, NY: Benchmark Education.

# Index

## A

absenteeism, 12, 14

Acadience, 70, 135

accountability, 63, 88, 152, 248
    collaboration and, 216, 220–221, 231
    expectations and, 28
    trust and, 235

accuracy, 162
    celebrating, 251
    in decoding, 167–168
    interventions and differentiation for, 174–177
    nonsense word fluency, 158–159
    oral reading fluency, 164, 171, 172, 174–177
    orthographic mapping and, 167–168

achievement, xv
    interventions' effect on, 88
    involvement of all educators in, xv–xvi, 2, 6–7
    principals' desire for, 23
    principals' effects on, 21
    school leaders in, 4

acquisition, 36

assessment of, 62–63, 69
    data analysis on, 118, 133, 138
    instructional strategies and, 150–151
    subskills in, 154, 156, 184
    vocabulary, 180, 184

administrators and staff
    inexperienced, professional development and, 194–195
    intervention calculator and, 102
    in interventions, 85
    involvement of all, xv–xvi, 2, 7, 85
    morale among, 12
    school leadership teams and, 231–232

Agarwal, P. K., 44

agenda setting, 224–226, 228–229

aimswebPlus, 57, 70, 83

Alameda Literacy Project, 5

Amber Guardian Series, 174

American School District Panel, 194

Amira, 96

announcements, 239

antonyms, 181

Archer, A. L., 27, 50

assemblies, 240

*Assessing Reading Multiple Measures* (Diamond & Thorsnes), 70

assessment literacy, 60–61, 62–64

assessments, 8. See also data analysis
    benchmark, 64–67, 118–123
    compliance and, 61, 251
    composite scores in, 118–122
    comprehensive, 6–7
    comprehensive, planning, 57–81
    comprehensive plan development for, 74–76, 248–249
    cost of, 61
    determining areas of difficulty with, 115–116
    diagnostic, 68
    effective vs. ineffective practices with, 62
    instructional levels and, 39
    interventions based on, 92–93
    in literacy evaluation, 24–26
    norm-referenced, 118
    off-level, 140
    organizational practices and procedures for, 72–74
    outcome/summative, 70–72
    overlooked ways to use, 76–79
    percentile ranks in, 118, 120–122
    principal's perspective on, 57–60
    progress monitoring, 68–69
    recommended, 68
    redundancy in, 61
    reliable, 62–63
    reproducible on, 80–81
    resources distribution and, 78–79

phoneme-grapheme correspondence, 41, 42, 156–157
phoneme-grapheme mapping, 104, 140, 157, 161, 267–268
phonemic awareness, 16–17, 41–42
    diagnostic surveys in, 68
    differentiated instruction and, 95
    in instructional hierarchy, 36–37
    interventions and differentiation on, 156–159
    kindergarten instruction in, 153–159
    research on teaching, 155–156
    science of reading and, 19–20
    time allotted for, in literacy blocks, 40–41
    unitizing and, 165
phonemic segmentation, 65
Phonicbooks.com, 174
phonics, 16–17
    diagnostic surveys in, 68
    differentiated instruction and, 95
    in instructional hierarchy, 36–37
    interventions and differentiation of, 161–164
    research on teaching, 160–161
    science of reading and, 19–20
    supplemental reading programs in, 183–184
    Tier 3 small-group instruction in, 168
    time allotted for, in literacy blocks, 40–41
phonics approach, 3
phonological awareness, definition of, 155
Phonological Awareness Screening Test (PAST), 68
phonological sensitivity, 155
Plain Talk About Literacy and Learning Conference, 5
policies and procedures
    for assessments, 72–74
    for dyad reading, 172, 173–174
    professional development and, 203–204
poverty, 88
*Powerful Teaching: Unleash the Science of Learning* (Agarwal & Bain), 44
practice, 6, 17, 19, 26, 38, 41–42. *See also* interventions
    explicit instruction and, 44–45
    lesson pacing and, 45–46
    in small-group instruction, 38–39, 95–96
practices
    classroom, student outcomes, and, 203–204
    effective vs. ineffective assessment, 62
    effective vs. ineffective data analysis, 116
    effective vs. ineffective literacy instruction, 30
    efficient school leadership team, 222
    efficient team, 222
    instructional, 91–92, 172, 173–174, 257
    maximizing literacy time through, 239–240
    science of reading and, 257
    pre-alphabetic phase, 150
preteaching, vocabulary, 19, 96, 180
Primary Phonics books, 4
principals
    action inspired by, 115
    burnout among, 191

coach role and, 205–208
    helpful resources for, 209
    as instructional leaders, 205–210
    overworked, xv
    role of in literacy instruction, 20–21
    self-reflection survey on trust, 236–238
    sharing control and, 230–231
    student achievement and, 21
    teacher observation by, 200–201
    trust, collaboration, and, 232, 235–238
    turnover among, 194
*A Principal's Primer for Raising Reading Achievement* (Montgomery, Ilk, & Moats), 4
print knowledge, 254
processing time, 46
professional development, 2, 6–7, 8, 22, 185–213, 249–250
    action-oriented feedback in, 208–210
    in assessment administration, 74
    assessments in guiding, 77–79
    characteristics of effective, 196
    classroom practices, student outcomes, and, 203–204
    criteria for systems of, 192–204
    definition of, 192
    implementing universal instruction and, 27–29
    instructional strategies and, 30–31
    on interventions, 84–85
    job-embedded, 202–203
    learning how to teach literacy and, 18
    legislation on, 17
    in literacy evaluation, 24–26
    making time for, 189
    observation and feedback in, 200–201
    planning considerations for, 191
    principals and, 205–210
    principal's perspective on, 185–190
    professional learning vs., 191–192
    reproducible for, 212–213
    school improvement plans and, 204–205
    school leadership teams and, 231
    school spotlight on, 207–208
    on standards, 84
    for structured literacy, 193
    student outcomes and, 197
    summary on, 211
    understanding the importance of, 190–192
    variety in avenues for, 199–200
    vision for literacy instruction and, 192–194
professional learning communities (PLCs), 117, 133
progress monitoring, 58
    assessments in, 68–69
    collaboration and, 232–233
    frequency of, 69–70
    interventions and, 85–86
    on letter naming, 153–154
    Tier 2 interventions and, 97

### A Leader's Guide to Reading and Writing in a PLC at Work®, Elementary
*Kathy Tuchman Glass and Karen Power*
Confidently lead literacy improvement in your PLC. With the support of this results-focused guide, you will learn how to take urgent action to address deficiencies and help your teachers ensure every student successfully reads and writes at or beyond grade level.
**BKF903**

### Read Alouds for All Learners
*Molly Ness*
In *Read Alouds for All Learners: A Comprehensive Plan for Every Subject, Every Day, Grades PreK–8*, Molly Ness provides a compelling case for the integration, or reintegration, of the read aloud in schools and a step-by-step resource for preK–8 educators in classrooms.
**BKG116**

### 40 Reading Intervention Strategies for K–6 Students
*Elaine K. McEwan-Adkins*
This well-rounded collection of reading intervention strategies, teacher-friendly lesson plans, and adaptable mini-routines will support and inform your RTI efforts. Many of the strategies motivate all students as well as scaffold struggling readers. Increase effectiveness by using the interventions across grade-level teams or schoolwide.
**BKF270**

### The Power of Effective Reading Instruction
*Karen Gazith*
Through research-supported tools and strategies, this book explores how children learn to read and how neuroscience should inform reading practices in schools. K–12 educators will find resources and reproducible tools to effectively implement reading instruction and interventions, no matter the subject taught.
**BKG104**

### Solving the Literacy Puzzle
*Norene A. Bunt*
Using graphic organizers, assessments, and reflection questions, educators can unpack five core components of literacy instruction within the science of reading framework. This comprehensive guide prepares teachers to confidently implement effective literacy instruction in their classrooms.
**BKG158**

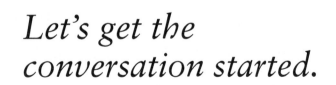